ETHICS OUT OF LAW

DANA HOLLANDER

Ethics Out of Law

Hermann Cohen and the "Neighbor"

UNIVERSITY OF TORONTO PRESS
Toronto Buffalo London

Toronto Buffalo London
utorontopress.com

ISBN 978-1-4875-0624-7 (cloth) ISBN 978-1-4875-3368-7 (EPUB)
ISBN 978-1-4875-3367-0 (PDF)

Library and Archives Canada Cataloguing in Publication

Title: Ethics out of law : Hermann Cohen and the "neighbor" / Dana Hollander.
Names: Hollander, Dana, author.
Description: Includes bibliographical references and index.
Identifiers: Canadiana (print) 20200307967 | Canadiana (ebook) 20200307991 | ISBN 9781487506247 (hardcover) | ISBN 9781487533687 (EPUB) | ISBN 9781487533670 (PDF)
Subjects: LCSH: Cohen, Hermann, 1842–1918. | LCSH: Jewish philosophy – 19th century. | LCSH: Jewish ethics – Philosophy. | LCSH: Law and ethics. | LCSH: Law – Philosophy. | LCSH: Ethics – Philosophy.
Classification: LCC B3216.C74 H65 2021 | DDC 296.3/6 – dc23

This book has been published with the help of a grant from the Federation for the Humanities and Social Sciences, through the Awards to Scholarly Publications Program, using funds provided by the Social Sciences and Humanities Research Council of Canada.

University of Toronto Press acknowledges the financial assistance to its publishing program of the Canada Council for the Arts and the Ontario Arts Council, an agency of the Government of Ontario.

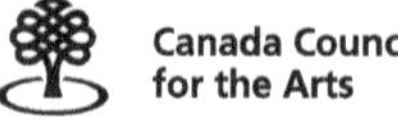

Contents

Acknowledgments and Preface

To understand Hermann Cohen's systematic philosophy in conjunction with his writings on Judaism has been an interest of mine for many years, beginning with the work that went into a chapter of my first book (*Exemplarity and Chosenness: Rosenzweig and Derrida on the Nation of Philosophy* [2008]) that looked at Cohen as a prime influence on Franz Rosenzweig's *Star of Redemption.*

My idea to work on this topic in a sustained fashion began to take shape thanks to a most stimulating year I spent as a postdoctoral fellow with the UCLA Mellon Sawyer Seminar on "The Ethics of the Neighbor," directed by Kenneth Reinhard. Subsequent stages of the project were enabled by a Standard Research Grant from Canada's Social Sciences and Humanities Research Council (SSHRC) and a fellowship from the Alexander von Humboldt Foundation. That fellowship allowed me to spend eighteen months at the Zentrum für Literatur- und Kulturforschung (ZfL, Center for Literary and Cultural Research) in Berlin, leading to a summer stay funded by one of the ZfL's own fellowships. I am most grateful to Kenneth Reinhard and Martin Treml, my hosts at UCLA and the ZfL, respectively, as well as to other colleagues and staff at both institutions, for providing such nourishing environments in which my thinking toward this book began to develop. Martin's and Ken's intellectual partnership allowed for many fruitful exchanges during my stays, and enabled us to collaborate on colloquia and workshops. My work on the book was further supported by two research leaves granted by McMaster University, and by the Canada Research Chairs Program, which funded my position and research activities during my first five years at McMaster, when I held the Canada Research Chair in Modern Jewish Thought. Most recently, I was able to complete the manuscript thanks to a research stay at the Selma Stern Zentrum für Jüdische Studien (Center for Jewish Studies) Berlin-Brandenburg.

Many colleagues and friends encouraged my ongoing work toward this book by inviting me to share my work in progress at conferences, workshops, invited lectures and in edited volumes, with many fruitful discussions on those occasions. These include Stephan Steiner; Klaus-Peter Adam and Paul Mendes-Flohr; Liliana Feierstein; Norbert Waszek; Robert Yelle; Nitzan Lebovic and Daniel Weidner; Leora Batnitzky; Eric Dreff; Sergey Dolgopolski; Elad Lapidot and Ron Naiweld; Ino Augsberg and Karl-Heinz Ladeur; Paula Schwebel; Paul North, Paul Franks, and Eliyahu Stern; Jeffrey Bernstein; Randi Rashkover and Martin Kavka; John Ackerman; Myriam Bienenstock; Rabbi Michael Stroh; Rodolphe Gasché; Aaron W. Hughes and Elliot R. Wolfson; Leonard V. Kaplan; Martina Urban and Christian Wiese; Till van Rahden; Kevin Hart; and Michael Zank.

My work has been greatly sustained over the years by the enthusiasm, curiosity, and friendship of Antonio Calcagno, David L. Clark, Astrid Deuber-Mankowsky, Louis Greenspan (z"l), Christoph Kasten, Rabbi Yonah Lavery-Yisraëli, Gesine Palmer, Randi Rashkover, Eugene Sheppard, Rabbi Asher Turin (z"l), and Arnd Wedemeyer.

I am grateful to Diane Perpich, Michael Morgan, Peter Fenves, and Michael Zank, who gave crucial support to my efforts to bring this work to publication. Roshaya Rodness provided invaluable research assistance and feedback on the manuscript at the final stages. Len Husband has been a wonderful and encouraging editor at University of Toronto Press. I am grateful to Jeff Tessier for allowing me to use his photography for the book cover.

I thank my partner, Nick Storch, and my daughters for the warmth of a home; and my mother, Vita Hollander, for her immeasurable, unwavering support of all my endeavors.

Lastly, I am most grateful to fellow Cohen scholar Christoph Kasten for instigating a daytrip to Hermann Cohen's birthplace, the picturesque town Coswig (Anhalt) on the Elbe River, and to Rolf-Dieter Rediess, who welcomed us on behalf of the Coswig-based Cohen-Gesellschaft – a society of citizens devoted to cultivating the legacy of this famous Jewish citizen of their town, and the worldly cultural heritage that his name evokes – and who generously shared his knowledge of the topography of Cohen's early life with us. This visit greatly sharpened my sense of the geographical, social and cultural-political spaces of Cohen's thought. Standing in front of the empty paved lot at Domstrasse 6 on which the house had stood that served as both the Cohen family home and the Jewish community and school building (it had been senselessly razed by the authorities in 1982) – a large gap in an otherwise intact row of historic houses – we could glance in one direction toward the site, some houses away along the same narrow street, of the former synagogue (destroyed on Kristallnacht and subsequently demolished) where Hermann's father Gerson had served as a cantor. Looking down the street in the other direction, a few houses down from the Cohens' old address, we faced the city's handsome abandoned castle – at one time inhabited by a branch of the family of the Dukes of Anhalt, and in later decades used as a military hospital, then for many years as a prison (which also held political prisoners and was the site of executions), including under both the Nazi and GDR regimes, and most recently as a state archive.

Cohen was fond of describing his parental home and hometown, which he continued visiting up until his mother's death in 1873. A 1902 letter to Kurt Eisner, the socialist author and politician who had befriended Cohen while living in Marburg in the 1890s and who acknowledged him as a key intellectual influence, makes reference to a period during which Cohen worked, in the "upper room" of his parents' house, on his book *Kants Theorie der Erfahrung* (submitted in 1871 as his Habilitation thesis). In honor of the philosopher's sixtieth birthday, Eisner had sent a landscape painted by his wife, Lisbeth Eisner, depicting a view of Coswig. The couple had evidently traveled to Coswig in order to create the painting. Cohen's letter acknowledging the gift as a tribute to his "love of my German home [*Heimath*], of my small hometown [*Vaterstadt*] as a living root of my being" not only contains a reminiscence that helps us to trace the philosopher-student's everyday pathways circa 1870 ("walking for hours down the Domgasse, often with [Kant's First] Critique in my hand and before my eye, afternoon nap on the Elbwiese [the low-lying river bank, located just the other side of the castle down the street]..., daydreaming under tall trees"), but also contains the observation: "Sometimes I think that only a small town can be a home [*Heimat*] because only there does one visit a *Volksschule*, grow up with the children of the middle and lower classes, and the countryside flows into the city."[1] It is easy to square this topography with Frederick Beiser's suggestion, in his recently published

1 Letter to Kurt Eisner, 14 August 1902, in Michael Zank, *The Idea of Atonement in the Philosophy of Hermann Cohen* (Providence, RI: Brown Judaic Studies, 2000), 467–9; this translation combines elements of Zank's translation (469–70) and that of Frederick Beiser in *Hermann Cohen: An Intellectual Biography* (Oxford: Oxford University Press, 2018), 7.

intellectual biography of Cohen, that Cohen's small-town vantage point allowed for a fundamental presumption of a stable, modern Jewish life-in-common with non-Jewish Germans.[2]

Like many educated and enterprising individuals whose life began in small towns, Cohen came to have strong connections to larger locales, in particular the metropolis of Berlin (the home city of his wife Martha Cohen, née Lewandowski), where he lived prior to becoming a university professor and also spent the last years of his life; and of course his home base for the greater part of his career was the university town of Marburg. Typically for a student of that era, his early studies had taken him to several cities, Dessau, Breslau (Wroclaw), Berlin, and Halle; and in his later life he engaged in the routine long-distance leisure travel that was typical of well-to-do Germans (the letter to Eisner, for example, bears the vacation address of Silvaplana in Switzerland).

Further explorations from the vantage of today's empty paved lot at Domstrasse 6 yield topographical insights that intersect with a cultural history bespeaking cosmopolitan openings of its own. It is intriguing, for example, to map onto the short stretch of (then) Domgasse beginning from the castle, passing in front of the Cohen home/Jewish school building at number 6, and up to the (now also empty) synagogue site, an episode of striking hospitality from the very period in which Cohen wrote his first Kant book in that upper room, a time at which the Jewish population of Coswig had dwindled to the point that out-of-towners had to be recruited to make a minyan for High Holiday services. Gerson Cohen, Hermann's father and the cantor and schoolteacher of the Coswig Jewish community, reports in a newspaper dispatch dated October 19, 1870, during the Franco-Prussian war: "Before ר"ה [Rosh Hashanah] I was approached by a Christian official in the name of Jewish prisoners [i.e., French prisoners of war] in Wittenberg, to intercede on their behalf with the commandant there, to obtain permission to hold the Holy Day services here with us (because Wittenberg has no Jews).... Thus *seven* Jews ... actually came here, escorted, for ר"ה, and after ר"ה returned, and came again for כ" [Yom Kippur]. Later on, 400 men were brought to stay here at our castle, of whom there were only six of the aforementioned Jews, who remain here to the present time. This has been and is a fine thing for us, insofar as they are well-versed Jews [*geschulte Juden*], and thus were able to complete our scarce minyan. These people were hosted on all the holidays by our families, which likely will occur again, if they remain here a long time." Upon Hermann Cohen's death, while the

2 Beiser, *Hermann Cohen*, 9.

Empty lot at Domstrasse 6 (at left), and view of the castle, in Coswig (Anhalt).

world war in which France and Germany were again enemies still raged, Salomon Steinthal, a younger friend of his from Coswig with a similar life path (after Abitur in Dessau and medical studies in Marburg, he became a doctor in Berlin), told of this same episode in a published reminiscence "Of Hermann Cohen's *Heimat*": The French-Jewish soldiers "were permitted to attend the synagogue escorted by a German officer, and for the first time in a long time, a service could be held on the Feast of Booths [Sukkot]. The few community members did not need to travel out of town to say Kaddish on *yahrzeit* (a death anniversary). Naturally, on the holidays, kosher food was sent to the prisoners staying in the castle. Later on they were permitted to go out alone and accept meal invitations."[3] Steinthal concludes this story of administrative hospitality toward Jewish soldiers of an enemy army which was surely foreign to the

3 Gerson Cohen, dispatch in *Allgemeine Zeitung des Judentums* (1 November 1870), and Salomon Steinthal, "Aus Hermann Cohens Heimat," *Allgemeine Zeitung des Judentums* (10 May 1918). Hartwig Wiedebach makes the connection between Steinthal's and Gerson Cohen's accounts in his editorial introduction to *Werke*, vol. 12: VII–VIII.

atmosphere of the waning days of World War I with the lament, "How far we have regressed in [matters of] culture!"

Beiser speculates that, if Cohen's early experience of coexistence among Jewish and non-Jewish small-town residents might have led to a naïveté about what was possible, it was also likely a source of "strength, self-confidence, and creativity" for Cohen as one who would later "have to fight" for the principles that such experiences represented. The investigations in this book present Cohen's philosophical thinking as a form of ordered struggle in the name of a cosmopolitan universality, or, in the idiom of Cohen and his compatriot, in favor of "matters of culture."

~

I gratefully acknowledge permission to include in this book material that was previously published in germinal form in "Love-of-Neighbor and Ethics Out of Law in the Philosophy of Hermann Cohen," in Christian Wiese and Martina Urban, eds., *German-Jewish Thought Between Religion and Politics: Festschrift in Honor of Paul Mendes-Flohr on the Occasion of His Seventieth Birthday* (Berlin: de Gruyter, 2012); "Understanding Law ('Gesetz' and 'Recht') in Hermann Cohen, With Help From the Early Strauss," *Idealistic Studies*, vol. 44 (2014), no. 2/3, special issue on "New Directions in the Thought of Leo Strauss," ed. Jeffrey Bernstein; "'Plato Prophesied the Revelation': The Philosophico-Political Theology of Strauss's *Philosophy and Law* and the Guidance of Hermann Cohen," in Randi Rashkover and Martin Kavka (eds.), *Judaism, Liberalism, and Political Theology* (Bloomington: Indiana University Press, 2014); and "'But Does He Really Not Remember?' Cohen's Revaluing of the Spinozan Politicization of Judaism," in *G.W.F. Hegel und Hermann Cohen. Wege zur Versöhnung. Festschrift Myriam Bienenstock*, ed. Norbert Waszek (Freiburg: Alber, 2018).

Abbreviations

Works by Hermann Cohen

BR	*Der Begriff der Religion im System der Philosophie* (Giessen: Töpelmann, 1915). Repr. in *Werke* 10.
Briefe	*Briefe*, ed. Bertha and Bruno Strauss (Berlin: Schocken, 1939).
CEM	"Charakteristik der Ethik Maimunis," in JS3 and in *Werke*, vol. 15: *Kleinere Schriften IV: 1907–1912*, ed. Hartwig Wiedebach (Hildesheim: Olms, 2009) (cited according to the JS3 pagination, which is included in the *Werke* edition). *Ethics of Maimonides*, trans. Almut Sh. Bruckstein (Madison: University of Wisconsin Press, 2004).
EmkN	"Einleitung mit kritischem Nachtrag zur 'Geschichte des Materialismus' von F. A. Lange," 2nd ed., in Lange, *Geschichte des Materialismus*, 7th ed. (Leipzig: Baedeker, 1902). 3rd ed. (1914), repr. in *Werke* 5/II, ed. Helmut Holzhey (Hildesheim: Olms, 2005).
ErW	*Ethik des reinen Willens*, 1st ed. (1904), 2nd ed. (1907), in *Werke*, vol. 7, ed. Helmut Holzhey (Hildesheim: Olms, 1981).
JS	*Jüdische Schriften*, 3 vols., ed. Bruno Strauss (Berlin: Schwetschke, 1924).
KBE	*Kants Begründung der Ethik*, 1st ed. (1877), 2nd. ed. (1910), in *Werke*, vol. 2 (Hildesheim: Olms, 2001).
LrE	*Logik der reinen Erkenntnis*, 1st ed. (1902), 2nd ed. (1914), in *Werke*, vol. 6 (Hildesheim: Olms, 1977).
RV	*Religion der Vernunft aus den Quellen des Judentums* (1919), 2nd ed., ed. Bruno Strauss (Frankfurt am Main: J. Kauffmann, 1929; repr. Wiesbaden: Fourier, 1978). *Religion of Reason Out of the Sources of Judaism*, trans. Simon Kaplan (Atlanta: Scholars Press, 1995).

SPZ *Schriften zur Philosophie und Zeitgeschichte*, ed. Albert Görland and Ernst Cassirer, 2 vols. (Berlin: Akademie-Verlag, 1928).

Werke *Werke*, ed. Helmut Holzhey (Hildesheim: Olms, 1977–).

Works by Other Authors

CM Leo Strauss, "Cohen und Maimuni" (1931), in *Gesammelte Schriften*, vol. 2: *Philosophie und Gesetz, Frühe Schriften*, ed. Heinrich Meier (Stuttgart: Metzler, 1997). "Cohen and Maimonides," trans. Martin D. Yaffe and Ian A. Moore, in Kenneth Hart Green, ed., *Leo Strauss on Maimonides. The Complete Writings* (Chicago: University of Chicago Press, 2013), 174–222. Cited according to the pagination in *Gesammelte Schriften*, which is included in Green's edition.

PG Leo Strauss, *Philosophie und Gesetz. Beiträge zum Verständnis Maimunis und seiner Vorläufer* (1935), in *Gesammelte Schriften*, vol. 2: *Philosophie und Gesetz, Frühe Schriften*, ed. Heinrich Meier (Stuttgart: Metzler, 1997). *Philosophy and Law. Contributions to the Understanding of Maimonides and His Predecessors*, trans. Eve Adler (Albany: State University of New York Press, 1995).

LrR Rudolf Stammler, *Die Lehre von dem richtigen Rechte*, 1st ed. (Berlin: J. Guttentag, 1902). *The Theory of Justice*, trans. Isaac Husik (New York: MacMillan, 1925).

AA Immanuel Kant, *Kant's gesammelte Schriften*, ed. Königlich Preußische Akademie der Wissenschaften (1900–) (Georg Reimer, later De Gruyter).

Note: I have drawn on the cited published translations to varying degrees and have modified them wherever necessary.

ETHICS OUT OF LAW

Introduction

If the impetus or imperative to philosophize begins from a wish to make sense of the conditions of our existence, beginning with the most elementary of those conditions, then it would seem that one of the central philosophical topics ought to be the realm of law. Law has, after all, a fundamental role in constituting our world and our existence and relationships within it.

In its typical organization, the university discipline of philosophy of course positions metaphysics, epistemology, or ethics as being more fundamental than the specialty called the "philosophy of law." That the field of ethics in particular is typically positioned as being more fundamental than that of legal philosophy aligns with our tendency to regard conceptions of morality and dilemmas concerning ethical decisionmaking as concerning initially an individual self who seeks thoughtfully to negotiate their own life in relation to other persons and in the social realm. But it is worth considering that, long before I might be enticed to think of myself as an autonomous agent of choice, I have in myriad ways already been negotiating and responding to a world organized, constructed, and regulated by means of legal institutions and other givens, such as rules about property; rules for right behavior in various spaces; distinctions between public and private; and rules for establishing identity, citizenship, affiliation, or belonging.

This book takes as its starting point the idea, put forward over 100 years ago by the Neo-Kantian philosopher Hermann Cohen, that ethics may be conceived as in some sense arising from law. This is an intriguing position to take, as it goes against our common intuition that law is defined and legitimized as a project of actualizing ethical principles and ideals, that, in other words, law is constructed – or is to be constructed – on the basis of ethics. Our very ability to challenge existing statutes as unjust rests on the idea that law should be just – and can be made more just – to the extent that it conforms to ethical norms.

In arguing for an ethics that is in some sense anchored in, or "generated" by, law or legal science, Cohen was motivated by several concerns. For him, philosophical ethics could only be a coherent project if it avoided several fallacies: It could not be anchored in an idea of goodness as a transcendent value, springing, for example, from the ancient Greek idea of "unwritten law" or from a determinate religious or theological source – those ideas, in other words, that are associated with traditional theories of natural law. An ethical philosophy is for Cohen defined as something human made, and thus as rooted in human autonomy (see EmkN 508/95, 511/98). On the other hand, the idea of the human source of ethics also needed to be dissociated from any attempt at naturalizing or psychologizing ethics, such as grounding morality in psychology or in affect. For Cohen, such attempts quickly approach the risk of physiologizing ethics: He associates the idea that morality could be a "law of nature" with the Pauline formulation of "a law in our members."

In elaborating a tenable model of ethics, Cohen posited the realm of law as its "scientific" basis or *Faktum,* and explored in myriad ways how legal principles, institutions, and dealings could be generative of morality. The realm of law – in German, the realm of *Recht* – here refers to the legal-political realm, the system of the rule of law. Thus, what Cohen conceptualizes as *Allheit,* the social realm that "all" inhabit, comprises the idea of the state, without the state having any conceptual priority or ultimacy in relation to other forms of public-political-juridical collectivity. As I go on to show in this book, the resulting ethico-legal philosophy is based on the idea of generation (*Erzeugung*) not only in that juridical concepts or institutions are thought of as "generative" of ethical concepts but also because Cohen is always guided by the principle that ethical action, and ethical theorizing, are to be thought of as an open-ended, futural "task" (*Aufgabe*), a project of achieving justice and peace in the world.

Reading across Two Corpuses, Jewish and Philosophical

This book develops an argument spanning Cohen's philosophy of ethics and law – as articulated chiefly in his work *Ethik des reinen Willens* (*Ethics of Pure Will*) – and his Jewish philosophy. The argument develops, in other words, out of readings that traverse two bodies of work produced by Cohen – his philosophical writings (comprising his works on Kant and his systematic philosophical works) and his "Jewish writings." The latter category derives from the posthumous publication, under the editorship of Bruno Strauss, of Cohen's shorter works on Jewish topics in the three-volume *Jüdische Schriften* (1924). (This remains a solid edition for scholarly purposes, even as the critical *Werke* edition launched by

Helmut Holzhey in 1977 has been since 2002 gradually supplemented by five volumes of Cohen's "shorter works," *Kleinere Schriften*, in an integrated chronological sequence, edited by Hartwig Wiedebach.) The classification "Jewish writings" is a useful one for referring to the very large corpus of shorter works that Cohen clearly produced for a Jewish readership or audience, often in Jewish periodicals or as lectures at Jewish venues, culminating in his two systematic works of "Jewish philosophy of religion"/"philosophy of Jewish religion" (*jüdische Religionsphilosophie*): *Der Begriff der Religion* (1915; *The Concept of Religion*) and the posthumously published *Religion of Reason Out of the Sources of Judaism* (1919/1929; *Religion der Vernunft aus den Quellen des Judentums*).[1] Earlier receptions of Cohen's thought approached his systematic-philosophical work quite separately from his Jewish writings. Such interpretations also often viewed Cohen's 1912 retirement from his post at the University of Marburg, and his move to Berlin – where he joined the faculty of the Lehranstalt für die Wissenschaft des Judentums and taught the material that he developed for *Begriff der Religion* and *Religion of Reason* – as a break, a turn or "return" to Judaism after a long academic career spent solely on general philosophical pursuits.[2] Franz Rosenzweig, who encountered and was influenced by Cohen's teaching during those Berlin years and who wrote a comprehensive introduction to the posthumously published "Jewish Writings," is the most famous originator of such an interpretation – and his version of it influenced the reception of Cohen's oeuvre for many years.[3] Today's scholarship, by contrast, overwhelmingly

1 However, see Michael Zank's discussion of the different character and discursive contexts of these two late "religion" books by Cohen. *The Idea of Atonement in the Philosophy of Hermann Cohen* (Providence, RI: Brown Judaic Studies, 2000; repr. Brown Judaic Studies Open Humanities Book Program, 2020), 37ff., https://repository.library.brown.edu/studio/item/bdr:1111035.

2 A list of titles of the courses Cohen taught at the Lehranstalt is included in the appendix to Hermann Cohen, *Briefe an August Stadler*, ed. Hartwig Wiedebach (Basel: Schwabe, 2015).

3 See Franz Rosenzweig, "Einleitung" to Hermann Cohen, *Jüdische Schriften* (1924) in JS1. I discuss Rosenzweig's influential characterization of Cohen's oeuvre in chapter 1 of *Exemplarity and Chosenness: Rosenzweig and Derrida on the Nation of Philosophy* (Stanford: Stanford University Press, 2008). For an example of an early-generation interpreter who echoes Rosenzweig's schema, see chapter 2 of Samuel Hugo Bergmann, *Faith and Reason: An Introduction to Modern Jewish Thought*, trans. and ed. Alfred Jospe (1961; New York: Schocken, 1963). Steven S. Schwarzschild's famous essay debunking "F. Rosenzweig's Anecdotes about H. Cohen" analyzes those anecdotes for how they construct or project the figure of Hermann Cohen in accordance with specific self-interested interpretations of Cohen's positions on Judaism and their ongoing implications. In *Gegenwart im Rückblick*, ed. Herbert A.

recognizes the significant continuities between Cohen's philosophical and "Jewish" corpuses, and that to treat them as completely separate realms means to miss important aspects of what is going on in each.

Jewish Philosophy: Ethics and Law

Jewish philosophical and other Jewish "thought" traditions are confronted with the question of the relationship between ethics and law in notable ways. Jewish law (*halakhah*) is often theorized in terms of the question of whether or not there is a necessary relationship between laws and morality or goodness, or, in other words: to what extent there can be a rational explanation of laws along such lines. In modern times, this question has in large part been shaped, first, by the history of Christian or Christian-influenced depictions and denunciations of Judaism as an empty legalism, and second, by the struggle of Jewish intellectuals and Jewish religious reformers to insist against that challenge on an "ethical" meaning of Judaism. Indeed, we will see that Cohen's own efforts to grasp the relationship between law and ethics in general are best understood in relation to that religio-cultural-historical horizon.

In contemporary Jewish thought, not only do we see rich ongoing discussions of the relationships and tensions between halakhah and ethics in Jewish frameworks, but also many noteworthy initiatives to pose, or re-cast, classic "general" political or juridico-ethical questions while engaging with Jewish legal, ethical, and political traditions.

With these lively domains of inquiry in mind, it might appear that we could present Cohen as a member of a class of thinkers who have provided intellectual resources for thinking politics or law from out of "Jewish sources." In doing so, we could pick up from Cohen's own careful methodological elaborations in his *Religion of Reason Out of the Sources of Judaism* on what the "sources of Judaism" are, and on how to engage with a "source" without either reducing it to being a mere illustration

---

Strauss and K.R. Grossman (Heidelberg: Lothar Stiehm Verlag, 1970); also included in Schwarzschild, *The Tragedy of Optimism: Writings on Hermann Cohen*, ed. George Y. Kohler (Albany: State University of New York Press, 2018). This interpretative debate was also taken up, in conjunction with the question of the relationship between the main philosophical oeuvre and the *Religion* works, by Dieter Adelmann in *Einheit des Bewusstseins als Grundproblem der Philosophie Hermann Cohens* (1968), 2nd rev. ed., ed. Görge K. Hasselhoff and Beate Ulrike La Sala (Potsdam: Universitätsverlag Potsdam, 2012), part 2, "Der Zweck des 'Systems der Philosophie'"; and in Zank, *The Idea of Atonement*, 165–77. See also Daniel H. Weiss, introduction to *Paradox and the Prophets: Hermann Cohen and the Indirect Communication of Religion* (Oxford: Oxford University Press, 2012).

of a philosophically self-sufficient discovery, or historistically elevating a manufactured notion of "context" to being an arbiter of philosophical validity.[4] But this kind of framing of Cohen, or of any number of other modern Jewish thinkers or intellectuals, by referring to some mode of Jewish "tradition" poses problems. Work by modern Jewish authors – by which I mean authors living not in an exclusively Jewish milieu – emerges and exists as part of a network of intellectual discourses whose link to Judaism or Jewish traditions is by definition an open question. By "open question," I don't mean some task of determining the nature or strength of the link between a given discourse and something we call Judaism. I mean, rather, that in exploring or extending modern Jewish thought, we can never presuppose, but must always be discovering and interrogating, what is meant, in a specific context, by "Judaism" or "Jewish."

How, then, do we legitimately approach the work of Cohen – as of any author who may be said to be a modern "Jewish thinker" – in relation to, or as contributing to, something called "Jewish philosophy," without oversimplifying or overdetermining our object of study in any number of obvious ways? For example, we might be tempted to consider the oeuvre in terms of a divide between "Jewish" and "general" spheres of activity or influence and to organize its elements or discernible origins accordingly using the headings "Jewish" or – to take some examples that would be pertinent for Cohen's case – "German" or "idealist" or "Neo-Kantian" or "Protestant." Or we might instead operate with the "Jewish" as a fixed horizon or sphere of influence and understand the Cohenian oeuvre as either emerging from that influence, or as falling short of expectations as to what a properly "Jewish" thought ought to look like – perhaps "explaining" this divergence by imputing to the author an overidentification with, or "assimilation" to something not-Jewish. (This latter sort of approach was for a time a fixture across treatments of Cohen, up until a couple of decades ago.)

None of these options – of which we can find many exemplars in scholarship on Jewish thinkers – is satisfactory, of course. Indeed, the constraints that the associated potential pitfalls ought to impose on us should suggest that the very field of "modern Jewish philosophy" be understood and constituted from the start as one that interrogates, rather than presupposing, the myriad constructions of "Jewish" in relation to

4 See chapter 3 below, as well as my essay "Ethical-Political Universality Out of the Sources of Judaism: Reading Hermann Cohen's 1888 Affidavit In and Out of Context," in *New Directions in Jewish Philosophy*, ed. Aaron W. Hughes and Elliot R. Wolfson (Bloomington: Indiana University Press, 2009).

its others. Modern Jewish philosophy is, and must continually be, constituted as an inquiry into difference as such. It is an arena in which the orders of dependence between the universal and the particular, between the "general" and the "Jewish" are continually called into question, and in which such calling-into-question is an essential source or condition for creative thinking.

A conception of, or ambition for modern Jewish philosophy along such lines informs my approach to Cohen in this book.

Biographical Sketch

Before giving an overview of the argumentative trajectory of this book, a short sketch of Hermann Cohen's life is in order.[5]

Hermann Cohen was born in 1842 in Coswig, a small town in Anhalt, the only child of Gerson and Friederike Cohen. Gerson Cohen was a cantor and the sole teacher in the town's Jewish school (a supplementary school; Jewish children were since the emancipation required to attend public schools); and Friederike Cohen (née Salomon) supported the family with a store for women's hats. The elder Cohen had

5 The following biographical information draws chiefly on Ulrich Sieg, *Aufstieg und Niedergang des Marburger Neukantianismus: die Geschichte einer philosophischen Schulgemeinschaft* (Würzburg: Königshausen & Neumann, 1994), 107ff., and "Der frühe Hermann Cohen und die Völkerpsychologie," *Aschkenas. Zeitschrift für Geschichte und Kultur der Juden* 13, no. 2 (2003): 461–83; and Zank, *The Idea of Atonement*, 48ff. – all three of which refer to a wealth of further sources that illuminate various contexts and aspects of Cohen's life and work. Franz Orlik's catalogue of an exhibition he curated at the University of Marburg assembles many bibliographical details and documents: *Hermann Cohen (1842–1918). Kantinterpret, Begründer der "Marburger Schule," Jüdischer Religionsphilosoph. Eine Ausstellung in der Universitätsbibliothek Marburg vom 1. Juli bis 14. August 1992* (Marburg: Universitätsbibliothek Marburg, 1992). An invaluable sketch of Cohen's early life and family and their historical-geographical context was published after Cohen's death by Salomon Steinthal (1859–1927; a member of the Coswig branch of the Steinthal family, whose familiarity with Cohen was facilitated by his having pursued his [presumably medical] studies at the University of Marburg) in the Jewish weekly *Allgemeine Zeitung des Judentums*: "Aus Hermann Cohens Heimat," 82, no. 19 (10 May 1918); reprinted in *Jüdisches Gemeindeblatt für Anhalt und Umgegend* 3, no. 4 (4 November 1927). (Note that some of the scholarship on Cohen misattributes this essay to "H. Steinthal.") Hartwig Wiedebach surveys Cohen's early life in "Hermann Cohens Kindheit. Aus Anlaß seines 100. Todestages am 4. April 2018," in *Kalonymos. Beiträge zur deutsch-jüdischen Geschichte aus dem Salomon Ludwig Steinheim-Institut an der Universität Duisburg-Essen* 21, no. 1 (2018). Chapter 1 ("Early Years, 1842–1865") of Frederick C. Beiser's *Hermann Cohen: An Intellectual Biography* (Oxford: Oxford University Press, 2018) (which appeared too late for me to take full account of it in the present book) contains much important information.

studied in a yeshiva and was also well versed in secular learning. The family was observant, and the younger Cohen was proficient in Jewish religious learning and synagogue liturgy – he sometimes supported his father in performing cantorial duties. After attending primary school in Coswig and a *Gymnasium* in Dessau, in 1857, aged fifteen, Cohen moved to Breslau (today Wroclaw, Poland) to begin rabbinical studies at the Jüdisch Theologisches Seminar, which had been founded only three years earlier by Zacharias Frankel. This was a pathbreaking institution for rabbinical training and academic scholarship, with leading scholars (such as Heinrich Graetz and Jacob Bernays) among its faculty, which was to become highly influential across Europe, and in the United States as well, in subsequent decades. The 1904 *Jewish Encyclopedia* entry characterizes it as "proclaim[ing] freedom in theoretical research, but demand[ing] of its disciples a faithful adherence to the practices of traditional Judaism."[6] The 1972 *Encyclopaedia Judaica* characterizes the Breslau model as follows: "The seminary's basic aim was to teach 'positive historical Judaism.' The 'positive' stood for a faithful adherence to the practical precepts of Judaism, while 'historical' permitted free inquiry into the Jewish past, including even Bible criticism, though with some self-imposed limitations."[7] Beyond its role as a pathbreaking seminary for future rabbis and teachers, the Jüdisch Theologisches Seminar also quickly emerged as a preeminent center for the academic study of Judaism ("Wissenschaft des Judentums"), and also helped inaugurate and lead what has come to be understood to be a "middle movement" in Jewish religious life, a third denominational path between (Neo-)Orthodoxy and Reform.[8] In a tribute to this institution written in 1904, Cohen lauded the values it embodied for him of having "placed" scholarship

6 *The Jewish Encyclopedia* (1904), s.v. "Jüdisch-Theologisches Seminar (Fränckelscher Stiftung)."

7 *Encyclopaedia Judaica*, 2nd ed. (2007), s.v. "Juedisch-Theologisches Seminar, Breslau" (1972). For a fuller explanation of what the term "positive" means in Frankel's program for Judaism, see Ismar Schorsch, "Zacharias Frankel and the European Origins of Conservative Judaism," *Judaism* 30 (1981): 344–54.

8 Andreas Brämer, "Introduction: The Jewish-Theological Seminary of Breslau, the 'Science of Judaism' and the Development of a Middle-of-the-Road Current in Religious Judaism," *transversal* 14, no. 1 (March 2016), and "Jüdische 'Glaubenswissenschaft' – Zacharias Frankels rechtshistorische Forschungen als Herausforderung der Orthodoxie," in *Die "Wissenschaft des Judentums": eine Bestandsaufnahme*, ed. Thomas Meyer and Andreas Kilcher (Paderborn: Wilhelm Fink, 2015). Frankel came to be regarded as having "founded and shaped European Conservatism," in the sense of the American denomination of Conservative Judaism; see Schorsch, "Zacharias Frankel," 344.

(*Wissenschaft*) directly "into" "faith" – an "identification" which he regarded as vital for "true piety."[9]

Though his studies at the Breslau seminary were doubtless significant for Cohen's Jewish education and his orientation in the Jewish world, he remained enrolled there for only four years. In 1861, finding himself disinterested in "theology"[10] and drawn instead to university academics, he entered the University of Breslau full-time as a student of philosophy and philology (concurrently completing his *Abitur* [secondary school diploma] at a Breslau *Gymnasium*) and moved in 1864 to the Friedrich Wilhelms Universität in Berlin.[11] Cohen received his doctorate in 1865 with a dissertation on the antinomy between contingency and necessity in Greek philosophy.[12] In the following years, with no immediate prospects for advancement in a university, Cohen struggled to make a living as a private teacher in Berlin. He found an important mentor in Heymann Steinthal, who together with Moritz Lazarus was establishing a new academic discipline they termed *Völkerpsychologie*, a "psycho-ethnography" that combined the study of culture, language, myth, and religion and was a precursor of modern cultural anthropology.[13] Cohen published three major essays in their journal, *Zeitschrift für Völkerpsychologie und Sprachwissenschaft*, among which his essay on Plato's theory of forms

9 "Ein Gruß der Pietät an das Breslauer Seminar," JS2: 422, 423.

10 As per the letter he wrote to Eduard Steinthal (see *Briefe*, 12–13) and quoted by Sieg, *Aufstieg und Niedergang*, 107. In both this letter and the above-cited tribute to the Breslau seminary, Cohen also reports that the bitter feud between Zacharias Frankel, its director, and Samson Raphael Hirsch, the leader of Neo-Orthodoxy, provided the "external occasion" for his exit. For details of this conflict, see Brämer, "Jüdische 'Glaubenswissenschaft.'" Zank, *The Idea of Atonement*, 58–62, discusses the conflict and its impact on Cohen.

11 For information on how rabbinical students in this era, including those at the Breslau seminary, pursued their studies concurrently at local universities, see Carsten L. Wilke, "Talmudschüler, Student, Seminarist: Breslauer rabbinische Studienlaufbahnen 1835–1870," in *Aschkenas. Zeitschrift für Geschichte und Kultur der Juden* 15, no. 1 (2005).

12 Having encountered some resistance to his work at the Berlin university, Cohen submitted the dissertation instead to the University of Halle. Sieg, "Der frühe Hermann Cohen," 466–8. The dissertation is discussed by Beiser in *Hermann Cohen*, 17–20.

13 Marcel Stoetzler has introduced the term "psycho-ethnography" as a translation of *Völkerpsychologie* so as to capture the fact that "it is concerned with the 'souls' of peoples, not with ethnographic aspects of the psychology of individuals." Stoetzler, *The State, the Nation, and the Jews: Liberalism and the Antisemitism Dispute in Bismarck's Germany* (Lincoln: University of Nebraska Press, 2009), 2, 389n3. Ivan Kalmar describes this discipline and its impact in "The *Völkerpsychologie* of Lazarus and Steinthal and the Modern Concept of Culture," *Journal of the History of Ideas* 48, no. 4 (October–December 1987). Both Ulrich Sieg and Frederick Beiser trace the influence of

("Die platonische Ideenlehre, psychologisch entwickelt," 1867) had the greatest significance for the development of his own thought.[14] A major shift in Cohen's thinking away from the psychology-based approach to a Kantian methodological orientation is represented by two publications in 1871: an article responding to the controversy about Kant's "transcendental a priori" between his teacher Adolf Trendelenburg and Kuno Fischer ("Zur Kontroverse zwischen Trendelenburg und Kuno Fischer"),[15] and his first major book, *Kants Theorie der Erfahrung* ("Kant's Theory of Experience"),[16] which, in presenting Kantian theoretical philosophy as an essentially epistemological program – centering on the transcendental conditions of knowing – laid a foundation for what became known as the Marburg School of Neo-Kantianism.[17]

Völkerpsychologie on Cohen's thinking – in particular his changing understanding of the importance of psychology – in the years 1865–71. Sieg, "Der frühe Hermann Cohen," 469–75; Beiser, "The Young Hermann Cohen," chap. 12 in *The Genesis of Neo-Kantianism, 1796–1880* (Oxford: Oxford University Press, 2014), and "The Young Folk Psychologist," chap. 2 in *Hermann Cohen.* The relationship of Cohen to Steinthal is explored by Dieter Adelmann in "H. Steinthal und Hermann Cohen" in *Hermann Cohen's Philosophy of Religion: International Conference in Jerusalem, 1996,* ed. Stéphane Mosès and Hartwig Wiedebach (Hildesheim: Olms, 1997). The ups and downs of Cohen's relationship with Steinthal and Lazarus were also intertwined with Cohen's Jewish involvements, including his role in the growing field of Wissenschaft des Judentums, as explained by Zank, *The Idea of Atonement,* 66–9.

14 Included in SPZ 1 and *Werke* 12. See Beiser, "The Young Hermann Cohen," 471–4, and Andrea Poma, *The Critical Philosophy of Hermann Cohen* (1988), trans. John Denton (Albany: State University of New York Press, 1997), 22–4.

15 Included in SPZ 1. See Beiser, "The Young Hermann Cohen," 478ff., and Helmut Holzhey, "Hermann Cohen: der Philosoph in Auseinandersetzung mit den politischen und gesellschaftlichen Problemen seiner Zeit," in *Philosophisches Denken – politisches Wirken. Hermann-Cohen-Kolloquium Marburg 1992,* ed. Reinhard Brandt and Franz Orlik (Hildesheim: Olms, 1993), 16. In chapter 1 of *The Critical Philosophy of Hermann Cohen,* Poma introduces Cohen's early interpretations of Kant – including his response to the Trendelenburg-Fischer controversy – in the context of the Neo-Kantian philosophical movements (the "return to Kant") of the time.

16 A second, much longer edition appeared in 1885. The argument of the first edition is presented by Beiser, "The Young Hermann Cohen," 482–3, and by Poma, *Critical Philosophy,* chap. 1. All three editions are in *Werke* 1.

17 See Beiser, "The Young Hermann Cohen," 465–6. I take up these methodological questions and their role for Cohen's thinking – especially about ethics and law – in chapter 1. For a short introduction to Cohen's interpretation of Kantian philosophy, see Scott Edgar, "Hermann Cohen," *Stanford Encyclopedia of Philosophy* (Fall 2015 Edition), https://plato.stanford.edu/archives/fall2015/entries/cohen/. For brief introductory information on Neo-Kantianism and the Marburg School, see the introduction to Helmut Holzhey and Vilem Mudroch, *Historical Dictionary of Kant and Kantianism* (Lanham, MD: Scarecrow Press, 2005), 11–14, as well as the entry "Marburg School of Neokantianism," 174–5.

Cohen twice (in 1871 and in 1873) unsuccessfully sought the Habilitation degree (required for a university professorship) from the Berlin university on the basis of the latter work, to which he later added the manuscript of his book on Kant's ethics, *Kants Begründung der Ethik* (1st ed. 1877). His breakthrough to an academic career in philosophy was finally enabled by Friedrich Albert Lange, who became an important mentor and influenced Cohen in his embrace of Kantianism.[18] Lange's work *History of Materialism* was widely read and was influential for the establishment of Neo-Kantian philosophy as a leading force in the academy.[19] (Cohen would later go on to write an extensive introduction to Lange's book, which was included from the 1896 edition onwards. In its three editions [1896, 1902, and 1914], Cohen's introduction in fact provides a good introduction to his own philosophy[20]). Lange had been a professor, political activist, and journalist in Germany. He had a prominent role in the labor movement and in the development of social democratic thought. Having spent several years teaching in Switzerland, in 1872 he accepted a professorship at the University of Marburg – part of a wave of political liberalism that had taken hold in the German Reich.[21] By that time, Cohen and Lange were already acquainted, and in 1873 Lange successfully supported Cohen's Habilitation at Marburg, for which Cohen submitted (again) his first Kant book, as well as a manuscript on "The

---

18 See Beiser, "The Young Hermann Cohen," 477–8. In "Encounter with Friedrich Albert Lange," chap. 5 of *Hermann Cohen: An Intellectual Biography*, Beiser describes Cohen's ongoing engagement in acknowledgment of his personal indebtedness to Lange and provides a detailed consideration of this relationship. See also Helmut Holzhey, "Neukantianismus und Sozialismus," introduction to *Ethischer Sozialismus. Zur politischen Philosophie des Neukantianismus*, ed. Holzhey (Frankfurt am Main: Suhrkamp, 1994), 11–12; and Poma, *Critical Philosophy*, 26–9, 59, 281n23.

For an introduction to the person and work of Friedrich Albert Lange, see Nadeem J. Z. Hussain and Lydia Patton, "Friedrich Albert Lange," *Stanford Encyclopedia of Philosophy* (Winter 2016 Edition), https://plato.stanford.edu/archives/win2016/entries/friedrich-lange/; Thomas Willey, *Back to Kant: The Revival of Kantianism in German Social and Historical Thought, 1860–1914* (Detroit: Wayne State University Press, 1978), chap. 4; and Sieg, *Aufstieg und Niedergang*, 86ff.

19 F.A. Lange, *Geschichte des Materialismus und Kritik seiner Bedeutung in der Gegenwart*, 1st ed. (Iserlohn: Baedeker, 1866), 2nd ed. (1873–5), translated by by Ernest Chester Thomas as *The History of Materialism and Criticism of Its Importance* (London: Trübner, 1877), 3rd ed. (London: Kegan Paul, 1925).

20 See EmkN; Myriam Bienenstock, "Présentation," in *Hermann Cohen. Le concept de philosophie* (Paris: Cerf, 2014); and Helmut Holzhey, "Einführung des Herausgebers," in Cohen, *Werke* 5/II.

21 This was connected to the tenure of Adalbert Falk as Minister of Culture. See also note 24.

Systematic Concepts in Kant's Pre-critical Writings in Their Relationship to Critical Idealism."[22] The following year, Lange worked, without success, to have Cohen appointed to a professorship in his institute. Following the contentious deliberations – with, to be sure, some anti-Jewish undertones – which resulted in the appointment of a different candidate, support for Cohen's candidacy for a position at Marburg remained strong at the institute, with the result that, after Lange's own death in 1875, Cohen was nearly unanimously, and successfully, proposed as his successor.[23] Cohen thereby became the first Jewish chair-holding professor ("Ordentlicher Professor" or *Ordinariat*) for philosophy in Germany, at a time when it was very rare for (non-converted) Jews to hold university positions. (Indeed, his appointment to such a position could only have taken place during a very short-lived window of a few years, during which the Prussian state was open to Jews holding professorships, before the rise of political antisemitism beginning in 1879.)[24]

In 1876, Cohen married Martha Lewandowski (born 1860), whose Berlin family he had been friendly with for a number of years. Martha's

---

22 *Die systematischen Begriffe in Kants vorkritischen Schriften nach ihrem Verhältniss zum kritischen Idealismus* (Berlin: Dümmler, 1873), in SPZ vol. 1: 276–335.

23 Helmut Holzhey, *Cohen und Natorp* (see note 31 below), 1: 1–3; Sieg, *Aufstieg und Niedergang*, 113–18. The two dissenting votes came from professors who expressed concerns that appointing a Jew to a professorship would threaten the Christian character of the university.

24 See Steven S. Schwarzschild, "'Germanism and Judaism – Hermann Cohen's Normative Paradigm of the German-Jewish Symbiosis," in *Jews and Germans from 1860 to 1933: The Problematic Symbiosis*, ed. D. Bronsen (Heidelberg: Carl Winter, 1979), 135–6 (also included in Schwarzschild, *The Tragedy of Optimism*), 135–6; and Zank, *The Idea of Atonement*, 78–9, referring also to Ernest Hamburger's study (see below). On the political dimension of the appointments of Cohen and of a number of leading Neo-Kantian figures in 1876–8, see Klaus Christian Köhnke, *Entstehung und Aufstieg des Neukantianismus: die deutsche Universitätsphilosophie zwischen Idealismus und Positivismus* (Frankfurt am Main: Suhrkamp, 1986), 307–8; translated by R.J. Hollingdale as *The Rise of Neo-Kantianism: German Academic Philosophy between Idealism and Positivism* (Cambridge: Cambridge University Press, 1991), 202. On the complex and multiple trajectories of Jews' access to positions at German universities since the emancipation, see for example, Ernest Hamburger, *Juden im öffentlichen Leben Deutschlands* (Tübingen: Mohr Siebeck, 1968), 8–17, 27–9, 54–6. Both Zank and Hamburger refer to a 1911 survey of who held professorships from 1874/75 to 1909/10, conducted on behalf of the Verband der Deutschen Juden by Bernhard Breslauer: *Die Zurücksetzung der Juden an den Universitäten Deutschlands* (Berlin: Levy, 1911). On the complex conditions of Jews' pursuing university careers specifically in the humanities, see Ulrich Sieg, "Der Preis des Bildungsstrebens. Jüdische Geisteswissenschaftler im Kaiserreich," in *Juden, Bürger, Deutsche. Zur Geschichte von Vielfalt und Differenz. 1800–1933*, ed. Andreas Gotzmann, Rainer Liedtke, and Till van Rahden (Tübingen: Mohr Siebeck, 2001).

father was Louis Lewandowski (1821–94), the pathbreaking Jewish liturgical composer and musical director of the Neue Synagoge (on Oranienburger Strasse) in Berlin. Martha Cohen was a pianist, and music was an important part of the couple's life.[25] She was also intensively involved in the production of her husband's philosophical oeuvre, due to his diminishing eyesight beginning in 1892. Hermann Cohen wrote his later books by dictation to Martha, who transcribed them. His most important work on Jewish religion, *Religion of Reason Out of the Sources of Judaism*, appeared posthumously. As is explained by its editor, Bruno Strauss, Cohen was able to personally proofread the transcribed text only up to the middle of chapter 15, "Immortality and Resurrection," before he died.[26] (After Hermann Cohen's death in 1919, Martha Cohen continued living in their Berlin apartment, amidst his manuscripts and their other shared possessions. She lived long enough, indeed, to endure the end of the era of German-Jewish co-existence. At the age of eighty-two, in September 1942, she was deported to the Theresienstadt concentration camp, where she died shortly after arrival.[27])

With his university career secured, Cohen went on to publish two additional books developing his interpretations of Kant's philosophy: the above-mentioned *Kants Begründung der Ethik* (1877) and *Kants Begründung der Ästhetik* (1889). A new phase of Cohen's work consisted in moving past attempts to account for Kantian philosophy in terms of a "theory of knowledge" (*Erkenntnistheorie*) toward an independent project of "critique of knowledge" (*Erkenntniskritik*) and a program of "critical idealism."[28] This project begins to take shape in the second expanded edition of the first Kant book (1885) and in the long essay *Das Prinzip der Infinitesimal-Methode und seine Geschichte* (1883; *The Principle of the*

25 Liliana Ruth Feierstein remarks on the importance of music for Cohen's connection to Jewish tradition in *Von Schwelle zu Schwelle: Einblicke in den didaktisch-historischen Umgang mit dem Anderen aus der Perspektive jüdischen Denkens* (Bremen: Edition Lumière, 2010), 115–16. See also James Loeffler, "When Hermann Cohen Cried: Zionism, Culture, Emotions," in *Zionism as a Cultural Movement*, ed. Israel Bartal and Rachel Rojansky (Leiden: Brill, forthcoming).

26 Bruno Strauss, "Nachwort des Herausgebers" ("Editor's Remarks to the Second German Edition"), RV 623–4/xli.

27 Holzhey, "Hermann Cohen," 17, 22; Zank, *The Idea of Atonement*, 64n66. Ulrich Sieg, "Das Testament von Hermann und Martha Cohen. Stiftungen und Stipendien für jüdische Einrichtungen," *Zeitschrift für neuere Theologiegeschichte* 4 (1997): 260. Sieg, *Aufstieg und Niedergang*, 248n266.

28 See chapter 1. The notion of "critical idealism" is at the center of Andrea Poma's presentation of Cohen's philosophy in *Critical Philosophy of Hermann Cohen*, see esp. chaps. 3 and 4.

Infinitesimal Method and Its History).[29] The latter two works form a kind of turning point on the way to the three systematic works that Cohen subsequently authored, his *Logik der reinen Erkenntnis* (1902; *Logic of Pure Cognition*), *Ethik des reinen Willens* (1904; *Ethics of Pure Will*), and *Ästhetik des reinen Gefühls* (1912; *Aesthetics of Pure Feeling*). (In the latter volume, Cohen gestured to a possible fourth part of his philosophical system, a psychology, which he did not get around to writing, as the following years were devoted to consolidating his philosophy of [Jewish] religion.[30]) Helmut Holzhey has noted that *Prinzip der Infinitesimal-Methode* along with the second edition of *Kant's Theorie der Erfahrung* may be considered as supplying the philosophical doctrine of what came to be known as the "Marburg School of Neo-Kantianism," even though the School would not come to full fruition until after 1900, during the decade when Cohen was writing his three systematic works.[31] A decisive development for the formation of the Marburg School was the arrival in 1880 of Paul Natorp at Marburg, where he received the Habilitation degree in 1881 and was appointed a professor in 1893.[32] The school attracted attention from the German academic community and from across Europe.[33] The best-known philosophers who studied at Marburg were Albert Görland, Ernst Cassirer, Nicolai Hartmann, Wladyslaw Tatarkiewicz, Dimitri Gavronsky, Heinz Heimsoeth, Karl Vorländer, and José Ortega y Gasset.

---

29 *Das Prinzip der Infinitesimal-Methode und seine Geschichte. Ein Kapitel zur Grundlegung der Erkenntniskritik*, 1st ed. (1883); 2nd ed. in SPZ 2; 3rd. ed., ed. Werner Flach (Frankfurt: Suhrkamp, 1968); 4th ed., *Werke* 5/I (1984), ed. Peter Schulthess; 5th ed., ed. Johannes Kleinbeck (Vienna: Turia & Kant, 2013). On the second edition of *Kants Theorie der Erfahrung* in connection with *Prinzip der Infinitesimal-Methode*, see Poma, *Critical Philosophy of Hermann Cohen*, chap. 3. On *Prinzip der Infinitesimal-Methode*, see Astrid Deuber-Mankowsky, "Einleitung," to Kleinbeck's reedition of that work, as well as Marco Giovanelli, "Hermann Cohen's *Das Princip der Inifinitesimal-Methode*: The History of an Unsuccessful Book," in *Studies in History and Philosophy of Science* 58 (2016).

30 Holzhey, "Hermann Cohen," 19–20.

31 Holzhey, "Hermann Cohen," 17–18. Holzhey has published a full account of the interactions among the members of the Marburg School, including the correspondence among Cohen, Natorp, and other key players: *Cohen und Natorp*, vol. 1: *Ursprung und Einheit. Die Geschichte der "Marburger Schule" als Auseinandersetzung um die Logik des Denkens*; vol. 2: *Der Marburger Neukantianismus in Quellen. Zeugnisse kritischer Lektüre. Briefe der Marburger. Dokumente zur Philosophiepolitik der Schule* (Basel/Stuttgart: Schwabe, 1986). For a comprehensive history of the Marburg school, see Sieg, *Aufstieg und Niedergang*.

32 Holzhey, "Hermann Cohen," 17, and Köhnke, *Entstehung und Aufstieg des Neukantianismus*, 502n1.

33 *Historical Dictionary of Kant and Kantianism* (2005), s.v. "Marburg School of Neokantianism."

Famously, the author Boris Pasternak was a student there, as well as the socialist politician Kurt Eisner.[34]

The rise of political antisemitism in the German Reich beginning in the late 1870s could not fail to have had a tremendous impact on Cohen's life and thinking, and he increasingly authored writings that engaged with anti-Jewish polemics, especially with those that attacked or conspicuously ignored Jewish religious and ethical traditions.[35] His first major foray into this arena was his essay in response to the landmark 1879 attack on Jews by the historian Heinrich von Treitschke that launched the infamous Berlin Antisemitism Dispute.[36] Cohen's second major intervention in an antisemitism dispute, his participation as an expert witness in the 1888 Marburg Antisemitism Trial, is a focal point of chapter 6 in this book. Indeed, the chapters that follow offer a number of cases

---

34 On Kurt Eisner's intellectual debt to Cohen, see Eisner, "Hermann Cohen" (1912), *Die halbe Macht den Räten. Ausgewählte Aufsätze und Reden,* ed. Renate and Gerhard Schmolze (Cologne: Jakob Hegner, 1969); Albert E. Gurganus, *Kurt Eisner: A Modern Life* (Rochester, NY: Camden House, 2018), chap. 3; and Michael Brenner, "Between Hermann Cohen and Karl Marx: The Jewish Dimension of Kurt Eisner's Revolution in Bavaria, 1918–19," *Modern Judaism* 40, no. 1 (February 2020).

35 See Schwarzschild, "'Germanism and Judaism,'" 135–6.

36 The Berlin Antisemitism Dispute has received detailed scholarly treatment, for example in Stoetzler, *The State, the Nation, and the Jews*; Hans Liebeschütz, *Das Judentum im deutschen Geschichtsbild von Hegel bis Max Weber* (Tübingen: Mohr Siebeck, 1967), chaps. 5 and 6; Michael A. Meyer, "Great Debate on Antisemitism: Jewish Reaction to New Hostility in Germany 1879–1881," *Leo Baeck Institute Year Book* 11 (1966).

In addition to the compilation of texts making up the dispute by Walter Boehlich, ed., *Der Berliner Antisemitismusstreit* (Frankfurt am Main: Insel, 1965), there is also a critical edition: Karsten Krieger, ed., *Der "Berliner Antisemitismusstreit" 1879–1881. Eine Kontroverse um die Zugehörigkeit der deutschen Juden zur Nation. Eine kommentierte Quellenedition im Auftrag des Zentrums für Antisemitismusforschung,* 2 vols. (Munich: K.G. Saur, 2003).

Michael Zank notes that Cohen's published response, "Ein Bekenntnis in der Judenfrage" (1880; JS2: 73–94) was "the first text on Judaism Cohen published under his name." Zank discusses this work as a questionable defense of Judaism, as well as the criticism it received from fellow Jews, in *Idea of Atonement,* 77–97, as does Sieg in *Aufstieg und Niedergang,* 146–52. Both Zank and Sieg highlight that Cohen's "Bekenntnis" must be read against the background of two letters that Cohen initially sent to Treitschke, with the request that Treitschke publish them in his journal, *Preußische Jahrbücher* (in which he also published his initial attack). Those letters have also been published: Helmut Holzhey, "Zwei Briefe Hermann Cohens an Heinrich von Treitschke," *Bulletin des Leo Baeck Instituts* 12 (1969). See also Andrea Poma, "Hermann Cohen's Response to Anti-Judaism," in *Yearning for Form, and Other Essays on Hermann Cohen's Thought* (Dordrecht: Springer, 2006), chap. 1; George Y. Kohler, "German Spirit and Holy Ghost – Treitschke's Call for Conversion of German Jewry: The Debate Revisited," *Modern Judaism* 30, no. 2 (May 2010).

in point for how Cohen's efforts to analyze and expose anti-Judaism in the culture at large and in academic scholarship form a part of his philosophical thought. It should be noted that, despite Cohen's accession to a professorship (which, as mentioned above, was due to a period of short-lived openness in Prussia to Jewish and politically liberal academics) and despite his role in establishing an influential school of philosophy, there are indications that, as a Jew, he continued to be embattled and institutionally excluded in many respects. (Ulrich Sieg has analyzed the mode in which Cohen and similarly situated Jewish scholars functioned at German universities in Wilhelmine Germany as one of "established outsider" – with the accent on "outsider."[37])

As will become evident from the references to Cohen's "Jewish writings" in this book, Cohen's scholarly work on Judaism and related topics was ongoing, with the pace of his publications and activities in this area accelerating as of around 1900. The works collected posthumously in the *Jüdische Schriften* edition typically originated as lectures at meetings of Jewish popular or scholarly organizations (plus a couple of noteworthy instances of lectures at Christian or ecumenical gatherings, such as the Fifth World Congress of Free Christianity and Religious Progress or the Freie Wissenschaftliche Vereinigung, an anti-antisemitic organization), or as articles in Jewish newspapers and scholarly journals. Looking at the corpus of Jewish writings, we can see Cohen working out, continually over a long period, a number of themes that would become constitutive for his philosophy of Jewish religion. Drawing on biblical, rabbinic, and medieval Jewish philosophical writings, as well as on the insights worked out in his systematic-philosophical writings, we find him returning continually to discussing such themes as atonement, messianism, justice, and love-of-neighbor as the core elements of Jewish religion, in its ethical and universalist significance.[38] The opportunity to consolidate these ideas into a systematic philosophy of Judaism came, as already mentioned, in 1912, when Cohen retired from his professorship at Marburg and moved to Berlin to teach full-time at the Lehranstalt für die Wissenschaft des Judentums. This continued a longtime involvement of his with this

37 Sieg, "Preis des Bildungsstrebens," esp. 90–3.

38 In *The Idea of Atonement*, Michael Zank gives an indispensable detailed analysis of how Cohen's philosophical account of Jewish religion took shape against the background of his decisive interpretations of messianism and atonement in the early 1890s, in writings that remained unpublished until the posthumous *Jüdische Schriften* (101–51), as well as of how that account takes shape in the writings from 1899 onwards that develop the theory we see articulated fully in *Religion of Reason* (151–61).

historic institution of Jewish scholarship, on whose board he served, and at which he had held occasional lecture courses while still a professor at Marburg.[39] It was during this period that he worked on his two books on Judaism, *Der Begriff der Religion* (1915; *The Concept of Religion*), and the posthumously published *Religion of Reason Out of the Sources of Judaism* (1919/1929; *Religion der Vernunft aus den Quellen des Judentums*).

As has been much discussed, Cohen was a German patriot, who argued for a spiritual and intellectual affinity between German and Jewish thought and culture as beacons of universalism and humanity. The two works titled "Deutschtum und Judentum" ("Germanism and Judaism") along with related works written during the First World War, form a kind of high point of this mode of writing engaged in by Cohen.[40] At the same time, Cohen was also writing polemical essays that dissociated Judaism

39 Zank, *The Idea of Atonement*, 68–9; Sieg, *Aufstieg und Niedergang*, 258. Cohen's involvement with the centers of "Wissenschaft des Judentums" was multifaceted – beginning, of course, with his lifelong ties to the seminary at Breslau. For instance, in 1902, he helped initiate a new Gesellschaft zur Förderung der Wissenschaft des Judentums, whose goal was to sponsor an ambitious research and publication program (see Zank, *The Idea of Atonement*, 161–4). Part of the agenda he pursued as a member of that society was to argue for the inclusion of the disciplines of ethics and philosophy as part of "Wissenschaft des Judentums," and thus also in the curricula of academies such as the Lehranstalt. (See Cohen's presentation of this argument in "Die Errichtung von Lehrstühlen für Ethik und Religionsphilosophie an den jüdisch-theologischen Lehranstalten" [1904] in JS2.) Another example is that shortly before his death, through his intellectual exchanges with Franz Rosenzweig, Cohen enthusiastically responded to the latter's call for a new kind of "academy for Wissenschaft des Judentums." See Cohen's "Zur Begründung einer Akademie für die Wissenschaft des Judentums" (1918) in JS2: 210–17; and David N. Myers, "The Fall and Rise of Jewish Historicism: The Evolution of the Akademie für die Wissenschaft des Judentums (1919–1934)," *Hebrew Union College Annual* 63 (1992). Dieter Adelmann argues that Cohen's own writing projects elaborating a Jewish philosophy of religion, culminating in *Religion of Reason*, are integral to his involvement in the Gesellschaft zur Förderung der Wissenschaft des Judentums and its large-scale publication plans. "Kawwana (Andacht) und der kantorale Hintergrund in Hermann Cohens Begriff der Philosophie" (1997), 86–7; and "Die 'Religion der Vernunft' im 'Grundriss der Gesamtwissenschaft des Judentums'" (2000), in *"Reinige dein Denken." Über den jüdischen Hintergrund der Philosophie von Hermann Cohen*, ed. Görge K. Hasselhoff (Würzburg: Königshausen & Neumann, 2010).

40 *Deutschtum und Judentum. Mit grundlegenden Betrachtungen über Staat und Internationalismus* (1915; 2nd ed., 1916), JS2: 237–301, and in *Werke*, vol. 16. "Deutschtum und Judentum" (1916), JS2: 302–18, and in *Werke*, vol. 17. The *Werke* editions include pagination for the JS editions.

Marc B. de Launay, presenting this work to a French readership in *Pardès*, no. 5 (1987), called it a *texte maudit*, an "accursed text," a formulation later commented upon by Jacques Derrida in his reading of *Deutschtum und Judentum* in

and Zionism, most notably as part of a public exchange with Martin Buber.[41] Cohen's arguments against Zionism are, indeed, closely linked

"Interpretations at war. Kant, le Juif, l'Allemand" (1989), in *Psyché: Inventions de l'autre II*, rev. ed. (Paris: Galileé, 1987–2003). Translated by Moshe Ron and Dana Hollander as "Interpretations at War: Kant, the Jew, the German," in *Psyche: Inventions of the Other*, vol. 2, ed. Peggy Kamuf and Elizabeth Rottenberg (Stanford: Stanford University Press, 2007). (I briefly discuss this treatment by Derrida of Cohen's *Deutschtum und Judentum* in the context of Derrida's writings on "philosophical nationality," in *Exemplarity and Chosenness*, 127–8.)

Emil Fackenheim reflects on the ambivalent legacy of Cohen's *Deutschtum und Judentum* for Jewish philosophy in *Hermann Cohen – After Fifty Years*, Leo Baeck Memorial Lecture 12 (New York: Leo Baeck Institute, 1969), 7–8. For a more affirmative assessment, see Schwarzschild, "'Germanism and Judaism,'" esp. 138–9; and most recently, Miguel Vatter in "Nationality, State and Global Constitutionalism in Hermann Cohen's Wartime Writings," in *100 Years of European Philosophy Since the Great War*, ed. Rory Jeffs, Jack Reynolds, and Matthew Sharpe (New York: Springer, 2017). On the historic and ongoing relevance of the conjunction "German" and "Jewish" that figures in Cohen's text along with some other exemplars, see Christoph Schulte's introduction to his edited anthology *Deutschtum und Judentum: ein Disput unter Juden aus Deutschland* (Stuttgart: Reclam, 1993).

The "Deutschtum und Judentum" texts are to be understood in the context of World War I and the pressure on Jews to be vocal about their allegiance to Germany. See Cohen's October–November 1914 letters to Paul Natorp, and editorial notes by Helmut Holzhey, in Holzhey, *Cohen und Natorp*, 2: 432–5; Hartwig Wiedebach, *Die Bedeutung der Nationalität für Hermann Cohen* (Hildesheim: Olms, 1997), 18–22; translated by William Templer as *The National Element in Hermann Cohen's Philosophy and Religion* (Leiden: Brill, 2012), 11–15. As well, see the introduction by Görge Hasselhoff and Knut Martin Stünkel to a translated selection from the 1916 essay in *Religious Dynamics under the Impact of Imperialism and Colonialism: A Sourcebook*, ed. Björn Bentlage et al. (Leiden: Brill, 2017), 489–90. Ulrich Sieg discusses the response to the war on the part of the Marburg Neo-Kantians in *Aufstieg und Niedergang*, 373ff., and Cohen's wartime writings in particular at 392–402. Frederick Beiser argues that the pro-war writings of Cohen and other Neo-Kantians were a factor in the waning of the influence of this philosophical movement after 1918: "Weimar Philosophy and the Fate of Neo-Kantianism," in *Weimar Thought: A Contested Legacy*, ed. Peter E. Gordon and John P. McCormick (Princeton: Princeton University Press, 2013), chap. 6, 127–8. Most recently, Paul E. Nahme has focused on "Deutschtum und Judentum," among other texts, in order to analyze the role and meaning of "Protestantism" in Cohen's philosophy: *Hermann Cohen and the Crisis of Liberalism: The Enchantment of the Public Sphere* (Bloomington: Indiana University Press, 2019), chap. 1.

41 See "Religion und Zionismus. Ein Wort an meine Kommilitonen jüdischen Glaubens" (1916), JS2 and *Werke* 17; "Antwort auf das offene Schreiben des Herrn Dr. Martin Buber an Hermann Cohen" (1916), JS2 and *Werke* 17. I discuss this exchange in "Buber, Cohen, Rosenzweig, and the Politics of Cultural Affirmation," *Jewish Studies Quarterly* 13, no. 1 (March 2006): 87–103. See also Aharon Shear-Yashuv, "Darstellung und kritische Würdigung von Hermann Cohens Stellung zum Zionismus," *Aschkenas. Zeitschrift für Geschichte und Kultur der Juden* 10, no. 2 (2000): 443–57; Jeffrey Andrew Barash, "Politics and Theology: The Debate on Zionism between

to his embrace of Germanism's affinity with Judaism,[42] and, as I discuss in chapter 4 of this book, to his theory of Judaism as a form of messianic universalism.

An important context for the present study of Cohen's ethico-legal-political philosophy is the political alignment of Cohen and the Marburg School of Neo-Kantianism with democratic socialism – an orientation often called "ethical socialism." This refers to efforts at the time of the "revisionist" challenges to Marxist economic and historical determinism at the turn of the twentieth century, associated above all with Eduard Bernstein, to reformulate socialism based on Kantian ethics. A number of studies have examined how Cohen's *Ethik* along with other works authored by the Marburg Neo-Kantians supported and interacted with socialist democratic political currents, and also argued for the lasting value of a Kantian undergirding of socialism along the lines suggested by Cohen. (I touch on the "socialist" dimensions of Cohen's philosophy in chapters 1 and 2 below.)[43]

Plan of the Book

This book does not attempt to give a comprehensive overview of its topic. To attempt to capture the entirety of Cohen's philosophical work on ethics and philosophy of law, and in addition to explore the myriad of ways that Cohen investigates questions of ethics and law in his

---

Hermann Cohen and Martin Buber," in *Dialogue as a Trans-disciplinary Concept: Martin Buber's Philosophy of Dialogue and its Contemporary Reception*, ed. Paul Mendes-Flohr (Berlin: de Gruyter, 2015). A correspondence that illuminates the Buber-Cohen exchange on Zionism was published by Hartwig Wiedebach in "Hermann Cohens Auseinandersetzung mit dem Zionismus," *Jewish Studies Quarterly* 6, no. 4 (January 2000).

42 See Wiedebach, *Bedeutung der Nationalität*, 23–6/15–18.

43 A good starting point for understanding Cohen's views on socialism is part 5 of the introduction to Lange, *Geschichte des Materialismus* (EmkN). On the links between Neo-Kantianism – in particular Cohen and the Marburg School – and socialism, see Holzhey, "Neukantianismus und Sozialismus"; Holzhey and Mudroch, *Historical Dictionary of Kant and Kantianism* (2005), s.v. "Ethical Socialism"; Willey, *Back to Kant*, chap. 5 and 174–8; Steven S. Schwarzschild, "The Democratic Socialism of Hermann Cohen," *Hebrew Union College Annual* 27 (1956) (also included in *The Tragedy of Optimism*); Harry van der Linden, *Kantian Ethics and Socialism* (Indianapolis: Hackett, 1988); Dirk Lüddecke, "Staatsidee und Revolution bei Hermann Cohen. Ein Kapitel der sozialistischen Kant-Rezeption um 1900," in *Kants Lehre von Staat und Frieden*, ed. Henning Ottmann (Baden-Baden: Nomos, 2009); and Peter A. Schmid, "Das Naturrecht in der Rechtsethik Hermann Cohens," *Zeitschrift für philosophische Forschung* 47, no. 3 (1993): 420–1.

Jewish philosophy, would not be possible in one book. The former task has already been undertaken quite comprehensively and in detail by Eggert Winter's monograph, whose particular merit is to have taken into account many different argumentative contexts in the area of German jurisprudence and legal theory.[44] Meanwhile, many works have examined aspects of Cohen's Jewish philosophy separately from his systematic philosophy, with only a few scholars so far pursuing integrated projects that examine themes occuring in both the philosophical and the Jewish writings.

In the present work it has been my primary concern, in reconstructing Cohen's views about ethics and law, to draw out how those views take shape *across both corpuses*, and this has been at the cost of having to restrict somewhat the textual scope of the investigation. I am presenting here a series of interconnected arguments, by way of readings of key sections of Cohen's main work on ethics and law, *Ethik des reinen Willens*; key sections of his major book on Jewish religion, *Religion of Reason*; and key Jewish-philosophical essays pertaining to ethical questions. As announced in the title of this book, in working out Cohen's views about ethics and law, I especially focus (in the final chapter) on a subgroup within the latter category (the Jewish writings on ethical questions): the essays Cohen wrote concerning the problem of love-of-neighbor, which I believe are pivotal to understanding how the question of "ethics out of law" traverses Cohen's philosophical system and his philosophy of Jewish religion.

Here is what the chapters do in sequence:

Chapter 1 presents the basic argument from the core chapters of *Ethik des reinen Willens* as to what it means, according to Cohen, for ethics to be rooted in, or to be generated out of law or legal science. Drawing on a brief consideration of Kelsen's "Pure Theory of Law" (*Reine Rechtslehre*), I situate Cohen's theory between positivism and natural law theory, and then focus on Cohen's treatment of the notion of the "legal person" in order to examine the relationship between ethics and law that Cohen envisions.

An important vantage point for any investigation into Cohen's understanding of ethics and law is a pair of terms that are distinguished in other European languages but that in English are, confusingly, both rendered by the word "law": (1) *Recht* (German; akin to *droit* in French and *ius* in

44 Eggert Winter, *Ethik und Rechtswissenschaft: eine historisch-systematische Untersuchung zur Ethik-Konzeption des Marburger Neukantianismus im Werke Hermann Cohens* (Berlin: Duncker & Humblot, 1980).

Latin), referring to the rule of law or the system of law. (2) *Gesetz*, aligned with the Greek term *nomos*: a term that is used in various contexts to refer to a law that is imposed or to which I am accountable, including notably the historic notion of divine law, and the notion of "moral law" (*moralisches Gesetz*) that is central to Kant's philosophical ethics. Importantly for the present study, *Gesetz* has also historically been used to refer to religious bodies of law; and Cohen often follows the convention of referring to Jewish law as *jüdisches Gesetz*.

Although the meanings and functions of the terms *Recht* and *Gesetz* may often overlap in practice, the distinction between them is crucial in particular for understanding how Cohen's interest in law is articulated, respectively, in his systematic philosophy and his Jewish philosophy. Recht – the system of law, articulated in legal principles, norms and institutions – is the topic of Cohen's ethico-legal philosophy presented in the *Ethik*. Yet, as I show at the end of chapter 1 and especially in chapter 2, there is a supplementary notion of Gesetz at work in the *Ethik*, denoting a futural "otherness" of law, through which the self is constituted as a "hypothesis" or a task. Ethical self-consciousness is, importantly, not rooted in an individual "I," but is a task of the "unification of I and You."

Cohen's use of the term 'Gesetz' to evoke the paradoxical otherness and futurity of law can seem puzzling, unless we properly analyze two interlinked functions of this term in the *Ethik* and beyond – an analysis for which Leo Strauss's early reading of Cohen (emerging from the work that went into the writing of his book, *Philosophy and Law* [1935; *Philosophie und Gesetz*]) provides a helpful entry point: Cohen grapples with Gesetz insofar as he renegotiates the relationship between heteronomy and autonomy in conversation with Kantian ethics, and thus also questions Kant's critique of legality as coercive, and as going against the autonomy that is foundational for grasping ethical responsibility. As I show in this chapter, Cohen's recuperation of legality for ethics goes hand in hand with his – at once oblique and vehement – efforts to expose the anti-Judaism in Kant's critique of legality, which he places in the tradition of Pauline anti-Judaism. I find, therefore, that the argument of the *Ethik* calls for a Judaic source or meaning of law, even if it does not supply any account of Jewish law in that work.

With this insight, we are able to begin to connect Cohen's project of developing a philosophical account of Judaism to his philosophy of ethics and law. It is worth pausing at this point of transition between the philosophical system and the Jewish writings to consider what it means to trace the question of (Jewish) law (both Gesetz and Recht) in both those areas of Cohen's thought. This moment of transition is symptomatic of studies of modern Jewish thinkers in general, and key to my own procedure in this book: The oeuvre of a thinker such as Cohen – which presents itself as two separate corpora or projects, philosophical and "Jewish" – demands that we understand what takes place across that separation, without however reducing or projecting the claims of one domain to those of the other. Nor must we erase or ignore the distinction between those domains, in order to reconstruct a single philosophy out of the whole of Cohen's works. Given today's keen interest in questions of law and political existence in Jewish thought and life, it is worthwhile to notice that such questions become readable in the works of Cohen – again, to my mind symptomatically for Jewish philosophy in its modern Western idioms – not in either his Jewish philosophy alone, or in his systematic philosophy alone – and certainly not in both at the same time, since comparative exercises routinely lead to remarking on the tensions and contradictions between claims found in each domain. Rather, as I seek to show in chapter 2, we can understand Cohen's analysis of the notion of Gesetz and the problem of legality only in the *passages* or *relays* between the two corpuses or discourses.

The question raised by the analyses of chapter 2 is whether Cohen ever supplied the implied missing argumentative link: Do we find in his philosophy of Judaism anything resembling a theory of law in Judaism?

In order to be able to approach Cohen's treatment of law within his Jewish philosophy, in chapter 3 I lay the groundwork by focusing on the methodic framing and procedure of Cohen's main work on Judaism, *Religion of Reason*. Again, Strauss's early reading of Cohen provides a useful vantage point, as it raises the question of whether Cohen bridges what Strauss sees as the essentially heteronomous structure of law in Judaism – an understanding that is axiomatic for Strauss's own explorations in *Philosophy and Law* – and the demand, core to Cohen's purposes, that law be fundamentally ethical. Here, Cohen's theory of atonement as a kind of substitute for biblical sacrifice provides a focal point for his articulation of law with ethics, as well as a classic case, evocatively (if somewhat obscurely) pinpointed by Strauss, of how Cohen's method of philosophico-political theology allows him to elaborate the concept of a (Jewish) religion of reason.

If the intertwining of law and ethics has been established in Cohen's account of Jewish religion, what place, if any, does he accord to Jewish law as such? In chapter 4, I explore Cohen's rejection of attempts to politicize Jewish law along the lines most famously associated with Spinoza's *Theological-Political Treatise*, along with the fact that Cohen nevertheless criticizes classic attempts of his time to subsume law in Judaism to a "Jewish ethics" (a stance that can be traced to Cohen's 1899 polemic against Moritz Lazarus's *The Ethics of Judaism*). It is true that despite Cohen's declared embrace of law as having an indispensable meaning in Judaism, the "Law" chapter of the *Religion* does not offer a robust theory of halakhah or *mitzvot* (commandments). However, in insisting that Jewish law is nothing political in the Spinozan sense (that it is not, in other words, a law that exists for the sake of a particular people's material and political good fortune), Cohen effectively repoliticizes law. In his political history of Judaism, we find that law, and thus politics, takes on a new meaning as part of a universal and cosmopolitical messianic history of humanity.

If the "Law" chapter in the *Religion* does not conform to what one might expect from a full-fledged theory of Jewish law – and certainly not a theory of law that might accord with the heightened importance of law for ethics that Cohen elaborates in the *Ethik* – there is an alternative point of departure that allows us to recognize Jewish law in the sense not of Gesetz – law in the sense of halakhah, mitzvot, or the idea of law as nomos or revelation that is Strauss's interest in *Philosophy and Law* – but in the sense of Recht. I argue that we can identify in Cohen's philosophy of Judaism at least one noteworthy institution of law in that sense: the concept of the "neighbor," *der Nächste,* that, according to Leviticus 19:18, is to be "loved." This "neighbor" – which Cohen thinks together with the biblical notion of "stranger" (*ger*) and the rabbinic notion of the "Noahide" (*ben Noaḥ*) – can be understood, in line with the theory of the *Ethik,* as a juridical concept, as generating ethical comportment or principles.

In order for the neighbor-stranger to be graspable as an institution of Recht in Cohen's sense, it is necessary to follow his refutation of some widespread misconceptions. One is that love-of-neighbor is a kind of affect that allows us to charitably expand the scope of our ethical action to ever wider circles of those "near" to us, in line with the lexical field of the term "neighbor" as the "near(est) one" ("der Nächste") – which Cohen analyzes as a mistranslation of *re'a* in the Leviticus 19:18 formula. In chapter 5, I return to the *Ethik* to showcase Cohen's argument against any ethical philosophy based on this sort of "affective expansiveness." Cohen articulates this argument above all in his vehement criticism of Rudolf Stammler's theory of "'right' law" (*richtiges Recht*) and its positing of "particular communities" as part of its guiding model for social ethics. I show that this argument, in connection with Cohen's interpretation of neighbor-love as a universal love of the "stranger," is a further important "seam" between Cohen's general philosophical ethics and his Jewish philosophy. In chapter 6 I continue tracing this "seam" by looking further at the brief treatment of love-of-neighbor in Cohen's *Ethik,* and then exploring Cohen's treatments of the problem of love-of-neighbor across his Jewish writings. I situate these in the discourses of "Jewish moral defense" that took shape in the late nineteenth century in the face of growing political antisemitism in Germany. A focal point of my discussion is Cohen's participation as an expert witness in the 1888 Marburg Antisemitism Trial and the affidavit he submitted to the court, which became his first published essay on love-of-neighbor, *Die Nächstenliebe im Talmud* ("Love of Neighbor in the Talmud"). I analyze Cohen's emphatically philosophical defense strategy as a response to the dispositives of supersessionist Christian universalism as it plays out in the setting of a classic antisemitism trial. Cohen's argument in his testimony becomes the blueprint for the several essays he went on to write on love-of-neighbor – which were early on grasped as an ensemble by Martin Buber, who saw to their publication, in abridged form, in a small volume published in 1935 in the famous "Bücherei des Schocken Verlags" series, with the title *Der Nächste.*[45] Diverging from prevalent Jewish defense strategies, Cohen presents the neighbor-stranger as a concept or institution of law in a universalist sense, in opposition to the ethically and politically insufficient notion of "tolerance."

In the "neighbor," then, Recht – the law of institutions oriented to *Allheit* that generates ethical concepts – intersects with Gesetz, Cohen's term for the futural and "other" dimension of law, as well as the conventional term for Jewish law, which Cohen idiosyncratically interpreted in light of a messianic and cosmopolitical universalism. To discover such a noteworthy and suggestive intersection is not to mistake Cohen's systematic philosophy of ethics and law for *part* of his Jewish philosophy, or vice versa, or to view both bodies of thought as part of a larger continuous whole. But in the passages and relays I trace in this book between the ethico-legal philosophy and the philosophy of Judaism, there emerges a shared disposition toward Jewish law (halakhah) and toward law as Recht – interrogated by the transcendental method of the "science of law" (*Rechtswissenschaft*). With respect to both realms, and in elaborating and championing some exemplary interconnections between them, Cohen performs and teaches an expectation that both should and shall be potential means of achieving a future justice.

45 See Buber's "Prefatory Remark" in Hermann Cohen, *Der Nächste. Vier Abhandlungen über das Verhalten von Mensch zu Mensch nach der Lehre des Judentums* (Berlin: Schocken Verlag, 1935), 6–7. Buber was an important consultant to Salman Schocken in his founding (in 1931) and running of the Schocken Verlag, which became the publisher of a new edition of the Buber-Rosenzweig translation of the Bible along with other works by Buber. See Volker Dahm, *Das jüdische Buch im Dritten Reich*, 2nd rev. ed. (Munich: C.H. Beck, 1993), 273–4, 288–9, 301–2, 305.

Chapter One

Cohen's "Methodistic" Founding of Ethics in Legal Science: Generation of the Legal Person

The core objective of the present book is to illuminate the meaning of Cohen's claim that "ethics is founded in law." It is a claim that is immediately intriguing. After all, we ordinarily imagine laws, or systems of law, to emerge out of, or be somehow undergirded by moral principles or intuitions. This sort of a principle can be seen as the basis of any attempt to argue that a law is unjust, to seek greater justice by challenging existing legislation. The idea that laws are founded in morality, or are accountable to morality is typically aligned with a natural law theory. A positivist theory of law, by contrast, would view the question of whether law emerges from, or is undergirded by something like morality as beside the point, since such a theory defines law as posited law pure and simple.

How, then, are we to make sense of Cohen's inverse vision of law undergirding ethics? What did he have in mind in structuring his systematic work of ethics, *Ethik des reinen Willens*, around this bold claim?

Between Legal Positivism and Natural Law Theory

This chapter will sketch out the main contours of Cohen's theory of ethics out of law. The approach I will take here, as suggested by these opening remarks, is to begin by attempting to situate that theory – which was an integral part of Cohen's philosophical system, his own attempt to articulate a Neo-Kantian path to understanding ethics in relation to law and politics – in relation to legal positivism and natural law theory. Given the evident disjunction between the idea that ethics proceeds from law and any kind of natural law theory, according to which law is, or ought to be rooted in morality, it makes sense to begin instead by exploring the possible affinity between Cohen's theory, as a preeminent account within the broad philosophical spectrum represented by the Neo-Kantianisms of the late nineteenth century and early twentieth century, and legal positivism. After all,

Neo-Kantian philosophies have historically been characterized, particularly from the point of view of phenomenology, as notoriously positivistic or scientistic attempts to reduce human existence and strivings to causal explanations that bypass concrete factical realities and necessarily fail to pose questions of meaning. (This picture can be traced partly to Husserl's attempts to set off phenomenology against the Kantian philosophizing of his day and may also have been influenced by the routine dismissals of Neo-Kantianism that one can find, for example, in the works of Heidegger or Gadamer.) In that sense, Cohen's attempt to understand ethics as rooted in law, and more precisely in the science of law (*Rechtswissenschaft*), would seem to be a classic case in point for a scientistic positivism.

Classic legal-positivist philosophies insist on a strict distinction between law and ethics, or at least on problematizing any supposed connection between law and ethics. A classic example is the philosophy of the preeminent legal positivist, Hans Kelsen, who argued for an absolute disjunction between morality and law. Kelsen's theory was in fact often associated with Neo-Kantianism – with its supposed reliance on positive scientific accounts in its approach to philosophical questions – and even with the thought of Hermann Cohen himself.[1] My first step in elucidating Cohen's argument for ethics-out-of-law will therefore be to consider it against the background of Kelsen's compelling and elegant attempt to provide a purely positive account of law.

Kelsen's brand of legal positivism is animated by a critique of what one might call, in Husserlian terms, a "natural attitude" with regard to what law is.[2] Guided by the principle of methodological "purity," in which law is treated as an autonomous realm of inquiry, Kelsen sets off "law" first against the realm of nature. Legal acts or processes cannot be adequately grasped if they are thought of as empirical phenomena taking place in time and space and governed by the laws of causality.[3] The "meaning"

1 See note 7 below.

2 In her comprehensive book-length introduction to the phenomenology of law, Sophie Loidolt identifies significant common presuppositions and lines of thinking about ethico-political principles and the foundations of law and legal institutions among thinkers aligned with phenomenology and with Neo-Kantianism. She finds that "phenomenology" is a helpful category with which to approach the work of Hans Kelsen, for example, whose brand of legal positivism is animated by a critique of what one might call, in Husserlian terms, a "natural attitude" with regard to what law is. Loidoldt, *Einführung in die Rechtsphänomenologie* (Tübingen: Mohr Siebeck, 2010).

3 Hans Kelsen, *Reine Rechtslehre*, 1st ed., ed. Matthias Jestaedt (1934; Tübingen: Mohr Siebeck, 2008), 15–19; translated by Bonnie Litschewski Paulson and Stanley Paulson as *Introduction to the Problems of Legal Theory* (Oxford: Clarendon, 1992), 7–10 (hereafter cited in text as RR).

of a legal phenomenon is intelligible only thanks to a "norm" that supplies the necessary "interpretative scheme" for assigning that meaning. It would be thanks to such a norm, for example, that we might assign the "meaning" of "contract" to a given instance of "a merchant writ[ing] a certain letter to another merchant, who writes back in reply" (RR 17/8). Further, Kelsen's "Pure Theory of Law" seeks to "break the connection" between law and that category with which it has traditionally been linked: that of morality. While we certainly may desire the law to be moral and can work to ensure that it reflects ethical principles, this cannot mean that law – as positive law – is *by definition* moral (RR 25/15). Unlike "moral norms," which have the form of "imperatives," a "legal norm" for Kelsen is a "hypothetical judgment" by which a given deed (*Tatbestand*) is "specifically linked" to a given consequence (RR 33–4/23). Kelsen understands this link as being conditioned by a pre-existing norm: the deed and the consequence are linked by virtue of "imputation" (*Zurechnung*, i.e., holding-accountable). With this, he rejects the idea that the link between a deed/*Tatbestand* and its legal consequence is a causal one (RR 34–5/23–5).

A problem widely recognized in relation to Kelsen's theory is whether a schema in which law is strictly divorced from morality would still allow for the possibility that a system of laws, or a regime founded on the rule of law could legitimately be contested on moral grounds. Taking a cue from Kelsen's evocation of Augustine's famous rhetorical question, "When there is no justice, what is the *state* but a *robber band* enlarged?" the political philosopher Wolfgang Kersting clears up a possible misunderstanding about Kelsen's project: Kelsen is not seeking to offer criteria by which I can recognize whether I live under the authority of a state or of a robber band. Rather, he is seeking to explain, in the event that I regard or treat a regime as legitimate, what is involved or presupposed in such a recognition. The "basic norm" that undergirds the hierarchy of norms that makes up a legal system is hypothetical. Insofar as I regard a state as a *Rechtsstaat*, I am presupposing such a *Grundnorm*. The system of norms as Kelsen understands it is purely descriptive.[4] Thus, it is possible that a robber band may gain the legitimacy of a state, that mere power may become justice.[5]

4 See also Geert Edel, "The *Hypothesis* of the Basic Norm: Hans Kelsen and Hermann Cohen," in *Normativity and Norms: Critical Perspectives on Kelsenian Themes*, ed. Stanley L. Paulson and Bonnie Litschewski Paulson (Oxford: Clarendon, 1998), 214, 219.

5 Wolfgang Kersting, "Neukantianische Rechtsbegründung. Rechtsbegriff und richtiges Recht bei Cohen, Stammler und Kelsen," in *Neukantianismus und Rechtsphilosophie*, ed. Robert Alexy, Lukas H. Meyer, Stanley L. Paulson, and Gerhard Sprenger

Scholarship on Kelsen paints a more differentiated picture of his understanding of the relationship of legality and legitimacy – exploring, for instance, his political theory as a counterbalance to his Pure Theory of Law.[6] I will not trace those attempts here. My brief look at the simple and compelling elegance of the transcendental method for cognizing law proposed by Kelsen was meant to prepare an exploration to the ethico-legal theory of Hermann Cohen. Cohen's ethical philosophy, as put forward in his *Ethik des reinen Willens* (*Ethics of Pure Will* [1904/1907]), famously roots ethics in jurisprudence, in the science of law (*Rechtswissenschaft*). (While some commentators have posited a straightforward continuity between the approaches of Cohen and the Pure Theory of Law developed by Kelsen, the affinities between the two theories are limited, as I hope will become clear here.[7]) The elegance and simplicity of Kelsen's transcendental theory of law – the qualities

---

(Baden-Baden: Nomos, 2002), 62–3, citing Hans Kelsen, *Reine Rechtslehre*, 2nd rev. ed. (Vienna: Deuticke, 1960) and Augustine, *City of God*, IV, 4. For an explanation of this issue, see also Detlef Horster, *Rechtsphilosophie zur Einführung* (Hamburg: Junius, 2002), 74. For a further useful exploration of the Kelsen-Cohen connection, see Agostino Carrino, *Das Recht zwischen Reinheit und Realität. Hermann Cohen und die philosophischen Grundlagen der Rechtslehre Kelsens* (Baden-Baden: Nomos, 2011).

6 See David Dyzenhaus, *Legality and Legitimacy: Carl Schmitt, Hans Kelsen and Hermann Heller in Weimar* (Oxford: Clarendon Press, 1997), chap. 3, "The Pure Theory in Practice: Kelsen's Science of Law"; and Lars Vinx, *Hans Kelsen's Pure Theory of Law: Legality and Legitimacy* (Oxford: Oxford University Press, 2007). For an attempt to draw a moral theory out of Kelsen's legal theory of norms, see Ota Weinberger, *Normentheorie als Grundlage der Jurisprudenz und Ethik. Eine Auseinandersetzung mit Hans Kelsens Theorie der Normen* (Berlin: Duncker & Humblot, 1991), chap. 5.

7 Grouping Kelsen together with Cohen, as an exponent of Neo-Kantianism, may in particular have served the aims of a critical assessment of Neo-Kantian philosophies of law, ethics, and the state such as the one offered by Ulrich Hommes, a philosopher with evident sympathies for phenomenology and existentialism, for whom "the Neo-Kantian restriction of philosophy to theory of cognition/knowledge [*Erkenntnistheorie*] lost the reference to the question concerning law as an originary reality [*ursprüngliche Wirklichkeit*] of historical community [*Gemeinschaft*]." That is to say, "political philosophy in Neo-Kantianism," in remaining possible only as "theory of legal science" (*Theorie der Rechtswissenschaft*), could no longer yield an "originary theory of political reality." Ulrich Hommes, "Das Problem des Rechts und die Philosophie der Subjektivität," *Philosophisches Jahrbuch* 70 (1962/63), 330, 331–2. (Hommes ultimately finds valuable reflections toward such an "originary theory" in Cohen's later works on religion and Judaism, but he posits a complete break between those works and the earlier philosophical works. See 332ff.) But such an interpretation was also greatly facilitated by Kelsen's own well-known remarks regarding parallels between his own theories and those of Cohen, among other Neo-Kantian philosophers, in the preface to the second (1923) edition of *Hauptprobleme der Staatsrechtslehre* (repr., Aalen: Scientia, 1960), XVII. For further details, along with

that make it compelling – are likely tied to the fact that, as I pointed out, he does not seek to incorporate into that theory an account of how to achieve ethical ends in the law. In considering Cohen's theory against the background of a sketch of Kelsen's theory, what we find is a theory that is far less elegant and compellingly simple than Kelsen's. However, I shall argue that what will look like the relative clutter of Cohen's theory is balanced out by the fact that Cohen intends his theory of ethics rooted in jurisprudence not simply to account for the concept of law or for law as a system of norms but also to show how legal concepts and institutions can serve as the generative origins of ethics, and how ethical aims can be realized by way of law.

As has been much discussed, Cohen's "critical idealism" is based on an interpretation of Kant that privileges thought and concept over intuition and that engages in a critique of knowledge (*Erkenntniskritik*) that asks about the conditions of possibility of objective experience.[8] The starting point for this line of inquiry is the so-called *factum*[9] of science: Based on his interpretation of Kant – especially the *Prolegomena to Any Future Metaphysics* – Cohen proposes a transcendental method of philosophy that takes the factum of mathematical natural science as a basis or source for discovering the a priori laws or principles that account for the objectivity of experience.[10] Although criticisms of Cohen and of Marburg Neo-Kantianism were often nurtured by the suspicion that what was being proposed was a kind of scientistic positivism, in which philosophy's own leading role in theorizing knowledge was being abdicated

---

remarks on the Cohen reception among Kelsen's students, see Eggert Winter, *Ethik und Rechtswissenschaft: eine historisch-systematische Untersuchung zur Ethik-Konzeption des Marburger Neukantianismus im Werke Hermann Cohens* (Berlin: Duncker & Humblot, 1980), 33–6, 33–4n100, 280–1.

8 Andrea Poma, *The Critical Philosophy of Hermann Cohen* (1988), trans. John Denton (Albany: State University of New York Press, 1997), focuses on presenting Cohen's philosophy as a "critical idealism." See also Paul Franks's discussion of Cohen in "Rabbinic Idealism and Kabbalistic Realism: Jewish Dimensions of Idealism and Idealist Dimensions of Judaism," in *The Impact of Idealism: The Legacy of Post-Kantian German Thought*, vol. 4, *Religion*, ed. Nicholas Adams (Cambridge: Cambridge University Press, 2013).

9 Although many render the term *Faktum*, used in German philosophical texts, with the English "fact," I have opted to use *factum* in order to make clear that this is a technical term that is distinct from the English word "fact" (whose standard German equivalent would be "Tatsache").

10 See Scott Edgar, "Hermann Cohen," *Stanford Encyclopedia of Philosophy* (Fall 2015 Edition), https://plato.stanford.edu/archives/fall2015/entries/cohen/; Geert Edel, "Kantianismus oder Platonismus? Hypothesis als Grundbegriff der Philosophie Cohens," *Il cannocchiale. Rivista di studi filosofici* no. 1–2 (1991): 60–4; and Poma, *The Critical Philosophy*, 48–9.

in favor of empirical science,[11] Cohen's efforts were in fact animated by a concern to conceive of philosophical method as an autonomous undertaking and to avoid the pitfalls of empiricism. As Michael Zank has pointed out, Cohen was writing in an age in which "empirical studies of brain function eclipsed intellectual inquiries into the nature of thought, and in many philosophy departments experimental psychology displaced traditional philosophy."[12] Cohen's critical idealism was meant to oppose this positivistic tendency; above all, he rejected attempts to reduce questions concerning logic and thought to questions of psychology. (In this, his project shares a fundamental impetus with those of other thinkers of the late nineteenth century and early twentieth century, notably Husserl's phenomenology.) As Geert Edel has effectively argued, what Cohen postulates in beginning from a factum of science is simply that a certain kind of experience, a cognition that takes place according to specific laws or principles, is present in certain sciences; this of course does not entail assigning some kind of a priori validity or legitimacy to the content of those experiences or cognitions. Rather, as is the case for Kelsen, the "transcendental method" takes the factum as a "problem" and asks about the conditions of possibility of the validity of the cognitions given in science.[13] Cohen takes law or legal science/jurisprudence (*Rechtswissenschaft*) to be the "factum of science" for ethics (see ErW 65ff.).[14] Law thus occupies an "analogous" role to that of mathematics for logic, and thus for theoretical philosophy (ErW 70).[15]

---

11 See Geert Edel, *Von der Vernunftkritik zur Erkenntnislogik. Die Entwicklung der theoretischen Philosophie Hermann Cohens* (Freiburg/Munich: Alber, 1988), 121–2, 121n11.

12 Michael Zank, "Cohen, Hermann," in *Routledge Encyclopedia of Philosophy* (London: Routledge, 1998).

13 Here I am drawing on the discussion in Edel, *Von der Vernunftkritik*, 121–3. See also Wolfgang Marx, *Transzendentale Logik als Wissenschaftstheorie. Systematisch-kritische Untersuchungen zur philosophischen Grundlegungsproblematik in Cohens "Logik der reinen Erkenntnis"* (Frankfurt am Main: Vittorio Klostermann, 1977), 17–18.

14 See Helmut Holzhey, "Analytische Hermeneutik und reine Rechtslehre. Die Transformation neukantianischer Theoreme in die reine Rechtslehre Kelsens," in *Hermeneutik und Strukturtheorie des Rechts*, ed. Michael W. Fischer, Erhard Mock, and Helmut Schreiner (*Archiv für Rechts- und Sozialphilosophie*, Beiheft n.F. no. 20 [1984], 103–4; Poma, *The Critical Philosophy*, 111, 121; Michael Zank, "The Ethics in Hermann Cohen's Philosophical System," in "Hermann Cohen's Ethics," ed. Robert Gibbs, special issue, *Journal of Jewish Thought and Philosophy* 13, nos. 1–2 (2004): 9n4. Cohen also discusses the idea of law as factum – including as a corrective to Kant's ethics, and in particular his dissociation of law from ethics – in the newly written part IV of the second edition of *Kants Begründung der Ethik*, published in 1910, and thus well after both editions of the *Ethik* were published. See KBE, 397–8.

15 Eggert Winter has identified Georg Jellinek as a precursor to Cohen, in that Jellinek had already equated the methodological rigor of the new legal science with that of mathematics. Winter, *Ethik und Rechtswissenschaft*, 295, 295n66.

As is the case for Kelsen, to follow the "method of purity," to acknowledge "scientific reason" as the guide for seeking truth (ErW 91), means for Cohen that ethics does not have an "external," transcendent grounding or foundation (ErW 87). Cohen's philosophical approach is emphatically "methodological" – or, as Steven Schwarzschild has put it, "methodistic."[16] We can see this "methodism" or centrality of method in the fact that at every stage of his philosophical demonstrations, Cohen is at the same time engaged in defending and affirming his proposition that legal science is the scientific basis for ethics – in other words, always defending the method. Underlying this method is the idea that truth – including the truth sought by ethical philosophy – is "the truth of cognition" (ErW 87).[17] "The search for truth *is* the truth"; thus, truth itself consists in and is founded on "the acknowledgment of scientific reason" (ErW 91). For the field of law in particular, it follows that, as Ulrich Hommes has put it, "only as an object of science 'is' there law in the first place."[18] As Helmut Holzhey notes, for legal science to provide the factum means that positive law is given not as a natural or ontic datum, but as something "intelligible," that is, as a medium for "investigating [its] conditions of validity" ("für die Ermittlung der Geltungsbedingungen durchlässig").[19] In other words – just as we saw for Kelsen's example

16 Not to say "methodomaniacal" – to quote Wolfgang Kersting's blanket characterization of the Neo-Kantians (Kersting, "Neukantianische Rechtsbegründung," 32n25). See Steven S. Schwarzschild, "Introduction" to Cohen's *Ethik*, in *Werke* vol. 7 (1981): VIII*; also included in Schwarzschild, *The Tragedy of Optimism: Writings on Hermann Cohen*, ed. George Y. Kohler (Albany: State University of New York Press, 2018).

17 Cf. ErW 93: "It is not the things [*die Dinge*] themselves that the examination of [those] things must primarily attend to. Rather it is cognition of the things, insofar as such cognition is given in a science, that must always be [attended to] first." "Nicht die Dinge sind das Erste, worauf die Untersuchung der Dinge selbst ... zu achten hat; sondern die Erkenntnis von den Dingen, sofern sie in einer Wissenschaft gegeben ist, muß allemal das Erste sein."

18 Hommes, "Das Problem des Rechts," 328.

19 Helmut Holzhey, "Die praktische Philosophie des Marburger Neukantianismus," in *Neukantianismus. Perspektiven und Probleme*, ed. H. Holzhey and E. W. Orth (Würzburg: Königshausen & Neumann, 1994), 149–50. See also Holzhey, "Analytische Hermeneutik," 103–4. As Holzhey points out, Cohen, in characterizing the "new position" that he intends to give to ethics, sets this plan off against the circumstance that Kant himself did not "apply" the "transcendental method" to ethics. Cohen adds that this lack – which he argues must be repaired by recognizing jurisprudence as the science with respect to which the possibility of ethics must be developed (by means of "deduction") – introduces an "irreparable fault into the concept of transcendental method," in that a procedure/investigation applied to logic was abandoned with respect to ethics. ErW 227; cf. Holzhey, "Analytische Hermeneutik," 104n28.

of the contract as a norm – it is on the basis of the "norm" that we may discover the meaning of the "facts" (*Vorgänge und Tatbestände*) of law, and "positive law" only gains its meaning in relation to the norms.[20] "Positivism" in Kelsen's sense thus does not mean taking the empirical law as a given, or as a basis for inquiry; to do the latter would amount to "sociology."

How does the transcendental method – the philosophical method that takes the facta of law and interrogates their legal presuppositions and principles – promote ethical theorizing and, with it, moral progress? Cohen upholds the principle that ethics has a constitutive share in "truth." But even though he also endorses Kant's principle of the "primacy of practical reason," such that "the interest in ethics" is at the "highest point," he insists that this primacy does not affect the "methodological" hierarchy in which ethics must be founded in logic, which determines the value of truth (ErW 22–3).[21]

Cohen's conception of ethics is just as much directed against relativist positions according to which "state and law are presented as something human, and accordingly as something erroneous/misguided and sinful," or, in a similar vein, as outgrowths of instinct or of a desire for power (ErW 91–2), as it is against classic approaches that have sought the foundation of ethics in God (ErW 87) or in a transcendent idea of the good. Cohen's ethical theory is thus meant to be a simultaneous refutation of two views:[22]

(1) The idea that "ethics has something to do with a transcendent shepherd's world" (ErW 28).[23] In contrast to such an image, for Cohen ethics has a "being," or a "reality." This leads Cohen to remark that even the Kantian dictum that "is" (*Sein*) must be divorced from "ought" (*Sollen*) is in need of qualification/modification:

---

20 Holzhey, "Die praktische Philosophie," 150. Holzhey here also draws on Winter, *Ethik und Rechtswissenschaft*, 289.

21 See the discussion in Eric Dufour, "Introduction: L'interprétation cohénienne de la 'Critique de la raison pure,'" in Hermann Cohen, *Commentaire de la 'Critique de la raison pure' de Kant*, trans. and ed. Eric Dufour (Paris: Cerf, 2000), 71.

22 Helmut Holzhey elegantly and compellingly expresses the dual purpose of Cohen's project that I lay out below when he describes the project, under the heading of "transcendental method," as a "critique of metaphysics" which "repeats" the Kantian critique of reason "explicitly" on two "fronts": it confronts both (1) the "idealistic overbidding [*Überbietung*]" and (2) the "psychologistic underselling [*Unterbietung*]" of that original Kantian critique. Holzhey, "Analytische Hermeneutik," 103. On Cohen's critique of psychologism, see also Marx, *Transzendentale Logik*, 19–21.

23 ErW 28. See also Cohen's discussion of the stakes of properly understanding Kant's notion of a "kingdom of ends," ErW 393–5.

> The fact that *Sollen* ["ought"] is distinguished from *Sein* ["is"] must by no means take away from *Sollen* the value of *Sein*/existing, or to shut off *Sollen* from *Sein.* (ErW 24)[24]

For this reason, Cohen argues for an "idea of the good" that has shed all noumenal trappings. The association with the "thing in itself" poses for Cohen a greater danger for the idea of the good than it does for the objects of theoretical reason. For the latter, he finds that the Kantian critique has made adequate provisions that the "thing in itself" will evermore be understood as "dissolving into the value of a [merely] methodological formula," a "regulative and heuristic maxim" (ErW 25–6). Ethical theory, by contrast, remains endangered by the continuing "suspicion that the idea [of the good] is indeed only an idea," such that *Sollen*/normativity would denote "if not a catechism of commandments, then at least a fantasy region of pious hopes" (ErW 26–7). The task of Cohen's ethical theory, then, is for the "idea" to be "taken up without remainder in *Sollen*," in normativity. That is, the idea of the good is to be understood as "nothing other than the precepts of the practical use of reason" (ErW 27).[25]

(2) The idea that ethics is something subjective or psychological. That the being of *Sollen* is distinct from the being of things in nature is consistent with the above-mentioned image of the human being as initially guided by instinct or a base drive for power, and could lead to the misguided project of grounding ethics in psychology (ErW 28, cf. 17) or in affect (ErW 99).[26] In this connection Cohen explains how the refutation of a naturalist approach to ethics goes hand in hand with the first refutation of a transcendent source of ethics: Evoking the Nietzschean critique of morality, he notes that it is no accident that such a "naturalistic" image of the human being – which in Nietzsche's terminology appears as an *Untermensch* – may appear in combination with a "supernaturalist" image of an "overman," *Übermensch*. Just as these two figures combine "in order to complement their mutual lacunae," we may see moral theologies that appeal to a transcendent source of goodness as the necessary counterpart of moral psychologies in which ethics is merely subjective (ErW 28).

---

24 However, similarly to Kelsen's approach to the "norm"/the "ought," Cohen still regards the being of *Sollen* as distinct from the being of things in nature, that is, "the nature of natural science"; ErW 24; cf. 13–14, 21, 176–7.

For further background, see Holzhey, "Neukantianismus und Sozialismus," introduction to *Ethischer Sozialismus. Zur politischen Philosophie des Neukantianismus* (Frankfurt am Main: Suhrkamp, 1994), 17–18.

25 Cohen explores the Sein/Sollen distinction also in his earlier work *Kants Begründung der Ethik* (1877), see, for example, KBE 137–9.

26 See also EmkN part IV, esp. 509/96, 511/98–9.

Thus, Cohen's "method of purity," according to which ethics is oriented to law as a scientific factum, is designed to avoid both "dangers": "the imprecision of psychology" and the "exclusive autarchy of religion" (ErW 66–7).

We can see from this that while for Kelsen, to dissociate law from the realm of nature and causality also entails dissociating it from morality, for Cohen, to deny that law belongs to the realm of nature, and to affirm the purity of method is instead a way of affirming the ethical nature of law.[27] In a discussion of the method of "apriorism," Cohen thus draws the following parallel between mathematics and physics on the one hand and legal science on the other:

> Just as mathematics and physics progress by means of experiences, but nonetheless in all these developments permeate [*durchwirken*] the original logical motifs/motivations [*Motive*], so too the development of law [*die rechtliche Entwickelung*, by which Cohen must mean the development of "legal science" – D.H.] already for its part comprises within itself the escalation of moral cultivation [*Gesittung*], by force of the basic ethical motifs/motivations that reside in it. (ErW 66)

Furthermore, and again in a manner "similar to natural science," the history of law may also be influenced "by other means of moral experience."

---

27 For Wolfgang Kersting, the fact that Cohen's project is to demonstrate that law has an ethical ground amounts to a departure from and challenge to positivism, despite the subtleties of the "foundational circularity" that Cohen discerns in the way that ethics and law are related to each other. Kersting takes this feature of Cohen's theory to mean simply that Cohen is taking a natural-law position in the traditional debate between natural law theory and legal positivism (Kersting, "Neukantianische Rechtsbegründung," 37). In fact, the question of whether Cohen's theory of ethics and law is dangerously close to a natural law theory recurs throughout the history of its reception. See, for example, Gianna Gigliotti's discussion of the interpretation of Cohen (and Kelsen) put forward by the legal theorist Fritz Sander (1889–1939), in "Ethik und das Faktum der Rechtswissenschaft bei Hermann Cohen," in *Ethischer Sozialismus*, ed. Holzhey, 181. For a nuanced discussion of the relationship of Cohen's ethico-legal theory to natural law theory and to Kelsen's positivism, see Peter A. Schmid, "Das Naturrecht in der Rechtsethik Hermann Cohens," *Zeitschrift für philosophische Forschung* 47, no. 3 (1993). Pierfrancesco Fiorato has reflected on the stakes of Cohen's distance from natural law theory in the sense of "unwritten laws" as the foundation of law in "Ungeschriebenes Gesetz und schriftliche Lehre. Hermann Cohen über den Palimpsest der Vernunft," *Deutsche Zeitschrift für Philosophie* 59, no. 2 (April 2011). The relationship of Cohen's theory to Kelsen is also discussed in Holzhey, "Analytische Hermeneutik." Relatedly, Stanley L. Paulson points out that Kelsen at least on one occasion dismissed both Cohen and Stammler as natural-law theorists, in Paulson, "Einleitung," in *Neukantianismus und Rechtsphilosophie*, ed. Alexy et al., 12–13.

In contrast to what we saw in Kelsen, Cohen thus rejects the absolute opposition of legality to morality. Instead, his project is to "acknowledge morality as an immanent force within legality" (ErW 66).

Ethics and Law: A Necessary Foundational Circularity

In grappling with the bidirectional relationship posited here between moral experience and legal science, it is helpful to recall the observation of Paul Natorp, Cohen's student and, later, colleague and collaborator at Marburg, that there is a "foundational circularity" (*Begründungszirkel*)[28] in the relationship between law and ethics envisioned by Cohen.[29] From his conception of legal science as the foundation of ethics, Cohen derives the task of "discover[ing]/investigat[ing] ethics from out of legal science" (ErW 227). Thus, it is at first glance puzzling why

> it is not only law that is dependent on ethics; rather, ethics too must take recourse to legal science, [i.e.,] must recognize in legal science the factum of a science for the continuation/further development of transcendental method. (ErW 228)

But as Natorp shows, the apparent circularity between ethics and legal science becomes acceptable once one looks more closely at the methodological parallel that Cohen is working from between the grounding of logic in "pure" (i.e., non-empirical) natural science and the grounding

---

28 The term is Wolfgang Kersting's ("Neukantianische Rechtsbegründung," 36). Paul Natorp, "Recht und Sittlichkeit. Ein Beitrag zur kategorialen Begründung der praktischen Philosophie. Mit besonderem Bezug auf Hermann Cohens 'Ethik des reinen Willens' und Rudolf Stammlers 'Theorie der Rechtswissenschaft,'" *Kant Studien* 18 (1913). On the significance of Natorp's review essay, see Winter, *Ethik und Rechtswissenschaft*, 267.

Similarly, Holzhey finds in Cohen an "ambivalence" as to whether law is dependent on ethics. See "Analytische Hermeneutik," 104, also discussed by Gigliotti, "Ethik und das Faktum der Rechtswissenschaft," 179n15.

Natorp published his essay, a study of "law and morality" "with special reference to" both Cohen's *Ethik* and Rudolf Stammler's *Theorie der Rechtswissenschaft* (1911), also as a review of the latter book (see Natorp, "Recht und Sittlichkeit," 1n1). Natorp classifies Stammler's book as a contribution, as per its title, to the "theory of legal science" in the sense that Cohen found lacking when he undertook to theorize ethics in 1904 ("Recht und Sittlichkeit," 26). (The interactions between Cohen's *Ethik* and Stammler's philosophy of law will be the focus of chapter 5 in this book.)

29 See ErW 65, where Cohen describes the relationship of ethics and legal science, in analogy with that of logic and mathematics, as a "reciprocal relationship" (*Wechselverhältnis*).

of ethics in "pure" legal science. Cohen, appealing to Kant, presumes a systematic unity between theoretical and practical philosophy; both must be approached via the "transcendental method." Thus,

> just as physics ... is rooted in logic, so too law must have its root in ethics; and therefore too, ethics must be discovered/investigated out of legal science and must be grounded/founded [*begründet*] in legal science. (ErW 227)

Natorp points out that there is a limitation, however, on the parallel that Cohen can draw between natural and legal science. For Cohen, the science in question is supposed to constitute the factum, the given material with which the work of foundation/*Begründung* can then engage. The criterion of methodological "purity" means, further, that the science in question must be considered apart from that science as a "positive" or empirical science. Just as Kant's transcendental logic drew not on mathematics or natural science in general, but on "pure" mathematics/natural science – that is, on their "fundamental concepts" rather than on any "positive" claims or content – so Cohen must seek the science that is to serve as the factum and thus as the foundation for ethics not in legal science in general, but in the "*pure* theory of law" ("*reine* Rechtslehre"). The foundations or principles of mathematics/natural science, the science that underlies theoretical philosophy, are at least in part available or visible to us. Those sciences exist as positive sciences, and by studying those positive sciences, we may discern the principles on which they are founded. But the same cannot be said, Natorp explains, for the "pure foundations of positive law," because the "pure science/theory of law" is not available in the same way as mathematics is. To expose the hidden foundations or "roots" of positive law is the task of philosophy – and, in particular of ethics. This, for Natorp, is the very good reason behind the circular foundational relationship between law and ethics in Cohen's theory:[30] Ethics can only be approached in a "foundational" manner – using the pure "scientific" method – by reference to law. That is, while mathematics is a science outside philosophy, the pure theory of law, since it can only be developed as ethics, is itself

30 Thus, unlike Manfred Pascher, I do not read Natorp's discussion here as having exposed the foundational relationship that Cohen is positing in *Ethik des reinen Willens* between ethics and law as being meaningless, despite the corrective to Cohen's theory that Natorp goes on to propose later in his review. Manfred Pascher, *Hermann Cohens Ethik als Gegenentwurf zur Rechtsphilosophie Hegels* (Innsbruck: Verlag des Instituts für Sprachwissenschaft der Universität Innsbruck, 1992), 40. Cf. Natorp, "Recht und Sittlichkeit," 38ff.

already philosophy. "For this reason, ethics itself in fact becomes in Cohen philosophy of law."[31] The circularity of the law-ethics relationship is thus a necessary one. It entails a certain congruence or overlap between ethical philosophy and its scientific factum. And Natorp has a persuasive explanation of why this overlap should not be worrisome: legal science may still be understood to have an "independence" vis-à-vis philosophy akin to that of mathematics, in that, even if (or while) the basic concepts of law are not (yet) established with certainty, "they are still themselves on hand in positive legal science in [their] factical, i.e., 'positive,' *use*," that is, in their concrete employment or applications. (These may also be latent possibilities, to be developed further as part of a trajectory of moral progress [ErW 66].) This allows ethics in its turn to be "independent" of "the historical material of law" to the extent that it proves itself capable of applying "its methodical critique to the great institutions of law [*Rechtsinstitute*]" (ErW 270).[32] Positive legal science, comments Natorp, has been lax in working out its pure foundations – in this it lags behind mathematics and natural science. Thus, the project of ethical philosophy – in order to achieve its own ends – must also take over the task of supplying foundations on behalf of legal science.[33] In theorizing ethics, Cohen must also theorize law.[34]

Legal Person and *Genossenschaft*

In order to develop his theory of how ethics emerges from law, Cohen examines some key legal institutions, in particular that of the "legal person," in conjunction with the institution that he believes best represents legal personhood, the *Genossenschaft* or association. Cohen's considerations of *Genossenschaft* will ultimately also ground his understanding of the role of the state in ethics.

---

31 Natorp, "Recht und Sittlichkeit," 23–5.

32 See Dufour, "Introduction," 76–7, who in this connection also gives a helpful explanation of the necessary foundational circularity between ethics and law.

33 Natorp, "Recht und Sittlichkeit," 25–6.

34 Referencing a 1903 letter by Natorp, in which the latter comments that Cohen does not recognize "law" (Recht) apart from "morality," Schwarzschild comments as follows: "Cohen wanted what might be called a tactical separation between ethics and jurisprudence, so that strategically the two could mutually improve and strengthen one another the more in advancing toward their common goal." "Introduction" to Cohen's *Ethik*, p. XVI*, commenting on Natorp's letter to Albert Görland of 26 May 1903, letter no. 82 in Holzhey, *Cohen und Natorp*, vol. 2, *Der Marburger Neukantianismus in Quellen. Zeugnisse kritischer Lektüre. Briefe der Marburger. Dokumente zur Philosophiepolitik der Schule* (Basel/Stuttgart: Schwabe, 1986).

The notion of the "legal person" (*juristische Person*) in the German legal tradition is supposed to capture the circumstance that individual ("natural") persons can act in concert and can be, collectively, the bearer of legal rights and obligations. The concept arose and became a central topic of German legal scholarship in the latter half of the nineteenth century, an era dominated by aspirations to establish a constitutionally based democratic state in place of the prevailing absolute-monarchical orders. Particularly with the 1867 and 1871 constitutions, it became important to develop definitions of sovereignty that kept pace with the dissolution of the absolute monarchy and its hierarchical governmental structures and the increased access to political power within broader strata of society.[35] As part of this movement, the idea that the state itself was an organism or "legal person," made up in turn of numerous bearers of power conceived as its "organs," became a way to envision a state governed not from above, hierarchically, but from below, guided also by private interests. According to Michael Stolleis, the notion of "legal person" thus became "a way of dissolving the antinomy of princely sovereignty and popular sovereignty by means of the neutralizing [force of] state sovereignty."[36] In particular, legal scholars such as Otto von Gierke mined German historical traditions in order to champion the cooperative association/fellowship/corporation (*Genossenschaft, Körperschaft*) as the ideal model of social-political organization to be applied to state and society, from its lower to its upper echelons,[37] and in accordance with popular

---

35 Cf. Michael Stolleis, *Geschichte des öffentlichen Rechts in Deutschland*, vol. 2, *1800–1914* (Munich: C.H. Beck, 1992), 364–5. See also Ekkehard Kaufmann, "Körperschaft (juristische Person)," in *Handwörterbuch zur deutschen Rechtsgeschichte*, vol. 2, ed. Adalbert Erler et al. (Berlin: Erich Schmidt, 1978), 1147–55.

36 Stolleis, *Geschichte des öffentlichen Rechts in Deutschland*, 2:368.

37 See Kaufmann, "Körperschaft," 1149–50. Kaufmann also notes that the work of the so-called Germanists, of whom Gierke was the most prominent member, on corporate entities and legal personhood was the most significant contribution of this school to nineteenth-century legal scholarship (1148).

As Michael Stolleis explains, the "Germanist" legal scholars were known for ascribing especially positive qualities to the German legal tradition, e.g., community-centeredness, concreteness, organicist and vitalist principles, and, with respect to the idea of *Genossenschaft*, a commitment to "social" (i.e., social welfare) principles that transcend the division between state law and private/civil legal relationships. See Stolleis, "Sozialrecht," in *Handwörterbuch zur deutschen Rechtsgeschichte*, vol. 4, ed. Adalbert Erler and Ekkehard Kaufmann (Berlin: Erich Schmidt, 1990), 1732. As part of his major study on the Germanist legal tradition, Frank L. Schäfer discusses the methodology of Gierke on the *Genossenschaft* and its central significance for the field as a whole. See Schäfer, *Juristische Germanistik. Eine Geschichte der Wissenschaft vom einheimischen Privatrecht* (Frankfurt am Main: Klostermann, 2008), 496–9.

consciousness of social realities, as opposed to learned jurisprudence, which relied on authoritarian Roman legal traditions.[38] Accordingly, the *Genossenschaft*, as "legal person," was a category that encompassed both state law and private (civil) law, realms that are strictly separate in Roman jurisprudence.[39] A main thrust of Gierke's *Genossenschaft* theory was to set off this specifically German idea from concepts in Roman law that similarly described collective legal formations or intentions. In the words of one commentator, Gierke argued that "technical jurisprudence, though it was influenced by German as well as Roman ideas and sought to come to terms with existing social realities, never gave satisfactory legal formulation to the German [concept of *Körperschaft*, or corporation], as this was unreflectingly held in everyday life." For Gierke, Roman, Latin, "foreign" ideas and state-centered sovereignty theories had come to replace "such genuinely corporative and associative ideas as had been sporadically germinated in the high and later Middle Ages," a development whose effects were now to be undone by jurisprudential attempts "to formulate satisfactorily [the] concept of group personality, based on [*Genossenschaft*]."[40]

The virtue of the legal person as represented by the *Genossenschaft* was supposed to be that in it "there was no complete division of the legal spheres" of the members on the one hand and of the corporate entity on the other.[41] The "tie" (*Band*) that binds together the "person of the whole" (*Gesamtperson*) and the "individual person" – the member of the *Genossenschaft* – is one which is unique to corporate entities (*Körperschaften*).[42] For the contemporary notion of legal personhood, this means that an association of persons that has the capacity to act on its own behalf is "as a matter of law [*rechtlich*] something different than the sum

38 See Antony Black, "Editor's Introduction" to Otto von Gierke, *Community in Historical Perspective: A Translation of Selections from* Das deutsche Genossenschaftsrecht (Cambridge: Cambridge University Press, 1990), xxvii.

39 Stolleis, *Geschichte des öffentlichen Rechts*, 2:360, 369. Frederick William Maitland, "Translator's Introduction" to Otto von Gierke, *Political Theories of the Middle Age* (Cambridge: Cambridge University Press, 1927), xxviii. (This book is a partial translation of vol. 3 of *Das deutsche Genossenschaftsrecht*.)

The notion of "Genossenschaft" had a significant role in the history of socialism; and the cooperative form of the "Genossenschaft" was established by law in Prussia as of 1867. See Winter, *Ethik und Rechtswissenschaft*, 295–7nn68–9; and Stolleis, "Sozialrecht," 1731–3.

40 Black, "Editor's Introduction," xxvii. See also Maitland, "Translator's Introduction," xxviii.

41 Winter, *Ethik und Rechtswissenschaft*, 311.

42 Otto von Gierke, *Deutsches Privatrecht*, vol. 1 (Leipzig: Duncker & Humblot, 1895), 479, quoted in Winter, *Ethik und Rechtswissenschaft*, 311.

of the members [*Genossen*]."[43] As we will see, this structure, in which the will and action of the whole is inseparable from the will and action of the constituents, is what makes the *Genossenschaft* attractive to Cohen as a specification of legal personhood.

Self, Unity of Consciousness, and the Ethical Subject

Cohen presents the allied categories of "legal person" and *Genossenschaft* as part of chapter 4 of the *Ethik*, entitled "The Self-Consciousness of the Pure Will." Two aspects of Cohen's understanding of "self-consciousness" and the "self" are important for understanding the role of "legal person" as part of Cohen's theory of ethics out of law: First, self-consciousness is a "unity." Second, this unity must be understood not as a pre-supposed, readymade entity, an already constituted self, but as something generated, that is to say, open-ended. This open-ended generation is oriented toward the achievement of a collective subject, or toward *Allheit*. Below I discuss these two aspects in further detail.

The Self as a Unity

In the introduction to the *Ethik*, which gives a sweeping overview of its central themes, Cohen prepares us for this aspect of his theory: Ethical-legal theory rests on the ability to perceive action ("action is the basic problem of ethics," ErW 72),[44] and a given action is cognized by grouping multiple things done by someone into a "unity" (*Einheit*), one action, to which we can retrospectively refer (ErW 73, 80). Thus, "the unity of action constitutes the concept of action," *Handlung*. In other words, it is a task of ethics to understand action as a unity (ErW 73); and law, too, treats an action as a unity (ErW 184).

The value of unity is of central importance to Cohen's ethics.[45] Cohen distinguishes unity (*Einheit*) from singleness or individuality (*Einzelheit*)

43 Kaufmann, "Körperschaft," 1147–8.

44 As has been highlighted by Helmut Holzhey, Cohen criticizes Kant for not making the concept of action into the focal point of his practical philosophy. On this point and on the centrality of action (*Handlung*), see ErW 168–9. Cf. Holzhey and Mudroch, *Historical Dictionary of Kant and Kantianism* (2005), s.v. "Action"; and Michael Zank, *The The Idea of Atonement in the Philosophy of Hermann Cohen* (Providence, RI: Brown Judaic Studies, 2000; repr. Brown Judaic Studies Open Humanities Book Program, 2020), 275–8, https://repository.library.brown.edu/studio/item/bdr:1111035.

45 The significance of unity is already established in Cohen's *Logik* (LrE); see ErW 4, 73, 184.

(e.g., ErW 73).[46] Thus, in the introduction to the *Ethik*, he consigns the "individual" human being to being a matter for psychology. Psychology is a kind of naturalism that looks at the ego in a way that can only lead to solipsism. Ethics, by contrast, is aimed at Allheit (totality), which is distinct from the plurality (*Mehrheit*) that is the aggregate of individuals. Allheit[47] is not a matter of number at all, but is qualitatively distinct from plurality (ErW 11–12, cf. 10, 4–5). Cohen presents his ethical theory as a way of transcending the "ambiguity" inherent in the concept of the human being – to resolve the question of whether the human being, as it concerns ethics, is a singular or a plural entity (ErW 4, 188–9). This goes along with his project of formulating an ethics that will demonstrate the self to be in "correlation" with Allheit (ErW 71), such that Allheit is shown to be "the true unity [*Einheit*]" (ErW 183).

The Self as Generated (erzeugt*), toward Collectivity* (Allheit*)*

What is at stake for Cohen in insisting on unity in place of individuality is that for him unity is something generated (*erzeugt*). The object of ethics is not a readymade, preexisting "unified" self, of which ethics could subsequently ask, what must that self do? (Again, Cohen attributes to psychology the naturalist view and "egoistical prejudice" that a person constitutes a "unity," such that psychology has already constituted persons as its object [ErW 188, cf. 73].) Accordingly, the Allheit into which Cohen resolves the "ambiguous" concept of the human being (ErW 4–5) represents the achievement of collectivity, it is an "infinite gathering/summary/summation [*Zusammenfassung*]," a process by which

> the *Allheit* of human beings forms at some time the "universe-ity" [*Universität*, which is here not meant as "university" – D.H.] of an estate/class [*Stand*] or of a city, at another time that of a state, and at another time finally that of humanity. (ErW 5)

46 Later on, when he develops in full his philosophy of Judaism, a similar disinction informs Cohen's understanding of God's unity, see RV chap. 1.

47 The category of Allheit is already developed by Cohen in *Logik der reinen Erkenntnis* (1902/1914). See, for example, LrE 179 regarding Allheit as "infinite summation," LrE 180 regarding the contrast with plurality (Mehrheit), and LrE 176 and 186 regarding the connection between Allheit and unity (Einheit). As has been pointed out by Winter, Cohen already in the *Logik* used the example of the legal person and the corporative person in explaining Allheit, and also accords ethical significance to Allheit in contrast with Mehrheit. Cohen writes there: "All progress that law has accomplished regarding the problem of the legal person rests on the logical power/force of Allheit." See LrE 204–5, and Winter, *Ethik und Rechtswissenschaft*, 313–14, 310–11n120, 316n135.

Since Allheit is not a matter of number, it represents an *achievement* or infinite generation of collectivity. Such an infinite summation is the model for imagining the formation or "hypothesis" of a collective (or corporate) will, decision (*Beschluß*), or legal action in which the individual member is not "in question" (ErW 230–1). (I shall return to Cohen's use of the term "hypothesis" below.)

Ethics is the domain of "will" and "action." Just as unity is distinguished from individuality, Cohen stipulates that the "single individual" does not will or act – that is, willing and acting do not pertain to the single individual. Rather, the individual "can only desire [*begehren*] and do [*tun*]" (ErW 189). This last notion, mere "doing" (*Tun*), serves as a contrasting term to "action," *Handlung*, in the sense that "doing" is directed at a "finished" (*fertig*) product, whereas for action, there can be no such thing as something "finished" or "completed" ("Die Handlung ist dadurch vom Tun unterschieden, dass es für sie nichts Fertiges gibt," ErW 171). Thus, just as the self that is the object of ethics is not a readymade, unified self, and just as Allheit is an infinite process or task of summation, so ethics does not deal with actions as completed unities, but is engaged in the task of "generating" or achieving concepts of self and of action. (Linked to this is Cohen's conception of "thinking" itself as the activity of generating concepts, his view that concepts are thus never completely "given," but that the concept as such is a "task," *Aufgabe* [ErW 170–1].)

Accordingly, Cohen excludes any use of the term "self-consciousness" that would proceed from the assumption that "consciousness" is something already given: Like consciousness, self-consciousness is to be "generated" "by way of will." Thus, consciousness is to be taken as a "problem" to be "worked on" or treated (ErW 136). Another way that Cohen expresses this is that since "consciousness" refers to "the purity of consciousness in pure will,"[48] that which is to be cognized is consciousness "as it unfolds in action." That is, action "accomplishes itself" (*vollzieht sich*) as consciousness; it is in this sense that consciousness or self-consciousness become a matter of interest for ethics (ErW 203).

Cohen distinguishes his reliance on the notion of "self-consciousness" from the way this notion is employed by Kant and in post-Kantian philosophies. He routinely raises objections to what he terms "romanticism," as represented in the philosophies of Schelling, Fichte, and Hegel – which

48 The term "purity" here, as always, signals that we are dealing with something non-empirical, something to be approached as a problem of transcendental method. As Michael Zank well explains in his commentary to this chapter, "self-consciousness is not an empirical reality. Established as the condition of pure will it participates in the purity of the will; it is pure self-consciousness." Self-consciousness becomes a topic in Cohen's *Ethik* "as the condition of will and action." Zank, *The Idea of Atonement*, 279.

he often also groups with Spinoza under the heading of "pantheism." For example, he finds in those philosophies a failure to distinguish "is" from "ought," logic from ethics. Further, he warns, in a Kantian vein, against a "dogmatic-psychological" misunderstanding of "self-consciousness," which subsequently evolved into the "magic word of self-consciousness" that is found in the "philosophy of romanticism." Cohen notes that what is at stake here is not only maintaining the methodological distinction, discussed above, between psychology and ethics. For the "ethical constitution" of the moral and legal subject to be consistent with the "method of purity," "the moral person may not be assumed as being given, or as determined by certain natural dispositions and conditions" (ErW 95–6). It is with the help of these provisos that Cohen makes a case that the "honor" of "the rejected expression 'self-consciousness'" should be "restored" (ErW 205). The notion of a unified will, and thus of "ethical cognition" requires a notion of "self-consciousness" – as long as this notion is properly understood.[49]

For Cohen, ethics is directed at overcoming "particularity" – not only insofar as it attaches to individual persons but also insofar as it inheres in collectivities such as peoples and states. This has consequences for the role of the state in Cohen's ethical theory: The state can be ethically significant only if it is conceived as a generation of Allheit and a transcending of particularity (ErW 32–5, cf. 60, 81).[50] (In chapter 4, I return to Cohen's understanding of such collectivities – peoples, nations, and states.)

In sum, Cohen's characterization of the unity of action informs his notion of the unity of the legal subject (i.e., the subject of law, *Rechtssubjekt*). Determining the unity of the legal subject is the central problem to be addressed by legal science (ErW 74, 75). Again, this philosophical task of determining the legal subject as a unity is distinct from any possible

---

49 See the discussion in Poma, *The Critical Philosophy*, 113–14.

50 For a broader discussion of Cohen's general positive attitude to the state, including its relationship to his socialist politics, see Schmid, "Das Naturrecht," 417–19. Andrea Poma has written an appreciative reflection on this aspect of Cohen's ethics in "Autonomy of the Law," chap. 13 of *Yearning for Form and Other Essays on Hermann Cohen's Thought* (Dordrecht: Springer, 2006). Harry van der Linden discusses the Allheit of the state in "Hermann Cohen's Political Philosophy and the Communitarian Critique of Liberalism" (1994), available at https://digitalcommons.butler.edu/facsch_papers/66, pp. 4–5; published in French translation in "L'École de Marbourg," ed. Fabien Capeillères and Jean Kahn, special issue, *Cahiers de philosophie politique et juridique* 26 (1994): 93–118.

task of psychology, such as determining, out of the manifold of psychic processes, a unity of consciousness (ErW 75).

The Unity of the Subject in the Association and the "Union of Ethics with Legal Science"

Having clarified in the previous section what is at stake in determining the subject as a unity allows us now to return to Cohen's investigations into legal personhood. Cohen turns to legal categories such as the "legal person" or the association/*Genossenschaft* in order to develop his understanding of the ethical subject. Legal science, the study of law, provides the ideal means to ask about the correlation of the individual and Allheit because it is the discipline that poses the following sort of question: What is the unity of the subject in the case of the association (*Assoziation*)?

> Now a not merely large and important, but also fundamental and epoch-making part of legal transactions consists in the *associations.* Who in these alliances [*Verbindungen*], which diverge into multiple juridical significations, who, in the pluralities in which each of these alliances consists, is the unity of the subject? (ErW 75)

Legal science is the discipline that faces up to the challenge of determining, in the case of the association as a legal actor, whether and in what sense that actor is a unified subject. The unity of the subject in this case must be demonstrable despite the apparent circumstance that we are dealing here with a "pathological double-I," or even with an aggregate of "I"s (ErW 75).

Let us underscore the methodological, "methodistic" shape that Cohen gives to this question – again, keeping in mind the "foundational circularity" between ethics and law discussed above: Consistently with the transcendental-methodological meaning of the "factum" of science, for Cohen it is not a matter simply of pointing to the empirical "association" – or to depictions of such associations – in order to observe that, in fact, here we find many individuals acting as a unified subject. Rather, the example of the association is here given in order to show "the decisive value that we are to recognize in the union of ethics with legal science." Cohen proceeds from the stipulation that "the human being of ethics may not be constituted merely as individual." Instead, "the correlation of individual and *Allheit*" is to be recognized as the "actual problem of ethics," and thus the ethical subject must be "at once *Allheit* and individual" (ErW 75–6). When Cohen mentions the concepts of "association," "legal person," and

Genossenschaft (and his discussions of these, when he does mention them, are quite brief[51]), it is not in order immediately to present them as empirical instances of, or evidence for individual-Allheit correlation, but as evidence that legal science can usefully serve as the factum for ethics. "Here now is revealed the decisive value that we must recognize in the conjunction of ethics with legal science," Cohen concludes after his initial discussion of the "association" example; and versions of this claim become a regular refrain throughout the book (ErW 75).

This is also to say that the phenomenon of the association is not put forward by Cohen as an immediate "solution" to the problem of how to achieve unified ethical subjectivity on the basis of Allheit, though it may well be part of a welcome reform of state law along "social" (i.e., social justice) principles. Rather, Cohen is interested in showcasing the "juridical method and technique" that is in evidence in legal concepts (with respect to the achievement of "social" ideals, Cohen points to the concept of *societas*, as a precursor to the association), which "prepares the way" for reform (ErW 77). Thus, legal science, in that it confronts concepts such as "legal person" or "association," frames the question of the unity of the ethical subject in a way that is distinct from the individual-centered way ethical theory would approach this problem if it did not allow itself to be informed by jurisprudence.

The Legal Person as a Non-Natural Non-Fiction

For Cohen, it is significant that the notion of legal person arose "only late in the development of legal science," and that it goes along "with the modern development of morality." Legal science offers the legal person – in particular in the form of the Genossenschaft – as an "example," even a "model," for ethics. (Nowhere else, in no "form of altruism,"[52] can we find such a compelling example, Cohen adds.) With the concept of Genossenschaft, what is referred to is "immediately" the "persons" who make up the membership – as opposed to, say, the non-personal assets that are controlled by the Genossenschaft.[53] But the members, the

51 I hope hereby to be supplying an explanation for why, as Pascher has observed, "contrary to what one would expect based on his talk of the/a 'Faktum' of legal science, [Cohen] makes no efforts to delve more deeply into positive law." Pascher, *Hermann Cohens Ethik*, 40.

52 I discuss in chapters 5 and 6 Cohen's objections to conventional ideas of altruism.

53 Andreas Heusler, whose account of the legal person Cohen follows at many crucial points, explains why there arises a need for the concept of legal person by pointing to the growing need for goods/commodities to be exploitable for purposes beyond

Genossen, are "immanent" to the Genossenschaft; the Genossenschaft is not "made up of" its members as pre-existing individuals. For this reason, the legal person as represented by the Genossenschaft is also not to be thought of as a *physical* person, the person "as it is normally thought of as an individual creature [*Einzelwesen*]" (ErW 229). That is, the legal concept of "legal person" is irreducible to any physical or natural entity; it is "an abstraction from the start" (ErW 230, cf. 78), in accordance with Cohen's stipulation, discussed above, that ethical theory is not directed at the human "individual" (cf. ErW 234–5). Hence, Cohen strictly distinguishes the notion of "person" from that of "human being."[54] The "natural" individual, we recall, was deemed by Cohen to be the purview of psychology; and Cohen considers the rejection of any naturalist foundations for ethics to be the "meaning" of Kant's distinction between "is" (*Sein*) and "ought" (*Sollen*) (ErW 12).

In this connection, Cohen underscores that family, which we grasp as a "natural" or physical entity, has never been defined as a legal person (ErW 78).[55] (In line with the tradition of conceiving the people/*Volk* as an organism, Cohen argues that Volk constitutes a similar case.[56]) This appears to conflict, Cohen notes, with our initial sense (one, we may add, that goes along with the ethical philosophy developed above all by Hegel) that family is a morally significant entity. We already saw that Cohen deliberately avoids constructing his ethical theory on the basis of an already-constituted individual self. Similarly, Cohen's preference for the abstract, non-physical legal category of "person" over the "natural" entity entails a rejection of any model whereby ethics is directed toward Allheit by means of a dialectical process that allows the particular individual to culminate in a universality. This negative side of the ethical lesson is summed up by Cohen at the end of chapter 4, where the legal person emerges as also constituting the concept of the state:

> Guided by the state-concept of the legal person [i.e., the concept of the legal person as a concept of the theory of the state, or of political theory – D.H.],

individual interests, that is, for the common good, which calls for a body (*Träger*) that will "own" and dispose over such goods, as a legal subject (*Rechtssubjekt*). Neither the assets (*Vermögen*) themselves, nor the "purpose" (*Zweck*) toward which they are administered, nor the ultimate beneficiaries can be thought of as such a "subject." Andreas Heusler, *Institutionen des deutschen Privatrechts*, vol. 1 (Leipzig: Duncker & Humblot, 1886), 253–4. It was Eggert Winter who first established that Heusler was a prime source for Cohen; cf. Winter, *Ethik und Rechtswissenschaft*, 311n120.

54 ErW 230. See the parallel point in Heusler, *Institutionen des deutschen Privatrechts*, 1:255.

55 See the discussion in Heusler, *Institutionen des deutschen Privatrechts*, 1:258ff.

56 Cf. ErW 34, 250–3, 255.

> I learn to recognize, and to put into practice, that I cannot, in my natural individuality, produce the self-consciousness of the will. (ErW 256)

In his invaluable comprehensive study of Cohen's ethical and legal philosophy, Eggert Winter shows how Cohen's use of the Genossenschaft concept builds on and responds to late-nineteenth-century and early-twentieth-century debates in German legal theory, which grappled with the notion of the "corporative legal person." Initially, in accordance with the "naturalist-substantialist" orientation of the discipline of law, the legal person was construed as a "fictional person" (*persona ficta*). To ascribe "fictional" "personhood" to an entity was deemed to be the prerequisite for recognizing that entity as empowered to engage in legal transactions. The problem of legal personhood therefore consisted in the question of how to make sense of a person that is merely a "fiction." Applied to the problem of the Genossenschaft, such a theory would mean that the "will" that would ensue from the collectivity would be an artificially produced will, and thus would be merely derivative of the will of a natural person, which would thus represent an "authentic" will.[57]

Given that Cohen so strenuously objects to any identification of Genossenschaft – or, more generally, of emergent ethical self-consciousness – with natural persons, it makes sense that he also explicitly confronts this alternative possibility that has been entertained by legal theory: that the legal person is a fiction. But he rejects this possibility as well: For to consider the legal person as "merely the fiction of a person" amounts to reinforcing the assumption that "only the person, the physical person can be a legal subject."[58] Instead, Cohen wants to see legal science or legal philosophy to be "creating," in the concept of the legal person, "a new kind of will, a new kind of self-consciousness, and accordingly a new kind of legal subject" (ErW 232). That is, in the legal-philosophical debate about the physical/natural reality or fictionality of the legal

57 Winter, *Ethik und Rechtswissenschaft*, 295; Kaufmann, "Körperschaft," 1151; and Bernd Schildt, "Genossenschaft, Genossenschaftsrecht," in *Handwörterbuch zur deutschen Rechtsgeschichte*, ed. Albrecht Cordes et al., 2nd rev. ed., vol. 2 (Berlin: Erich Schmidt, 2012).

58 Andreas Heusler puts this point as follows: "Das ist mehr als blosse Fiction: eine solche, wenigstens wenn wir das Wort in seiner technischen Bedeutung nehmen, würde die rechtliche Gleichstellung mit der physischen Person gerade negieren und durch ihre eigene Vorschrift, daß es gegebenen Falles so solle angesehen werden, als wäre eine (physische) Person vorhanden, eingestehen, daß in Rechten keine Person vorhanden sei." *Institutionen des deutschen Privatrechts*, 1:256.

person, Cohen takes the position that the legal subject must be neither natural nor fictional.[59] The following passage by the Swiss legal scholar Andreas Heusler (1834–1921) – identified by Eggert Winter as closely corresponding to and a possible source for Cohen's stated position[60] – well illustrates what is at stake in the difference between the notion of the person as a fictional entity, and the idea of the "legal person," which is essentially a legal subject from the outset:

> Greater abstraction and a higher degree of legal education (*Rechtsbildung*) is needed in order to arrive at the proposition: the union of persons, the institution, the foundation is a legal subject, than in order to content oneself with: It is not a legal subject, but we imagine that in the present case it is a physical person who is acting. For in the latter case the law stops at the fact that only physical persons can be legal subjects, whereas in the former case, the law expands the concept of "person" and creates a new type of legal subject.[61]

We can further illuminate the significance of Cohen's position in the context of the legal debates about legal personhood if we consider that what distinguishes Gierke's pioneering Genossenschaft theory and what gave the Genossenschaft idea its tremendous appeal and influence was the "anti-individualist" conception of the human being that undergirded it, as expressed for example in the oft-cited opening line of *Das deutsche Genossenschaftsrecht*: "Man owes what he is to union [*Vereinigung*] with his fellow man" ("Was der Mensch ist, verdankt er der Vereinigung von Mensch und Mensch"). Further, for Gierke, the Genossenschaft was a "reale Verbandsperson" (roughly: a real associative person) – in the

59 "Aber das Recht schützt solche Gebilde, die wir juristische Personen nennen, nicht unter der Annahme, sie seien physische Personen, sondern stellt sie den letzteren gleich, verlässt also das Gebiet der Fiction." Heusler, *Institutionen des deutschen Privatrechts,* 1:256.

60 Winter underscores that although Heusler's study dated back to 1885, Cohen was certainly taking up an issue of contemporary relevance, as fiction theories of legal personhood remained widespread and influential at the time of Cohen's writing.

61 Heusler, *Institutionen des deutschen Privatrechts,* 1:256–7, cited by Winter, *Ethik und Rechtswissenschaft,* 317n136. The very newness of the idea of legal personhood – or the far distance that had to be traversed – accounts, according to Heusler, for why "the concept of the legal person was in all systems of law brought into a clear form relatively late" (257). This point is echoed by Cohen when he observes that it is instructive that the concept of legal person "arises only late in the development of legal science" (ErW 78).

words of one commentator, a "living reality." Thus, he rejected the idea that such a collectivity should be thought of as a "fiction."[62]

We saw earlier that Cohen in the "Self-Consciousness" chapter of the *Ethik* emphasizes unity (Einheit) as a defining feature of ethical subjectivity, that he understands this unity as a "correlation of individual and *Allheit*," and that this correlation is the "problem of ethics" to be investigated, notably in view of the category of the legal person. In the same chapter, we can see Cohen critically responding to Gierke's idea that the Genossenschaft represents unification (*Vereinigung*), specifically in passages in which he argues for an originary and fundamental relationship between "I" and "you." Similarly, to Gierke, Cohen regards the I/You relationship as undergirding the possibility of collectivities/legal persons such as the Genossenschaft and ultimately the state:

> You and I belong together as such. I cannot say "You" without referring/relating you to me, without in this respect/reference/relationship [*in dieser Beziehung*] *uniting* you with the "I." (ErW 248, emphasis added)

And a couple of paragraphs later, in explaining in what sense the state is the "task of self-consciousness," Cohen determines this self-consciousness as "the *unification* [*Vereinigung*] of I and You" (ErW 249, emphasis added).[63]

Thus, Cohen may be seen to appropriate the anti-individualism championed by Gierke, and he of course also agrees with Gierke that the legal person ought not to be understood as a "fiction." But this appropriation and agreement is nevertheless based on a reasoning that departs from that of Gierke. This is because it is wholly at odds with, and explicitly seeks to avoid, the organicism which is also the hallmark of Gierke's theory. (That Cohen avoids organicism or naturalism is also evident in his systematic rejection of the term *Gemeinschaft* [community] to capture the kind of collectivity that he sees as essential to defining ethical subjectivity, as well as in his insistence that "state," insofar as it can be an ethically relevant category, emerges not properly from the notion of peoplehood

62 Otto von Gierke, *Das deutsche Genossenschaftsrecht*, vol. 1 (Berlin: Weidmann, 1868), 1; translated by Mary Fischer as *Community in Historical Perspective* (Cambridge: Cambridge University Press, 1990), 2. Cited by Kaufmann, "Körperschaft," 1150. The terms "anti-individualist" and "living reality" are borrowed from Kaufmann's characterization of Gierke.

63 I return to Cohen's understanding of self-consciousness as a unification of I and You in chapter 2.

or Volk, but along the same methodological lines as the legal person of the Genossenschaft.[64])

In fact, Cohen's double rejection of the naturalist theory and the fictionalist theory exposes the fictionalist theory as the flip side of the naturalist or organicist theory: To cast the legal person as a "mere" fiction serves to reinforce the idea that natural persons are the authentic legal subjects and thus serves to devalue the legal subjectivity of the Genossenschaft and of the legal person in general.[65]

Genossenschaft as the "Hypothesis" of the Self, and the Futurity of Law as *Gesetz*

By a kind of substitution, Cohen suggests that the "legal person in the *Genossenschaft*" "creates a new kind of will" and "a new kind of legal subject" – one that is a "*hypothesis*" rather than a fiction (ErW 232, 243).[66] By attending to Cohen's use of the notion of "hypothesis," we can complete our initial review in this chapter of how he theorizes ethical subjectivity and ethical action as emerging, or being generated out of law. Attending to the role and meaning of "hypothesis" will also allow us to focus attention on another aspect of Cohen's ethico-legal theory: his characterization of law as something *futural*. What this means will be more fully explored in the next chapter, where we turn to the facet of law known as "Gesetz" (in addition to the notion that principally orients Cohen's thinking, that of "Recht.")

That Cohen understands ethico-legal subjectivity in terms of hypothesis goes along with the idea that the "method of purity," or transcendental method in ethics "seeks to discover those conditions and concepts that bring about" the notion of ethico-legal subject or "moral person" (ErW 95–6). Since pure thought does not have a "given,"[67] the ethical

64 ErW 250–6. For more on the problematic category of Volk, as well as the role of Gemeinschaft, see chapter 5.

65 That an "organicist" or psychologist theory of the will may be understood as the flip-side of an "anorganic" fictionalist one was also subsequently demonstrated by Kelsen regarding the "will of the state," which Kelsen, similarly to Cohen, also sees as a legal person. Kelsen, *Hauptprobleme der Staatsrechtslehre,* 162ff. Winter points to this section of Kelsen's work as accomplishing something akin to Cohen's reflections on will. Winter, *Ethik und Rechtswissenschaft,* 311n120.

66 At most, Cohen at one point suggests, the concept of "legal fiction" can be valuable only *insofar* as it *is* a hypothesis (ErW 242, 243).

67 cf. ErW 91: "Truth consists in the unified method of logic and ethics. It cannot be revealed as a datum. It can also not be presumed to be available or revealable as a fact [*Tatsache*] of nature or of history. It is not a treasure, but a treasure seeker. It is a method ..."

subject may also not be "presumed as given, or as determined by certain natural dispositions and conditions" (ErW 95–6). Instead, ethical subjectivity must be "constituted" or generated – which is also to say that this constitution "accomplishes itself" – "by force of" the method of purity (ErW 95). In aiming to understand ethical subjectivity as oriented to Allheit, we must follow the "logical directive [*Befugnis*, authorization] of infinite gathering/summary/summation [*Zusammenfassung*]." This is where the notion of hypothesis proves a useful one for Cohen.

As has been shown by Geert Edel and others, Cohen developed the notion of hypothesis out of an engagement with Plato's theory of ideas. Edel traces how in his 1878 essay on Plato's theory of ideas, Cohen critically examines Plato's depiction of the "hypotheses" or presuppositions (*Voraussetzungen*) of the geometers as a deficient basis for knowledge that is to be "overcome" by way of an *anhypotheton*, a presuppositionless absolute. In contrast to this, the new notion of "hypothesis" advanced by Cohen as part of his own transcendental method refers to a kind of presupposition that is not a metaphysical foundation (*Grundlage*), but is a dynamic, generative "founding" (*Grundlegung*) – generative because the reflection on presuppositions that it entails is, as Edel underscores, open-ended in principle.[68] This notion of hypothesis, the "determination of foundations [*Grundlagen*] as foundings [*Grundlegungen*]," was "increasingly emphasized in the course of the development of [Cohen's] philosophy."[69]

As Edel has pointed out, the work of *Grundlegung* is the unifying feature of Cohen's philosophical "system." Just as the work of the *Logik* is to "found" cognition, the work of the *Ethik* is to "found" will;[70] and ethical philosophy is the open-ended interrogation of the presuppositions of "pure will." As Cohen characterizes the project at one point: "We will have ... to trace how the method of unity is to generate/produce [*erzeugen*] the concept of will, of pure will" (ErW 101). (The qualifier "pure" here simply names the inquiry as a transcendental one.) Thus, Cohen identifies the "purity of method" with "hypothesis as the instrument

---

68 Edel, "Kantianismus oder Platonismus?" 72–5, reading Cohen, "Platons Ideenlehre und die Mathematik" (1878) in SPZ 1:336–66.

Cohen offers a compelling account of the sense in which "foundations" (*Grundlagen*) must be "foundings" (*Grundlegungen*), specifically with reference to the relationship of logic and ethics, at ErW 84–5, and brings the idea of *Grundlegungen* together with "hypothesis" at ErW 97–8.

69 See Edel, "Kantianismus oder Platonismus?" 75, which gives detailed evidence for this assessment. Regarding the centrality of *Grundlegung* to logic and the cognition of nature, see ErW 85.

70 Edel, "Kantianismus oder Platonismus?" 76.

[*Werkzeug*] of truth" (ErW 100) and, taking up the methodological tools of the *Logik*, with the "judgment of origin" (ErW 101).[71]

According to this transcendental method, "nothing may be regarded as given for pure thought; even what is given thought must generate for itself" (ErW 101). An important consequence of Cohen's application of this principle to ethics in particular is that Cohen determines law as something *futural*. This is to say that in critiquing the metaphysical dogmatism of certain conceptions of law that are mistaken in the sense of being unsuited to promoting moral progress, Cohen groups together various traditional (or entrenched habitual) conceptions of law as caused by, or rooted in something *past*, determinate, or fated: If ethical theory makes the "dogmatic" – whether naturalist or empiricist – mistake of beginning from a given of thought as a certainty (ErW 98), Cohen argues, this entails a host of metaphysical presuppositions that foreclose the possibility of moral progress. Thus, the "moral person" is not to be thought of as "given." No "prejudice" about "character" should form the starting point of our reflections on the ethical subject, for example, that it has a "good or an evil will," or a "soul" – a notion that "ethically so easily becomes a specter [*Gespenst*]." As we saw with respect to the legal person, this subject is not "natural" – hence, it is not determined by either inborn or inherited traits (ErW 95–6). Cohen links such common prejudices with certain ancient Greek notions of law or justice as fated, meted out or whose existence is exhausted in mere convention (*syntheke*), and which is thereby encountered as something arbitrary, contingent, incontrovertible – and "eternal" in the sense of being immutable and of unknown origin (ErW 96–7).[72]

71 Cohen argues strenuously for a "unity of method," that of hypothesis, for both logic and ethics (ErW 100–1), as he must do if ethics is to be a matter for objective philosophizing at all. Gianna Gigliotti has emphasized the significance of this and has in particular brought out the contrast between this unity of method envisioned by Cohen and the philosophies of Dilthey and others who insisted that human science/ *Geisteswissenschaft* and natural sciences are distinct realms that call for distinct approaches. Gigliotti, "Ethik und das Faktum der Rechtswissenschaft," 173.

72 Cohen here means specifically a certain "Greek" notion of "eternity," which he goes on to contrast with a prophetic-Jewish notion of eternity, in line with his conception of messianism as a human ethical "task," and against mythical conceptions of a "golden age" or a "lost paradise." ErW, 400–11. See the discussion by Francesca Yardenit Albertini, *Das Verständnis des Seins bei Hermann Cohen: Vom Neukantianismus zu einer jüdischen Religionsphilosophie* (Würzburg: Königshausen & Neumann, 2003), 144–8. Cohen takes a similar approach in developing his notion of messianism as part of his theory of Judaism. See RV 289–92/247–50.

Similarly, Cohen recalls the Pauline formulation of a "law in our members"[73] as representing commonly held beliefs about how morality may be thought as a "law of nature" anchored psycho-physiologically in our selves (cf. ErW 97–8). In Cohen's diagnosis, this line of thinking has subsequently become bifurcated into different variants, according to which, for instance, we are fundamentally motivated toward moral deeds by sympathy, or by revenge – by some sort of affect or drive (ErW 99, cf. 101). (We will see in chapter 6 that this point is also mobilized by Cohen in his critical reception of traditions concerning neighbor-love.) For Cohen, all these "dogmatic" conceptions of law – often modeled after ideas of laws of nature (ErW 261–2) – have had a historic negative impact on ethical theory.

Conceiving the Genossenschaft as "hypothesis" is a way of theorizing its collective action as a kind of infinite gathering/summation and open-ended "task." This infinite gathering/summation (*Zusammenfassung*), which we already encountered in Cohen's notion of a "correlation" of individual and Allheit, is envisioned as a collective action undertaken by the Genossenschaft, in which "multiple wills become unified [*vereinigen sich*] in a will of the whole [*Gesamtwille*]" (ErW 230–1).[74] This is then the sense in which the legal person as Genossenschaft is a hypothesis. Conversely, the hypothesis of ethical self-consciousness, of the ethical subject, "accomplishes itself [*sich vollzieht*] in the legal person of the *Genossenschaft*" (ErW 231–2; cf. 243).

Cohen's attention to the "prejudices" about ethical subjectivity as something determined psycho-physiologically by a "self" or by an immutable order or "law" of nature (*Naturgesetz*) also lead him to problematize the notion of the "moral law" – a key term in Kant's practical philosophy. If the "moral law" is conceived along the lines of a "law of nature," then that represents a "mistaken view of *Gesetz*/law" in its possible significance for ethics in general (ErW 98).

The next chapter will examine further what it is that concerns Cohen about this "mistaken view of *Gesetz*." In fact, it is initally puzzling that this term is present at all alongside Recht – Cohen's principal term for what in English is called "law" – in his main argument that ethics is generated out of law. Making sense of the presence of Gesetz in that argument will allow me to begin to explore the passages between Cohen's ethico-legal philosophy and his philosophy of Judaism.

---

73 ErW 99; cf. Rom. 7:23.

74 Cf. ErW 224: It is "in [the sphere of] law [*im Rechte*]" that ethically significant action (*Handlung*) becomes manifest in the form of legal action (*Rechtshandlung*), which requires "unification [*Vereinigung*] toward/for the purpose of legal action, i.e., for the generation [*Erzeugung*] of a legal content, a legal relationship."

Chapter Two

"For the Idea of Law [*Gesetz*] He Substitutes Morality": Understanding Law in Cohen's *Ethik*, with Help from the Early Strauss

Many commentators have observed a convergence or a possible affinity between the central claim of Cohen's ethical philosophy – that ethics is rooted in law or in legal science – and the centrality of law in Judaism. Yet when we look at Cohen's works on Jewish religion, law (halakhah, mitzvot, etc.) does not appear to have a constitutive or core role in his understanding of what Judaism or "religion of reason" is.[1]

It is noteworthy that Steven Schwarzschild, the foremost, and formidable commentator on Cohen in the immediate postwar period, sums up the implications of Cohen's unified approach to law and ethics as follows:

> The Jew Cohen has thus salvaged his fundamental commitment to halakhah, the law, for his ethics of rational autonomy.

Yet Schwarzschild does not explain what he means by this statement.[2] The same is true for other scholars of Cohen. Although many have suggested

---

1 Michael Zank makes a related point when he notes a certain disjunction between the central role of law in the *Ethik*, as well as Cohen's "evident interest in the principles of a legal theory that is expressly oriented toward Judaism," and the fact that Cohen "does not claim for himself any special knowledge of the legal teachings (i.e., halakhah), which after all do markedly dominate the Talmud." Zank, "Hermann Cohen und die rabbinische Literatur," in *Hermann Cohen's Philosophy of Religion*, ed. Stéphane Mosès and Hartwig Wiedebach (Hildesheim: Olms, 1997), 266. However, see George Y. Kohler's recent study "Against the Heteronomy of Halakhah: Hermann Cohen's Implicit Rejection of Kant's Critique of Judaism," which, while it agrees in many respects with my readings of Cohen's treatments of law in Judaism (in the present chapter and in chapter 4), indeed does see in those treatments a philosophical argument for a commitment to halakhah. *Dine Israel* 32 (2018), 208*–9*.

2 See Steven S. Schwarzschild, "Introduction" to Cohen's *Ethik*, in *Werke* vol. 7 (1981): XVII*; also included in Schwarzschild, *The Tragedy of Optimism: Writings on Hermann Cohen*, ed. George Y. Kohler (Albany: State University of New York Press, 2018). In his

or intimated that there is in Cohen's thought a connection between law in Judaism and ethical philosophy, such suggestions are often lacking in explanation as to what that connection might be.[3]

The question of whether Cohen, as a formative influence on modern Jewish thought (indeed, arguably the key inaugural figure

---

essay from the same period, "An Agenda for Jewish Philosophy in the 1980's" (1980), Schwarzschild intimates that the "Jewish, halachic issue" that is operative in Cohen's understanding of jurisprudence as "the positive science from which philosophy transcendentally deduces ethics" (an idea I explored in the last chapter) would be a connectedness between halakhah and ethics, "in contrast to Kant's sharp dichotomy between 'virtue' and law." While Schwarzschild does not develop this interpretation in detail, it is consistent with my findings in the course of this chapter. *Studies in Jewish Philosophy*, ed. Norbert Samuelson (Lanham, MD: University Press of America, 1987), 106.

3 (Kohler's above-referenced study, "Against the Heteronomy of Halakhah," is a recent exception.) Gesine Palmer, taking up Schwarzschild's interpretation, also views "halakhic thinking" as a central element of Cohen's *Ethik*. See Palmer, "'Freud vermoralisiert die Psychologie'. Eine Randnotiz von Franz Rosenzweig im Lichte der Antinomismusdiskussion von Jacob Taubes" (lecture held at a workshop on Jacob Taubes, Zentrum für Literatur- und Kulturforschung Berlin, 21 February 2011), https://gesine-palmer.de/wp-content/uploads/2017/07/taubes.vortrag2.pdf. A general observation along these lines is also made by Liliana Ruth Feierstein in *Von Schwelle zu Schwelle: Einblicke in den didaktisch-historischen Umgang mit dem Anderen aus der Perspektive jüdischen Denkens* (Bremen: Edition Lumière, 2010), 122.

A further reflection of this explanatory gap is David Novak's contrarian proposal to "take the philosophical and theological strengths of Cohen's political thought and use them to give the agenda of cultural Zionism" today "an intellectual focus and conviction it might never have had before" – despite Cohen's own anti-Zionism. To this end, Novak "translates" "Cohen's term" "law" into the "cultural Zionist" notion of *mishpat ivri*. With this translation, Novak is supplementing "law" as a key term in Cohen's thought by drawing on a notion of Jewish law that lies outside the Cohenian corpus, so as to make the term fruitful for his task of reflecting on a particular vision for contemporary Jewish political existence in "a post-Zionist age." It is symptomatic of the general deficit in inquiry into the precise role of Jewish law in Cohen's thought that Novak does not justify this choice by showing whether there exist any resources *in* the Cohenian corpus for thinking law in Judaism, or in the Jewish state. Novak, "Hermann Cohen on State and Nation: A Contemporary Review," in *Hermann Cohen's Critical Idealism*, ed. Reinier Munk (Dordrecht: Springer, 2005), 271ff.

Several commentators have highlighted, more broadly, the significance of the *Ethik* as a key work in which Cohen also conveyed his philosophy of Judaism. For example, Michael Zank identifies in the *Ethik* a "defense of Judaism" and also finds Cohen's valorization of law to be significant in this connection. See Michael Zank, "The Ethics in Hermann Cohen's Philosophical System," in "Hermann Cohen's *Ethics*," ed. Robert Gibbs, special issue, *Journal of Jewish Thought and Philosophy* 13, nos. 1–2 (2004): 2, 10–15; see esp. 14 regarding the importance of law.

By means of what is from today's perspective a tendentious reading, Cohen's contemporary Benzion Kellerman praised the *Ethik*, in his review of the book for a Jewish readership, as an ingenious Jewish apologetics, a "scientific verification of Judaism." Kellermann, "Hermann Cohens 'Ethik des reinen Willens,'" *Allgemeine Zeitung des Judentums* (1905, printed serially in issues no. 3, 5, 7, 9, 11, 14, 17, 18, and 21), 250; cf. 32–3.

for twentieth- and twenty-first-century Jewish thought), articulated a connection between law in Judaism and ethics is, furthermore, of special relevance today, given the intense contemporary interest in the place of law, politics, and practice in Judaism, and in looking at Jewish thought as a resource for contemporary thinking about law, politics, and justice.[4]

As a way into this question, I want to present the early, incisive reading of Cohen offered by Leo Strauss in *Philosophy and Law* in order to suggest that that reading can help frame and sharpen our analysis of Cohen's approach to law in both his ethics and his philosophy of Judaism. In this chapter, I will thereby be showing to what extent I view Cohen as invoking or involving an understanding of Jewish law, or of law "out of the sources of Judaism," in his *philosophical* ethics, that is, in *Ethik des reinen Willens.*

The subsequent chapters (3 and 4) will go on to explore Cohen's understanding of law in the context of his theory of (Jewish) religion, as laid out in his "Jewish writings."[5]

~

Leo Strauss's early reading of Cohen is embedded in Strauss's own project during the early 1930s of trying to articulate together questions directed to a philosophy of Judaism – or, more accurately, to an understanding of revelation – with general philosophical questions, which is to say, with the question of philosophy in general. We find this reading in parts of the book *Philosophy and Law* (*Philosophie und Gesetz*, 1935), and especially in Strauss's notes for the lecture on "Cohen and Maimonides" ("Cohen und Maimuni") that he gave at the Hochschule für die Wissenschaft des Judentums in Berlin in 1931.[6] Strauss wrote this text the same year as he

4 A helpful survey of some recent literature in this area is Julie E. Cooper, "The Turn to Tradition in the Study of Jewish Politics," *Annual Review of Political Science* 19 (2016).

5 I explain what I mean by Cohen's "Jewish writings" in the introduction to this book.

6 For analyses of Strauss's early references to Cohen in relation to Strauss's own intellectual development, see, for example, David Janssens, *Between Athens and Jerusalem. Philosophy, Prophecy, and Politics in Leo Strauss's Early Thought* (Albany: State University of New York Press, 2008); Leora Batnitzky, "The Possibility of Premodern Rationalism: Strauss's Transformation of Hermann Cohen," *Leo Strauss and Emmanuel Levinas: Philosophy and the Politics of Revelation* (Cambridge: Cambridge University Press, 2006), chap. 5; Corine Pelluchon, "Strauss and Cohen: The Question of Enlightened Judaism," *Interpretation* 32, no. 3 (2005); Chiara Adorisio, "Politische Philosophie als Philosophia Prima. Leo Strauss' Transformation von Hermann Cohens philosophischem Projekt," in *Links. Rivista di letteratura e cultura tedesca / Zeitschrift für deutsche Literatur- und Kulturwissenschaft* 7 (2007).

did the essay that became chapter 3 of *Philosophy and Law*, "Maimonides's Doctrine of Prophecy and Its Sources," and the lecture text overlaps significantly with both that chapter and chapter 1, the critical review of Julius Guttmann's *Die Philosophie des Judentums.*[7]

In *Philosophy and Law*, Strauss argues that Jewish thinkers of the medieval period (who for him exemplify Jewish philosophy as such) are, along with Islamic thinkers of the same period, in a unique position to teach us about a certain congruence of philosophy, politics, and revelation/theology.[8] By revelation, Strauss means revelation as "law," "Gesetz." For the purposes of Strauss's study of philosophy, politics, and revelation, "law" thus refers to a law of divine origin; and revelation refers to a situation of heteronomy, of being subject to a transcendent law. One of Strauss's central preoccupations in *Philosophy and Law* is to interrogate the notion and the origin of this idea of being subject to a law, which for him is a notion that is both theological and political. He identifies this notion as the "nomos" tradition,[9] which he sees as having been originated in Plato and – depending on how one reads his rather intricate treatment of this issue – as having been either retrieved or instantiated

7 The essay on Guttmann was written in 1933. See Heinrich Meier's editorial preface to Strauss, *Gesammelte Schriften*, vol. 2: XII–XIII. The title of chapter 3 of *Philosophy and Law* is "The Philosophical Foundation of Law"; the original essay title, "Maimonides's Doctrine of Prophecy and Its Sources," appears in parentheses after the new main chapter title. Chapter 1 is entitled "The Quarrel of the Ancients and the Moderns in the Philosophy of Judaism (Remarks on Julius Guttmann, *The Philosophy of Judaism*)."

Thomas Meyer and Michael Zank have called attention to an even earlier phase of Strauss's readings of Cohen, dating from around 1925 and centered on his review of the posthumous edition of Cohen's *Jüdische Schriften.* Though I have taken account of that review insofar as it helps us understand and situate Strauss's treatment of Cohen in the 1930s, it does not serve as a basis for my discussion in this chapter. Thomas Meyer and Michael Zank, "More Early Writings by Leo Strauss from the *Jüdische Wochenzeitung für Cassel, Hessen und Waldeck* (1925–1928)," *Interpretation* 39, no. 1 (2012).

8 For a helpful characterization of this work and its legacy, as well as the interpretative challenges it poses, see Michael Zank, "Arousing Suspicion Against a Prejudice: Leo Strauss and the Study of Maimonides' *Guide of the Perplexed*," in *Moses Maimonides (1138–1204): His Religious, Scientific, and Philosophical* Wirkungsgeschichte *in Different Cultural Contexts*, ed. Görge K. Hasselhoff and Otfried Fraisse (Würzburg: Ergon, 2004).

9 For some helpful reflections on the impact on Judaism and Jewish philosophy of the Septuagint's translation of the term *Torah* as *nomos* (instead of the available term *didache*, meaning "teaching"), see Paul Franks, "Sinai since Spinoza: Reflections on Revelation in Modern Jewish Thought," in *The Significance of Sinai: Traditions About Sinai and Divine Revelation in Judaism and Christianity*, ed. George J. Brooke, Hindy Najman, and Loren T. Stuckenbruck (Leiden: Brill, 2008).

for the first time by the medieval Jewish and Islamic thinkers. (In chapter 3, I will be looking in some detail at this aspect of Strauss's argument in *Philosophy and Law*, in order to illuminate Cohen's own interpretative method of "political theology.")

For Strauss, the nomos tradition represents two interlinked claims that characterize this medieval tradition:

(1) The claim that philosophy is conditioned by revelation/theology, which is also to say that it is authorized and made possible by revelation as law. (Strauss is fascinated by the phenomenon that the medieval Islamic and Jewish thinkers argue for an authorization of philosophic inquiry by the very tradition of revelation that ought to have no need of philosophical insight.)
(2) The claim that philosophy's task, and thus its essence, is essentially moral and political.

Taken together, these two claims propose a philosophical pursuit of truth that is "authorized" by revelation. This revelation is also a nomos, a law, and this fact goes hand in hand with philosophy's task being essentially moral and political. These claims together thus denote a kind of philosophico-political theology or theo-philosophical politics.

Strauss's Search for the Nomos Tradition in Cohen

Strauss names Hermann Cohen as an important resource for his views along these lines about the lasting contribution and status of (medieval) Jewish philosophy. Strauss credits Cohen with having identified an ethical-political program in Maimonides's philosophy, that is, of having given a reading of Maimonides that Strauss takes as "guidance" for his own reading. For Strauss, this identification of an ethical-political program in Maimonides by Cohen goes along with the general orientation of Cohen's own ethics. That is, Strauss at least to some extent also credits Cohen for giving his ethics a jurisprudential, "nomos" orientation. However, as we will see, Strauss also thinks that the commitment of Cohen's ethics to this principle falls short.[10]

For the purposes of this chapter, Strauss's ambivalence regarding Cohen's ethico-political thought is significant. Examining this

10 For a brief sketch of Strauss's argument, see Micha Brumlik, "*... ein Funke des römischen Gedankens ...*" *Leo Strauss' Kritik an Hermann Cohen* (Heidelberg: Universitätsverlag, 2008), 22–5.

ambivalence will help me pursue the question I raised at the beginning: How does Cohen's theory of ethics-out-of-law relate to the idea of law relevant to Judaism, which Strauss frames as the nomos tradition?

To see how this question arises in Strauss's reading of Cohen on ethics and law, let us consider a passage from the "Cohen and Maimonides" lecture, in which Strauss affirms that all great topics of thought, or matters for thought, are by definition "political" and sets up Cohen as an ally in this affirmation (CM 394, 406). Strauss writes that two things hold true for Cohen's understanding of philosophy (both of them being views that Strauss seems to share): (1) that ethics/politics holds a central place in philosophy (CM 394, 406),[11] that is, that "politics is the field on which philosophical, moral, inner oppositions come to *decisive expression* [or externalization: *Äusserung*]"; (2) that in the field of politics, "regarding these oppositions, it is a matter of the *whole* (*es geht aufs Ganze*)." That is, in the political, "all" is at stake. It is the field in which "it *becomes evident/revealed* [*offenbar*] what those oppositions" – the "philosophical, moral, inner oppositions" – "are all about" (CM 406). Understood in such a way, politics is the essential purpose of philosophy, the direction toward which philosophy essentially strives. For Strauss, Cohen's *Ethik* is fundamentally based on this idea of the concurrence, or shared direction, of politics and philosophy (CM 406).

In Strauss's view, if Cohen's ethical philosophy evidences a recognition of the concurrence of philosophy and politics, this is not only because Cohen recognizes that ethical-political questions are central or essential to philosophy. Rather, to recognize that politics is the field on which philosophical truths become expressed/externalized/revealed entails recognizing that this kind of "becoming-revealed" or becoming externalized is not a secondary phenomenon – it does not, strictly speaking, come "after" the original event of the truth to be revealed or externalized. Instead, philosophy, defined as "that which is internal/inward [*das Innerliche*]" (i.e., as the field of the aforementioned "inner oppositions"), just is that which "presses toward expression/externalization [*die Äusserung*], toward deed, toward realization." This insight is one that Strauss attributes to Cohen; he calls it "the fundamental idea of Cohen's ethics" (*der Grundgedanke der Cohenschen Ethik*), and he links it to a key move in Cohen's *Ethik*: namely that, as Strauss puts it, Cohen "replaces the point of view of *conviction* [Gesinnung] with that of *action* [Handlung]" (CM 406).

---

11 See also a passage from the 1931 essay version of chapter 3 of *Philosophy and Law* that explains further "Cohen's view of the opposition between Platonic and Aristotelian philosophizing" and in which Strauss also notes his disagreement with this view (PG 610).

"No Conviction without Action"

This observation by Strauss refers to an argument that Cohen makes repeatedly in the *Ethik:* that action should not be seen as the (secondary) result of a (primary) internal conviction. Cohen sometimes articulates this view in the formula "no conviction without action" ("keine Gesinnung ohne Handlung"). The self for Cohen must not be thought of as being rooted in a psyche or a conviction – as if the conviction were the cause of the action, and the action merely the externalization of a conviction. Instead, Cohen envisions the self as an ethical task/project whose action is geared to Allheit, and is directed to the future. Cohen's account of ethics as rooted in law (Recht) signifies that action in some sense issues from law and Allheit.

Cohen thus breaks with the traditional way of thinking of a will to action as, for instance, latently contained in a conviction, such that the conviction would take primacy over the will in understanding action. As discussed in the previous chapter, Cohen objects to psychologically based accounts of ethics as "metaphysical." In "naturalizing" the human being, they at the same time also posit a transcendent, supernatural counterpart to that natural human being, such that moral psychology can be seen as the flip side of moral theology (ErW 16–17, 28). This diagnosis of the "error of psychology" has consequences for Cohen's analysis of the relationship between thinking, willing, and acting (ErW 16–17). The insufficiency of psychology consists in its "metaphysical" overemphasis on willing over thinking in understanding what motivates us to act – and thus in attributing our actions primarily to natural tendencies such as drives (ErW 18–19). Thus, Cohen finds that the interest of psychology in drives and motivations as the source of willing is indicative of psychology's engagement with "the metaphysics of things-in-themselves" (ErW 103). (The "metaphysics" inherent in this psychology is for Cohen also manifest in affirmations such as those of Arthur Schopenhauer of the "will" as the "absolute" and the "thing in itself," and thus as utterly distinct from the intellect [ErW 103].)

Based on such considerations, Cohen discerns a slight problem in Kant's use of the terms "will" and "practical reason," which he says is likely to lead us to the mistaken assumption that Kant views only theoretical reason as the realm of thought, while the will, or practical reason is not actually reason and does not involve thought (ErW 169). In this connection, Cohen suggests that in order to clarify that practical reason as will (pure will, the "good will") indeed must involve thought, Kant ought to have placed a greater emphasis in his practical philosophy on "action" – as J.G. Fichte later did (ErW 169–70), and as Cohen does in his own *Ethik.*

In identifying moral psychology's problem of overemphasizing willing over thinking, Cohen uses the term "Gesinnungs-Ethik": such an ethics would neglect the "intellectual moment" in action and would locate action in conviction (Gesinnung) (ErW 17).[12] This criticism of the "perspective of Gesinnung" is also used by Cohen to argue against any attempt to understand action as a mere "expression" or extension of something that is actually "inside" us. Such a quasi-spatial understanding mistakenly frames action (which for Cohen designates "the fundamental problem of ethics"; ErW 72) as derivative of willing or conviction. Cohen wants to turn this relationship around: If anything, it is the "inner" willing or intention that should be thought of as "belonging to" the "outward" action (ErW 176, 177–8). Another way of putting this is to say that action is for Cohen *immediately* at issue whenever we think of an ethical willing. "Pure will accomplishes itself, completes itself in pure action"; it is not conceivable apart from action (ErW 177).[13] Cohen in particular reminds us of the dangers of such a misunderstanding for criminal legal theory/criminal law (ErW 17, 72). Conviction, furthermore, does not really get us very far in understanding the complex problem of the will; it names "something interior, the interior as such," and thus is "a profound moment of will," but it is not essentially constitutive of will (ErW 72, cf. 118). For will is defined by its being directed to "the external," which is the same as saying that it is defined by its "becoming an action" (ErW 72). Will as an object of ethical inquiry – unlike will as an object of psychology – is not an "immediate natural fact"[14] but a "concept" whose analysis involves that of action. "For ethics there cannot and must not exist a willing that does not accomplish itself in action." To study the will thus must involve not only looking at the impetus for willing, but above all "attending to [its] end" (ErW 103).[15] Cohen thus critiques the entire enterprise of moral psychology – the inquiry into motives for action – as "metaphysical." He goes so far as to say that "so-called *intention* and *conviction* withdraw/shrink from [i.e., are unavailable to] human insight" (ErW 103).

---

12 Cohen's use of this term should not be confused with Max Weber's famous distinction between "ethic of conviction" (*Gesinnungsethik*) – meaning acting based on one's convictions – and "ethic of responsibility" (*Verantwortungsethik*) – meaning acting in order to achieve desired results.

13 Affect has a somewhat ambiguous status in the *Ethik*, in particular in the development of the concept of "pure will." Cf. ErW, 116–24, 133–43, as well as the study by Ursula Renz, "Affektivität und Geschichtlichkeit: Hermann Cohens Rehabilitierung des Affekts," in *Affekte und Ethik. Spinozas Lehre im Kontext*, ed. Achim Engstler and Robert Schnepf (Hildesheim: Olms, 2002).

14 Cf. KBE (1st ed.), 140, where Cohen already warns of the confusion of will with physical processes, which amounts to making will into a thing-in-itself.

15 Thus, ethics must not "separate the beginning of willing from its end," the action (ErW 103–4). Cf. ErW, 120.

The "Limit of [Cohen's] Understanding" According to Strauss: Morality or Politics/Law?

The precedence Cohen accords to action over conviction in determining ethics is a focal point for Strauss in his reading of Cohen's landmark essay on Maimonides, "Charakteristik der Ethik Maimunis" (1908) (which Cohen wrote shortly after the *Ethik*[16]). Strauss links this precedence of action over conviction to Cohen's characterization of Maimonides as a philosopher who, in philosophizing, "always focuses his attention on the *aktuell* [i.e., currently relevant, topical – D.H.], living meaning of the concepts." This topicality, *Aktualität*, Cohen specifies, "lies in ethics."[17]

From Strauss's analysis of this claim, there also emerges a criticism or correction: Strauss remarks that what Cohen calls "morality" should really be called "politics" – or rather, that *Cohen* should have called it "politics" or "law"/"Gesetz" (CM 394, 428–9). Accordingly, Strauss qualifies Cohen's valuable "understanding of Rambam [Maimonides] as a Platonist" as follows:

> The *limit* of his understanding is given in the fact that for the idea of *law* [*Gesetz*] he substitutes that of *morality* [*Sittlichkeit*]. (CM 429)[18]

---

16 The edited volume to which this essay was a contribution (*Moses ben Maimon, sein Leben, seine Werke und sein Einfluss* [Leipzig: Fock, 1908]) was published in honor of the 700th anniversary of Maimonides's death, which would have been 1904; but its publication wound up being delayed by four years. Cohen evidently composed his contribution in 1905 and submitted a version in August of that year, though he revised that version in the following year and resubmitted it by late 1906. See Hartwig Wiedebach's editorial remarks in *Werke* 15, XXIII–XXV. Thanks to Michael Zank for pointing out to me the chronological proximity of this essay to the *Ethik*.

17 CEM 248/78; cited at CM 394 and alluded to at CM 406. Though Strauss breaks off his quote here, the remainder of Cohen's original sentence designates this very quality of maintaining focus on *Aktualität* as a kind of inwardness, *Innerlichkeit*. This recalls the reversal that Strauss has said he values in Cohen, by which action, and "actuality," in the sense of making things current and ethically relevant, gains primacy over conviction.

18 As Corine Pelluchon points out, Strauss argues this point against Cohen also with reference to their respective interpretations of Maimonides on God's attributes. Pelluchon, *Leo Strauss. Une autre raison, d'autres lumières* (Paris: Vrin, 2005), 153. Cf. CM 419. Strauss further interprets Cohen's substitution of ethics for politics as representing a "fundamental critique" of Plato. He cites Cohen's statement in the *Ethik* "that while [Plato] orients the I toward the state, he at the same time dissolves the I in the state" (ErW 584, cited at CM 429). Cohen originally makes this statement in the context of an argument for the ethical importance of the legal institutions of family and marriage, which in Cohen's view ought not to be obscured in favor of according ethical importance exclusively to the state.

This is the critique that lurks behind Strauss's recommendation of Cohen as a "guide" to the "topical-current [*aktuell*] political" meaning of Maimonides's philosophy: that Cohen is himself

> guided by a topical-current [*aktuell*]-ethical, or, more pointedly, by a political interest. (CM 394)

For Strauss, Cohen obscures the political dimension of philosophizing by putting an emphasis on ethics and thus (typically for latter-day Jewish philosophers, and for modern philosophy in general) obscuring the role of the nomos tradition for philosophy. In that sense, Cohen is too "modern" for Strauss; and Strauss views Cohen's politics as a "determinate" politics of the individual and of "the left," and thus as political in an inadequate "party-political" sense.[19]

When we look closely at this assessment of Cohen by Strauss, we can see that it is not simply a criticism, but that it also conveys, with all necessary qualifications, what Strauss appreciates about Cohen. For with his assessment that Cohen, in describing Maimonides's topicality (*Aktualität*), said "morality" when he should have said Gesetz, Strauss is suggesting that we ought to tacitly correct Cohen on that score, to hear Cohen say what he *ought* to have said. If we hear him correctly, we will hear an endorsement of the nomos tradition, of the "idea of Gesetz," the idea of a "*concrete* binding order of life" that is shared by the Jews and the Greeks (and that is subsequently covered over by intervening Western philosophical and theological traditions). Cohen is to be recruited as an ally in bringing us onto "the path of reclaiming" Gesetz/nomos as "this fundamental concept of humanity" not only because he "substitutes the point of view of action for that of conviction" but in particular because he accomplishes that substitution "by orienting his ethics in principle to jurisprudence." Cohen is thereby a political philosopher, even if he fails to say so himself, even if he persists in saying – or in appearing to say – ethics when he should be saying – or is perhaps actually saying – politics (CM 428–9).

We may now reformulate the opening question of this chapter by reframing it in the terms of Strauss's reading of Cohen: If what Cohen affirms as Maimonides's recognition and retrieval of the ethical is actually bound up with Maimonides's understanding of revelation as Gesetz, what becomes of Gesetz in Cohen? Is it a part of, or does it have any kind of key role in Cohen's theory of ethics out of law?

---

19 Cf. CM 429, as well as the opposition Strauss draws between politics as such (as "the field on which philosophical, moral, inner oppositions come to decisive expression," etc.) and the "wretchednesses [*Erbärmlichkeiten*] of party politics." CM 406; cf. CM 412.

Terminological Note: *Recht* and *Gesetz*

To look at the role of Gesetz in Cohen's ethico-legal theory, we need to keep in view a matter of terminology: We have been looking at Strauss's interest in the category of "Gesetz," which is aligned with the Greek term *nomos*. Strauss is concerned with how that Greek notion *nomos* is retrieved in medieval Islamic and Jewish texts to mean a kind of revelation or divine law to which human beings are subject. By contrast, in Cohen's theory of ethics out of law, it is a matter of "Recht," which refers to something like a system of law, comprising the totality of legal institutions and norms (equivalent to the Latin "ius" and the French "droit"). As I laid out in the previous chapter, in developing an ethics out of the science of law, *Rechtswissenschaft*, Cohen wants to explain how legal concepts and institutions relate to ethical principles and concepts, and thus to moral progress.

In addition, historically and to this day, Jewish law, or law in Judaism is typically referred to in German as "Gesetz"; so that for Cohen and Strauss and their contemporaries, when they discuss the role of law (halakhah, mitzvot, observance) in Judaism, the relevant notion is Gesetz. (By contrast, now that the study of Jewish law is finding its way, to a very minimal extent, into German law school curricula, the term used for that field of study is *jüdisches Recht*.[20])

In sum, with Recht and Gesetz, we have a difference of genealogies and conceptual emphasis, though of course these two terms constantly cross each other in legal, political, and ethical philosophy.

Gesetz and the Problem of Autonomy in Kant and Cohen

The significance of the notion of Gesetz in Cohen's ethico-legal theory – his theory of ethics out of Recht – comes to the fore in connection with Cohen's treatment of the problem of autonomy. Cohen's investigations into whether and in what sense the self may be autonomous go along with his conception of the ethical subject that I elaborated in chapter 1: This self, or "self-consciousness" is not pre-constituted or readymade, but

20 See the activities in the area of "Jüdisches Recht" since 1998 at the Faculty of Law of the Humboldt University in Berlin, documented at https://www.rewi.hu-berlin.de/de/lf/oe/bsjr, and of the Forschungsstelle für jüdisches Recht Marcus Cohn at the Faculty of Law of the Goethe University in Frankfurt am Main, described at http://www.juedisches-recht.de/home.php; as well as the terminological framing of Justus von Daniels's monograph *Religiöses Recht als Referenz. Jüdisches Recht im rechtswissenschaftlichen Vergleich* (Tübingen: Mohr Siebeck, 2009). Similarly, Islamic law, "Islamisches Recht," is present in today's German law school curricula, while the term frequently used to refer to sharia law has been "Gesetz."

is a hypothesis, an open-ended task, something to be generated or that accomplishes itself. Cohen is continually dealing with and reworking the philosophical legacy of Kant, for whom determining human moral capacity meant understanding agents to be "autonomous." Cohen therefore also grapples with the notion of autonomy, a term that itself involves that of law/Gesetz, since auto-nomy literally means self-legislation, giving oneself one's own law (nomos).[21] Kant is an inheritor of a long tradition of seeing morality as a function of Gesetz, the idea of a "moral law" (*moralisches Gesetz*) that obliges us to action. Early modern traditions according to which moral comportment is a matter of one's actions being consistent with the law of nature may be seen as the background to the centrality of the terminology of Gesetz in Kant's ethical theory. Such traditions have their origin in the idea that moral law stems from divine law, such that there would be a close relationship between moral law and laws of nature, both of which are founded in God's plan for the world.[22] That historic use of Gesetz, whether with or without reference to a divine legislator, entails understanding ethical action in view of a law imposed by something or someone.

For Kant, the idea that the moral agent is autonomous goes along with the criterion of *universality* that is at the heart of the categorical imperative: In its so-called basic formulation, the categorical imperative states that I must act in such a way that I can will that the maxim of my action be a universal law (*allgemeines Gesetz*). Kant combines this criterion of universality with the requirement that moral duties be performed out of reverence for the law, that is, for the sake of the law (AA4: 400, 390). He further combines (a) the idea that to act morally is to act in conformity with a universal law with (b) the idea that the will is *self-legislating* or *autonomous* – that I give myself my own law.[23] Autonomy, or self-legislation is the guarantee of universality; that is, only if I will myself (and not only others) to be subject to this law is it a truly universal law.[24]

---

21 For the idea that the will is self-legislating or autonomous, see Immanuel Kant, *Grundlegung zur Metaphysik der Sitten*, in AA4: 431–3; translated and edited by Mary Gregor as *Groundwork of the Metaphysics of Morals* (Cambridge: Cambridge University Press, 1997), which includes the AA pagination.

22 See W. Bartuschat, "Gesetz, moralisches," *Historisches Wörterbuch der Philosophie*, vol. 3, ed. Joachim Ritter, Karlfried Gründer, and Gottfried Gabriel (Basel: Schwabe, 1974), cols. 516–19.

23 AA4: 431–3.

24 AA4: 431, and commentary on this passage by Jens Timmermann in Immanuel Kant, *Grundlegung zur Metaphysik der Sitten*, ed. Jens Timmermann (Göttingen: Vandenhoeck & Ruprecht, 2004), 130.

"Autonomy of the will" as the "highest principle of morality" can thus be thought of as underwriting the universality of Gesetz that is required by the categorical imperative.[25]

Cohen is similarly guided by the view that Kant's principle of autonomy serves to secure the universality of the categorical imperative. He presents this view in his book on Kant's ethics, *Kants Begründung der Ethik* (1877/1910), working from the second formulation of the categorical imperative (sometimes termed the "humanity formula") in the *Groundwork of the Metaphysics of Morals* (1785):

> Act in such a way that you use humanity, whether in your own person or in the person of any other, always at the same time as an end, never merely as a means. (AA4: 429)

This is for Cohen the most significant of the formulations of the categorical imperative, because it names "humanity" (*Menschheit*) as the ultimate end or telos (*Zweck*) of human action. Cohen argues that "humanity" here denotes a universality that goes beyond a generalization over, or an aggregate of human individuals and their respective ends. This universality is thus akin to the universality or Allheit toward which, as we saw, ethical theory should be oriented.[26] Cohen calls attention to a passage in the *Groundwork* in which Kant explains that the principle of humanity as an end in itself is universal in that as a law it is "the supreme limiting condition of all subjective ends" (AA4: 430–1). If humanity is a supreme limiting condition of subjective ends, Cohen suggests, a new requirement

---

25 Thus, the following statement of Kant about the principle of autonomy takes up the exact wording of the basic formula of the categorical imperative: "The principle of autonomy is, therefore: to choose only in such a way that the maxims of your choice are also included as universal law in the same volition/willing" (AA4: 440, cf. 421). Onora O'Neill has made a similar point by emphasizing that the universality called for here is not just one of "mere adherence to the form of law," but also one of "scope." O'Neill, "Self-Legislation, Autonomy and the Form of Law," *Recht – Geschichte – Religion. Die Bedeutung Kants für die Gegenwart. Deutsche Zeitschrift für Philosophie,* Sonderband 4, ed. Herta Nagl-Docekal and Rudolf Langthaler (Berlin: Akademie Verlag, 2004), 22.

26 As Andrea Poma points out, in the *Ethik,* Cohen credits Kant with having "renewed Platonic ethics" by making "exceptionless universality [*Allgemeinheit*]," comprising humanity (*Menschheit*) (which was "thought up" by the prophets), into its content. See ErW 146 and the discussion in Poma, *The Critical Philosophy of Hermann Cohen* (1988), trans. John Denton (Albany: State University of New York Press, 1997), 112. See also "Religion und Sittlichkeit," JS3: 150, where Cohen specifies that the moral individual stems from the Allheit of "humanity."

is thereby added to the "formal" law of the categorical imperative: that humanity be an end in itself.[27]

In a move that is significant for understanding autonomy as self-legislation, Cohen extends this requirement to mean that humanity is "the ground of law [*der Grund des Gesetzes*]." In other words, "the will of humanity in itself [*in sich selbst*] accomplishes the only possible end in itself [*Zweck an sich*]" (KBE 223–4). Cohen sees this interpretation, which links humanity as an end to legislation, confirmed in the third formulation of the categorical imperative (sometimes termed "the autonomy formula"): "the idea of the will of every rational being as a will giving universal law [als eines allgemein gesetzgebenden Willens]" (AA4: 431). In this formulation, not only is the formal universal law maintained, but the *self-legislating* will – the idea that the will is the author of the law to which it is subject (AA4: 431, paraphrased by Cohen) – is shown to be key to that universality:

> The will is no longer merely subjected [*unterworfen*], but is at the same time "itself legislating" [or "self legislating," *selbst gesetzgebend*], the *author* of the law to which it is subject.[28]

Here the categorical imperative is being recast by Cohen in view of the task or generation of self-consciousness. This reinterpretation avoids understanding the categorical imperative as a heteronomous law, or understanding law as heteronomous at all. The value of the divergence of the third formulation of the categorical imperative from the earlier formulations lies in the fact that it abandons the very "form of the imperative." In fact, the universality of humanity as an end in itself has already with the second formulation supplanted the importance of the formality of the law, in the form of the imperative. "The form of the *imperative*," Cohen writes, "now no longer makes sense/now no longer has any meaning/is now pointless

27 See Poma, *The Critical Philosophy*, 112. Manfred Pascher also comments on Cohen's preference for the aforementioned formulation of the categorical imperative. For Pascher, this preference is a version of a critique against the formalism of Kant's ethics, following in Hegel's footsteps, and offering an alternative to Hegel. Pascher, "Hermann Cohens praktische Philosophie und die Ethik Kants," in *Einführung in den Neukantianismus* (Munich: Fink, 1997), 84.

28 KBE 225, paraphrasing the following passage by Kant: "Hence the will is not merely subject to the law but subject to it in such a way that it must be viewed also *as giving the law to itself* [or: "as itself lawgiving," *als selbstgesetzgebend*] and just because of this as first subject to the law (of which it can regard itself as the author)" (AA4: 431). In the directly quoted term from Kant's original passage, Cohen has separated out the compound "self-legislating" (*selbstgesetzgebend*) into two words, "selbst gesetzgebend," thus stressing that the will *itself* becomes legislating.

[*hat nun keinen Sinn mehr*]."[29] What has supplanted the form of Gesetz and the form of the imperative is the idea that "universal legislation," due to the "rational nature" of agents, "belongs to" that rational nature.[30]

In the *Ethik*, Cohen similarly gives exorbitant praise to the above-quoted second formulation ("autonomy formula") of the categorical imperative: It expresses "the most profound and most powerful meaning of the categorical imperative," "contains the moral program of the new age and of all the future of world history," and represents "the new meaning of freedom." To give priority to humanity as an "end" is for Cohen "the idea of socialism," for which each human being is a final end-in-itself (*Endzweck*), is its own purpose (*Selbstzweck*) (ErW 320–1).[31] In a tribute to Kant he wrote for a Jewish newspaper on the occasion of the centenary of Kant's death in 1904 (the same year in which Cohen published the first edition of the *Ethik*), Cohen adds that this formulation is significant for having placed the idea of a cosmopolitan, "international" humanity at the center of the modern "social" ethics that Kant inaugurated.[32]

Returning to Cohen's earlier work on Kant's ethics, *Kants Begründung der Ethik*, Cohen emphasizes that in Kant, the principle of autonomy gives an additional, explicitly universalist meaning to Gesetz – to the

29 Cohen is here presumably interpreting the passage in which Kant further explains what has been added with the third formulation, namely a solid criterion for understanding what distinguishes a categorical from a hypothetical imperative, that is, for recognizing an imperative (AA4: 431–2). If the imperative can now be recognized by means of the criterion of a will that universally legislates, Cohen implies with his interpretation, we may also say that the legislating will supplants the imperative as a characteristic of ethical action.

30 KBE 224: "Die allgemeine Gesetzgebung ist, unter der Idee der vernünftigen Natur, eine derselben '*eigene*.'"

31 Cohen also highlights the connection between this second formulation of the categorical imperative and socialism in EmkN, 525/113. Andrea Poma comments on the importance of the second formulation as a point of reference in German socialist thought in *The Critical Philosophy*, 296n15. For further commentary, see Steven Schwarzschild, "The Democratic Socialism of Hermann Cohen," *Hebrew Union College Annual* 27 (1956), 432–3 (also included in *The Tragedy of Optimism*). For a more extended treatment, see Harry van der Linden, "Cohen's Socialist Reconstruction of Kant's Ethics" (1994), http://digitalcommons.butler.edu/facsch_papers/42/; published in German translation as "Cohens sozialistische Rekonstruktion der Ethik Kants," in *Ethischer Sozialismus. Zur politischen Philosophie des Neukantianismus*, ed. Helmut Holzhey (Frankfurt am Main: Suhrkamp, 1994). See also Pierfrancesco Fiorato, "Notes on Future and History in Hermann Cohen's Anti-Eschatological Messianism," in *Hermann Cohen's Critical Idealism*, ed. Reinier Munk (Heidelberg: Springer, 2005), 152–3.

32 Hermann Cohen, "Immanuel Kant. Zu seinem hundertjährigen Todestage (12. Februar 1904)," *Allgemeine Zeitung des Judentums* (12 February 1904), 77.

point that autonomy supersedes Gesetz in importance for understanding Kant's ethics:

> Thus there now comes about, as a further consequence [*Folgerung*] of the "formal" moral law [*Sittengesetz*], by way of the idea of humanity as rational nature ..., the concept of *autonomy*. (KBE 224)

The insistence that the categorical imperative must not comprise any element of heteronomy further leads Cohen to argue that law as such may not be understood in terms of coercion (*Zwang*). (This again leads him to oppose a view of Kant's, as we will see further on.)

In explaining this point in the *Ethik*, Cohen draws on a debate in legal theory about how to conceive a norm, particularly in the context of criminal law: Criminal statutes state what actions are illegal; they are hypotheticals, in that they indicate what punishment will follow in case a given action is performed. Legal scholars puzzled over how to conceive of the relationship of statute to the corresponding norm, which would be a formulation of what one ought to do. We might be tempted to define the norm as the result of a reformulation of the statute (the hypothetical statement) grammatically/syntactically into an "imperative."[33] But this would imply viewing the law as a heteronomous imposition of a purpose/end on my will by the will of another. For Cohen, by contrast, it is essential to the definition of norm that the other that "wills" me to act in accordance with the norm is equally bound by that norm, by the general law. In line with Cohen's understanding of the realm of law/Recht as the orientation toward Allheit, "coercion" must be replaced with the idea of the "unification of the one and the other." Thus, not only can we conceive of a norm that functions non-coercively, but insofar as there is ultimately "no one left who has not been ordered" to do something – that is, no one exempted from the law – it might just as well be "anyone" who issues the order to him- or herself. The norm is thus the "ground of law" (*Rechtsgrund*) and may be understood as part of the task/generation of self-consciousness (ErW 269–71).

However, despite Cohen's reservations about a notion of Gesetz that risks being reduced to heteronomy, we will see further on that the notion of Gesetz nevertheless remains important to Cohen's own ethics, in a

33 The conception alluded to here by Cohen, which, he writes, relies on an analysis of "linguistic, gramatical stylistic form," is traced by Eggert Winter to the views of Karl Binding and August Thon. Winter, *Ethik und Rechtswissenschaft: eine historisch-systematische Untersuchung zur Ethik-Konzeption des Marburger Neukantianismus im Werke Hermann Cohens* (Berlin: Duncker & Humblot, 1980), 361–5.

meaning that is set off against Kant's own use of this category. Thus, Cohen will be able to assert, in the above-referenced newspaper tribute to Kant, that Gesetz and freedom – in the sense of the "very difficult concept" of autonomy – mutually imply each other, that is, that their opposition is to be balanced out and overcome in the notion of autonomy, and in the "self of humanity": "No law [*Gesetz*] without freedom; no freedom without law."

Ultimately, then – or at least in this text that lauds Kant's ethics for a Jewish popular readership – Cohen will still praise Kant for having "discovered" "the concept of law" "for the moral law," by means of the categorical imperative, a discovery that has allowed freedom to "shine forth from" law.[34] Yet we will see that Cohen finds it necessary to correct some of Kant's thinking about law and freedom in order for their essential connection to be assured, in particular by honing the notion of autonomy in relation to Kant's notion of freedom.

Autonomy and the Ends of Action

Consistently with the passage discussed above from *Kants Begründung der Ethik*, Cohen notes in the *Ethik* that the concept of autonomy is "the center of Kant's ethics" (ErW 324).[35] For Cohen, Kant's use of this term is an effort to surpass "freedom" as an ethically relevant category (see also EmkN 510–1/97–9). Cohen clarifies his objection to freedom as an ethical category by recalling the "metaphysical" conflict between freedom and causality that Kant in the First Critique expressed in the Third Antinomy of Pure Reason – the antinomy of the claims (1) that "there is no freedom, rather everything in the world occurs only according to the laws of nature"; and (2) that causality according to laws of nature does not explain all phenomena, but that a "causality by means of freedom" is required for such explanation.[36] Freedom "metaphysically" conceived as a counterpart to causality is imagined "as a force and power," as a "soul-spirit [*Seelengeist*] of freedom" (ErW 315). Kant's resolution of this antinomy restricts the application of principles of causality to the explanation of phenomena and demonstrates that the principle of freedom thus pertains only to noumenal "things in themselves" (which cannot be objects of experience). But for Cohen, this resolution does not make a complete

34 Cohen, "Immanuel Kant," 76–7.

35 Cohen underscores this also in his essay "Autonomie und Freiheit" (1900) in JS3: 37.

36 Immanuel Kant, *Kritik der reinen Vernunft*, ed. Raymund Schmidt (Hamburg: Meiner, 1956), A444/B472; translated by Paul Guyer and Allen W. Wood as *Critique of Pure Reason* (Cambridge: Cambridge University Press, 1998).

transition away from the notion of freedom – which Cohen regards as inherently metaphysical – to that of autonomy.

In an essay written a few years before the *Ethik*, contributed to a volume commemorating the scholar of medieval Jewish philosophy David Kaufmann, "Autonomie und Freiheit" (1900), Cohen expresses his views about this insufficiency more compactly than in the *Ethik* and in a way that helps illuminate his discussion in the later book. The distinction between causality and freedom in the First Critique, he writes there, was merely a preparation for the achievement of the Second Critique, "the elaboration of freedom into autonomy."[37] (Hence, Kant was mistaken in terming "autonomy" a "reciprocal concept" [*Wechselbegriff*] of – and thus as referring to the same thing as – "freedom."[38]) In the *Ethik*, Cohen explains the insufficiency of the term freedom by pointing out that it promotes the idea of an "absolute," "free" "I" (ErW, 316–17).[39]

As has been pointed out by Myriam Bienenstock, reading another essay of Cohen's from the same period, "Religion und Sittlichkeit" (1907), Cohen's objection to the idea of a pre-constituted self – which he counters, as shown above, with the idea of the self as hypothesis and task – goes along with his critique of the notion that "freedom" is the origin of action:[40]

> Freedom is supposed to be the faculty of beginning an action "from itself."[41] *But where is this self?* Is it really already there? [*Wo aber ist dieses Selbst? Ist es etwa schon da?*] If so, it would after all be the absolute substance that is asserted by the dogmatist side, but which is here [i.e., by Kant] critically denied.

In this mistaken view, the notion of freedom as the absolute origin of action is intertwined with that of the self as absolute originator. The passage continues:

> And if [the self] were already there, then that freedom would also already be there which exists in [the self] as [the self] exists in freedom.

---

37 "Autonomie und Freiheit," JS3: 38.

38 "Autonomie und Freiheit," JS3: 37, citing AA4: 450. Cited by Myriam Bienenstock, "Hermann Cohen über Freiheit und Selbstbestimmung," in *Religious Apologetics – Philosophical Argumentation*, ed. Yossef Schwartz and Volkhard Krech (Tübingen: Mohr Siebeck, 2004), 523.

39 See also the related discussion of the notion of "intelligible character" in ErW 318, 341, and the discussion in Poma, *The Critical Philosophy*, 113.

40 Bienenstock, "Hermann Cohen über Freiheit und Selbstbestimmung," 524, citing Cohen, "Religion und Sittlichkeit," in JS3: 149–50.

41 In the *Critique of Pure Reason*, Kant defines "freedom in the cosmological sense" as "the faculty of beginning a state [*Zustand*] from itself." *Kritik der reinen Vernunft*, A533/B561.

For Cohen, "freedom," like the self, must instead be thought of as a "task."[42] Even to juxtapose freedom with, or to place it alongside causality would mean to treat it as though it were a quasi-natural force or origin of human action. It would mean – and here Cohen implicitly recalls in "Religion und Sittlichkeit" the lessons of the *Ethik* – treating the self "as a physiological organism."[43]

In the *Ethik*, Cohen summarizes the problem as follows:

> All treatments of the problem of freedom to date were caught up in a mistaken posing of the question. One asked about a first cause, and [consequently] had to take umbrage at the fact that this [first cause] in the end could only ever be a last effect. (ErW 322)

In other words, Cohen substitutes for the notion of freedom – which still risks being misunderstood as a quasi-cause of action in the self – that of autonomy, and thereby shifts the focus away from the imperative/"the laws" (*den Gesetzen*) to a concern with the "purpose" or "ends" (*Zweck*) of action (ErW 321–2).[44]

At stake in this emphasis on purpose/ends is, indeed, the very question of whether ethics is conceived as something realizable. Cohen finds Kant lacking in this regard, particularly in Kant's framing of moral purposes/ends as a "kingdom of ends." In the *Groundwork*, this is Kant's name for the "concept of every rational being as one who must regard himself as giving universal law through all the maxims of his will." This being "think[s] of a whole of all ends in systematic connection" with each other, that is, a "kingdom of ends." It thinks itself as universally legislating (through "common laws") toward that systematic whole of all ends (AA4: 433). But for Cohen, Kant's notion of "kingdom of ends" remains a version of the religious Christian notions "reign of grace" or "kingdom of God" (ErW 393–4). This undermines the project of philosophical ethics insofar as those

---

42 Cohen, "Religion und Sittlichkeit," JS3: 149. To construe the self as a task is to avoid its being misunderstood as a homo noumenon, a thing-in-itself (ErW 341).

43 Cohen, "Religion und Sittlichkeit," JS3: 150.

44 See Paul Nahme's related discussion of Cohen's effort to distinguish "is" and "ought" (*Sein* and *Sollen*), which focuses particularly on Cohen's corrective to Kant's "typic of practical reason" in the *Critique of Practical Reason*. Nahme, "From Critical to Prophetic Idealism: Ethics, Law, and Religion in the Philosophy of Hermann Cohen" (PhD diss., University of Toronto, 2013), 58–63, centered on ErW 390–2. Nahme analyzes this corrective as the basis of Cohen's critique of Kant's separation of legality from morality. See his more recent *Hermann Cohen and the Crisis of Liberalism: The Enchantment of the Public Sphere* (Bloomington: Indiana University Press, 2019), chap. 3.

notions convey "the illusion ... that perhaps morality is not of this world at all" (ErW 394).

Self-Determination and the Origination of Self from Other

As has been demonstrated by Myriam Bienenstock,[45] in elaborating self-consciousness as a hypothesis and as a task, Cohen is countering post-Kantian conceptions of self-determination (*Selbstbestimmung*), particularly that of Fichte's "I-philosophy," as well as critically extending Kant's own conception of the role of autonomy in ethical decision.

Bienenstock's analysis underscores that Cohen's ethico-legal theory – his theory of the ethical self as being directed toward Allheit – requires him to reject models of subjectivity that construe ethical decision in terms of "self-determination" understood as the absolute freedom of the human individual.[46] She particularly focuses on Cohen's critique of Fichte's philosophy of the "I," which Cohen had described as a "theoretical step backwards" vis-à-vis Kant.[47] For Fichte, consciousness is spontaneous and determines itself purely from itself. This characterizes the self both logically and ontologically, but also in its ethical capacity. Self-determination is understood as autonomy and thus as "self-legislation" (*Selbstgesetzgebung*). But for Fichte the law/Gesetz involved in self-legislation is without content. Instead, Gesetz means "absolute self-sufficiency" (*Selbständigkeit*) and entails an absolute indeterminateness of the self.

Bienenstock finds in this association of self-legislation/Gesetz with an absolutely indeterminate self a prioritization of the self, rather than of Gesetz as a constitutive part of autonomy, which is what Cohen emphasizes in his treatment of autonomy. Bienenstock further shows that Cohen uses the notion of "self-determination" in a sense that runs counter to Fichte's.[48] For Cohen it does not refer to the action or the self-sufficient decision of an "isolated" or "abstract individual." Rather, the self-consciousness that leads to action and decision must from the

---

45 Bienenstock, "Hermann Cohen über Freiheit und Selbstbestimmung." Cf. chap. 5 of Myriam Bienenstock, *Cohen face à Rosenzweig. Débat sur la pensée allemande* (Paris: Vrin, 2009).

46 See also the discussion in Michael Zank, *The Idea of Atonement in the Philosophy of Hermann Cohen* (Providence, RI: Brown Judaic Studies, 2000; repr. Brown Judaic Studies Open Humanities Book Program, 2020), 287, https://repository.library.brown.edu/studio/item/bdr:1111035.

47 Bienenstock, "Hermann Cohen über Freiheit und Selbstbestimmung," 516, citing "Deutschtum und Judentum," JS2: 282–3. Cf. ErW 343.

48 Bienenstock, "Hermann Cohen über Freiheit und Selbstbestimmung," 516–17.

first be achieved in relation to others (cf. ErW 356–7) – to society, Allheit, state, and thus, as we have seen, in relation to law/Recht.

Notwithstanding his reservations about Fichte's theory of self-consciousness, an aspect of that theory that in fact proves useful for Cohen is the idea that the I arises from a non-I. Cohen puts this idea in the service of his own vision of ethical self-consciousness as a task of "unification of I and You." Using the notion of a "judgment of origin" that he developed in the *Logik*, Cohen appropriates Fichte's idea of I as arising from non-I, arguing that despite its mistaken understanding of self-consciousness as a matter of logic or the cognition of nature, it represents a promising path for conceptualizing ethics. Cohen envisions the idea of a "non-I" or other human being that is the generative origin of the "I," of ethical self-consciousness as a kind of "progress," in which the other person becomes a You, and in which the ultimate unity of humanity, and thus the idea of the human being as such, may be confirmed (ErW 208–10, 248–9, cf. 258).[49]

Cohen envisions the self as something generated out of the "hypothesis" of the other human being (*Nebenmensch*) or out of the concept of the "other" (*der Andere*) or "alter ego" (ErW 211–12). Like the ethical subject in general, this other is also not derived from experience;[50] and in keeping with Allheit as the orienting point of ethics, the others are not to be understood as a plurality (*Mehrheit*), lest the multiplicity or diversity of the others be perceived as a "historical sin" or offense to be overcome (ErW 211).[51] That the other person is the origination of ethical subjectivity is discernible in the principle that "pure will takes place in [an] action [*Handlung*]," and in the circumstance that an action, which Cohen envisions as a "legal action" or transaction, requires "two subjects" – a subject "referring to" another subject (ErW 212, 213, 248–9).

Cohen distinguishes this "reference" of self to other from a model whereby the self would "include"/"encompass"/"comprise" (*einschliessen*) or "sublate" (*aufheben*) the other, thereby apparently guarding against any confusion between his model and a certain understanding of Hegelian recognition or dialectic. "Both [self and other] must remain in isolated

---

49 Cf. the discussion in Zank, *The Idea of Atonement*, 280, and Helmut Holzhey, "Die Religion im System der Philosophie Cohens," in *Hermann Cohen und die Erkenntnistheorie*, ed. Wolfgang Marx and Ernst Wolfgang Orth (Würzburg: Königshausen & Neumann, 2001), 159–60.

50 Thus, the complementarity between self and other, or "progression" from self toward other, is not a function of "mere affect" (ErW 213).

51 Similarly, the legal action of the "contract" serves not only to remove mistrust between parties, but, more fundamentally, to "dissipate" foreignness that "seems" to emanate from the other (ErW 248).

existence" (ErW 212, cf. 258). The "belonging together as such" of You and I signifies at the same time an "othering" (for this purpose Cohen uses the coinage *Anderung*) of the I (ErW, 212, 213, 249). Another term for this, which we encountered in the previous chapter as a term for the relationship between individual and Allheit, is "correlation": The correlation of self and other in reference to each other is what "generates" the self-consciousness of the pure will (ErW 212, 213).[52]

We find here, then, a noteworthy concurrence between the function of the sphere of law and that of the other-than-self: Both are understood by Cohen to be the generative origin of the ethical self. We will see that this concurrence is also what centrally drives Strauss's analysis of Cohen's *Ethik* in view of the role of Gesetz, an analysis which in turn will allow us to examine the connection between the argument of the *Ethik* and Cohen's understanding of law in Judaism.

The Self as Task and the Futurity of Law (*Gesetz*)

Cohen is concerned to safeguard the idea that "the 'I' of ethics is and remains a task" – a task in relation to which we work at creating (*schaffen*) its solution, but that thereby "always again becomes a task anew" (ErW 343); this task is self-consciousness in its "ethical meaning" (ErW 325). That task of constituting the moral self is to be accomplished "*in* the juridical person, *by* the law [*Recht*]" (ErW 342, emphasis added). This means that for Cohen, the origination of the self from the other-than-self – or, to put it another way, self-consciousness as a project oriented to Allheit – is always at the same time an orientation toward the *future*.

We can bring out the meaning of futurity and task in this connection by again looking at Cohen's analyses of the categorical imperative. As we have seen, Cohen in *Kants Begründung der Ethik* had highlighted "humanity" as the core idea contained in its second formulation ("Act in such a way that you use humanity ... always at the same time as an end, never merely as a means.") This represents a kind of universality that, akin to Allheit, goes beyond generalization over individuals. Later, in the *Ethik*, Cohen additionally highlights the motif of the "end in itself" (*Zweck an sich selbst*, *Selbstzweck*, autotely).[53] As we saw, Cohen emphasizes purpose/end as an alternative to positing the question of freedom as a first cause or

52 Cf. Zank, *The Idea of Atonement*, 280, and Robert Gibbs, "Jurisprudence Is the Organon of Ethics: Kant and Cohen on Ethics, Law, and Religion," in *Hermann Cohen's Critical Idealism*, ed. Munk, 207–10.

53 Note that Cohen's reflections on this motif culminate in an observation in which he uses a Greek equivalent of *Selbstzweck*, "autotely" (ErW 322). See also Cohen, "Problem der jüdischen Sittenlehre," JS3: 17–18.

origin. Freedom is conceived along the lines of autonomy as a futural task, without any initial "metaphysical" positing of a free root/source of action.

Having itself as an end, moreover, defines human being as such. The second formulation of the categorical imperative implies that all things can be properly used as means as well as ends, but that the human being has the distinction of being properly usable as a means only to the extent that it is also an end. Thus the mark of human being is to be an end in itself. Autotely is "the new meaning of freedom"; and it is in autotely that the concept of the "person," as the one to whom "respect" is due, is grounded (ErW 320–1, 322). Kant's claim in the First Critique that freedom pertains only to noumena is acceptable to Cohen so long as it is understood that noumena can only be ends (ErW 316–18). The "elaboration of freedom into autonomy" that Cohen highlighted in his earlier book on Kant's ethics is thus now in the *Ethik* explained as the transformation of autonomy into autotely (ErW 322).

This point brings us to Cohen's understanding of law – both the "Gesetz" of auto-nomy, and even the more general notion, Recht – as itself *futural*. To insist on this futurity goes hand in hand with Cohen's elaborations on what distinguishes the notion of Gesetz from the idea of a "law of nature": The "law" of self-consciousness must not be thought of as governing self-consciousness in the manner of a "law of nature" – not as a "constitution," as Cohen also puts it (ErW 261, 263, cf. 272–3).[54] Here, Cohen repeats the caution that to conceive law/Gesetz as "law of nature" entails thinking of law as a "law in our members" (ErW 262); we saw in the previous chapter why he thinks such a conception is unsuitable for ethical philosophy (cf. ErW 99).

This futural meaning of law is not restricted to the notion of Gesetz, but extends to that of Recht. This can be made evident by referring back to the concept of the legal norm, discussed above. Law (Recht) is not a static "description" of legal relationships and institutions; rather, law names the process in which "demands" or "claims" are made, and in which the "fulfillment" of those claims has "legal effects" or "consequences" (*zur Folge*). Seen from this perspective of "(con-)sequence" (*Folge*), norms are distinct from judgments about nature. Thus, the

54 Cohen similarly distinguishes hypothesis from "law of nature" and notes the significance of this distinction for understanding properly the role of Gesetz in morality (ErW 98–9). Cf. Cohen's 1904 newspaper tribute to Kant, in which he praises Kant's "discovery" of the "concept of Gesetz" "for the moral law" – a discovery represented by the categorical imperative – but then immediately cautions against conflating moral law with the "law of nature" as that kind of "law" that holds sway in philosophy and in science: "It would not be any help to my morality if I could simply be assured that, like an animal or an automated machine [*Automat*], I will not lose my way if I blindly allow myself to be guided by my instinct or by the clockwork of my bodily machine." Cohen, "Immanuel Kant," 76–7.

norm – as a matter of ethics, and not only of logic – is, unlike a law of nature, not a logical condition (*Bedingung*): if *x*, then *y* (ErW 271–2).

This (con-)sequentiality that demarcates the norm from the law of nature means that the difference between law of nature and juridical law here is one of *temporality*. The relationship between natural causes and effects may be "thought entirely without regard to time." By contrast, when we think of the effects of norms, "the regard [*Rücksicht*] to time steps into the foreground." In particular, the "concept of the future" is of decisive importance for understanding what a legal norm is:

> *Legal norms are not indicatives, not judgments, not statements about a true being [*ein wahrhaftes Sein*] which must as such refer to all of time, because they [legal norms] primarily refer to the future.* They may, they must refer to the future, because they refer to *actions*, and not to movements, processes, and occurrences. Such a regard to the future – let alone a priority of such a regard – is absent from the law of nature. (ErW 279–80)[55]

In aligning law with futurity, Cohen is also insisting that both law and ethics require a "turning away from the past" as well as from the idea that the present is "determined" by the past (ErW 280). He calls for an "emancipation" of self-consciousness (in its ethical meaning) "from past and present," and from all "sentimental romantic" attachment to the past (ErW 281). Cohen describes his project of understanding ethical self-consciousness as one of "placing all of morality upon the future" (ErW 282).[56]

---

55 Cohen expands here on his earlier point that when we consider the laws, or realm of nature, the "regard to time" – the question of temporality as such – remains in the background: Even distinguishing the present from the past "falls outside the purview" of the laws of nature, let alone the "regard for the future that is required by the concept of action" (ErW 280). My understanding of this part of Cohen's argument was aided by the reading offered by Gianna Gigliotti, "Ethik und das Faktum der Rechtswissenschaft bei Hermann Cohen," in *Ethischer Sozialismus*, ed. Holzhey, 175–6.

56 Similarly, Cohen demarcates the law of the task of self-consciousness from the Greek idea of law as an arbitrary or fateful decree (ErW 262; cf. 96). Here, Cohen also considers the Greek idea of the "unwritten laws" that place the individual in conflict with the "written laws" of the community (ErW 262–3). Rather than seeing the "unwritten laws" and the self, defined in its conflict with the arbitrary decrees, as being in opposition to state and collectivity, Cohen wants to see the collectivity as the source of the self. Thus, he cites the death of Socrates as representing an "interpretation of the [Athenian] law" that "repairs the rift" between the individual law by which he was condemned and the "moral world." For Cohen, Socrates repairs this rift by refusing the idea that there is a "collision" between the community and the individual. Here, Cohen writes, the self is guided and "generated" (*erzeugt*) by the state (by Allheit), out of reverence for the law that flows from the state (ErW 264–5).

The Paradox and Otherness of Law (*Gesetz*)

The language of futurity that Cohen applies to the generation of Allheit and to law dramatically exceeds Cohen's positing of "purpose" and "autotely" as an alternative to freedom understood as a cause of the self's action. In the preceding section, I have argued that in Cohen's ethical theory, the auto-nomous self is self-legislating in the sense of being a dynamic future-directed self that is generated and realized in the activity of legislation. Implicit in this characterization is an understanding of law/Gesetz as something other than constraint or coercion, Gesetz as a kind of possibility. Even more than Kant, for whom following the moral law is the same thing as being "autonomous," Cohen thus needs a notion of Gesetz that is something other than constraint, that is generative and futural, a task – *even though* Gesetz also retains the traditional meaning of something that is located outside the self's action. In directing us to ethical self-consciousness, Gesetz – although it is not to be thought of as an arbitrary decree – is nevertheless something "other" and "foreign." It represents a "paradox."

Cohen describes this paradox of law as follows: "We initially/primarily do not seek the law [*Gesetz*] as our own law," that is as something already belonging/pertaining to ourselves from the outset. We seek it instead as something that is "apparently foreign [*ein scheinbar fremdes*]" (ErW 266).

In this sense, Gesetz as the open-ended task or hypothesis of self-consciousness belongs to the self in guiding the self *and* is at the same time other than that self.[57] It is as this "paradox" that Gesetz is supposed to direct us onto the "new path" of establishing self-consciousness as an ethical principle (ErW 266).

Cohen further analyzes this paradox of Gesetz as an ethical task in light of the idea, discussed above, that "there is no self without You or We" (ErW 266). The rejection of an "absolute 'I'" or individual as the basis of ethics and the affirmation of Allheit as the direction of the ethical task means that the law that, by means of hypothesis, constitutes the self, represents the otherness and foreignness of the non-self: the "we" and the "you" (which for Cohen is also to be recognized in the state). Thus, I am to recognize/acknowledge the task of self-consciousness "as law/ Gesetz," just as "I can find my Self not in the 'I,' but in the 'You' and the 'We'" (ErW 266, cf. 248–9), that is, with the affirmation of Allheit as the direction of ethics. In other words, the law that constitutes the self also represents the *otherness and foreignness of the non-self.*

57 See the discussion in Zank, *The Idea of Atonement*, 285.

A "Targeting" of Jewish Religion That "One Could Perhaps Live With"? Kant's Suspicion of Legality

This last insight brings us back to Cohen's dictum, which as we saw becomes the crux of Leo Strauss's presentation of Cohen's philosophy: "No conviction without action" ("keine Gesinnung ohne Handlung"). This slogan is ultimately articulated by Cohen in the same breath with the principle that ethical action is essentially legal and communal, that is, directed to Allheit by definition and from the start:

> For there is no conviction without action; *no individual in the ethical sense without legal community* [Rechtsgemeinschaft].
>
> Denn es gibt keine Gesinnung ohne Handlung; *kein Individuum im ethischen Sinne ohne Rechtsgemeinschaft.* (ErW 225)

What this pairing of formulas conveys is that Cohen's objection to conviction (or to will understood merely as a function of inner conviction) as a basis for understanding action is at the same time an objection to understanding the *individual* as the locus of action, or as the paradigmatic ethical subject. This in turn opens the way to Cohen's analysis of Recht as the domain in which ethical concepts and principles are generated. Within the argument of the *Ethik*, the "paradox" of Gesetz is in a sense neutralized, by becoming part of the constructive account of Recht as the horizon and ground of ethics.

On one level that would be the whole story for Gesetz in Cohen's *Ethik* – that is, we could conclude that Gesetz has no great role in Cohen's theory of ethics out of law – were it not for the fact that woven into the accounts of Gesetz in the *Ethik*, there is a forceful and in some ways puzzling contestation of what Cohen calls Kant's suspicion toward legality. For in valorizing action over conviction, Cohen strenuously and repeatedly objects to Kant's characterization of law as coercion (*Zwang*), as well as to his strict demarcation of morality from legality.[58] For Kant, to fulfill a moral obligation – to act morally – is not the same as obeying a law imposed on me. The "moral law" is the law I "give myself" – such that I am "auto-nomous." We may see this idea from Kant's *Groundwork of the Metaphysics of Morals* as the basis for the distinction Kant draws in the *Rechtslehre* (*Doctrine of Right*) between

58 As discussed in Helmut Holzhey, "Analytische Hermeneutik und reine Rechtslehre. Die Transformation neukantianischer Theoreme in die reine Rechtslehre Kelsens," in *Hermeneutik und Strukturtheorie des Rechts*, ed. Michael W. Fischer, Erhard Mock, and Helmut Schreiner (*Archiv für Rechts- und Sozialphilosophie*, Beiheft n.F. no. 20 [1984]), 110.

legality as coercion, and morality.[59] This opposition between legality and morality is the one to which Cohen objects. But note that Kant's opposition between legality and morality on the one hand, and, on the other hand, his characterization of the self as self-legislating and of ethical comportment in terms of the "moral law," represent two distinct views. They are not articulated by Kant in conjunction with each other, and they do not depend on each other, but belong to different areas of his thought. Nevertheless, Cohen pinpoints these two views as being in a clear tension with each other.

Quite improbably given the minor role he himself has accorded to Gesetz, Cohen claims that the "ambiguity" he finds in Kant regarding Gesetz has "dire consequences" (*verhängnisvoll*) for the "concept of Recht and the state" – that is, for Cohen's theory of ethics-out-of-Recht – and thus for "the problem of ethics" as a whole (ErW 267–8). Cohen asserts that

> *It is precisely Gesetz that distinguishes morality from legality.*
>
> *Denn Gesetz gerade unterscheidet die Moralität von der Legalität.* (ErW 267)

Accordingly, Cohen calls for the protection of Gesetz as a core concept for ethics from the "suspicion" that has been cast on legality: "Such an ambiguity must not be allowed to adhere to the concept of Gesetz; it [i.e., the ambiguity] must be removed from it" – that is, from the concept of Gesetz (ErW 268).

Cohen has a straightforward means at his disposal for accomplishing this: For he finds that the problem to be solved is not a philosophical one at all (nor a juridical one, a problem concerning Recht), but rather a problem of religion or religious history.[60] Asking about the "meaning" of legality in Kant, Cohen diagnoses it as "targeting" "religion, statutary religion, which institutes and entrenches itself according to the letter of the divine word" (ErW 267). About this targeting and striking of Judaism by the critique of legality, Cohen says initially that

> This is something one could perhaps live with. [Das liesse man sich gefallen.]

---

59 Kant's "Doctrine of Right" is Part 1 of Kant's *Metaphysics of Morals* (1797; *Die Metaphysik der Sitten*), entitled "Metaphysical First Principles of the Doctrine of Right" ("Metaphysische Anfangsgründe der Rechtslehre"), in AA6; translated by Mary Gregor as *The Metaphysics of Morals*, ed. Lara Denis (Cambridge: Cambridge University Press, 2017). See the discussion of the legality-morality distinction in Pascher, *Einführung in den Neukantianismus*, 86–7.

60 The ambiguity, he writes, "as a matter of fact has an origin that is not juridical [*rechtlich*] and not philosophical, but an indubitably religious one" (ErW 268).

He then proceeds to give the sort of explanation about Kant that one would expect:

> This in fact is the point of view from which Kant evaluated the religions, in accordance with his literary knowledge about their documents and their history.

In other words: Were Kant's legality-morality opposition merely a critique of Judaism – in line with his predictable and well-known misunderstandings of Judaism – they would not be worth discussing further. But, in fact, "the opposition does not stop at religion, but it also extends to *law* [*Recht*]" (ErW 267).

Since the problem with Kant's suspicion of legality appears to threaten the notion of Recht, the solution to it ought to be, and indeed is, provided by the analysis of ethics out of Recht, that is, in Cohen's *Ethik*. This suggests, then, that there is something excessive about Cohen's treatment of the "suspicion" he sees as having been cast on the term Gesetz. That is, Cohen's work to expose and undo this suspicion might in fact not be called for strictly from the point of view of his ethico-legal-philosophical project. In that case, Cohen's disclaimer that the targeting and striking of Judaism by the critique of legality is "something one could perhaps live with" were it not for the risks to the ethico-legal theory could be understood as a kind of screen for the circumstance that, in addition to the ethico-legal project, what is just as genuinely at issue for Cohen is a critique of Western-Christian anti-Judaism, a critique that he at the same time puts in the service of philosophical objectives. In other words, because Cohen's critique of anti-Jewish prejudice for philosophical purposes is not conducted in a straightforward, transparent manner, but often involves disclaimers and tangents about religion such as the one I have described, the result is that at times the accompanying *philosophical* arguments become excessive.[61]

61 I take it that this is what Robert Gibbs, for example, is responding to when he notes that when Cohen criticizes Kant's assimilation of moral law to law as coercion, he does so in a "truly flamboyant manner." Gibbs, "Jurisprudence Is the Organon of Ethics," 204.

This strand of what Cohen is doing in the *Ethik* is also what leads Myriam Bienenstock to describe Cohen's thought as an "apologetic thinking" in Rosenzweig's constructive sense of that term. (That is, in line with Rosenzweig's observation that apology can be "one of the most noble human activities" if it means going to the foundation/root of things [den Dingen auf den Grund gehen] and "apologizing" – that is, *ent-schuldigen*, meaning disburdening something or someone from guilt or blame – "with truth itself, that is, with the whole truth.") Franz Rosenzweig,

The Devaluation of Deeds as an "Ambiguity" of Religion

Thus, while in his discussion of Kant's mistaken suspicion of legality, Cohen had relativized the importance of anti-Jewish prejudice, subordinating it to the importance of rescuing the significance of law itself, in the context of his argument that action has priority over conviction, that religious dimension is foregrounded. Instead of pinpointing the "religious" reason as perhaps negligible, while presenting the "philosophical" reason as the real one for dwelling on the issue, here he presents the philosophical reason as secondary. Discussing the mistaken tendency to reduce will to "the element of thought in will" and the concomitant reduction of will to "intention" (which he traces to the juridical terminology of the Roman Empire), Cohen writes that this factor by itself was of limited significance. The real danger came only with a new "complicated religious motif" that entered the scene:

> However the juridical moment of intention would not have brought the theoretical element of the will to an overarching [point of/state of] danger and ambiguity, had it not been the case that a complicated religious motif became an additional factor and a very pressing [*vordringlich*] additional influence. (ErW 117)

This "religious prejudice" that conviction was the sole or decisive factor in will is not characterized by Cohen as an aspect merely of the *history* of the concept of "will." Rather, he argues that it remains "the densest and *most harmful prejudice* with which the pure will must contend" (ErW 117). Cohen finds that religion is for its part right to valorize conviction. (He links this to the history of the elimination of sacrifice as a form of worship in biblical religion, as well as to the New Testament valorization of "conscience" over "moral deeds"; ErW 118–19.) But he argues that ethics must not follow religion in this, and warns that the religious "attack on law" has had negative effects beyond the bounds of religion itself. Religion's emphases on conviction and conscience have spilled, and continue to spill out into ethical philosophy and into culture as a whole.

"Apologetisches Denken," in *Der Mensch und sein Werk. Gesammelte Schriften*, vol. III, *Zweistromland* (The Hague: Nijhoff, 1984), 686, cited by Bienenstock, "Hermann Cohen über Freiheit und Selbstbestimmung," 512. Translated as "Apologetic Thinking" in Franz Rosenzweig, *Philosophical and Theological Writings*, trans. and ed. Paul W. Franks and Michael L. Morgan (Indianapolis: Hackett, 2000).

We may similarly see this strand of what Cohen is doing in the *Ethik* as being in line with Zank's analysis of that book as Cohen's quintessential Jewish book. Zank, "The Ethics in Hermann Cohen's Philosophical System."

The devaluation of deeds, the overemphasis on conviction – these are "ambiguities" of religion that exceed the bounds of religion itself.

Moreover, although at one moment Cohen accords legitimacy to religion's stance vis-à-vis the law as long as this stance remains confined to the domain of religion, Cohen then goes on to condemn as "ambiguous" the religious "attack on the law" for being itself excessive – itself a mark of religion's excessiveness, its spilling out into the domains of philosophy and culture to which it does not belong, and in particular into a properly "moral" aspect of religion:

> The attack against the law itself already overshoots its mark [*schießt über das Ziel hinaus*], insofar as under the [heading of] law it is not only rite that is combated, rather ... the moral law in the Ten Commandments is also struck. (ErW 119)[62]

In sum, there is an ambiguity and an unease here in Cohen's treatment of the role of religion in promoting an individualist, conscience-based ethics to which his own ethical philosophy is opposed. If Cohen himself finds that religion's attack against Gesetz is excessive – that is, that it misses the mark by exceeding its target – the multiplicity of tacks that he takes in his own account suggest that he himself has difficulty negotiating between the ethico-legal-philosophical project – in relation to which the account of legality/Gesetz, as well as the debunking of the religiously motivated error regarding conviction, ultimately seems tangential – and his perception that the grave cultural-religious misunderstanding about conviction and action must be systematically exposed.

Conclusion and Outlook

In this chapter, we were guided by Strauss's inquiry into the presence of a question concerning nomos/law in the argument of Cohen's *Ethik*, and have been led to a "paradox" of Gesetz that persists in Cohen's ethico-legal philosophy, not having been entirely resolved in the account of Recht. This paradox of law is what allows Strauss to press Cohen regarding the true meaning of nomos/Gesetz in ethics, at the same time that he also dismisses Cohen's *Ethik* for having subsumed Gesetz into the politically "modern" notion of Recht.

---

62 This sort of observation in the *Ethik* has frequent parallels across Cohen's Jewish writings. Cohen habitually exposes attempts to distinguish in Jewish religious history/tradition a legalistic from a properly moral content as untenable and as ultimately implying an attack on Judaism at its purported core.

What Strauss's reading allows us to see is that, although Cohen clearly implies that a critique of Christian attitudes to law and to the role of conviction in morality, undertaken from a Jewish standpoint, would be an important component of a robust theory of ethics out of law, Cohen does not actually offer that full critique in the *Ethik.* Strauss's reading thus reveals that Cohen's argument implies or involves a theory of Judaism and the law that it does not itself articulate beyond defending the law from a polemic that he characterizes as having anti-Jewish motives and impulses.

Strauss's early, ambivalent engagement with Cohen's writings thus opens up an invaluable view onto the stakes of Cohen's ethico-legal theory in its interactions with his theory of Judaism. Strauss performs a fundamental uncertainty about whether a valorization of law as nomos can or cannot be found in Cohen's works – and thus also about the sense in which Cohen is or is not a Jewish philosopher.

For the purposes of the argument of this book, the next logical step must be to ask: Do we find the implied missing argumentative link – a possible theory of law in Judaism – in Cohen's philosophy of Judaism? This question will need to be pursued by focusing on Cohen's main work on Judaism, the posthumously published *Religion of Reason.* In reading the *Religion,* including the key chapter on "Law" (chapter 16, "Das Gesetz"), a great deal hinges on how one understands Cohen to be making an argument about Judaism as such (Judaism of the present and of the future) by engaging with biblical sources.

A further detour through Strauss's early readings of Cohen will again prove fruitful here: The next chapter (chapter 3) will show how Strauss's great theme in *Philosophy and Law,* "political theology," and his reflections on Cohen's method within his own project provide a vantage point for understanding the methodology and hermeneutic with which Cohen approaches biblical religion and which thus enables him to explore the concept of a "religion of reason." In chapter 4, then, I turn my attention more specifically to exploring what role Cohen accords to law in Judaism, as part of his account of a "religion of reason."

Chapter Three

Philosophico-Political Theology as Method: From Strauss's *Philosophy and Law* to Cohen's "Philosophy of Jewish Religion"

In an essay on contemporary theories of halakhah, Menachem Kellner lays out two opposing schematic viewpoints, which he draws out of the philosophies of two twentieth-century thinkers, both of whom, he explains, "placed halakhah at the center of their vision of Judaism":[1] Yeshayahu Leibowitz and Steven Schwarzschild. The latter thinker is of special relevance to my project in this book, given his crucial role in the postwar reception of Cohen's philosophy, and because many of his writings are devoted in particular to explicating and making fruitful Cohen's ethical and political thinking. (As mentioned in the opening to the previous chapter, Schwarzschild discerned in Cohen's ethico-legal philosophy a "salvag[ing]" of "his fundamental commitment to halakhah," to Jewish law.)[2] The first position, which Kellner associates with Leibowitz, is that

(1) halakhah must be understood as consisting of absolute commandments that serve "no end beyond themselves" and that "are to be performed simply because they are God's commands."[3] Those

1 Menachem Kellner, "Torah and Science in Modern Jewish Thought: Steven Schwarzschild vs Yeshayahu Leibowitz," in *Torah et science: perspectives historiques et théoriques: mélanges offerts à Charles Touati*, ed. Gilbert Dahan, Gad Freudenthal, and Jean-Pierre Rothschild (Leuven: Peeters, 2001), 230.

2 Kellner, in his turn, laid the early foundation for a proper reception of Schwarzschild's writings as a coherent body of work by publishing the collection *The Pursuit of the Ideal: Jewish Writings of Steven Schwarzschild*, ed. Menachem Kellner (Albany: State University of New York Press, 1990).

3 Leibowitz presents this understanding of halakhah, for example, in "Religious Praxis: The Meaning of Halakhah" (1953; "Mitzvot Ma'asiyot"), trans. Eliezer Goldman, in *Judaism, Human Values, and the Jewish State*, ed. Eliezer Goldman (Cambridge, MA: Harvard University Press, 1992).

commands are not informed by any insights or demands arising from knowledge of the world, or from moral reflection. One who takes it upon themselves to fulfill them makes a "commitment" ("faith") that "does not result from any information one has acquired"[4] and does not, in its turn, yield any such "information" for extra-halakhic purposes.

An implication of this understanding of halakhic Judaism that is not especially highlighted by Kellner, but that is of importance to the present discussion, is that Jews are as capable and free as anyone else to draw on knowledge and insight from any source whatsoever in the pursuit of truth and justice. There is no such thing as a more or less "Jewish" knowledge or reason or morality, and no specifically Jewish mandate or tendency to pursue truth or justice. (While Kellner finds it sufficient to point out that Leibowitz has with his definition of halakhah "bought" an "industrial peace" between science and religion, that formulation obscures the positive potential that Leibowitz's definition of halakhah opens up to seek scientific or moral knowledge by any means that might be deemed suitable.)[5]

Kellner juxtaposes this view with the one he attributes to Schwarzschild of

(2) halakhic Judaism as a "consistent, rational system primarily characterized by the primacy it gives to ethical concerns." If Judaism is construed as such a system, it follows that a given religious or philosophical position can be more or less consistent with Judaism. (Indeed, this definition of Judaism leads Schwarzschild to a definition of Jewish philosophy, and even – invoking Hermann Cohen – to a view of "Judaism as intellectually philosophical.")[6] Halakhah, then, is continuous with a system of thought, rather than a priori indifferent to the realm of knowledge and moral reasoning, as it is for Leibowitz. In particular, halakhah would on Schwarzschild's view thereby be consistent with the "centrality of ethics" in Judaism.[7] By virtue of this, halakhah is also inherently linked to a striving to realize a better world, or, in Schwarzschild's Kantian-Cohenian idiom, to the "task of scientific and ethical man ... to bring [the empirical

4 Kellner, "Torah and Science," 231–3, quoting Leibowitz, "The Reading of the Shema" (1981), in *Judaism, Human Values*, 37.

5 Kellner, 232–3.

6 Kellner, 235, and Schwarzschild, afterword to *The Pursuit of the Ideal*, 252.

7 Kellner, 234–5.

> universe] increasingly into conformity with [the rationally constructed ideal model of a universe]."[8]
>
> Schwarzschild claims Cohen as a guide for this view of the meaning of halakhah, as we can see in a key passage of one of his seminal essays on Cohen's philosophy, "The Democratic Socialism of Hermann Cohen" (1956). There Schwarzschild cites Cohen's early lecture on "The Sabbath," in which the latter defends the endeavor of seeking to "explain" the cultural and moral meaning of the Sabbath against those who would find it sufficient to base Sabbath observance on its having been instituted by God. In a very Kantian vein, Cohen argues against those who would wish to explain a religious institution merely by deriving it from a divine creator: Since anything, even "the most diabolical phenomenon" can be attributed to God, not to seek the moral purpose of a religious institution is at best arbitrary and at worst "offensive" to religious feeling. This principle then clears the way for Cohen's analysis of the Sabbath as a social-ethical institution.[9] Schwarzschild underscores that "the tendency to explain social institutions and historical facts in terms of divine revelations or ordinances" stands in the way of such social-ethical analyses. If the "humane purposes of the origin" of an institution such as the Sabbath is "disguised," this "makes impossible the humane improvement of the future."[10]

Kellner's juxtaposition of these two opposite ways of understanding halakhah suggests a range or continuum of views of how Jewish law might relate to or might express ethical concerns. It is instructive to compare these two poles to the model of Jewish philosophy that Strauss articulates

8 Schwarzschild, "An Agenda for Jewish Philosophy in the 1980's" (1980), in *Studies in Jewish Philosophy*, ed. Norbert Samuelson (Lanham, MD: University Press of America, 1987), 109, quoted in Kellner, "Torah and Science," 235.

9 Cohen, "Der Sabbat in seiner kulturgeschichtlichen Bedeutung" (1869/1880), JS2: 48, and Schwarzschild, "The Democratic Socialism of Hermann Cohen," *Hebrew Union College Annual* 27 (1956): 431–2, included in Schwarzschild, *The Tragedy of Optimism: Writings on Hermann Cohen*, ed. George Y. Kohler (Albany: State University of New York Press, 2018).

10 Schwarzschild, "Democratic Socialism," 431–2. Kellner, "Torah and Science," 234–5, calls attention to Schwarzschild's characterization of his project in "A Note on the Nature of Ideal Society – A Rabbinic Study" (1969) as one of "crystalliz[ing] a systematic consistent conception of the ideal, Messianic society out of some Rabbinic sources," which is a general project that demands to be pursued for "all of Jewish-Rabbinic theology." Schwarzschild laments "the general view" that "the Talmud is a welter of unsystematic thought.... How unsystematic thought is supposed to underlie, or result from, what is conceded to be an extraordinarily systematic legal system is incomprehensible." Schwarzschild, *Pursuit of the Ideal*, 108, 293n64.

in *Philosophy and Law*, read, as we began to do in the previous chapter, in conjunction with his related lecture "Cohen and Maimonides." This model is based on Strauss's conception of the medievals (or of Maimonides) as blending the authority of divine law with philosophy and politics – defined as activity toward a good living-together. In Strauss's account, then, we find a blending of (1) law or halakhah as an arbitrary command or revelation (akin to Leibowitz's definition) with (2) a prophetic philosophizing authorized by that same revealed law or nomos, which is political in that it pursues the "good life." We can recognize in Schwarzschild's view, which invokes Cohen, an embrace of this sort of prophetic philosophizing.

In chapter 2, we saw that Strauss recruits Cohen (based on his readings of Cohen's *Ethik* and of the 1908 Maimonides essay) as an ally in this philosophico-political-theological project that is centered on revelation as law. We saw, too, that Strauss identifies a limitation to Cohen's project: "that for the idea of law [*Gesetz*]" or politics, "he substitutes that of morality" (CM 429). That is, there is for Strauss a fundamental tension between Cohen's ethical project and the heteronomy of nomos or revelation. Strauss's observation here is akin to Leibowitz's argument that no ethics or knowledge of any kind is derivable from halakhic Judaism, which is absolute command without reason.

In this chapter, I wish to take this vantage point of Strauss's as a way of putting a crucial question to Cohen's theory of law and ethics – which is, as we see in Kellner's treatment, an ongoing question for law and ethics in Judaism, namely: Can we find in Cohen a bridging of the tension between the heteronomous structure of law in Judaism and the demand that law be fundamentally ethical?

My answer is that if there is such a bridging, it takes place at the level of *method*. Again, it will be by examining Strauss's reading of Cohen – this time, focusing on Cohen's theory of Jewish religion in *Religion of Reason* – that we will be able to identify the hermeneutic logic that links these two conceptions of what law should do. My plan for this chapter is, first, to examine Strauss's treatment of the circumstance that the Platonic institution of the philosopher comes to be combined, in medieval thought, with that of the prophet, and that philosophico-politics becomes theologized as divine law or revelation. While I sketched out this link briefly in the last chapter, I now want to look more closely at how Strauss, in *Philosophy and Law*, comes to discover and describe it, and at what his descriptions owe to his engagement with Cohen.

Second, I will show that Cohen serves as a methodological guide (albeit an unacknowledged one) for Strauss's understanding of the theologization of philosophy by the medievals. Strauss's reading, and his adoption of Cohen's hermeneutic logic, allows us to see that Cohen's way of elaborating an ethical-philosophical meaning of law relies on a specific way of charting a "transformation" between earlier and later forms of (Israelite-Jewish) religiosity. This transformation is pinned by Cohen onto the evolution of the "legal" (*rechtlich*) institution of sacrifice into that of atonement.

Similarly to his remarks about the pitfalls of ethical individuality that we looked at in the previous chapter, Strauss's analysis brings Cohen's method for discerning this "transformation" into view while casting suspicion on Cohen's valorization of the ethical notion of atonement over the political dimension of nomos, understood as revelation – that is, of autonomy over heteronomy.

Strauss on Plato's "Prophecy" of Revelation

As discussed in the previous chapter, the question that animated Strauss's reflections on the relationship between philosophy and law had been: Why does philosophy continue to thrive among the medievals, even though it has apparently been reconceived as a pursuit occurring only under the authority of divine law/revelation, and thus presumably restricted in its freedom of inquiry? As we have seen, Strauss, in part, takes over Cohen's answer to that question: Because the medievals were philosophizing in the framework set by Plato, they understood the purpose of philosophy to be political, which means that they understood philosophy as a law-bound pursuit, called to responsibility before the project of living-together in the "true state."

The second reason given by Strauss for why philosophy continues to thrive is that the law becomes divine, that is, revealed law. Maimonides and the Falasifa pursue philosophy in a Platonic framework but with an additional un-Platonic "presupposition": that philosophy is "authorized" and even mandated by revelation. What does this second part of Strauss's answer owe to Cohen?

In order to answer this question, let us look at Strauss's descriptions of the structural transformation between the Platonic framework in which philosophy is limited by its responsibility to the state or to law, and the medieval "situation," in which revelation becomes the source of this limit, this command to responsibility. This structure that Strauss discerns in the relation between Plato and the medieval philosophers is the core idea around which the overall argument of *Philosophy and Law* is constructed.[11] For the medievals, according to Strauss, the law has become a

11 Strauss's most dense and gripping version of this description may be found in the closing passages of chap. 3 of *Philosophy and Law*, that is, the 1931 essay on Maimonides and prophecy (PG 122–3/131–3, with variants from the earlier essay version

revealed law and, concurrently, the position of the philosopher-king becomes that of the prophet. In this connection, Strauss concedes Cohen's claim that one can speak of a Platonism of the medievals in the sense that Plato calls philosophy to responsibility before human living-together, before the ideal state.

Taking together the relevant passages in chapters 1 and 3 of *Philosophy and Law* and in the associated lecture "Cohen and Maimonides," we find a great variation in the terms used by Strauss to describe the change and the relationship between Plato's view and its medieval counterpart. At times, Strauss makes it sound as though in describing this development, he is not particularly interested in whether it was a necessary or contingent one: he speaks of a "modification" or "transformation" of the Platonic conception. The task he sets himself is accordingly a neutral one of "illuminating the relationship" between the earlier view and the later one (PG 118/127–8). In connection with these sorts of characterizations, we also find descriptions in which it appears that what took place between Plato and the medievals was a mere modification, and not a radical transformation: Strauss speaks of Plato having provided a model (*Entwurf*) that was then "modified" (*verändert*), or (in many places, and as already mentioned) of Plato having set a "framework" (*Rahmen*) that was "changed" by the medievals (PG 118–19/128–9). On one occasion, Strauss further underscores that this framework or frame was merely modified or altered, perhaps "expanded" (*ausgeweitet*), but not exploded (*gesprengt*); that is, its original scope was not exceeded (PG 119/128).

Much of Strauss's depiction, however, revolves around the idea that the earlier Platonic conception is, in fact, to be understood in view of the later medieval development. Thus, he several times says of the "framework" not that it was changed or modified, but that it was "filled in" (*ausgefüllt*) (PG 62/74, 118/127), suggesting that in Plato it had been a mere frame, empty and in need of filling or completing by the medievals, in light of the fact of revelation. Similarly, Strauss speaks of a "question" asked by Plato, of the relation between law/politics/the ideal state and

at PG 611–12). This same description is found verbatim in the 1931 "Cohen and Maimonides" lecture notes (CM 426). *Philosophy and Law* is a work whose development took several years, and it is remarkable that what we may term its core idea, around which its overall argument is constructed, may be found verbatim, without significant changes or rewordings all the way from early drafts to the final version of the book published in 1935. The discussion that follows is based on those passages, on a section of chapter 1 (PG 61–4/73–6), and on another section of chapter 3 (PG 118–19/127–9); there are some significant parallels in wording between the latter two passages as well.

philosophy as something "in question" or "worthy of question" (*fragwürdig*) in Plato, to which an answer is to be "sought" (*gesucht*); the question is then ultimately "answered" (or loses its status of being about something *fragwürdig*, about something truly in question) in and by virtue of the medieval situation. What had been merely sought after, desired, and even "demanded" (*gefordert*) now becomes "given," in the sense that law is then "given" (i.e., by or through the prophet, as "the binding and absolutely perfect order of human life") or becomes "actual" as revealed (PG 62–3/74–5, 123/132–3; CM 427).[12] Strauss depicts the Platonic conception as offering an "approach" (*Annäherung, Ansatz*; PG 64/76) to the matter at hand, which is later to be taken up and built upon; or again writes that Plato's *Laws* "hint" at, or "point to" revelation ("but *only* point to it") – this then is a "hint" to which the medievals will supply "the next step" (PG 64/76). Thus, Plato's "demand" or call (*Forderung*) for a philosophy responsible to politics is later "fulfilled" (*erfüllt*, akin to the "filling" [*ausfüllen*] of the frame mentioned above) (PG 61/74, 123/132; CM 426). Further intensifying this idea, Strauss then also says that the desideratum of a law "under" which philosophy will find itself, and by virtue of which it will be responsible, is Plato's *Weissagung*, his "foretelling," "divination," or prophecy of such a law that is ultimately "fulfilled" (*erfüllt*) in the medieval situation. Revelation itself is actually "foretold" or "prophesied" (*geweissagt*) by Plato (PG 119/128–9).[13] The later prophetologies are thus to be seen as the "completion" or "consummation" (*Vollendung*) (PG 62/74) of the earlier theory of politics, of the ideal state and the philosopher-king.

At times, Strauss puts this juxtaposition between the earlier and the later view even more starkly by suggesting, for example, that the earlier doctrine becomes, in light of revelation, "obsolete" (*überkommen*; PG 62/74).[14] Thus, for medieval prophetology it is no longer merely

12 Similarly CM 427: "The *Platonism* of these [i.e., the medieval] philosophers is given in/in virtue of their *situation* [ist mit ihrer *Situation* gegeben]."

13 In "Cohen and Maimonides," it is the prophet who "fulfills what Plato called for, what he foretold/divined" (CM 427).

14 The adjective *überkommen*, which I am here rendering as "obsolete," is indeed an ambiguous term in the phrase "die Vollendung einer aus der Antike überkommenen Lehre," which Adler translates as "the consummation of a teaching handed down from antiquity." Functionally, it should be and does denote "transmitted," as is reflected by Adler's translation, "handed down." But that translation obscures the other unmistakable meaning captured by Strauss's choice of the rather unusual *überkommen* instead of a more straightforward and conventional term such as *übermittelt* (or *überführt*, consistently with *Überführung*, which Strauss chooses at PG 64 l. 24).

a matter of completing or fulfilling a lack or a demand inherent to the earlier theory, but of correcting a mistake that has come into view. Elsewhere, Strauss speaks of an "aporia" in Plato that had to be, and was "resolved" or removed (*behoben*) by the medievals (PG 64/76). Finally, at one point we learn that rather than Plato's theory having been mistaken in a way that only emerges in light of changing circumstances and new insights (the new insight that revelation brought), medieval prophetology actually performs a "critique" (*Kritik*) of Plato (PG 119/128). Thus, the lack that it fills is not visible only as of a certain point in history, but was presumably inherent in the original theory from its inception, even without the later "non-/un-Platonic" presumption of revelation. This would then go along with the idea that Plato himself in his theory of the state and of laws anticipated something like revelation or divine law, that he "foretold" (*geweissagt*) this divine law. After all, as Strauss points out, "in general, it is only the fulfillment that teaches a complete understanding of the divination [*Weissagung*]." It is according to this very logic, Strauss suggests, that the "Platonic model" of the ideal state had to be "changed" beginning from, or in light of "the factical revelation, the factical ideal state" (PG 119/128–9).

What stands out from this wealth of language, belonging to various registers, and that Strauss uses in these descriptions, is a tension between two interpretations: (1) That the old view harbors or anticipates the new one, and that the medieval presupposition of revelation thus affords a proper understanding or retrieval of the old view in its full meaning. (This interpretation, which casts the medieval view as a "completion" of the ancient view, entails for Strauss a task for his own time of recapturing or retrieving an obscured ancient understanding of divine law [*Wiederverständnis*], by systematically disregarding the "*modern* conception of 'religious consciousness.'" This task is oriented to the medieval presupposition of revelation [PG 66/69], in line with the idea that the medieval view is a "completion," perfection, or even logical conclusion [*Vollendung*] of the ancient one [PG 62/74].) (2) That the medieval presupposition of revelation was in some sense truly a "new" and unheard-of "answer" to an "admittedly ancient question" (PG 62/74), or even a "critique" of an "obsolete" position.

By a hermeneutic logic or method that one might term "prophetic," Strauss thus retrospectively grasps what Plato meant, in light of the purportedly "later" development of that meaning, but in such a way that the later meaning is at the same time also anticipated in the earlier one. A crucial aspect of this hermeneutic is illuminated if we attend to Strauss's use of the term "possibility," in a Heideggerian vein, to describe the relationship between earlier and later modes of philosophizing.[15] When Strauss repeatedly characterizes the ancient Platonic view as harboring a "possibility," he is employing this notion in an emphatic sense: In the ancient Platonic dialogue, the philosopher-king is "possible," "expected" (PG 62–3/75). Maimonides and the Falasifa, for whom the "fact [*Faktum*] of revelation is a given," "ask after the possibility of the actual law," meaning that they philosophize in a Platonic "horizon," about a possibility that is itself already given within that horizon (PG 118/128). Once the law is a "given," the philosophers' task is to "understand" it, and such understanding is "made possible by way of/through Plato" and "only by way of Plato" (PG 123/133). Consequently, the task of the interpreter is to "grasp the emergence of the [medieval] doctrine from out of Platonic philosophy *in its possibility*" (PG 63/76, emphasis added). The implication is that to understand the emergence of *x* from *y* is not the same as to understand this emergence or origination of *x from out of the "possibility"* that is harbored in *y*. Given the multiple ways in which Strauss portrays the relationship between Plato and Maimonides/the Falasifa, the notion of "possibility" with which Strauss is here operating is not the conventional one in which what is possible is "merely" possible, that is, in which "possibility" is to be understood primarily in what it lacks in relation to what is actual. Rather, this use of "possibility" is close to Heidegger's investigations in *Being and Time* into a sense of "possibility" that is "higher" than actuality – such that Dasein may be understood *as* its possibilities.

The "prophetic" hermeneutic I have been describing is essential to the philosophico-political theology that is the project of Strauss's *Philosophy and Law.* The "content" of that project is Strauss's demonstration of a philosophy-as-politics that is theologically grounded, a demonstration he makes by way of his readings of Maimonides and his Islamic counterparts or sources. But my contention is that that demonstration is inseparable

15 For some helpful initial speculations about the impact of Heidegger's thought on Strauss in the 1920s and early 1930s, as well as about the ongoing role of interlocutors who had been students of Heidegger (e.g., Gerhard Krüger, Karl Löwith, and Hans-Georg Gadamer), see Harald Bluhm, *Die Ordnung der Ordnung. Das politische Philosophieren von Leo Strauss* (Berlin: Akademie Verlag, 2002), 52–9. Bluhm rightly notes that the role of Heidegger for Strauss's thought has been insufficiently investigated (52). A promising approach to directly analyzing what Strauss's work during this period – including the core ideas that guide his interpretations in "Cohen and Maimonides" and *Philosophy and Law* – owes to his encounter with Heidegger's thought has been developed by Rodrigo Chacón in "Reading Strauss from the Start: On the Heideggerian Origins of 'Political Philosophy,'" *European Journal of Political Theory* 9, no. 3 (July 2010).

from the intricate hermeneutic or logic I have been calling attention to by virtue of which the purportedly "earlier" aspect of this philosophico-theological politics or politico-philosophical theology (philosophy as essentially political) corresponds to the purportedly "later" "addition" (revelation or divine law as re-founding philosophy).

We will see that with this method, Strauss is taking up, without especially acknowledging that he is doing so, a hermeneutic logic that is also key to Cohen's project in the *Religion.*

Strauss on Cohen's "Idealizing Interpretation"

In "Cohen and Maimonides," Strauss hinges his entire discussion of Cohen's *Religion* on a practice he ascribes to Cohen of "idealizing interpretation." Strauss has a twofold purpose in thematizing and discussing Cohen's interpretative practice. First, this discussion forms a part of his demonstration that Enlightenment – with which he aligns Cohen's philosophy, including Cohen's interpretation of the medievals – has a polemical purpose: that it is guided by modern moral-political aims, such as that of freeing rational ideas from mythical presuppositions. Second, Strauss discerns an affinity between Cohen's "idealizing interpretation" and the method of allegoresis in Maimonides's interpretation of the Bible, and he uses this affinity to explain both kinds of interpretation, as well as, as we shall see, the commonality of purpose between Maimonides and Cohen. This is consistent with Strauss's announcement at the beginning of his text that he is discussing Cohen and Maimonides together because Cohen, as an "Enlightener," can allow us to understand Maimonides's share in Enlightenment and rationalism (CM 394–5, cf. 398). According to Strauss, it is because Cohen himself belongs to Enlightenment thinking that he presents Maimonides as a "classic of rationalism."

Strauss asserts a "deep commonality" between allegoresis in Maimonides and Cohen's "idealizing interpretation." He explains that both methods proceed from the assumption that the text has an "ambiguous meaning." Both methods seek an "internal," "binding," "actual" meaning that is distinct from the text's apparent "literal," "non-binding" meaning. This common procedure aligns with a goal that Strauss identifies as common to Maimonides and Cohen: to "disburden" Scripture from the mythical meanings that it has (due to its origins in myth), in accordance with, or "in inner accord with" ("in innerem Einverständnis mit") its actual meaning (CM 401–2).

This sort of "demythologization" is indeed evident throughout Cohen's *Religion* book as a main goal of his interpretations of Judaism. Although the term does not have the prominence in Cohen's own discourse that is suggested by Strauss's reification of Cohen's method under this heading,[16] the link between "idealization" and Cohen's procedure of demythologization in coming to an understanding of religion is evident, for example, in Cohen's (often contradictory) efforts in the *Ethik* and in *Der Begriff der Religion* (1915; *The Concept of Religion*) to explain the sense in which religion can properly be said to be an autonomous domain. Thus, while in the *Ethik*, Cohen firmly denies such autonomy to religion – which he sees as defined by its ethical purpose – later in the two *Religion* books (*Der Begriff der Religion* and *Religion of Reason*) he discovers philosophical questions that he finds can only be addressed on the basis of a philosophical understanding of religion as its own domain. In all three books, however, Cohen clearly valorizes a concept of religion that would eschew its mythical contents and that would promote ethical progress. For example, Cohen uses the term "idealization" to refer to "the work of culture" by virtue of which morality is applied as a criterion to historical religion – a process that is also supposed to lead to a promotion of morality in religion (and thus to the "improvement" of religion) as well as in culture and in the sphere of politics.[17] Although we have no evidence regarding the precise source that Strauss was drawing on in calling Cohen's method of interpretation "idealizing," his analysis of Cohen's manner of interpretation is thus consistent with Cohen's usage in these passages, which signal Cohen's prevalent interpretative procedure in the *Religion of Reason*. That procedure always aims to understand the "sources of Judaism" according to the following criterion: what would be, and what should be, the, or a, religion of reason?[18]

16 CM 401; Strauss, "How to Study," 322 (see note 19 below).

17 See BR 119–20, ErW 587, and the discussion in Helmut Holzhey, "Die Religion im System der Philosophie Cohens," in *Hermann Cohen und die Erkenntnistheorie*, ed. Wolfgang Marx and Ernst Wolfgang Orth (Würzburg: Königshausen & Neumann, 2001), 158, 158–9n38. For related uses of the term "idealization," see, for example, RV 89/77 and 291/249. See also the extensive discussion of "idealization" in Cohen in Schwarzschild, "'Germanism and Judaism' – Hermann Cohen's Normative Paradigm of the German-Jewish Symbiosis," in *Jews and Germans From 1860 to 1933: The Problematic Symbiosis*, ed. David Bronsen (Heidelberg: Universitätsverlag Carl Winter, 1979); included in Schwarzschild, *The Tragedy of Optimism*; and commentary by George Y. Kohler in the introduction to *The Tragedy of Optimism*, xx–xxiii.

18 However, I would caution against taking Strauss's own characterizations of "idealizing interpretation" as straightforward descriptions of Cohen's ways of proceeding. While Cohen to be sure often analyzes a "tendency" or logic of "idealization" that he discerns *in* the movement of Jewish monotheism, he does not describe or recommend his own procedure as one of "idealization" in a systematic fashion, as is suggested by Strauss's usage. For example, in a later text, the 1965 preface to the English edition of *Spinoza's Critique of Religion*, Strauss defines "idealizing interpretation" as "the

Let us return to Strauss's association of "idealizing interpretation" in Cohen with allegoresis. Strauss notes that a modern historicist critique of allegoresis, in the manner of Spinoza, would assert that it fails to grasp the simple meaning of the text, that it transforms the meaning of the text (CM 400, 401). But he points out that historicism or historical-critical method also shares something with the allegoresis that it opposes: for both methods, interpretation has as its "sole task" "to discover how the author understood himself" (CM 401, cf. 400).

Readers of Strauss will find this formula quite familiar, as in subsequent works Strauss went on to vigorously endorse the idea that this ought to be the sole task of interpretation. Strauss's standard formula for the interpretative principle to which this idea is opposed is "to understand an author *better than* he understood himself." It is this latter "Kantian insight" that according to Strauss underwrites Cohen's "idealizing interpretation" (CM 401). This "Kantian insight" is thus also the source of the opposing formula that Strauss employs in future works in order to articulate his own preferred interpretative procedure: to understand authors as they understood themselves.[19]

---

interpretation of a teaching in the light of its highest possibility regardless of whether or not that highest possibility was known to the originator." Strauss, *Spinoza's Critique of Religion*, trans. E.M. Sinclair (New York: Schocken, 1965), 25. Martin Yaffe applies Strauss's definition to Cohen's procedure (without attributing it to Strauss), based on references to passages such as the ones I myself have pointed out above as representative of Cohen's usage of the term "idealization." But to designate Cohen's *method* using this term – especially given that Cohen was a thinker who dedicated much of his writing to explicating and reflecting on his method – would require further explanation or justification. See Martin Yaffe, "Autonomy, Community, Authority: Hermann Cohen, Carl Schmitt, Leo Strauss," in *Autonomy and Community*, ed. Daniel Frank (Albany: State University of New York Press, 1992), 145, 156n11. Yaffe's characterization is also taken up by James A. Diamond in "Exegetical Idealization: Hermann Cohen's Religion of Reason Out of the Sources of Maimonides," in "Ancients and Moderns in Jewish Philosophy: The Case of Hermann Cohen," ed. Aaron W. Hughes, special issue, *Journal of Jewish Thought and Philosophy* 18, no. 1 (January 2010): 62n51.

19 At the opening of the lecture "How To Study Medieval Philosophy" (1944), Strauss characterizes "historical understanding" in the sense in which he wishes to embrace it as being in opposition to the principle articulated in "a saying of Kant" that "it is possible to understand a philosopher better than he understood himself," and he cites Hermann Cohen's 1908 Maimonides essay as "the most outstanding example of such unhistorical interpretation which we have in the field of the study of Jewish medieval philosophy." There follows a kind of summary of Strauss's judgment about Cohen's procedure of interpretation articulated in "Cohen and Maimonides" thirteen years earlier. Strauss writes that Cohen called this procedure "'idealizing' interpretation," and that "it may justly be described as the modern form [of] allegoric interpretation." *Interpretation: A Journal of Political Philosophy* 23, no. 3 (Spring 1996): 321–2, cf. 337n5. See also the "more heavily edited" version (cf. editors' introduction to the

As others have pointed out, this formula derives from one of the early, preparatory sections of the Transcendental Dialectic in Kant's First Critique. The implication of Strauss's use of the formula is thus, as Corine Pelluchon puts it, that Cohen "has an idealizing interpretative principle which he got from" the passage in Kant.[20] The passage in question forms a part of Kant's argument for why he is justified in using the term "idea" (*Idee*) in coining his own term for concepts of pure reason that exceed the understanding or what we are able to experience: "transcendental idea." Kant considers the meaning of "idea" in Plato, in part in order to anticipate the objection that, in retrieving the term "idea," he might be introducing a term that carries with it the

---

Interpretation version, 319) of this lecture in *The Rebirth of Classical Political Rationalism: An Introduction to the Thought of Leo Strauss: Essays and Lectures*, ed. Thomas L. Pangle (Chicago: University of Chicago Press, 1989), 207ff.

Similarly to "How to Study Medieval Philosophy," Strauss's essay "Political Philosophy and History" (1949) criticizes historicism for "[taking] it for granted ... that it is possible and even necessary to understand the thinkers of the past better than those thinkers understood themselves." For Strauss this means, first, that the interpreter presumes from the outset that a claim to be interpreted is false, that is, that its author is "mistaken in making that claim," and, second, that that presumption necessarily becomes "the basis of [the] interpretation." Historical objectivity, by contrast, is guaranteed only if we construe the task of the historian of thought as being "to understand the thinkers of the past exactly as they understood themselves." In *What Is Political Philosophy*? (Glencoe, IL: Free Press, 1959), 67–8. Cf. "How to Understand," 322–3. There is also already in *Philosophy and Law* one instance in which Strauss employs the "to understand better" formula for his own polemical purposes (PG 18n9/137n9).

20 Immanuel Kant, *Kritik der reinen Vernunft*, ed. Raymund Schmidt (Hamburg: Meiner, 1956), A314/B370; translated by Norman Kemp Smith as *Critique of Pure Reason*, 2nd rev. ed. (New York: Palgrave Macmillan, 2007). Corine Pelluchon, "Strauss and Cohen: The Question of Enlightened Judaism," *Interpretation* 32, no. 3 (Summer 2005): 225. Also see Pelluchon, *Leo Strauss. Une autre raison, d'autres lumières* (Paris: Vrin, 2005), 149, where she presents Strauss's break with Cohen as part of Strauss's opposition to Neo-Kantianism. In the preface to her translation into French of "Cohen und Maimuni" (CM), Pelluchon explains that according to Strauss, Cohen's "idealizing interpretation" "sees in Kantian morality the realization or the truth of the morality of the prophets." Leo Strauss, "Cohen et Maïmonide," *Revue de Métaphysique et de Morale* (April–June 2003): 234.

Coincidentally, in a study of "Hermann Cohen's Concept of the Transcendental Method," Vladimir Zeman has used Kant's formula to pinpoint Cohen's procedure of "systematic reconstruction" vis-à-vis Kant, which was of course the founding presupposition of Cohen's own philosophy. Zeman, "Hermann Cohen's Concept of the Transcendental Method," in *Transcendental Philosophy and Everyday Experience*, ed. Tom Rockmore and Vladimir Zeman (Atlantic Highlands, NJ: Humanities Press, 1997), 112–13.

problems associated with Plato's understanding of "idea." His defense against such an objection takes the form of a mini-essay on why it is both possible and necessary, in trying to say something new in philosophy, to make use of old language.

Kant in this section makes appreciative comments about Plato's moral and political philosophy – that is, about the "practical" implications of Plato's theory of ideas – which indeed is quite fitting in view of what ultimately turn out to be the "practical" purposes of the Transcendental Dialectic. (This might have been a reason for Strauss to read this section closely, as he would have had to do in order to be able to notice and retrieve from it the formula "to understand an author better than he understood himself.") Describing and justifying his procedure in making use of a term of Plato's that might in some respects be foreign to his own purposes, Kant writes:

> I need only remark that it is by no means unusual, upon comparing the thoughts which an author has expressed in regard to his subject, whether in ordinary conversation or in writing, to find that we even understand him better than he has understood himself, in that he has not sufficiently determined his concept and has thus sometimes spoken or thought counter to his own intention [*seiner eigenen Absicht entgegen*].[21]

Kant here is describing the classic hermeneutical problem faced by philosophical authors who seek to make earlier thought and existing language productive for the purpose of advancing the understanding of some philosophical problem.

Hans-Georg Gadamer's discussion of the formula "to understand an author better than he understood himself" in *Truth and Method* (1960) is helpful here. Gadamer explains, with respect to Schleiermacher's use of it, in what sense this "formula that has been repeated ever since and in whose changing interpretation the entire history of modern hermeneutics may be observed," expresses an interpretative principle or desideratum "that contains the essential problem of hermeneutics."[22] Similarly to Strauss, Gadamer detects in this interpretative

---

21 Kant, *Kritik der reinen Vernunft*, A314/B370; *Critique of Pure Reason*, 310.

22 Hans-Georg Gadamer, *Wahrheit und Methode*, 6th ed., in *Gesammelte Werke*, vol. 1 (Tübingen: Mohr, 1990), 195–6; translated by Joel Weinsheimer and Donald G. Marshall as *Truth and Method*, 2nd rev. ed. (New York: Crossroad, 1989), 192. Gadamer presents the ways that this formula has been understood, for example, by Schleiermacher, Dilthey, Boeckh, and Steinthal (196–8/192–5).

principle, as it was promoted by Schleiermacher and consistently with the passage in Kant that is Strauss's source, the implication that the interpreter is "superior" (*überlegen*) to the object of interpretation.[23] Leaving open whether or in what sense this observation might be justified, Gadamer's characterization of Kant's employment of the formula seems to me to hit the mark:

> It is a matter there not of a principle of philology but of a claim [*Anspruch*] of philosophy to move, by way of greater conceptual clarity, beyond the contradictions that may be found in a given thesis.

The interpretative principle thus does not serve the understanding of an author or a text as an already-past or closed-off entity. Rather, Kant's use of the formula goes along with

> the demand ..., solely through thought, by developing the implications [*Konsequenzen*] that lie within an author's concepts, to achieve insights that correspond to the real intention of the author – insights he would have to share had his thinking been sufficiently clear and distinct.[24]

This "demand" (*Forderung*) is the "claim" or "entitlement" (*Anspruch*) to "objective philosophical critique" (*philosophischer Sachkritik*), which means that its purpose is not a hermeneutical one, but the "age-old" one of philosophical critique or philosophical treatment of some question. Indeed, we are dealing here with the demand of "scientific/scholarly [*wissenschaftlich*] critique" in general:

---

23 Gadamer, *Wahrheit und Methode/Truth and Method,* 198/195. Cf. CM 401. Similarly, Strauss argues in "Political Philosophy and History" that "our understanding of the thought of the past is liable to be the more adequate, the less the historian is convinced of the superiority of his own point of view." To avoid such a stance of superiority is for Strauss the prerequisite for "taking seriously" the thought we are studying, which in turn means "being willing to consider the possibility that it is simply true." "We cannot be ... seriously interested in the past if we know beforehand that the present is in the most important respect superior to the past." Strauss, "Political Philosophy and History," 68, 67, cf. "How to Study," 322–3. In the notes for the 1944 lecture "How to Study Medieval Philosophy," Strauss puts this point more strongly: "In the normal and most interesting case, the philosopher studied by the historian of philosophy is a man by far superior to his historian in intelligence, imagination, subtlety" and repeats the interpretation he gave of "Kant's saying" in "Cohen and Maimonides": that it "presupposes that the interpreter considers his insight superior to the insight of the old author" (322).

24 Gadamer, 198/195.

> Someone who is better able to think through what an author is talking about will be able to see what the author says in the light of a truth that is still hidden from the author himself.[25]

Indeed, since the sought-after insight is one that the author "*would have [had] to* share had his thinking been sufficiently clear and distinct," the "to understand better ..." formula may be taken to be a criterion for discerning philosophical "greatness" – that is, as a criterion for whether a work or an author merits philosophical attention or retrieval. This is the thrust of Martin Heidegger's employment of the formula in his 1927 lecture course *The Basic Problems of Phenomenology*. Heidegger gives the following explanation for his recourse to Greek ontology in seeking an understanding of Being – that is, for both why we ought to take this ontology as a starting point and why we are entitled to "extend" it:

> We not only wish to but must understand the Greeks better than they understood themselves. Only thus do we actually *have* the heritage/tradition [*Erbe*].... It is always a sign of the greatness of a productive achievement when it can let issue from itself the demand [*Forderung*] to be understood better than it understood itself. Irrelevancies have no need of a higher understanding.[26]

Thus, to "understand something better than it understood itself" is simply what it means to "have" a tradition, in a sense that I believe well describes the role of what we might call "tradition" in Strauss's constitutive claims about the medievals and the ancients in *Philosophy and Law*.

To return to Strauss's observations about "idealizing interpretation" in Cohen and its relation to allegoresis in Maimonides, what he highlights is that both methods seek to account for the specific sort of continuity that governs the relationship between the Bible and later

---

25 Gadamer, 199/195. Gadamer suggests that it was Schleiermacher who transformed the meaning of the formula from one pertaining to philosophical or *wissenschaftlich* critique to a principle of interpretation (199/195 and 199–200n47/195n47). In "Hermeneutics and Historicism" (1965), building on the background of his explication in *Truth and Method* of the formula and its origins, Gadamer argues against Strauss's polemical use of the formula as part of the latter's critique of historicism. "Hermeneutik und Historismus," in *Gesammelte Werke*, vol. 2, 2nd ed. (Tübingen: Mohr, 1993), 416–17; "Hermeneutics and Historicism," in *Truth and Method*, 534–5.

26 Martin Heidegger, *Die Grundprobleme der Phänomenologie*, in *Gesamtausgabe*, vol. 24 (Frankfurt am Main: Klostermann, 1975), 157; translated by Albert Hofstadter as *The Basic Problems of Phenomenology*, rev. ed. (Bloomington: Indiana University Press, 1988), 111, emphasis added.

(Jewish) thought. A certain conventional understanding of Maimonides's biblical interpretation would view it as being *exclusively* an "*external* assimilation of the Bible to Aristotelian philosophy" (CM 401, emphasis added). Strauss credits Cohen as a source for the insight that what is "decisive" (*maßgebend*) about Maimonides's employment of allegoresis is rather that it accomplishes a "*continuation* of the efforts of the prophets, the redactors, the Targumim" (CM 401, emphasis added). It is Cohen who allows us to see that the conventional view of allegoresis in Maimonides does not tell the whole story. According to the conventional view, Maimonides's method of allegoresis, which according to Strauss "seeks to understand the author as he understands himself," is trying to reconcile the interpreter's cosmology with that of the Bible, and thus imputes to the Bible a cosmological-scientific interest – an interest that according to Spinoza is foreign, or "external," to the Bible (CM 400). In practicing so-called idealizing interpretation – and, as we will see, in some reflections on his own interpretative procedure that Strauss calls special attention to – Cohen however allows us to see Maimonides's method of allegoresis as *both* representing a "continuation of the efforts" made evident in the Jewish sources *and* paving the way for the method that Cohen will ultimately see as setting the program for Jewish philosophy in general as just such a "continuation of efforts of the prophets," and others.

"Continuation" can of course mean many things, just as the formula "to understand an author better than he understood himself" leaves open in what sense the interpretation in question is supposed to be "better than" the "understanding" it imputes to the author (i.e., what sort of improvement or progress is supposed to characterize the relationship of the interpretation to its object), as well as what we mean when we refer, in relation to a passage we are interpreting, to an author's "understanding himself." Here it is important to note not only the similarity Strauss highlights between allegoresis in Maimonides and idealizing interpretation in Cohen – that both kinds of interpretation consist in "reinterpretation" (*Umdeutung*) in the sense of projecting new meanings onto their objects, and in thereby doing violence to the text (*sich an dem Text vergreifen*) – but also the divergence that he highlights: that unlike allegoresis, idealizing interpretation operates with a sense of superiority and distance vis-à-vis its object (CM 401). Ultimately Cohen is for Strauss an interpreter guided by Enlightenment principles and objectives, by a concern for progress and improvement. This, we saw, enables him to be a guide to understanding Maimonides as a rationalist/Enlightener (CM 395). But Strauss wants us to see Cohen's admiration for Maimonides as "paradoxical" (CM 403). Thus, Strauss does not restrict himself to presenting and analyzing Cohen's own interpretative method. He wants also to demonstrate that that method has Maimonidean allegoresis as a kind of model, despite the decisive difference between allegoresis, which "wants to understand the author as he understood himself" – for example by not imputing to the biblical author a scientific interest in cosmology – and Cohen as embodying the Enlightenment trait of self-superiority and distance – that is, the Enlightenment objective of improvement and progress. Strauss wants to highlight not only *what* Cohen finds in Maimonides – the ultimate "content" of his thought (Maimonides as providing an ethical philosophy in being a Platonist) – but also that the mechanism by which Cohen finds such content not only in Maimonides but in the sources of Judaism in general is itself a "salvaging" or "rescue," and a repetition-with-a-difference, a "more reflected" repetition, of Maimonides's method:

> Idealizing interpretation of Scripture fulfils the same function as RMbM's allegoresis: disburdening of Scripture from myth in inner accord with the *actual* meaning of Scripture. Idealizing interpretation repeats allegoresis in a more reflected form. Thus, Cohen accomplishes a *rescue [*Rettung*] of allegoresis.* (CM 401)

Strauss underscores that such a rescue of allegoresis is only possible for Cohen on the basis of a prior "concession" to the critique of allegoresis: Cohen is supposed to have conceded that allegoresis does not "understand the author as he understood himself," that it "does violence to" and "reinterprets" the text (CM 400–1). Just as Strauss depicts Cohen's own "idealizing interpretation" as one that projects foreign meanings onto texts, so this interpretation can be a "reflected repetition" or an "embracing" of allegoresis on Cohen's part only because Cohen is supposed to have waived his claim to interpreting "authentically," as it were – to interpreting the "simple meaning" of the texts (CM 401, cf. 431n26). While allegoresis seeks merely to find the true meaning of a text, "idealizing interpretation" seeks the true meaning of a text only in view of and for the sake of progress in thought (cf. CM 403). Cohen's "idealizing interpretation," again, is supposed to embrace the principle of "understanding the author better than he understood himself"; this procedure, which takes place from a position of superiority and distance vis-à-vis the text, is what yields Cohen's programmatic interpretations of Judaism. Cohen's program for an interpretation of Judaism is what Strauss refers to as Cohen's concern for an "enlightened Judaism" – "enlightened" in the same sense of "Enlightenment" that Strauss invokes as a heading under which heuristically to approach Cohen and Maimonides together

(CM 403, 395).[27] It is for the sake of an "enlightened Judaism" that Cohen "rescues" (Maimonides's) allegoresis by means of the "concession" that reinterpretation (*Umdeutung*) and violence to the text are necessary.

A "Transformation" That Is "the Best Kind of Destruction/ Annihilation"

In order to explain what this means in Cohen, Strauss looks at some passages in *Religion of Reason* in which Cohen reflects on his own interpretative method. As we discover, Strauss is here honing in on Cohen's discussions of the biblical institution of sacrifice and its transformations. By pointing to this part of Cohen's account of Jewish religion, Strauss touches on a theme that traverses, in a singular way, Cohen's systematic philosophy – in particular his ethics – and his Jewish writings: As others have noted, there are substantial argumentative links between Cohen's theory of atonement and justice in Judaism (some of which he articulated in the essay "Die Versöhnungsidee" ["The Idea of Atonement"], which dates from "the early to mid-1890's"[28]) and his analyses in the *Ethik* of the moral and juridical meanings of guilt and punishment.

Without revisiting the many detailed expositions and analyses that others have produced of these two areas of Cohen's thought,[29] it is

27 "Cohen begibt sich in die Nachfolge RMbM', weil es ihm um ein aufgeklärtes Judentum zu tun ist...." (CM 403).

28 Zank, *The Idea of Atonement*, 107 (see next note). "Die Versöhnungsidee" was first published in 1924 in JS1.

29 These include (in roughly chronological order): Martin Yaffe, "Liturgy and Ethics: Hermann Cohen and Franz Rosenzweig on the Day of Atonement," *Journal of Religious Ethics* 7, no. 2 (Fall 1979); Michael Zank, *The Idea of Atonement in the Philosophy of Hermann Cohen* (Providence, RI: Brown Judaic Studies, 2000; repr. Brown Judaic Studies Open Humanities Book Program, 2020), https://repository.library.brown.edu/studio/item/bdr:1111035; Gesine Palmer (see note 31 below); Astrid Deuber-Mankowsky, *Der frühe Walter Benjamin und Hermann Cohen. Jüdische Werte, Kritische Philosophie, vergängliche Erfahrung* (Berlin: Vorwerk 8, 2000); Rivka Horwitz, "Two Models of Atonement in Cohen's 'Religion of Reason': One According to Ezekiel, the Other 'Joyful in Sufferings' According to Job"; Aharon Shear-Yashuv, "Hermann Cohen über Chok und Mischpat"; and Lawrence Kaplan, "Hermann Cohen's Theory of Sacrifice in 'Religion of Reason Out of the Sources of Judaism'" – all three in *"Religion der Vernunft aus den Quellen des Judentums." Tradition und Ursprungsdenken in Hermann Cohens Spätwerk*, ed. Holzhey et al. (Hildesheim: Olms, 2000); Randi Rashkover (see note 33 below); Norman Solomon, "Cohen on Atonement, Purification and Repentance," in *Hermann Cohen's Critical Idealism*, ed. Reinier Munk (Dordrecht: Springer, 2005); Steven Kepnes, "Liturgical Selfhood: Hermann Cohen's Religion of Reason," chap. 2 of *Jewish Liturgical*

nevertheless important to recall that the question of what becomes of "sacrifice" lies at the heart of the entire Cohenian project of designating the progress-oriented trajectory of Judaism, its continual departure from myth and toward a universalist ethic. For Cohen, it is from sacrifice and its transformations that there emerges a human individual who can atone for their sin; such atonement thereby also becomes an institution of Recht, a function of a community's "juridical proceeding," a "public" institution.[30] Viewed from the perspective of Strauss's project, however, the institution of sacrifice can be taken to typify the problem of law as nomos: law as heteronomous, absolute, and arbitrary; law defined apart from the "liberal-individualist" ethical criteria that for Strauss typify Cohen's approach to both Jewish religious history and contemporary politics.

The other trajectory relevant to the passages we will be looking at that are highlighted by Strauss can be found in Cohen's *Ethik*: We saw in the last chapter that Cohen establishes the self's "autonomy" to mean a "self-determination" (*Selbstbestimmung*) that is other than freedom, to comprise a future-oriented task that is associated with a law (Gesetz) that is other than itself and that derives from Allheit. Cohen's next step in the *Ethik* is to explore that self's possibilities in view of its capacity for misdeeds. Cohen's analysis of juridical punishment, in particular, which enables but does not exhaust the self's capacity for taking responsibility for its own actions and for "preserving itself" (*Selbsterhaltung*), serves to complicate the relationship between heteronomy and autonomy in his ethico-legal philosophy.[31]

Reasoning (Oxford: Oxford University Press, 2007), 65ff.; Annika Thiem (Yannik Thiem), "Fate, Guilt, and Messianic Interruptions: Ethics of Theological Critique in Hermann Cohen and Walter Benjamin" (PhD diss., University of California, Berkeley, 2009); George Y. Kohler (see note 33 below).

30 RV 227/194, 234/200; cf. "Liebe und Gerechtigkeit in den Begriffen Gott und Mensch" (1900), JS3: 86.

31 ErW 372ff. Cf. Eggert Winter, *Ethik und Rechtswissenschaft: eine historisch-systematische Untersuchung zur Ethik-Konzeption des Marburger Neukantianismus im Werke Hermann Cohens* (Berlin: Duncker & Humblot, 1980), 396ff.; Zank, *The Idea of Atonement,* 295–301. For a particularly suggestive exploration of what Cohen might be after in trying to balance the logic of responsibility and accountability with a principle of "self-preservation," see Gesine Palmer, "Präskription und Deskription. Autonomie bei Sigmund Freud und Hermann Cohen," in *Torah – Nomos – Ius: Abendländischer Antinomismus und der Traum vom herrschaftsfreien Raum,* ed. Renate Haffke, Christiane Nasse, Gesine Palmer, and Dorothee C. von Tippelskirch (Berlin: Vorwerk 8, 1999), and "Die Hörner des Heidentums. Gesetz und Opfer bei Hermann Cohen und Sigmund Freud," in *Einbruch der Wirklichkeit,* ed. Jens Mattern (Berlin: Vorwerk 8, 2002).

Without forcing too strong an analogy, we can discern a parallel question of how autonomy is balanced with heteronomy in Cohen's concept of the "correlation" between God and human being as it is articulated in his theory of atonement.[32] This notion of correlation has either been read as Cohen's depiction of Judaism as achieving an essential balance between human autonomy and heteronomy, or alternatively, as introducing into his theory of Jewish religion an abiding, objectionable tension or indecision between autonomy and heteronomy.[33]

To sum up, while the domains of ethics and philosophy of religion are for Cohen methodologically distinct, and are guided by different questions and often diametrically opposed principles (e.g., the focus on collectivity in the *Ethik*, in contrast with the retrieval of the individual in the *Religion*), the analyses of guilt, punishment, and responsibility as ethical notions and of sin, expiation, and atonement as religious notions are intricately intertwined. Drawing on such analyses can perhaps offer a perspective onto a possible joint ethico-religious inquiry that draws on both Cohenian corpuses – though this is not an idea that we can pursue here.

Returning now to Strauss's discussion of Cohen's treatment of sacrifice in *Religion of Reason*: Strauss points out that Cohen regards his own employment of reinterpretation (*Umdeutung*) not as "an act of violence" (*Vergewaltigung*), but as a "transformation" (*Verwandlung*) (CM 401). With this observation, Strauss introduces a quote from *Religion of Reason*, chapter 10:

---

32 Much discussed in the Cohen literature, "correlation" is the technical term Cohen uses to describe the relationships between self and other and between God and the human being. A "correlative" relationship is one of reciprocity ("Wechselwirkung") in which the relata remain distinct. I discuss the God-man correlation in *Exemplarity and Chosenness: Rosenzweig and Derrida on the Nation of Philosophy* (Stanford: Stanford University Press, 2008), 15–16. Regarding the sequence of sin, punishment, and the "work of repentance [*Buße*]" in the logic of correlation, see also BR 68ff.

33 For an appreciative account, see Helmut Holzhey, "Gott und Seele. Zum Verhältnis von Metaphysikkritik und Religionsphilosophie bei Hermann Cohen," in *Hermann Cohen's Philosophy of Religion: International Conference in Jerusalem*, ed. Stéphane Mosès and Hartwig Wiedebach (Hildesheim: Olms, 1997), 92–3, drawing especially on BR 64, as well as Deuber-Mankowsky, *Der frühe Walter Benjamin und Hermann Cohen,* 138. Alternatively, see Randi Rashkover's critical evaluation of Cohen's theory of atonement in *Revelation and Theopolitics: Barth, Rosenzweig, and the Politics of Praise* (London: T&T Clark, 2005), 30, 37–46. Cf. the discussion in George Y. Kohler, "Finding God's Purpose: Hermann Cohen's Use of Maimonides to Establish the Authority of Mosaic Law," in "Ancients and Moderns in Jewish Philosophy: The Case of Hermann Cohen," ed. Aaron W. Hughes, special issue, *Journal of Jewish Thought and Philosophy* 18, no. 1 (Jan. 2010): 92–3.

> And it may be asked whether such transformation [*Verwandlung*] is not the best kind of destruction/annihilation [*Vernichtung*].[34]

In order to situate this quoted sentence in its original function within Cohen's argument about sacrifice, as well as to understand the use that Strauss makes of it in the "Cohen and Maimonides" lecture, let us recall the role of that argument in Cohen's philosophy of Jewish religion. In his study of *The Idea of Atonement in the Philosophy of Hermann Cohen*, Michael Zank notes that in confronting "the position of the sacrificial institutions in the context of Israelite and Jewish religion," Cohen's "solution was to correlate the intensification and regulation of the sacrificial cult during and after the Babylonian exile with the emergence of the idea of atonement." According to this solution, if atonement is acknowledged to be "the aim of biblical sacrifices," then "early Judaism provides sacrificial legislation with a constructive and valuable role."[35] On one level, in quoting Cohen's pronouncement that "transformation" is "the best destruction/annihilation," Strauss is calling attention specifically to the argumentative sequence in which that pronouncement appears: the thesis that atonement emerges as the "replacement" of sacrifice. Strauss is referring, then, to an argument that bears out, in obvious fashion, his overall criticism that Cohen espouses an individualist ethical philosophy. If we recall Strauss's juxtaposition of Cohen's "modern idea of the individual" with the nomos tradition that he traces to Plato (CM 429), then Cohen's argument for the centrality of the idea of atonement on one level seems to typify just such an individualism. In that sense, Cohen's account of how the institution of atonement emerges from the sacrifice legislation is a prime site for pursuing the guiding question of this

---

34 RV 204/175, cited in CM 401. This quotation of Cohen by Strauss is also discussed by Leora Batnitzky, "The Possibility of Premodern Rationalism: Strauss's Transformation of Hermann Cohen," *Leo Strauss and Emmanuel Levinas. Philosophy and the Politics of Revelation* (Cambridge: Cambridge University Press, 2006), chap. 5, 105–7, with special attention to Strauss's accompanying remark that this "question" is of course only "rhetorical," and to Strauss's redeployment of this quotation in his 1965 preface to the English translation of his 1930 Spinoza book, *Die Religionskritik Spinozas.* See Leo Strauss, *Spinoza's Critique of Religion,* trans. E.M. Sinclair (New York: Schocken, 1965), 24–5; and note 43 below. It does appear to me, however, contrary to Batnitzky's suggestion, that Strauss's reference to the source of the quotation is correct in both places.

35 Zank, *The Idea of Atonement,* 114. Zank traces the argument that Cohen presents for this view in "Die Versöhnungsidee" at 107–51.

The core chapters of *Religion of Reason* in which Cohen argues for this role of sacrifice in the emergence of atonement are chapters 10 ("The Individual as the I") – from which Strauss's one-sentence quotation is taken – and 11 ("Atonement").

chapter: Does Cohen offer a way of lining up the heteronomy of the concept of law (as envisioned by Strauss) with ethical autonomy?

Cohen assigns a central value to the notion that guilt becomes individuated in "the soul that sins," an idea found above all in Ezekiel and that Cohen finds to be "an expression for the person and for the individual" (RV 222/190).[36] The account of the emergence of the notion of sin and repentance/atonement is at the same time an account of the emergence of the individual as something like an ethical agent. For Cohen, these ideas replace the "mythical" one to be found in the biblical stipulation that the children are to be punished for the guilt of the fathers (RV 221–2/189–90).[37]

Let us now shift our attention to how the single-sentence quote in which Cohen asks rhetorically whether "transformation" is the best kind of "annihilation" functions once it has been embedded into Strauss's own text. Strauss's topic is Cohen's interpretative method. He is asking us, therefore, to read the quoted pronouncement for what Cohen conveys in it about *method.* In this part of chapter 10, Cohen looks at two kinds of prophetic response to the problem of sacrifice. The first response, evidenced in Isaiah 1, in Amos 5:25, and in Jeremiah 7:22 – which, Cohen points out, Maimonides's critique of sacrifice in the *Guide of the Perplexed* III.32 builds upon[38] – is one of "rejection" or "condemnation" (*Verwerfung*) (RV 200–4/172–5). In what follows, I will, for convenience's sake, refer to this tradition as that of "Jeremiah-Maimonides." The

36 See the discussion with reference to the key essay "Die Versöhnungsidee" and to Cohen's early treatment of this idea in "Die Nächstenliebe im Talmud" (1888), in Zank, *The Idea of Atonement*, 118ff., as well as Deuber-Mankowsky's discussion with reference to "Die Nächstenliebe im Talmud" and to the argument in the *Ethik* against original sin in *Der frühe Walter Benjamin und Hermann Cohen*, 130–8. As others have explained, what is partly at stake in Cohen's retrieval of Ezekiel's significance is his polemic against an implication of Wellhausen's influential thesis that, in the words of Zank, "the priestly theocracy of the second Temple period" was "a phenomenon of decline during which the erstwhile popular religion of Israel is forced into the mold of a proto-Catholic priestly institution that dominates through an elaborate sacrificial law and practice" (*The Idea of Atonement*, 110), which would amount to a post-biblical decline from the ethical values of the prophets. Wellhausen "characterized the Pentateuch as the founding document of post-exilic Judaism [,] distinguishing it from the pre-exilic folk religion of Ancient Israel," while "the New Testament represented ... a restoration of the original religion of Israel or of a religion on its par: the expression of a simple, immediate, and popular religiosity as opposed to the sickly sophistication of priestly or rabbinic institutions" (112). See also Kaplan, "Hermann Cohen's Theory of Sacrifice," 200–1, 201n40.

37 See also "Liebe und Gerechtigkeit in den Begriffen Gott und Mensch," JS3: 77–8; and "Die Versöhnungsidee," JS1: 127–8.

38 See also RV 381, 413. Cf. my discussion in the next chapter.

second response is one of "transformation" (*Verwandlung*) or "reshaping" (*Umgestaltung*), and Cohen links it to Ezekiel, whom he regards, in this respect, as exceptional among the prophets (RV 204/175). Ezekiel "does not condemn sacrifice" but combats it by means of "critique" and "reform" (RV 203/174). Cohen regards this second response as a necessary supplement to the first – necessary because the uncompromising rejection and abandonment of sacrifice based on the rationale provided by Jeremiah-Maimonides would risk doing away with cult or observance – and even with law (Gesetz) – altogether (RV 203–4/175–6, 205/176).[39]

Indeed, for Cohen, Ezekiel's response may be understood as an intervention at a specific "difficult historical crossroads." By this, Cohen means that point at which Judaism either could have abandoned cult along with sacrifice, or could have gone down a path that embraces cult by showing or discovering that cult "stands in accordance with the fundamental idea of the fellow human being, that is, with the idea that the path to the individual goes by way of the fellow human being." This latter path would end up at the realization that the self's "absorption in God can only be founded in the connection" with the fellow human being (RV 203/175).[40] In particular, Cohen wants to argue that worship/service to

39 Lawrence Kaplan has also pointed out that Cohen seeks here to mount an argument against sacrifice that would not entail a critique of cult/observance. Kaplan, "Hermann Cohen's Theory of Sacrifice," 195.

For another reading of this section of *Religion of Reason* in view of the problem of Jewish law and observance, see Kohler, "Finding God's Purpose," 92–6. The general concept of "ceremonial law" is discussed in relation to Cohen by Aharon Shear-Yashuv, "Hermann Cohen über Chok und Mischpat."

Cohen's grappling with the status of law in view of the demise of sacrifice has been analyzed in view of his response to Wellhausen's innovations in biblical philology. See Kaplan, "Hermann Cohen's Theory of Sacrifice," 200–2; Zank, *The Idea of Atonement*, 109–10, 112–13. In this connection, Ran HaCohen has highlighted the influential history of Israelite religion envisioned by Wellhausen – who, as a polemical target of Cohen's account, represents the anti-Jewish pitfalls of the modern historiographic progress of Protestant biblical criticism – as framing Jewish legal traditions as latter-day obstacles to the continuity of "authentic, pre-legal, prophetic, Israelite religion." HaCohen, "'Gehörst du zu uns oder zu unsern Feinden?' (Josua 5,13). Die jüdische Auseinandersetzung mit der 'Höheren Bibelkritik,'" trans. Görge K. Hasselhoff, in *Die Entdeckung des Christentums in der Wissenschaft des Judentums*, ed. Görge K. Hasselhoff (Berlin: de Gruyter, 2010), 74–5.

40 Cohen frames his turn to Ezekiel in the context of the question of whether cult would remain in the absence of sacrifice. Having identified the possible unwanted side effect of the Jeremiah-Maimonides argument – that it might call the legitimacy of cult into question – he adds that, lest he be misinterpreted as pointing out "merely speculative consequences," "Ezekiel and his successors" indeed portray just this "historical problem" (RV 203/174).

God (*Gottesdienst*) was understood by the prophets not as being directed to a "pietistic" "solitude," but rather as serving the collectivity – the "assembly" (*Versammlung*) or "congregation" (*Gemeinde*) (RV 202/174). (This prepares the reader for what he will argue later: that atonement involves the collectivity and in particular worship in the congregation [cf. RV 228/196 and 230/197].) Thus, what is at stake in the task of properly interpreting Ezekiel's response to sacrifice, of showing why this "exception" in the history of prophecy is nevertheless not a break with the "fundamental idea of prophetism," with the "prophetic spirit" (RV 203/174), is the idea that the self-other correlation founds the path to God,[41] which is represented by the "social spirit" (*sozialer Geist*) or social ethics of the prophets in general.

Interwoven with Cohen's treatment of the prophetic response to sacrifice are methodological considerations: How did that response entail a legacy or ongoing "historical-religious meaning" for sacrifice (RV 204/175)? In order for the second response, that of critique/reform, not to have been a complete break with the first response of condemnation, it must have allowed for the discovery of a "new idea," that of the fellowman as founding the path to God. Moreover, the second response of critique/reform must be shown to have yielded this new idea as a "necessary" one – "necessary," in particular, "for the concept of the human being." Here, then, we have a question regarding the "necessity" of the discovery or emergence of an idea, a question that asks about the "historical necessity of ideas." Philosophers encounter such questions as part of their efforts to make philosophical sense of the transformations or successions of ideas. "The philosopher can permit the course of history to prescribe for him neither the posing of nor, certainly, the solution to his problems," nor "can he prescribe to history the course it should have taken" (RV 204/175).

Cohen had in the Introduction the *Religion of Reason* formulated his approach to this methodological dilemma as it informs his procedures in the book for grasping and explaining the concept of Judaism in its emergence from the "sources of Judaism": "History as such is not decisive about the essence and distinctiveness of the concept," in part because the concept "has perhaps not yet been brought about and accomplished in the course of history thus far." Thus, while the "literary sources" or "literary history" of Judaism may be seen as "the factor by virtue of which the *factum* is accomplished," those historical sources "never [have] the value of criterion – which can reside only in the concept, as problem

41 See note 32 above.

and method, as task and presupposition." For this reason, to approach a source with a view to understanding its significance for a concept is to "pro-ject" (*vor-werfen*) that concept ahead, or to anticipate it in the sense of "foreclosure" (*vorwegnehmen*), in one's treatment of the source.[42] We can understand along similar lines Cohen's concern in chapter 10 to establish the "necessity" of the emergence of the "new idea" of the self-other correlation founding the path to God, and to do so by demonstrating the coherence between what appears at first glance to be the "standard" prophetic view, and what appears to be merely an "exception."

The response associated with Ezekiel, that of reform or critique, in itself guarantees for Cohen the emergence of the fellowman, which is decisive for the relationship of human beings to God. It does so by saving cult/observance from the threat of abandonment that was contained in the Jeremiah-Maimonides condemnation of prophecy. Let us return now to Strauss's quotation in "Cohen and Maimonides" of what he apparently regards as the signature sentence from Cohen's exposition of the prophetic response to sacrifice in its role for the emergence of atonement and the fellowman: "And it may be asked whether such transformation [*Verwandlung*] is not the best kind of destruction/annihilation [*Vernichtung*]." Strauss introduces this sentence as representing a specific trait of Cohen's interpretative method, a method (along with that of allegoresis) that according to Strauss makes it possible to "criticize/critique the old without breaking with the old" ("ohne Bruch mit dem Alten Kritik am Alten zu üben," CM 401). It is a method of "reinterpretation" (*Umdeutung*) in the very sense of the "transformation" that Cohen evokes in his sentence – a sentence that Strauss has transformed into a dictum, and now imputes to Cohen as a dictum, by reproducing it out of context.

In Cohen's text, the "transformative," "reformist" "critique" that is Ezekiel's response to sacrifice is the "better" "destruction" of sacrifice in that it avoids the side effect of the Jeremiah-Maimonides response, even though, on the face of it, it is the latter that would appear to be more effectively – because more completely – "destructive." It turns out that what Strauss terms *Kritik ohne Bruch* (critique of the old without a total break with the old) is in this instance the more effective and productive

42 RV 3–4/3. I have discussed this point previously in "Ethical-Political Universality Out of the Sources of Judaism: Reading Hermann Cohen's 1888 Affidavit In and Out of Context," *New Directions in Jewish Philosophy*, ed. Aaron W. Hughes and Elliot R. Wolfson (Bloomington: Indiana University Press, 2009), 230. Robert Erlewine also underscores Cohen's non-historicist approach in *Religion of Reason* in *Monotheism and Tolerance: Recovering a Religion of Reason* (Bloomington: Indiana University Press, 2010), 144.

critique. Cohen's "philosopher" aims to interpret "historically," or to make proper interpretative use of historical sources, in just the same sense as does Strauss's ideal interpreter, whom Strauss characterizes as a "historian" by virtue of his "ambition" "to understand the author as he understands himself" (CM 400). Cohen discerns in the "reinterpretation" of the old text on the part of the new text a "transformation" that Strauss – in what emerges as a very compelling reading of Cohen – describes as follows:

> Diese Umdeutung ist ... eine "Verwandlung": eine Anverwandlung des Früheren, Mythischen an das Spätere. (CM 401)

A coherent translation into English of this sentence unfortunately must obscure the fact that Strauss here reinterprets Cohen's word "Verwandlung" (transformation) as "*An*verwandlung des Früheren ... *an* das Spätere," thus making the transformation into one that adapts what is earlier *to* what is later, that reorients the earlier toward the later. The best translation I can come up with is:

> This reinterpretation is ... a "transformation": a transformation that assimilates/approximates that which is earlier, mythical, to that which is later.

This is the sentence with which Strauss leads in the sentence he quotes from Cohen, "And it may be asked whether such transformation [*Verwandlung*] is not the best kind of destruction/annihilation [*Vernichtung*]." Given the way in which he embeds it into his own text, then, this latter sentence is meant to represent Cohen's interpretative method. In this sense Strauss's use of the sentence is in fact very much in line with Cohen's methodological reflections as they enter into the context of Cohen's original sentence: It is quite right to say that Cohen is concerned to portray the "later" "critique" as revealing the way in which the "earlier" "adapts itself," as it were, to the "later." By virtue of the *Kritik ohne Bruch* that Strauss argues is revealed – and also enabled – by Cohen's interpretative method, it is as though the earlier text or view strains forward to accommodate the later one. In Cohen's formulation, this is what underwrites the ability of the interpreter to understand the later development or "new idea" as a "necessary" one.

We saw a similar interpretative concern governing Strauss's argument about Plato and the medievals. Strauss calls for an interpretation of revelation in medieval thought that "grasps" "the *emergence* of this teaching out of Platonic philosophy ... in its possibility." He distinguishes such a procedure from one that would merely trace the roots or sources of medieval teachings back to Platonic philosophy (PG 63/76). (I have called this use of "possibility" by Strauss an emphatic one, akin to Heidegger's use of the term in *Being and Time.*) We saw the specific way in which Strauss realizes this desideratum or ambition, with an interpretation according to which the later is at the same time harbored by what is earlier, while also serving as a critique of what is earlier, and is thereby also the necessary way out of the aporia or paradox constituted by what is earlier.

In light of what here emerges as a methodological convergence between Strauss and Cohen, we can refer again to the passage in Kant's First Critique that served as the inspiration for Strauss's criterion for interpretative failure – to understand an author better than he understood himself – along with its reworkings by Gadamer and Heidegger. Kant offers a characterization of what happens when philosophers draw on past ideas in order to explicate new ones that, while it is not identical to the methods espoused or practiced by Strauss and Cohen, nevertheless brings out the fundamental assumptions that must be in place for those methods to be operative at all. Only if one's purpose vis-à-vis the old text is not to reconstitute it, or the author's intention, as a past artifact, but to make its meaning productive for thinking about philosophical questions that lead one to read the text in the first place, can one go on to ask, regarding such texts, about the "necessity" or "possibility" (in an "emphatic" sense) of the emergence of ideas within them.[43]

We have seen that in its original context Cohen's sentence conveys that the "transformation" of Jeremiah-Maimonides's condemnation of sacrifice into Ezekiel's "reform" is the "best destruction" of sacrifice in that it recognizes and rescues the significance of cult/observance for the idea of the human being in its path to God. Doubtless, Strauss must also have been attending to this argumentative function of the sentence in Cohen's exposition. In particular, Strauss would not have missed Cohen's seamless transition in chapter 10 from arguing for his method for

43 This sort of interpretative principle is, in fact, echoed by Strauss himself in his redeployment of the "And it may be asked ..." sentence in the 1965 preface to the English edition of *Spinoza's Critique of Religion.* Looking back across the distance of three decades at the role of Cohen in his own intellectual experiences in Germany and their lasting impact on his thinking, Strauss implies that "'idealizing' interpretation," which (as mentioned above) he defines as "the interpretation of a teaching in the light of its highest possibility regardless of whether or not that highest possibility was known to the originator" – as opposed to "historical interpretation proper, which understands a teaching as meant by its originator" – is the mark of a "genuine fidelity to a tradition" (which Strauss opposes to "literalist traditionalism"). Strauss, *Spinoza's Critique of Religion,* 24–5.

treating the difference between the two prophetic responses to sacrifice – in order thereby to accord legitimacy to the rescue of cult/observance/ceremonial law effected by the second response – to making an analogous observation regarding a further "controversy," one in which the controversy concerning sacrifice is itself "quintessentially" "included" (*inbegriffen*): This further controversy concerns whether in the idea found in Deuteronomy that the "law" in the sense of mitzvah/commandment is "in the heart" – whose continuation Cohen sees in Jeremiah's idea of a "new covenant" to be "written on the heart" – there is a conflict with the "original" law, with law as such.[44] Cohen suggests his interpretative principle regarding "transformation" as a means to resolve also this difficulty, and thus to rectify a problem of the biblical scholarship of his time, which, in its efforts to properly understand Deuteronomy "wavers unsteadily [*haltlos*, i.e., "without support," "unsubstantiated"] back and forth in the distribution of light and shadow." Such scholarship

> does not take into consideration how in actual/real history [*in der realen Geschichte*] light and shadow belong together; how it is the matter [*Materie*] of human things and relationships/circumstances [*Verhältnisse*] to which light and therefore also shadow attach. (RV 205/176)

Cohen calls this principle of the co-belonging of light and shadow in "real" (*real*) history an "emergency law" or "emergency decree" (*Notgesetz*) to which "all great reformers ... had to submit." He underscores that, while this is of course true of reformers in "real history," who we might most readily expect to have had a need for such emergency decrees, in this instance he means instead the reformers in "intellectual history," or in the "history of ideas," *Geistesgeschichte*, such as were the prophets in their role as discoverers and developers of the religion of reason.[45]

In this passage in *Religion of Reason* we see a consideration of law in Judaism that is formulated as a methodological question. The reformers of law or of religious ideas are methodologians and historians of

44 Deut. 30:11–14; Jer. 31:31–3. Cohen discusses this connection at RV 94–5/81–2, and builds upon it in the passage that is my focus here, at RV 205/176.

45 To elucidate the subsequent sentence, which doubtless also has much to offer to the project of understanding Cohen in conjunction with Strauss's interpretation of him in "Cohen and Maimonides" and *Philosophy and Law*, is not something I can undertake here:

> And the greatest and purest of all idealists, Plato, has even in his *Republic*, and not only in his *Laws*, paid tribute to this anomaly, to this fate [or fateful circumstance, *Verhängnis* – D.H.] in the realm of *Geist*. (RV 205/177)

ideas who, like Cohen himself in his study of Jewish religion, must come to decisions of how to weight, and articulate together, the "light and shadow" of their material. What emerges from the dual consideration of Strauss's treatment of Plato and the medievals and Cohen's treatment of the responses of "Jeremiah-Maimonides" and "Ezekiel" to sacrifice – as a representative example among others for how Judaism emerges through reworkings of key concepts and institutions in a succession of sources – is that just as for Strauss the relationship of philosophy and law becomes fully elaborated by virtue of the medieval response to the ancients, understood as a kind of interpretative method, so in Cohen "Ezekiel," in his transformative response to earlier tradition, is to be understood as an interpreter – an interpreter who employs just the same method that Cohen suggests we ought to employ in approaching the sources of Judaism. The sentence, "And it may be asked ..." makes up part of Cohen's demonstration that Ezekiel's way of combating sacrifice is apparently "weaker" than that of Jeremiah-Maimonides. But Strauss's quotation of that sole sentence, and his reframing of it as a dictum about interpretation in general, allows us to see that already in Cohen's text, Ezekiel's critique and reform is not only a *matter* for interpretation. Rather, Ezekiel's critique and reform is also itself a *method* of interpretation. This is why Cohen can continue his thought about transformation-as-destruction as follows:

> In that case [i.e., in case the best destruction/annihilation is in fact the one by way of transformation], with this retaining [of sacrifice], the old combat [against sacrifice] would remain in force. Such questions [i.e., questions concerning *our* activity as interpreters] are posed by the exceptional figure [*Sondergestalt*] of Ezekiel among the prophets. (RV 204/175)

Just as we struggle to understand whether and in what sense Ezekiel is an exception or particular case (*Sondergestalt*), and thus to interpret the continuity and development among the (prophetic and other) sources, Ezekiel himself is portrayed by Cohen as being "at a crossroads" regarding the continuity of the "prophetic spirit" when he mounts his own combat against sacrifice in the wake of the earlier combat. It is only from the point of view of "Ezekiel" that the interpretative question makes sense as to whether

> the old idea, if it is combated in a traditional/historic/age-old [*hergebracht*] institution, ... also thereby *ought to be* completely repressed and removed, or whether instead it becomes a problem that a new idea seeks to unite itself with the old institution. (RV 203/175, emphasis added)

The prophet's situation is here articulated as a dilemma of interpretation – a dilemma of interpretation of just the same sort as the one that Cohen in the *Religion of Reason* continually needs to solve in seeking to lay out the development of the Jewish "religion of reason." In the chapters on sacrifice and atonement in particular, we can understand this also as a question about the ongoing status and significance of law (Gesetz) in Judaism, vis-à-vis the emergence of ethical autonomy. In not condemning sacrifice, Ezekiel prepares a path toward the "new idea" of atonement; he accords to the new idea "greater value" than to the old, or, more particularly, decides or discovers that the "old idea only requires supplementing by the new one," so that the new idea, instead of simply opposing or replacing without remainder the old idea, can "deepen [the old idea] and bring it to completion" (RV 203–4/175).

Strauss was critical of the outcome of Cohen's "idealizing interpretation" of Judaism for its privileging of a certain kind of "progress" in Judaism that aimed, in Strauss's view, at establishing the individual as the locus of morality. What I have tried to show here is that we can also find in Strauss's texts evidence of a profound preoccupation with and appreciation of Cohen's philosophical interpretative method. I have traced the convergence between the method that Cohen is espousing and enacting in passages to which Strauss calls attention (of which I have been able to discuss only one in detail) and Strauss's own method in formulating the relationship between Plato and the medievals. Both approaches are oriented toward the problem of accounting for the ongoing importance of law/heteronomy (even) in view of the ascendance of ethical autonomy. Further, I have suggested that Strauss's presentation of Cohen's method as enabling a "critique without a break" (*Kritik ohne Bruch*) and an "approximative transformation of the earlier to the later" (*Anverwandlung des Früheren an das Spätere*) points to a kind of theoretical underpinning to Strauss's procedure in understanding the relationship between Plato and the medievals as one that involves *both* "critique" of the earlier by the later *and* a harboring, anticipation, or prophecy of the later by the earlier. This method emerges as essential both to the philosophico-political theology of *Philosophy and Law* and to the argumentative procedure of *Religion of Reason*.

Law (*Recht*) between Heteronomy and Autonomy

I am suggesting, then, that philosophico-political theology is itself something methodological. It can only be a thesis about the relationships between and among philosophical, political, and theological propositions if it also comprises a method for positing or making visible the analogies or congruences that constitute those relationships. It is by such a method or hermeneutic that Cohen bridges the divide questioned by Strauss between an autonomous ethics of the individual and a heteronomous, divinely instituted law.

While Strauss's and Cohen's argumentative aims differ, both of them are concerned to understand the relationship between "earlier" (Plato/biblical sacrifice) and "later" (the medievals/atonement in Judaism) as a way of accounting for and legitimating the ongoing importance of heteronomous law, even in view of the ascendance of ethical autonomy. This ascendance was, of course, explicitly embraced by Cohen, while Strauss harbored great reservations about it. We must recall, too (as discussed in the previous chapter), that "autonomy" for Cohen means not a force that inheres in the origin of a pre-constituted self, but denotes the futurity of Gesetz and of Allheit as the ethical task to which law as Recht is oriented.

Indeed, this dimension of Recht is also present in Cohen's account of the transformation from sacrifice to atonement, as he makes clear that atonement retains a "legality" or law-like character as it emerges from the legislation of sacrifice. For example, Cohen on more than one occasion endorses Maimonides's interpretation that the substitution for the sacrifice legislation is the Sabbath – which Cohen conceives as essentially a matter of law in the sense of Recht and of justice (*Gerechtigkeit*) – and the institution of Recht/laws in general.[46] That the idea of atonement invokes a dimension of public law/Recht – that is, that it is a continuation of the public and law-like character of sacrifice – is further underscored in Cohen's detailed depiction. As discussed above, this is in part evident in Cohen's casting of atonement as a "juridical proceeding" (*Rechtsverfahren*) – in line with the idea that *teshuvah* is the sinful individual's "turning" in a "concrete" sense that is akin to what happens in the criminal courtroom once the judge has delivered the sentence: While the juridical proceeding is not itself a mechanism that leads to justice, the sentence or punishment delivers to the guilty party (the "criminal") the "support" and "consolation" that enables them to acknowledge their own guilt, which is the means to their "liberation from this almost unbearable burden." Confession and taking on of the sin is at the same time the "beginning" of a process of punishment in the juridical sense, while

46 "Liebe und Gerechtigkeit," JS3: 79–80; RV 202/173, 381/328, 413/355. I discuss this view of Maimonides, along with Cohen's use of it, in greater detail in the next chapter. See also the detailed discussion in George Y. Kohler, *Reading Maimonides' Philosophy in 19th Century Germany: The Guide to Religious Reform* (Dordrecht: Springer, 2012), chap. 7, "The Law," 235–7; and "Finding God's Purpose," 94–5.

the Yom Kippur service (worship, liturgy) takes shape as a public institution that is allied with the purpose of a juridical proceeding.[47]

The proceeding of teshuvah is thus envisioned by Cohen also as a bridging of the realm of individual ethical autonomy and the *rechtlich*, communal-political realm. (We saw in both this chapter and the previous one that even as Strauss is continually probing whether the heteronomy of law/Gesetz can be compatible with the idea that the self as an ethical agent is autonomous, that public-political realm is for him not a domain of what Cohen calls Recht, but rather a facet of heteronomous divine law and the "revealed" requirement to prophesy-philosophize, which also comprises the "political" task of working toward the "good life" in common.) Indeed teshuvah itself establishes a need for community. Cohen underscores that the resulting political entity, the "congregation," in line with the Hebrew term for it (*qahal* or *qehila*) denotes a union or unification (*Vereinigung*), as distinct from the principle inhering in the state, which is that of leadership and sovereignty.[48] As mentioned above, this model of atonement closely resembles Cohen's discussion of punishment in the *Ethik*, and also stands as an exemplar of what he envisions to be an ethics that emerges from law/Recht (the topic of chapter 1 above).

Recapping the sequence of the inquiry of this book thus far: In chapter 1, I traced Cohen's understanding in his *Ethik* of the idea of Recht (law) that can generate ethics. In chapter 2, I discerned in the *Ethik* a further strand, a question of whether there is a sense of Gesetz – what Strauss calls "the nomos idea," or an idea of heteronomy – and found in Cohen's elaborations on the auto-nomy of the self a sense of law/Gesetz as futural, denoting Allheit or universality as the task of law/Recht. At the same time, these elaborations opened up the question of whether Cohen's philosophy of ethics and law calls for a concept of law/legality/Gesetz in a Judaic sense that he does not supply in the *Ethik*. I then turned, in the present chapter, to Cohen's theory of Jewish religion. Again with the help of Strauss's interpretative interventions, I found Cohen to be developing a method of political-philosophico-theology that he applies to the relationship between sacrifice and atonement in a way that yields a further model for the idea that ethical life emerges in conjunction with legal/*rechtlich* institutions. The link between the autonomy of the self and the heteronomy of divine law that I first asked about with respect to

47 RV 227–9/194–5, 234/200. See also Cohen's discussion of atonement in conjunction with the concept of retribution, which, like sacrifice, is also a source of the emergence of law (Recht), in "Liebe und Gerechtigkeit," JS3: 84–6.

48 RV 230/197. The Hebrew term is not mentioned by Cohen, but is implied by his explanation.

Cohen's principal work on ethics and philosophy of law (the *Ethik*) thus appears to have been filled out further by attending to Cohen's philosophy of Jewish religion.

It is now clear where one might position Cohen on the axis posited by Kellner between Leibowitz and Schwarzschild: Cohen would affirm that thinking about law is an essential part of thinking about ethics and political life. But this still leaves open the question posed at the close of chapter 2: What resources, if any, does Cohen supply, as part of his theory of (Jewish) religion, toward a theory of law?

Chapter Four

Isolation and Universalism: Cohen's New Messianic Politics of Jewish Law

We pick up now the second question that we posed at the close of chapter 2: If Cohen's ethico-legal theory, as articulated in his *Ethik*, seems to call for a theorizing of law that is informed by Judaism, do we find such a theorizing in Cohen's philosophy of Judaism? What if anything do Cohen's works on Judaism have to offer by way of an account of law and politics in Judaism that might serve to fill out the call for a Jewish-informed understanding of legality that emerges in the *Ethik*? My answer to this question will be twofold. The first step, undertaken in the present chapter, will be to look closely at the only sustained study we have by Cohen of the nature and role of law in Judaism: chapter 16 of *Religion of Reason*. We will see that Cohen's rather idiosyncratic defense of law in Judaism entails a new understanding of the role of politics in Judaism and of the political significance of Judaism. The second step – undertaken in chapter 6 – will be to look at Cohen's treatments of love-of-neighbor, an idea that, I will show, is both a general concept of law in the sense of Recht, and a core concept of Cohen's philosophy of Judaism.

In examining chapter 16 of the *Religion of Reason*, I shall also occasionally draw on another key text by Cohen that contains analyses that are pertinent to our topic – his highly critical review from 1899 of Moritz Lazarus's book *The Ethics of Judaism* (*Die Ethik des Judentums*).[1] Although this review dates from much earlier than the writing of *Religion of Reason*, there are significant continuities between the questions pursued, and

1 "Das Problem der jüdischen Sittenlehre. Eine Kritik von Lazarus' Ethik des Judentums," in JS3 (hereafter cited in text as PJS), a review of Moritz Lazarus, *Die Ethik des Judentums*, vol. 1 (Frankfurt am Main: Kauffmann, 1898); translated by Henrietta Szold as *The Ethics of Judaism*, part 1 (Philadelphia: Jewish Publication Society, 1900).

views expressed in the two texts[2] – just as in general the "Jewish writings" and the two late *Religion* books represent a sustained, continuous unfolding of Cohen's *jüdische Religionsphilosophie* (Jewish philosophy of religion/philosophy of Jewish religion).

Defending Jewish Law's Compatibility with Morality: Autonomy as Duty

Cohen's treatment of law in chapter 16 can in part be read as an extension of Cohen's discussion of prophetic Judaism's turn away from sacrifice (discussed in the last chapter). We saw that Cohen prefers Ezekiel's way of overcoming sacrifice over that of Jeremiah as viewed through Maimonides's interpretation because it does not abandon cult/observance altogether. Here again, Strauss's early reading of Cohen helps put certain points in relief. On one level, Strauss's sometime complaint that Cohen ethicizes Jewish religion – his pronouncement (which I discussed in chapter 2) that "the *limit* of [Cohen's] understanding is given in the fact that for the idea of *law* [*Gesetz*] he substitutes that of *morality* [*Sittlichkeit*]" (CM 429)[3] – seems to be borne out by large

2 Hans Liebeschütz makes a strong general case for seeing the Lazarus review as a key early text in which Cohen raises questions that become the core impetus for the later systematic-philosophical treatments of Jewish religion in the two *Religion* books, investigations he began in his 1913/14 lectures at the Lehranstalt. He also points to Cohen's past affiliation with Lazarus's and Steinthal's *Zeitschrift für Völkerpsychologie und Sprachwissenschaft*, and his having turned away from sharing their faith in "the fundamental significance of psychology for the progress of philosophical thinking," as well as earlier public disagreements with Lazarus in connection with the 1880 Berlin Antisemitism Dispute, as relevant background to Cohen's critique. Liebeschütz, "Hermann Cohen: Seine Philosophie und die Zeitgeschichte," in *Von Georg Simmel zu Franz Rosenzweig. Studien zum Jüdischen Denken im deutschen Kulturbereich* (Tübingen: Mohr Siebeck, 1970), 47, 44–5. For a general introduction to Lazarus's book and a sympathetic presentation of Cohen's criticisms, see Ingrid Belke, introduction to *Moritz Lazarus und Heymann Steinthal: Die Begründer der Völkerpsychologie in ihren Briefen* (Tübingen: Mohr Siebeck, 1971), LXXIII–LXXX. For a sympathetic presentation of Lazarus's book, and a brief defense against Cohen's criticisms, see David Baumgardt, "The Ethics of Lazarus and Steinthal," in *Leo Baeck Institute Year Book* 2 (1957), 210ff. Franz Rosenzweig found in Cohen's review of Lazarus an "advance sketch" by Cohen of the path Cohen would take in his *jüdische Religionsphilosophie* and noted in particular that *Religion* chapter 16 on "Gesetz" continues an inquiry begun in the Lazarus review. Franz Rosenzweig, "Einleitung," JS 1: XXXVII and LI.

3 For the purposes of the present discussion, I am leaving aside my finding in chapter 2 that Strauss's complaint about ethics taking the place of politics/law in Cohen is an ambivalent one, given that Strauss also makes a forceful argument for Cohen as a political thinker, for example, in the "fundamental orientation" of his ethics "to jurisprudence."

portions of *Religion* chapter 16. Thus, from the outset of the chapter, Cohen's determination that law (Gesetz) in Judaism seeks to be understood as the "basic law of the moral world" (RV 393/338) announces that the task of the chapter will be to examine the extent to which, if at all, Jewish law can be seen as relevant to morality or ethics. Indeed, Cohen makes clear that in this, his inquiry continues one of the major overall demonstrations that the book has been pursuing all along: Recalling his earlier discussions of the "overcoming" of sacrifice – which he calls "the first form of law" – and its replacement by the institution of atonement (which we looked at in the previous chapter), he underscores that law remains a "necessary means" of the God–man correlation that is effected by the human accomplishment of atonement (RV 394/339). This sort of insistence that law in Judaism is necessary to the aims of morality, rather than being either incidental to those aims, or even a hindrance to their accomplishment, is one of the chapter's core themes.[4] In that sense, Cohen continues to wrestle with the dilemma we first encountered in the *Ethik* between a heteronomous law (Gesetz) and the autonomy of the ethical subject, a dilemma that Cohen there seeks to overcome with his notion of Gesetz (discussed in chapter 2) as futural, other than itself, and deriving from Allheit. Accordingly, Cohen opens chapter 16 by invoking an earlier demonstration, in which

> We have already considered that God's law does not contradict the autonomy of the moral will. (RV 395/339)

This refers to the argument in the previous chapter (chapter 15 on "Immortality and Resurrection") that divine commandment is consistent with – and indeed must properly be understood as – "duty," as humanity's "moral task" (RV 376–7/323–4) and thus, implicitly, as consistent with moral comportment understood along Kantian lines. Let us look more closely, then, at that argument before turning our attention to how Cohen builds on it in the "Law" chapter.

In support of the equivalence he has proposed between divine command and duty, Cohen cites several classic biblical and rabbinic formulations and interprets them so as to make apparent their value for

4 George Y. Kohler has underscored this aspect of the "Law" chapter and finds in Cohen's "insistence on the inextricable interwovenness of ritual and moral *mitsvot*" "an original defense of halakhah both against Jewish reform and against Christian, or even against the Kantian critique of Jewish legalism." See "Against the Heteronomy of Halakhah: Hermann Cohen's Implicit Rejection of Kant's Critique of Judaism," *Dine Israel* 32 (2018): 207*–8*.

ethical theory. For example, the people's response to God that "We will do and we will hear" (Exodus 24:7) and the Talmud's interpretation of that response according to which "the order of the words" indicates that the doing comes first, and "only thereupon the hearing and understanding" does not, for Cohen, indicate a situation of heteronomy.[5] Rather, it means that the "moral task" of taking up God's command, in not being *subsequent* to "knowing" God, makes moral action from the beginning a part of both knowing and loving God.[6]

Cohen gives a similar interpretation of the Talmudic pronouncement "Better is the one who acts as one who is commanded [*als Befohlener*] than the one who is not commanded and acts."[7] Only at first glance can it seem as though in this formulation the action is *entselbstet*, deprived of its very "self" – that is, deprived of the very status of being an action[8] – "by the command" ("durch den Befehl"). Instead, Cohen suggests a more qualified reading: It is only the "final origin" of the action that is "posited" as being "in God's command."

This interpretation expresses an argument against the notion that egotism is an impetus of action, an argument that is fully in line with the anti-individualism and anti-psychologism that we saw in the *Ethik*. Additionally, Cohen draws out of this Talmudic adage the classic Kantian principle that "reward" is irrelevant to the morality of an action (RV 377/324).

Cohen's procedure, then, in arguing that the fact that an action is "commanded" does not detract from its morality but is instead a part of, or constitutive of its morality, is to marshall Jewish sources in support of what he presents as its corollary: that the notion of "reward," along with that of happiness, is morally spurious and even "dangerous,"

5 Cohen's interpretation of the relevant passage in Tractate bShabbat 88a thus diverges from that of its most famous latter-day philosophical interpreter, Emmanuel Levinas, e.g., in "La tentation de tentation," in *Quatre lectures talmudiques* (Paris: Minuit, 1968); translated by Annette Aronowicz as "The Temptation of Temptation," in *Nine Talmudic Readings* (Bloomington: Indiana University Press, 1990).

On this general argument in *Religion of Reason* and related works, see Kenneth Seeskin, *Autonomy in Jewish Philosophy* (Cambridge: Cambridge University Press, 2001), chap. 6.

6 Cf. "Innere Beziehungen der Kantischen Philosophie zum Judentum," in JS1: 303, and in *Werke* 15. (Page references to the JS edition are included in the *Werke* edition.) We will return below to the equivalence between moral action and knowing God in connection with Cohen's reading of Maimonides.

7 "Besser der, der als ein Befohlener handelte, als der, der nicht befohlen ist und handelt." Tractate bBava Kamma 38a, Tractate bKiddushin 31a, at RV 377/324.

8 Cf. Simon Kaplan's non-literal translation of this phrase: "The act loses its autonomy."

because "eudaemonistic." That for Cohen the presence of this insight within the Talmudic corpus represents a true convergence with Kant's own discoveries in moral theory comes across most clearly in his lecture in 1910 at the Lehranstalt für die Wissenschaft des Judentums entitled "Innere Beziehungen der Kantischen Philosophie zum Judentum" ("Inner Affinities of Kant's Philosophy with Judaism").[9] The "surprising" convergence that Cohen presents there between Kant's philosophy and Judaism lies in the rejection of eudaemonism, of happiness as a goal of, or factor in ethics. As an alternative to understanding happiness as that which psychologically motivates the ethical will, Kant introduces the "universal law" (*allgemeines Gesetz*) as the objective "principle of will."[10] Cohen next cites Kant's remark in the *Critique of Practical Reason* that this role of the universal law means that "we must not be 'volunteers of morality,'"[11] and notes that this has striking parallels with Jewish philosophy and with the Talmud:

> It is as if Kant had heard this expression from a Jewish philosopher and in the Talmud itself.

---

9 This lecture, along with the closely related tribute to Kant on the 100th anniversary of his death in 1904 that Cohen published in the Jewish weekly *Allgemeine Zeitung des Judentums*, are noteworthy occasions on which Cohen explicitly addresses, and attempts somewhat to explain to a Jewish audience or readership Kant's flawed understanding of Judaism. See "Innere Beziehungen der Kantischen Philosophie zum Judentum," JS1: 284–7, and "Immanuel Kant. Zu seinem hundertjährigen Todestage (12. Februar 1904)," *Allgemeine Zeitung des Judentums* (12 February 1904), 76–7. I discuss both these essays in "Some Remarks on Love and Law in Hermann Cohen's Ethics of the Neighbor," in "The Ethics of the Neighbor," ed. Dana Hollander, special issue, *Journal for Textual Reasoning* 4, no. 1 (November 2005), http://jtr.shanti.virginia.edu.

10 Here, as he does in the *Ethik* (which appeared in the same year as this lecture), Cohen equates this principle of moral will with "autonomy" as "self-legislation." (See my discussion in chapter 2.) "Innere Beziehungen," JS1: 292.

11 "Innere Beziehungen," JS1: 292, quoting from a passage in the *Critique of Practical Reason* in which Kant cautions that those who in acting morally think of themselves as "volunteers" (*Volontäre*), rather than as doing their duty, are engaged in the self-flattery of imagining themselves the "sovereign" of the "kingdom of morals," rather than as its subjects, and that this is itself a "defection in spirit" from the "holy law." Immanuel Kant, *Kritik der praktischen Vernunft*, AA 5:79; translated and edited by Mary J. Gregor as *Critique of Practical Reason*, in *Practical Philosophy* (Cambridge: Cambridge University Press, 1996), which includes the AA pagination. Cohen also refers to Kant's principle that "the human being is not a volunteer of the moral law" at RV 401/345; and he similarly links this principle to the "it is better to act as under a commandment" principle in "Über den ästhetischen Wert unserer religiösen Bildung," JS1: 231. See the discussion in Kohler, "Against the Heteronomy of Halakhah," 197*–200*.

and then substantiates this claim with the line from Tractate bKiddushin 31a that we cited above, but which in this instance Cohen translates somewhat differently:

> Greater is the one who acts under the commandment [*Gebot*] than the one without commandment.[12]

In the closely related 1904 tribute to Kant on the 100th anniversary of his death published six years earlier in a Jewish weekly,[13] Cohen articulates this line of thinking by linking the fact that Kant's categorical imperative is "called a commandment [*Gebot*]" to the foundational role of law/Gesetz in Kant's understanding of morality (*Sittlichkeit*): "Law founds the concept of the moral human being.... [The categorical imperative] is called a commandment [*Gebot*] because this commandment brings the law – the law with which the concept of the human being stands and falls."[14]

In *Religion* chapter 15, Cohen continues his demonstration of the compatibility between being under God's command and anti-eudaemonistic ethics by citing two additional formulations from Mishnah Pirkei Avot: (1) the exhortation "Be not like servants that minister to the master on the condition of receiving a reward";[15] and (2) "The reward of duty is

---

12 "Größer der unter dem Gebot handelt als der ohne Gebot." "Innere Beziehungen," JS1: 292. See my longer discussion in "Some Remarks on Love and Law." This passage is also discussed in conjunction with Cohen's treatment of the legality problematic in the *Ethik* by Myriam Bienenstock, "Hermann Cohen über Freiheit und Selbstbestimmung," in *Religious Apologetics – Philosophical Argumentation*, ed. Yossef Schwartz and Volkhard Krech (Tübingen: Mohr Siebeck, 2004), 525–6.

Cohen takes care to add the caveat that while in Judaism it is the one God that is the "eternal origin" of the moral law, for Kant the moral law must continually generate the universal law anew for itself (JS1: 292). However, as is underscored by Bienenstock, Cohen also goes on to note the importance of God for Kant's understanding of the moral law (JS1: 293).

A further translation variation can be found in Cohen's posthumously published lecture, "Über den ästhetischen Wert unserer religiösen Bildung": "Besser, wer gebotenerweise handelt, als wer ohne Gebot handelt," JS1: 231.

13 See note 9 above.

14 Cohen, "Immanuel Kant," 76–7. I discuss the significance of this meaning of Gesetz in Kant for Cohen's ethical theory in chapter 2 above. For Kant's use of the term *Gebot* in his elaboration of the categorical imperative, see Immanuel Kant, *Grundlegung zur Metaphysik der Sitten*, e.g., at AA4: 413, 416; translated and edited by Mary Gregor as *Groundwork of the Metaphysics of Morals* (Cambridge: Cambridge University Press, 1997), which includes the AA pagination.

15 Mishnah Pirkei Avot 1:3, cited in RV 376/323. Translations from the Mishnah draw on Philip Blackman, ed., *Mishnayoth*, 2nd rev. ed., vol. 4, *Order Nezikin* (New York: Judaica Press, 1963), with adjustments where necessary.

duty."[16] This allows Cohen to spell out a further corollary to the principle that reward or happiness have no bearing on the morality of an action: that reward is in fact "identical" to duty (RV 374/321). What he is arguing for, he adds, is "the autarchy of duty" (RV 377/324). The very term for "law" or "command" in Judaism, *mitzvah,* has as its other meaning "duty," *Pflicht.* Building on his notion that the relationship between God and human being is one of "correlation," Cohen portrays the two correlates as being characterized by "law" from God's side and as "duty" from the human side. This, then, is a further way of accounting for the convergence or equivalence between autonomy and commandedness: "God commands man, and man in his free will takes upon himself the 'yoke of the law.'" The "yoke of the law" is at the same time the yoke of the Kingdom of Ends, and "the law is at the same time duty, just as duty is law" (RV 401/345).[17]

For Cohen, then, "God's command" must be viewed as equivalent to the "fundamental law of autonomy." The difference between the two is "methodological," which is to say that "God's command" is the religious analogue to what autonomy is in the realm of ethics. Where, in the realm of ethics, the morality of an action can be described from the point of view of "pure will," which is by definition free of "affect" (Cohen's version of the anti-eudaemonistic principle that he finds in Kant),[18] the "analogous" accomplishment in the realm of religion would be to understand the moral law *as* "God's command." This analogy is what Cohen tries to draw out of the biblical and rabbinic formulations he has cited, such that to "submit" to duty emerges as the very definition of autonomy (RV 377/324). When Cohen recalls, close to the beginning of chapter 16, that "the law of God does not contradict the autonomy of the moral will" (RV 395/339), it is this demonstration in the previous chapter that he is invoking.

16 Mishnah Pirke Avot 4:2, quoted at RV 376. Cohen here translates *mitzvah,* which in translations of this saying is sometimes rendered as "good deed," as *Pflicht,* "duty." (This is in line with his explanation of the word *mitzvah* as having two meanings, "Gesetz" [law] and "Pflicht" [duty] [RV 401/345].) See also the discussion of reward and commandment at RV 374; the parallel passage in "Liebe und Gerechtigkeit," JS3: 85; and the unpublished note, "Blatt 89" in Cohen, *Reflexionen und Notizen,* ed. Hartwig Wiedebach, *Supplementa* vol. 1, ed. H. Holzhey and H. Wiedebach (Hildesheim: Olms, 2003), 78.

17 Here too, Cohen invokes Kant's formulation that "the human being is not a volunteer of the moral law" in order to show the equivalence between being subject to God's command and performing one's duty (RV 401/245).

18 See, for example, ErW 99, 101, 165ff.

A Difference among the Laws

Cohen now links the equivalence between divine law and human autonomy to traditional Jewish discourses about law. He casts his understanding of the relationship of law and ethics in Judaism as continuous with the traditional rabbinic debate about the "reasons for the commandments" (*ta'amei ha-mitzvot*), particularly as it is pursued by the medieval thinkers.[19] These inquiries into the "reasons for the commandments" yield criteria for the "difference" (to use Cohen's oft-repeated term) among the divine commandments. Already in "Inner Affinities," Cohen refers to the "difference" in "ancient Judaism" "between the moral and the ritual legislation." Again rendering a rabbinic topos or idea in Kantian terms, he says that this difference between moral and ritual laws "is thought in ancient Judaism similarly to the *difference between pure and applied doctrine of morals* [zwischen reiner und angewandter Sittenlehre]."[20]

The best-known distinction in the historic tradition of exploring "reasons for the commandments" is that between "statutes" (*ḥuqqim*; *Satzungen*) and "ordinances" (*mishpatim*; *Rechte*). This rabbinic distinction is established in a Talmudic passage that explicates the meaning of Leviticus 18:4 as follows:

> Our Rabbis taught: "My ordinances [*mishpatai*] you shall do ..." [Lev. 18:4], i.e., such commandments which, if they were not written [in Scripture], they should by right have been written and these are they: [the laws concerning] idolatry [star-worship, *avodat kokhavim*], [sexual] immorality [*gilui arayot*] and bloodshed, robbery and blasphemy [*birkat ha-shem*]. And "... My statutes [*ḥuqqotai*] you shall keep" [Lev. 18:4, cont'd], i.e., such commandments to which Satan objects, they are [those relating to] the eating of pork, the

---

19 For an explanation and a brief history, see *Encyclopaedia Judaica,* 2nd ed. (2007), s.v. "Commandments, Reasons for." For a comprehensive study, see Isaac Heinemann, *The Reasons for the Commandments in Jewish Thought: From the Bible to the Renaissance* (1949–56), trans. Leonard Levin (Boston: Academic Studies Press, 2008).

We find a parallel treatment of this topic to the one in *Religion* chapter 16 in Cohen's major study of Maimonides, "Charakteristik der Ethik Maimunis" (1908). CEM 232/27, 235ff./35ff.

The discussion of *ta'amei ha-mitzvot* in *Religion* chapter 16 is the focus of Aharon Shear-Yashuv, "Hermann Cohen über Chok und Mischpat," in *"Religion der Vernunft aus den Quellen des Judentums": Tradition und Ursprungsdenken in Hermann Cohens Spätwerk, Internationale Konferenz in Zürich 1998 ["Religion of Reason Out of the Sources of Judaism": Tradition and the Concept of Origin in Hermann Cohen's Later Work],* ed. H. Holzhey, G. Motzkin, and H. Wiedebach (Hildesheim: Olms, 2000), 387ff. Shear-Yashuv notes omissions in Cohen's presentation of Maimonides on this topic at 397–8.

20 "Innere Beziehungen," JS1: 289.

> putting on of *sha'atnez* [fabrics of mixed linen and wool], the *ḥalitsah* [performed] by a sister-in-law [ritual by which a widow could become exempt from the duty to marry her brother-in-law, cf. Deut. 25:5ff.], the purification of a "leper," and the he-goat-to-be-sent-away [the scapegoat, see Lev. 16:7–10]. And perhaps you might think these are vain things, therefore Scripture says: "... I am the Lord" [Lev. 18:4, conclusion], i.e., I, the Lord have made it a statute and you have no right to criticize it. (Tractate bYoma 67b)[21]

In the words of Lenn E. Goodman, the operative distinction here is between the *ḥuqqim* as those "commandments that would have been unknown without revelation" and the *mishpatim* as "those we should have been obliged to invent had they not been revealed." In medieval Jewish thought, this distinction came to be taken to mean that the *mishpatim* could be discovered by reason alone, while the *ḥuqqim* could not have been anticipated by, and cannot even be understood on the basis of reason alone.[22] The latter category is often associated – including by Cohen – with religious ritual or "cult" and has sometimes been termed "ceremonial law" (a term that is likewise used by Cohen). As Cohen notes, the latter term, as an equivalent to the biblical-Talmudic category of *ḥuqqim*, arises in the early-fifteenth-century writings of Simeon Duran and Josef Albo.[23] It was also used notably by Moses Mendelssohn in his theory of Judaism in *Jerusalem*; in choosing this term, he followed Spinoza's account of Judaism and Jewish law in his *Theological-Political Treatise.* There, the term "ceremonies" (*ceremoniae*) denotes those

---

21 Quoted from the Soncino translation (ed. I. Epstein), incorporating biblical quotations from the New Revised Standard Version. Discussed by Shear-Yashuv, "Hermann Cohen über Chok und Mischpat," 387. Daniel Krochmalnik comments that the *mishpatim* are here justified as "natural law," whereas the justification given for the *ḥuqqim* is positivist. Krochmalnik, "Der Streit um das jüdische Naturrecht. Maimonides, Spinoza, Mendelssohn und Cohen" (2000) in *Interesse am Judentum. Die Franz-Delitzsch-Vorlesungen, 1989–2008*, ed. Jacobus Cornelis de Vos and Folker Siegert (Berlin: Lit Verlag, 2008), 246–7.

22 L.E. Goodman, "Rational Law/Ritual Law," in Daniel H. Franked., *A People Apart: Chosenness and Ritual in Jewish Philosophical Thought* (Albany: State University of New York Press, 1993), 109, cf. 139–41. David Novak comments that "for most of the medieval theologians, both rationalist and nonrationalist, the unintelligibility of the *ḥuqqim* is only apparent. Inherently they are *ratio per se*, even though they are not *ratio quoad nos*, i.e., immediately intelligible to us." Novak, "The Election of Israel: Outline of a Philosophical Analysis," in Frank, ed., *A People Apart*, 45n89.

23 RV 415/356. Cf. Kaufmann Kohler, "Ceremonies and the Ceremonial Law," in *The Jewish Encyclopedia*, vol. 3 (1902), and Shear-Yashuv, "Hermann Cohen über Chok und Mischpat," 390–1n27. Shear-Yashuv briefly points out the important polemical uses of this term, 390–1.

revealed laws that were commanded only to the Jews, for their temporal and physical well-being (as opposed to "divine law," which is universal and based on the true knowledge and love of God).[24] While Cohen does not comment on Spinoza in the *Religion* chapter on "Law," in his 1915 landmark essay on Spinoza, he criticizes Spinoza for his failure to grasp "ceremonies" such as the Sabbath in their social-ethical significance.[25]

Cohen begins from Maimonides's definition of this "difference within the concept of law," which he discusses along with brief mentions of the understandings of Saadya Gaon, Ibn Daud, Bahya ibn Pakuda, and Yehuda Halevi (RV 395/339–40; 408–15/351–6). For Maimonides, who, as "Judaism's rationalist" is committed to applying the "critique of rationalism" to the laws and to show the share of reason in those laws (RV 410/352), the "statutes" (*ḥuqqim*) concern the "ritual sphere" – that is, "exclusively or primarily the inner sphere of worship/service to God [*Gottesdienst*]" – while the "ordinances" (*mishpatim*) concern the "purely moral and political sphere," that is, "the moral laws for human life under law [*Recht*] and the state" (RV 395/339–40; cf. 408–9/351). However, Cohen also states that it is the Talmud itself that undertakes the "differentiation" in question, and that Maimonides builds on that Talmudic distinction (RV 408–9/351). This difference (*Unterschied*) within or among the laws/commandments is the same one, Cohen explains, as the one at the root of the historical rejection of sacrifice; indeed, Cohen notes that within the "statutes" category, the sacrifices are a prominent example.

For Cohen, that there is a perceived "difference" within or among the laws indicates the general tendency in the historical development of cult and law toward a more stringent monotheism and a more developed ethical meaning of the law, with a concurrent diminishing of the laws' merely "religious" significance (RV 395–7/339–41). He thus underscores that

24 See Alexander Altmann's "Commentary," in Moses Mendelssohn, *Jerusalem, Or on Religious Power and Judaism*, trans. Allan Arkush (Waltham, MA: Brandeis University Press, 1983), 220–1; Altmann's introduction to the German edition of that work in *Gesammelte Schriften. Jubiläumsausgabe* vol. 8: *Schriften zum Judentum II*, ed. Alexander Altmann (Stuttgart/Bad Cannstatt: Frommann-Holzboog, 1983), lii–liii; and chaps. 4 and 5 of Baruch Spinoza, *Theological-Political Treatise*, 2nd ed., trans. Samuel Shirley (Indianapolis: Hackett, 2001). Cf. *Spinoza's Theologico-Political Treatise*, trans. and ed. Martin D. Yaffe (Newburyport, MA: Focus Publishing, 2004).

25 Hermann Cohen, "Spinoza über Staat und Religion, Judentum und Christentum" (1915), JS3: 340. Also in *Werke* 16. Translated by Robert S. Schine as *Spinoza on State and Religion, Judaism and Christianity* (Jerusalem: Shalem Press, 2014), which includes the JS pagination. See my essay, "'But Does He Really Not Remember?' Cohen's Revaluing of the Spinozan Politicization of Judaism," in *G.W.F. Hegel und Hermann Cohen. Wege zur Versöhnung. Festschrift Myriam Bienenstock*, ed. Norbert Waszek (Freiburg: Alber, 2018).

the distinction, *Unterschied*, among the laws is not a *Differenz*, meaning that it does not bring any kind of "internal contradiction" into the "unity of the laws":

> Of course there is a distinction among the laws; this is not to deny such a distinction. But this distinction is not a difference [*Differenz*] of the sort which would introduce an internal contradiction into the unity of the laws. (RV 401/345)

Similarly, although the Talmud doubtless made a "distinction" between the purely moral commandments and the "religious commandments in the narrower sense," this was by no means a "separation" (*Trennung*) (RV 408/351). Indeed, for Cohen, the moral laws have precedence over the "religious commandments," such that even "what is not in itself moral law is at least thought of and expressly characterized as a means to the promotion of, and education in, the moral law" (RV 401/345). Sometimes, it is the "collision" between cult and the "pure moral laws" that ultimately yields to further moral and social-political progress (RV 396/340–1). Accordingly, much of Cohen's discussion is aimed at showcasing commandments with a social-ethical purpose, including those whose significance he deems to be social-ethical, even though they appear to have solely ritual significance.[26]

This priority of moral laws over "religious" ones is evident as well in Cohen's discussion of atonement and Yom Kippur. Here he maps the distinction between *ḥuqqim* and *mishpatim* onto the distinction between solely "religious" sins, that is, sins against God, and "purely moral" sins against other human beings (RV 405/348). Reconciliation between persons is required before atoning before God can take place.[27] In his early essay on "the idea of atonement," "Die Versöhnungsidee," Cohen praises the Yom Kippur laws for privileging the individual's sinfulness and its atonement, and "that we do not find [in the scope of the sin that is to be acknowledged] even a single slight hint regarding the transgression of a ceremonial law." Even the sin of desecration of the divine name, as the counterpart of the virtue of sanctifying the divine name,

26 RV 405–6/348–9, 407–8/350–1.

27 RV 257/220, referring to bYoma 85b. The point is recalled by Cohen at 405 and 408, and is also mentioned by him in his early essay, "Die Versöhnungsidee," JS1: 134. See the discussion by Steven Schwarzschild in "The Title of Hermann Cohen's 'Religion of Reason out of the Sources of Judaism'" (1986), in Hermann Cohen, *Religion of Reason Out of the Sources of Judaism*, trans. Simon Kaplan, 2nd ed. (Atlanta: Scholars Press, 1995), 19–20; included in Schwarzschild, *The Tragedy of Optimism*.

is not to be understood as concerning God alone, as it were, but is the "highest human virtue" and thus signifies "the moral law."[28] In sum, Cohen presents the inquiry into the "difference" among the ("reasons for the") commandments as being essentially a drive toward recognizing the moral value of the commandments, and as documenting the tendency of Judaism toward an ethicization of its laws, or of their significance.[29]

---

28 "Die Versöhnungsidee," JS1: 134–5.

29 See Cohen's discussion of Maimonides's account (in *Guide of the Perplexed*, III.32) of sacrifice as a concession to human psychology in the pursuit of God's purpose of forming or educating the people to worship of God at RV 413/354. Cohen cites Maimonides's analogy between the earlier concession of sacrifice and the continued human need for prayer, fasting, supplicating in times of peril, and engaging in other forms of worship, which suggests that ritual observance, too, is in Maimonides's view a necessary concession for the sake of the pursuit of God's moral purpose. Maimonides, *The Guide of the Perplexed*, trans. Shlomo Pines, 2 vols. (Chicago: University of Chicago Press, 1963) (hereafter cited in text as *Guide*).

Cohen presents Maimonides's answer to an objection that is parallel to the one voiced by Cohen himself two pages earlier about the "danger" of the law being relativized: If the laws/mitzvot are merely a means (in Maimonides's words: not "intended for [their] own sake, but for the sake of something else" [*Guide*, III.32, p. 527]), does this not mean that they are superfluous and have no value of their own? Cohen dwells at length on that part of Maimonides's answer that is in line with the theme that is for Cohen the central point of interest in discourses about the "reasons for the commandments": the way that they "distinguish" among the laws. "A great difference has been made between the two kinds" of worship, writes Maimonides – between sacrifice, which falls under God's "secondary purposes" and prayer (here Maimonides repeats the enumeration from the earlier analogy: "supplications, prayers and similar kinds of worship"), which are in accordance with God's "primary purposes" (RV 413/355; *Guide* III.32, p. 529). But by reviewing this difference and a further series of such distinctions made by Maimonides (RV 413–14/355–6), culminating in the partition between "laws between man and God" and "laws between man and man," Cohen underscores that in the most essential respect, that final distinction – and perhaps by extension also the prior succession of differentiations – is not ultimately decisive. For although it might seem as though "laws between man and God" should cover only religious actions, whereas "laws between man and man" would cover ethical actions, it would be a misunderstanding to view those realms as separate. The sacrificial laws, and "those [laws] that resemble them" do not only concern the relationship of human beings to God, but are "intermediate ends" en route to the "sole true purpose of knowing God and true reverence of God in human morality." Similarly, from the other side, "the moral laws also do not remain isolated; rather, they too concern mediately, in their final purpose, only the relationship between human being and God" (RV 414–15/356).

This discussion, then, is an elaboration/explication of the above-quoted principle announced early in chapter 16 regarding the interpretation of the *ta'amei ha-mitzvot*: that despite the presence of a "distinction" among the laws, they are to be thought of as a "unity" (RV 401/345).

Yet this account of the ethical meaning of the mitzvot leaves a fundamental problem unresolved, one which we already encountered in the *Ethik*. Just as there, Cohen lauded Kant for having recognized, at least to some extent, the share of legality in morality, here he regards Jewish religion as the analogue of ethics due to its recognition that autonomy is a submission to duty, to God's command – or, we might also say, to law (Gesetz). Regarding the earlier argument, we had noted that Cohen's criticism of those passages in which Kant appears to negate the very thing he is supposed to have accomplished – to have denounced legality in a manner that Cohen deems "Pauline" (a point Cohen repeats here as well [RV 399–400]) – seems to entail the demand that ethics be supplemented somehow by a robust "Jewish" concept or theory of law. Now, in *Religion* chapter 16, Cohen re-embeds the argument for the share of legality in autonomy into an account of Jewish law. He does so in particular by showing the argument for legality to be continuous with rabbinic pronouncements about moral behavior, and with inquiries into the ethical status of particular commandments or of classes of commandments.

Viewed in this new framing, we now have a definition of Jewish law as a divine command that is equivalent to autonomy – and that indeed is indispensable for understanding autonomy. This is, in other words, in some sense a repetition of the argument from the *Ethik* that legality is essential to autonomy. Within the terms of Cohen's *jüdische Religionsphilosophie*, his philosophy of Jewish religion, what we learn is that a full-fledged theory of ethics – or its perfect "analogue" – may be found within the Jewish sources, within the Jewish understanding of law. From the point of view of understanding or situating Jewish law and jurisprudence per se, however, it seems that nothing in the account we have been looking at thus far substantially goes beyond what Cohen had already established by means of philosophical argumentation in the *Ethik*. Rather, all that is added is a presentation of the quoted Jewish sources as having been prescient in recognizing what Kant, followed by Cohen, would later spell out philosophically: that autonomy is submission to duty.

We might here apply the terms of Strauss's complaint about the limits of Cohen's understanding of Maimonides, and thus of philosophy understood in terms of its political-theological task: In simply aligning or equating command and duty, Cohen has not resolved the tension between the "nomos" element – the idea that in acting morally toward living-together we are "under God's command" – and the idea that I am duty-bound, as a human individual, to act. Does Strauss's question, then, point to a danger that the nomos tradition is, in Cohen's reception and reworking of it, "ethicized" and individualized, or depoliticized?

A version of this concern indeed permeates Cohen's writings on Jewish religion and law as well. For example, in *Begriff der Religion* (1915), Cohen's first effort to methodologically account for the concept of (Jewish) "religion" and its place in relation to his philosophical system, we find him preoccupied with the "danger" that arises from Kant's philosophy of religion, which relates religion so closely to ethics that it threatens to dissolve religion into ethics so that it is no longer a distinctive entity (*Eigenart*) (BR 94).[30] In that earlier book, Cohen writes that "interpreting" the "moral law" as "divine commandment" "can only be explained and justified out of the view that I accomplish it from out of my own reason and therefore by virtue of autonomy" – something that is necessary "because and insofar as I seek to define, create, and ground religion" (BR 117). As is well known, in both *Begriff der Religion* and in the posthumously published *Religion of Reason*, Cohen's project of delineating religion from ethics is founded on the notions of the suffering and sinful individual, of compassion as an affect that generates that individual, and, following from those, the correlation of human being and God – all of which cannot be adequately grasped by ethics, but only by virtue of a "concept of religion." But given that law (Gesetz) is not a constitutive part of that systematic definition of religion, when Cohen confronts the problem of law in Judaism, the question of autonomy is reopened, taking the form of an anxiety that is voiced periodically throughout *Religion* chapter 16.

Looking past this anxiety, however, we will see that Cohen develops a larger argument in this chapter that puts the terms of the question about ethics and law in his philosophy of Jewish religion on a different footing. This argument brings the political dimension of Jewish law into focus; and we will see that in it, the notion or logic of "messianism" has a central role.

Judaism Outside the Reason/Revelation Opposition

Cohen's argument about law/Gesetz takes shape as a rejection of two diametrically opposed alternatives. Similarly to Moses Mendelssohn before him, Cohen finds that Judaism, unlike Christianity, is not a dogma;

30 This remark can be taken as Cohen's corrective to his earlier views about religion and ethics, as in *Begriff der Religion* he recalls that in the *Ethik* he followed Kant's understanding of religion as a function of ethics, to the point of drawing the "methodic consequence" that "religion must be dissolved into ethics" (BR 42). *Begriff der Religion* is an attempt – by way of clarifying the "points" that remained "obscure" in the *Ethik*'s "formulation" of the relationship between religion and ethics (BR 42) – to present religion as a methodologically distinctive field, independent of ethics.

it does not present a doctrine or a faith that poses as an alternative to philosophical reason. This is because Judaism already contains within itself the ethico-philosophical tradition that, for Christianity, historically functioned as a challenge to faith – such that "Christian ethics" would have developed as the answer to the challenge from philosophy. Cohen develops this point chiefly in his 1899 highly critical review of Moritz Lazarus's book *The Ethics of Judaism.* Lazarus (1824–1903) belonged to an older generation of Jewish intellectuals than Cohen, and was a prominent Jewish political leader in late-nineteenth-century Berlin. He shares in a widespread stance during that period (which I describe in greater detail in chapter 6) that sought to solidify Jewish civil equality by promoting a "moral defense" or "ethical" interpretation of Judaism. But paradoxically, despite Cohen's own commitment to demonstrating the moral content of Judaism, his review actually attacks Lazarus for underselling Judaism's ethical significance. Cohen pins this attack on Lazarus's characterization of his book as the first ever attempt to present an "ethics of Judaism." This is termed an "insult" of Judaism by Cohen (PJS 3), who accuses Lazarus of having failed to acknowledge and draw on Jewish philosophers, especially those of the medieval era and especially Maimonides, for their contributions to ethics.

Within his forceful polemic against what Cohen views as Lazarus's wayward attempt at drawing an ethics out of Jewish tradition, Cohen seeks methodological clarity by juxtaposing Christianity and Judaism in view of their respective relationships to philosophy, and thus to moral philosophy.

In the history of Western thought, Christianity is defined by its relationship to philosophy – or, to put it another way, it is defined by the opposition between reason and revelation, or between reason and dogma. "Christian ethics" is grounded in "the revelation in the old and the new covenant"; and it is at the same time determined by its opposition to philosophical ethics, which is to say, by the fact of being challenged by philosophical, reason-based ethics (PJS 1). "Dogma" is central to Christianity; and since dogma is defined by its "conflict" with the methods and content of reason, Christianity perpetually asserts itself in opposition to human, scientific reason (PJS 4). The result of this conflict is termed by Cohen "the problem of the Christian doctrine of morals [*Sittenlehre*]," Christian ethics as an ongoing topic or path of inquiry that is nourished by the opposition of dogma and reason.

Cohen titles his review essay on Lazarus "The Problem of the *Jewish* Doctrine of Morals" ("Das Problem der jüdischen Sittenlehre"), and a focal point of its opening pages is whether such a "problem" is something one can coherently ask about. For alongside Christianity – which is based on revelation and is challenged by a reason-based philosophical ethics and concomitant skepticism about the claims of revelation – Cohen presents Judaism as having *no* dogma, as having nothing that would call for a philosophy or an ethics to oppose or skeptically challenge it. Cohen considers four possible candidates for such a "dogma" and shows why each would not be worthy of such a challenge – of skepticism – by philosophical ethics: (a) ceremonial laws; (b) mythical motifs such as resurrection or immortality, (c) revelation in opposition to reason; and (d) the idea of one God: (a) The ceremonial laws have no inherent value, since they are traditionally seen as merely a "fence around the teaching [*Lehre, Torah*]":[31] "A fence is not a garden.... All zeal about the preservation and securing of the fence could not dissimulate the fact that it is merely a protection, but cannot itself be the treasure" (PJS 4–5). This is to say that Judaism already produces its own proto-philosophical skepticism about the value of its ceremonial laws, making an external challenge to them unnecessary. It is similar with (b) mythical ideas such as resurrection or immortality: In keeping with his general attitude of excluding from consideration all "irrational" elements in Judaism, Cohen deems such ideas to be marginal. (c) Revelation is in Jewish teachings not strictly opposed to the principle of reason; and (d) the unique God is for the medieval Jewish thinkers (at once Jewish "dogmatists" and "our philosophers") just as much the God of morality as he is the God of faith.

Cohen's idea here is that Jewish religion, rather than being subject to external reason-based challenge, supplies its own ethical/philosophical corrective from within itself, such that ethics – reason as ethics – is always a part of religion (PJS 1, 4).

Cohen is, of course, guided in many respects by the philosophy of Kant; and this point can be understood as a repetition-with-a-difference of Kant's criterion for a "religion within the limits of reason," which denotes a religion insofar as it could be capable of playing the role in ethics that Kant accords to religion. Just as Cohen describes Christianity as a dogma/faith that is determined by a perpetual dialectical or agonistic relationship with philosophy or reason, so for Kant the criterion

31 Cohen is referring to the concept of *seyag ha-Torah*, an expression that appears in Mishnah Avot 1:1 and is traditionally understood as a "preventive rabbinic injunction whose purpose is to safeguard the observance of biblical commandments" ("Seyag La-Torah," in *The Oxford Dictionary of the Jewish Religion*, 2nd ed., ed. Adele Berlin [New York: Oxford University Press, 2011]). Whereas this expression is often translated as "fence around the law [*Torah*]," Cohen reads *Torah* here in its other meaning, "teaching," rendering the expression as "fence around the teaching." This enables him to say, at the end of chapter 16, that with this expression, "the Mishnah distinguishes the Law [*das Gesetz*] from the Teaching [*von der Lehre*]" (RV 430/370). Cf. Blackman, ed., *Mishnayoth*, 4:489.

for a "good religion" was a criterion for sorting out what is mere dogma, or spurious service to God/worship, from that in religion which can be rationally defended or which can support ethical action. Kant excluded Judaism, as statutary religion, from this model of religion. We can see that Cohen instead employs Kant's own criterion for reasonable religion to argue for the inherent philosophical reasonableness of Judaism.[32]

Judaism Is Not a Polity

As Cohen routinely reminds us whenever he mentions Kant's attitudes to Judaism, the conclusion to which this sort of disjunction of Judaism and dogma or doctrine has typically led is exactly the politicizing interpretation of Judaism that Cohen rejects. That is, when Judaism is portrayed as a religion without dogma, as not consisting *essentially* of beliefs that may be subject to rational critique, the alternative interpretation that is usually embraced is the one we associate with Spinoza: that Judaism instead is a people following God's law – a political entity, a theocracy, that consists essentially in the divine laws that guide its life, and not in a body of convictions. This view is the one that Cohen pinpoints as Spinoza's great misinterpretation of Judaism – a misinterpretation that Cohen also (mistakenly, I think) ascribes to Mendelssohn.[33] In fact, when Cohen comments on Kant's mistaken understanding of Judaism, he frequently blames it on Kant's reception of Spinoza and Mendelssohn.[34] As

32 This is also the point of departure of Kenneth Seeskin's treatment of Hermann Cohen in his study of *Autonomy in Jewish Philosophy*. Seeskin presents Cohen against the background of Kant's philosophy of religion and ethics, as undertaking a "reconstruction of Judaism along Kantian lines" (155). On this reading, Cohen is pursuing a question that is implicitly "posed by Kant": What would Judaism "look like if it saw itself as a rational religion in [Kant's] sense"? "If Kant could look past the sectarian disputes, forced conversions, and statutory excesses of Christianity to find the core of a religion devoted to the highest moral principles, what would happen if someone took a similar approach to Judaism?" (154). See also Seeskin, "Jewish Neo-Kantianism: Hermann Cohen," in *History of Jewish Philosophy,* ed. Daniel H. Frank and Oliver Leaman (London: Routledge, 1997), chap. 33.

George Kohler makes some parallel points about Kant's understanding of Judaism in relation to Cohen's theory of Judaism and autonomy in "Against the Heteronomy of Halakhah," 192*–4*.

33 Cf. *Deutschtum und Judentum. Mit grundlegenden Betrachtungen über Staat und Internationalismus,* 2nd rev. ed. (1916), sec. 23, JS2: 258–9. Also in *Werke* 16 (page references to the JS edition are included in the *Werke* edition). Here Cohen also "excuses" this mistake of Mendelssohn's by referring to the oppressive situation under which Mendelssohn had to present his theory of Judaism in *Jerusalem.*

34 See for example "Innere Beziehungen," JS1: 284–7. See Ernst Simon's pathos-laden analysis of this view of Cohen's, which reads it as a symptom of Cohen's severe

we noted above with respect to Cohen's comments on the "difference" among the (reasons for the) laws, Cohen does understand Jewish law as comprising a state law, a juridical code or a rule-of-law that governs the life-in-common of a people. In speculating about the "reasons for the commandments," Cohen mentions that some of these may have their root in the absence of a boundary in ancient Judaism between "religious" life and "all other branches of public culture," such that "religion becomes the basic constitution of the state," and, concurrently, "rights and state laws become at the same time religious laws."[35]

But while Cohen sometimes presents this circumstance as non-problematic, at other times these sorts of observations are for him dangerous territory. In his famous 1915 essay on Spinoza, Cohen criticized Spinoza for his view that the Jews were elected by God not due to any distinction of "knowledge or piety," and not for "the true life nor for any higher understanding," but only contingently, for material advantage and good fortune, for a limited time. The law that was given to the Jews was thus for Spinoza bound to a promise of "prosperity/happiness for [their] state,"[36] a political advantage. Cohen complains bitterly about this politicization of the biblical story of the Israelites by Spinoza. The critique he mounts against this politicization is based on calling into question "the *concept* of law [*Gesetz*]" applied by Spinoza. In particular, Cohen counters that the laws in question were not "only *state laws*," but also "laws of *faith/belief* [*Gesetze des* Glaubens]."[37] Now, in the "Law" chapter of the *Religion*, Cohen briefly suggests a criticism that, rather than promising ethical gains if we properly understand political laws as religious laws, warns that when religion becomes a state "constitution," that is, if state laws were to be at the same time religious laws (i.e., a theocracy), this poses a danger for the "purity" of the "purely moral laws" (RV 395–6/340).[38]

---

disappointment in Kant for having taken on, thanks to Mendelssohn's mediating role, Spinoza's understanding that the Jewish laws pertain only, particularistically, to the state – a prevalent medieval antisemitic prejudice. Simon writes that here Cohen, despite his full agreement with Kant's systematic philosophy as well as with Kant's lack of sympathy for Spinoza, was disagreeing with Kant on the only point on which Kant agreed with Spinoza, "the question of Judaism." "Zu Hermann Cohen's Spinoza-Auffassung," *Monatsschrift für Geschichte und Wissenschaft des Judentums* 79 (1935): 192; also included in *Brücken. Gesammelte Aufsätze* (Heidelberg: Lambert Schneider, 1965).

35 RV 395–6/340. Cf. "Innere Beziehungen," JS1: 289, in which Cohen points out that "ritual legislation" (*Ritualgesetzgebung*) comprises "for example" the laws of the state – belonging to the idea of law as Recht: "die staatlichen Rechtsgesetze."

36 Spinoza, *Theological-Political Treatise*, chap. 3, trans. Shirley, 38; trans. Yaffe, 34.

37 Cohen, "Spinoza über Staat und Religion, Judentum und Christentum," JS3: 328–9.

38 Benjamin Pollock has highlighted the ambiguity of Cohen's occasional usage of the term "theocracy" in the *Religion*: Cohen writes that if the "constitution" represented

Reason as Inherent to Judaism

It was Mendelssohn who had in *Jerusalem* elegantly lifted Judaism out of any possible parallelism, and thus out of any possible dogmatic competition with Christianity, by determining that unlike Christianity, Judaism does not consist of any "eternal truths" or involve belief in any dogmas, but consists only of a "revealed" legislation that Jews are obliged to follow.[39] So when Cohen posits just the same sort of asymmetry between Christianity as a religion of dogmas, and thus a religion that can be philosophically contested, and Judaism as having no dogma, he actually incorporates a part of Mendelssohn's famous core insight about Judaism. (Mendelssohn had himself put forward this insight as a way of asserting the philosophical-moral value of Judaism in the face of Christian supersessionism – an aim which Cohen of course shares; the reasons why Cohen either cannot or chooses not to acknowledge this purpose of Mendelssohn's conceptualization of Judaism need not concern us here. For the purposes of my discussion here, I shall focus on Mendelssohn as Cohen portrays him.)

In *Religion* chapter 16, Cohen accuses Mendelssohn of having "[obscured] the concept of Judaism by limiting it to a religion of law.... The specific character of the Jewish religion consists [according to Mendelssohn] in being duty-bound to the law" (RV 415/357). In having deemed ceremonial law to be the essence of Judaism, Mendelssohn represents for Cohen a throwback, an "apparent regression" (RV 416/258) that takes no account of the progress made by the medieval thinkers in having recognized (in their deliberations about the "reasons for the

---

in the Noahide laws is "theocratic," this is to be understood in the sense of those laws' being founded "not on the unity of state and religion, but on that between state and morality." The "harmony" that this represents, however, between "religion on the one hand and law and state on the other" is something Cohen also terms "the principle of theocracy" (RV 143/123, 144/124; cf. 498/430). Pollock, "'Every State Becomes a Theocracy': Hermann Cohen on the Israelites under Divine Rule," *Jewish Studies Quarterly* 25 (2018): 1–19. Commenting on Cohen's use of the term "theocracy" in a description of prophecy, Steven Schwarzschild similarly appreciates the fact that it has not only a negative valence but "describ[es] the laudable permeation of politics with ethics in historical as well as in the messianic society." Schwarzschild, "The Democratic Socialism of Hermann Cohen," *Hebrew Union College Annual* 27 (1956): 434, commenting on RV 300/257 and ErW 61; included in Schwarzschild, *The Tragedy of Optimism: Writings on Hermann Cohen*, ed. George Y. Kohler (Albany: State University of New York Press, 2018).

39 Mendelssohn, *Jerusalem oder über religiöse Macht und Judentum*, in *Jubiläumsausgabe* 8: 191–3; *Jerusalem, or on Religious Power and Judaism*, 126–7.

commandments," that is, about the "difference" among the commandments) that the ceremonial law is inessential:

> [Mendelssohn's] inner religious teaching and practice appeared to make primary [to make into the *Hauptwerk*] that which long ago, in the Middle Ages, had been recognized to be secondary [*Nebenwerk*]. (RV 415/357)

Recall that in the Lazarus review, Cohen had dismissed the possibility that ceremonial law would be a sufficiently robust Jewish counterpart to "dogma" in Christianity and had accorded to ceremonial laws only secondary value (citing the idea that they are a "fence around the teaching/*Torah*"). But if Cohen in the early Lazarus review contrasted Judaism with Christianity by casting it as somehow exempt from any dispute between reason and revelation, this was not because he wished to dissociate Judaism and reason, but rather, as he makes plain in the argument of the *Religion*, because reason, and with it morality or moral teaching (*Sittenlehre*) is already a part of Judaism. This is why, in the Lazarus review, Cohen objects strenuously to what he sees as a failure to take account of the philosophical contribution of the medievals, who for him represent the unequivocal recognition that it is legitimate to try to understand the truths of Judaism as being in line with philosophical truths (PJS 7–8). (This, we recall, is part of what Strauss appreciated about Cohen.) Such an omission, from Cohen's point of view, amounts to a forfeiture of universalism in Judaism. Thus, when Lazarus claims in his elaboration of a Jewish ethics to draw on an "all-encompassing spirit of Judaism" (or "spirit of Judaism as a whole"; *Gesamtgeist des Judentums*), Cohen objects: "Such a ghetto has, thank God, never existed." For Cohen, Judaism cannot be particularist; he cites Maimonides's famous declaration that "We hear the truth, from whoever says it" (PJS 8–9).[40]

Knowledge/Critique of the Laws

Cohen spends several pages in *Religion* chapter 16 explicating Maimonides's pronouncements on the inquiry into the "reasons for the commandments." We can understand this as an elaboration of his conception of Judaism as comprising a principle of reason within itself. For Cohen, Maimonides's engagement in this inquiry belongs to his "rationalism" – albeit to a "rationalism of monotheism," a rationalism that presupposes a God whose giving of the commandments calls for human inquiry into

40 This declaration of Maimonides is in his "Eight Chapters," in Maimonides, *Ethical Writings of Maimonides*, ed. and trans. Charles E. Butterworth and Raymond L. Weiss (New York: Dover, 1983), 60.

its "reasons" (RV 412/354). (Cohen cites approvingly Maimonides's argument in the *Guide of the Perplexed* III.31 against those who reject this enterprise, who "consider it a grievous thing that causes should be given for any law; what would please them most is that the intellect would not find a meaning for the commandments and prohibitions."[41])

We can read Cohen's account of Maimonides's rationalism, as applied to the *ta'amei ha-mitzvot*, as a specific illustration or performance of what Cohen means by the idea that reason is inherent to Judaism: Cohen calls what Maimonides is doing here a "critique"; we can understand his use of this term in Kant's sense, to mean a critique of the nature and bounds of reason.[42] The object of Maimonides's critique is "the laws," the commandments/mitzvot. To engage in critique is to ask whether the laws originate in, or are "caused" solely by reason.[43]

But we can only inquire about "causes" in the realm of natural science, and not in the *Geisteswissenschaften* ("sciences of the spirit," i.e., "human sciences"), and this has consequences for any inquiry into reasons for laws, whether those laws are human-made laws or divine commandments. Cohen suggests an instructive contrast between the idea of laws as "natural right" and the "rationalist" critique of the laws that he identifies with Maimonides: If we were to conceive laws on the model of "natural right," we would dogmatically understand them as having reasons or as a priori grounded in reason. (Similarly, according to natural law theory, the definition or ideal of a law is that it should be grounded in reason in the sense of morality.) Rationalist critique must not presuppose such a grounding, but consists instead of an *inquiry* into the laws' "reasons" in the sense of their "purposes" or "ends" (*Zwecke*) (RV 410–1/353).[44]

41 *Guide* III.31, p. 523. RV 412/354.

42 In "Charakteristik der Ethik Maimunis," Cohen uses similar language to describe Maimonides's inquiry into the "reasons for the commandments": "The sought-after *reasons* [*Gründe*], insofar as they are sought, summon the laws before the forum of reason." CEM 238/46.

43 "Ob deren Ursache allein die Vernunft ist, oder ob noch andere Ursachen dabei mitwirken" (RV 410/352). For some other examples of Cohen's "Kantianizing" renditions of Maimonidean views, see Arthur Hyman, "Maimonidean Elements in Hermann Cohen's Philosophy of Religion," in *Hermann Cohen's Critical Idealism*, ed. Reinier Munk (Dordrecht: Springer, 2005), 368. Cf. George Y. Kohler, *Reading Maimonides' Philosophy in 19th Century Germany: The Guide to Religious Reform* (Dordrecht: Springer, 2012), chap. 8 ("Maimonides and Kant"), esp. 286–96.

44 See the helpful discussion of Cohen's argument by George Y. Kohler in "Finding God's Purpose: Hermann Cohen's Use of Maimonides to Establish the Authority of Mosaic Law," in "Ancients and Moderns in Jewish Philosophy: The Case of Hermann Cohen," ed. Aaron W. Hughes, special issue, *Journal of Jewish Thought and Philosophy* 18, no. 1 (Jan. 2010).

(This is akin to the procedure of understanding law/Recht laid out in Cohen's *Ethik* that I discussed in chapter 1: Through legal science, the law is given as a factum, as something intelligible, allowing us to investigate its conditions of validity.) In this sense, Maimonides can be said to conduct his inquiry into the "reasons for the commandments" as a "teleology," an inquiry into their purposes. (This is in line with an aspect of Maimonides's theology that Cohen often emphasizes: that the essence of God is knowable only by means of God's "attributes of action," and thus only as "archetype [*Urbild*] of morality" [RV 411/353].[45])

Another way that Cohen puts this is to say that the laws cannot *themselves* be purposes or ends. They have no inherent value (unlike, again, laws conceived as natural laws or natural rights) (RV 411/353). Thus, rationalist critique inquires into the laws "relative" to their "absolute purpose": God as morality. (For Cohen, following Maimonides, God is the God of morality, and morality is "contained in the essence of God.")

But if the laws are thereby understood only as "means" to God's morality as an end, does this mean that the laws have been demoted in importance, that is, relativized (RV 411/354)? Cohen argues against such a relativization by recalling that for Maimonides it is a "commandment" "to know God" – and in particular, to cognize God as God of morality. (That Maimonides understands the knowledge of God in conjunction with the identity of God and morality is also a strong thesis that Cohen argued for in his Maimonides essay [CEM 247/74].) Building on the idea (introduced in our last section) that reason is inherent to Judaism, we now learn that this reason is practical/moral at the same time as it is theoretical: Cohen cites Maimonides's statement that knowing God is the same as "worshipping" God, so that "the reasons for the laws" become "recognizable as a means of worship of God" (RV 412/354, 414–15/356).

Thus, we must not think that a merely theoretical requirement of "critiquing" the laws subsequently gives rise to understanding them as means to realizing God's moral purpose – as if the laws were to be thought of as part of a causal process. Rather, "critique" here is understood as something that *in itself* aims at furthering God as morality. This idea of Maimonides's rationalist teleology of the laws as "critique," then, helps fill out what it means to understand reason as inherent to Judaism. This is in line with an overarching theme in *Religion* chapter 16: that in the performance of a commandment, moral action goes hand in hand

45 Thus, in his major study of Maimonides, "Charakteristik der Ethik Maimunis," Cohen stresses that the "attributes of action," as *Vorbilder* – models for emulation – must be understood in their role for knowledge – knowledge of God, and knowledge of ethics. CEM, 246–7/71–2.

with knowledge, practice with theory (RV 430/370). (Chapter 16 ends by newly posing the question as to which commandments actually fulfill this combined requirement, and the question is taken up again in chapter 17, whose purpose is to show that "prayer" uniquely fulfills this desideratum [RV 431/371].)[46]

The key strand of the argument about "law" that we have been drawing out of *Religion* chapter 16 so far, is that after having noted a disjunction/asymmetry between Christianity as defined by reason as its perpetual opponent, and Judaism as incorporating reason within itself, Cohen has identified the concurrent movement toward knowledge and worship of God, who is "identical" with morality, as the meaning of law in Judaism.

Cohen's Repoliticization of Jewish Law

However, in depicting Jewish philosophy as embodied by the great rationalist Maimonides, Cohen does not merely underscore that for Maimonides religious law is essentially ethical. He also regularly makes a point of saying that there is a political, public dimension to Maimonides's appreciation of the law or the commandents. For example, when he approvingly discusses, in the "Law" chapter of the *Religion*, Maimonides's justification for why one may and ought to inquire into the "reasons for the commandments" (a justification Maimonides directs against the detractors of such an enterprise, who hold that at least some of the commandments need to be thought of as not having any "reasons"), Cohen highlights the following statement within that justification:

> All [the commandments] are bound up with three things: opinions, moral qualities, and political civil actions. (*Guide* III.31, Pines translation, p. 524)

Or, in an English approximation of Cohen's German rendering:

> All depends on three things: knowledge [*Erkenntnis*], morality [*Sittlichkeit*], and citizen engagement [*staatsbürgerliche Betätigung*]. (RV 412/354)

That is to say, despite Cohen's determined rejection of the Spinozan idea that Judaism is a polity, with the third term in this enumeration, "citizen engagement," he also brings out the sense in which the commandments,

---

46 This chapter is briefly discussed by Steven Kepnes in *Jewish Liturgical Reasoning* (Oxford: Oxford University Press, 2007), chap. 2, "Liturgical Selfhood. Hermann Cohen's Religion of Reason," 75–7.

in that they are means of knowing God in his "identity" with morality, also involve our existence in relation to political and legal institutions, institutions of Recht.

In other words, having taken pains to clear the category of "law" (Gesetz) in Judaism of any suspicion that it might refer to political laws directed at the temporal good fortune of a people, and having insisted that Jewish tradition has consisted of continually consolidating and enhancing the ethical content/essence of "the commandments," Cohen here begins to argue that this content of the commandments has core "political"-*rechtlich* aspects. In place of the "politicization" of the law that he has rejected, he now reinstates, as it were, a legitimate politics of Recht. This shows up, for example, in the fact that, as George Kohler has noted, Cohen on several occasions highlights one of Maimonides's explanations for endorsing Jeremiah's outcry against sacrifice,

> For on the day that I brought your ancestors out of the land of Egypt, I did not speak to them or command them concerning burnt-offerings and sacrifices. (Jer. 7:22)

Maimonides's explanation, on which, according to Cohen, he "constructs his entire critique of sacrificial law," is that because the biblical verse makes reference to "*the day* that I brought your ancestors out of the land of Egypt," it refers to, to quote Kohler, "the first act of divine lawgiving in Mara," i.e., to Exodus 15:25: שָׁם שָׂם לוֹ חֹק וּמִשְׁפָּט, "and gave them there statutes and ordinances," and further to the Talmudic interpretation of this verse according to which on that day – that is, before receiving the Decalogue at Sinai – the Israelites received

> (1) the commandments to keep the Shabbat and to honor one's parents, both precepts identified by Maimonides in the *Guide* with statutes (חקים, [*ḥuqqim*]); and (2) *dinim*, legal regulations, according to Maimonides' understanding, that protect society against crime and injustice, identified with the biblical ordinances (משפטים [*mishpatim*]).[47]

For Cohen, it is significant that for the sacrificial legislation Maimonides "has substituted the legislation of statute and ordinance at Marah" (RV 202/173). *Dinim* denotes the first of the seven Noahide laws, the institution of courts of law, or, put more broadly, "the injunction to establish

47 Kohler, "Finding God's Purpose," 93–4; cf. Kohler, *Reading Maimonides' Philosophy*, chap. 7, "The Law," 235–6.

a legal system."[48] (We will return in chapter 6 to the category of the Noahide, which is for Cohen among the most important elements of Judaism.) Cohen's German term for *dinim* is *Gerichtsverfassung*, the constitution/institution of courts; for him, this belongs to the sphere of Recht – law as a system of law or of governance. Discussing this first Noahide law in *Religion* chapter 15, Cohen notes that

> Law [*Recht*] is the foundation of human morality.... Only the formulation of rights [*Rechte*] and the establishment of a court [*Gerichtshof*] and of judicial organization [*Gerichtsverfassung*] gives a sufficient foundation [for morality]. (RV 381/327–8)[49]

The first of these quoted sentences could come straight out of Cohen's theory of ethics-out-of-law in the *Ethik.*[50] That Maimonides interprets Jeremiah 7:22 as a reference to the institution of statutes and ordinances at Marah is understood by Cohen as Maimonides's affirmation that "Law [*Das Recht*] is the true foundation of Torah" (RV 381/338). Similarly, in chapter 16, Cohen cites Maimonides's interpretation of "statutes and ordinances" in Exodus 15:26 – an application of a Talmudic interpretation of the verse[51] – that "statute" (*ḥoq*) refers to the Sabbath laws, and "ordinance" (*mishpat*) refers to *Rechtsverfassung*, the constitution of laws – *dinim* according to the Talmudic source invoked by Maimonides.[52]

For Cohen, an additional merit of Maimonides's interpretation is that it implies that "even the statutes should be counted under the category of moral laws, since the Sabbath represents social legislation" (RV 413/355). Here again, Maimonides's treatment of the "difference" among and within the commandments is taken by Cohen to convey the insight that that difference tends to become obsolete, and that the

48 See Klaus Müller, *Tora für die Völker. Die noachidischen Gebote und Ansätze zu ihrer Rezeption im Christentum* (Berlin: Institut Kirche und Judentum, 1994), 87–94; and David Novak, *The Image of the Non-Jew in Judaism: The Idea of Noahide Law*, 2nd ed., ed. Matthew Lagrone (Oxford: Littman Library of Jewish Civilization, 2011), chap. 2. Steven Schwarzschild presents this law as "the injunction to establish a legal system" in his contribution to the entry on "Noachide Laws" in the *Encyclopaedia Judaica.*

49 This first Noahide law thus signifies the principle that the state should be directed toward justice (RV 498/430).

50 Kohler also makes the connection between these passages in the *Religion* and Cohen's theory in the *Ethik*, in *Reading Maimonides' Philosophy*, chap. 7, 237.

51 The Talmudic source is bSanhedrin 56b. Kohler clarifies the connection in "Finding God's Purpose," 94, and *Reading Maimonides' Philosophy*, chap. 7, 236.

52 *Guide* III.32, p. 531. Pines translates the term corresponding to *dinim* as "civil laws." and has Maimonides gloss these as "the abolition of mutual wrongdoing."

ultimate meaning of all the laws is moral. But if Cohen here underscores again that the commandments are a means of knowledge, and that this knowledge goes hand in hand with moral deed, or action, this is also to say that "truthful knowledge," as the "first purpose" of the laws, goes hand in hand with "the removal of injustice from humankind" (*Guide* III.32, cited in RV 413/355). Another pertinent example of Cohen's insistence on a political dimension to Maimonides's ethical insights is his appreciation for Maimonides's statements about the messianic times as reflecting a hope for a historical future, rather than a utopianism or a reference to a paradise beyond the end of time: Cohen says about those statements that they recognize in messianism the basic traits of an "ethical socialism" (RV 361/311).

If Strauss had remarked about Cohen's reading of Maimonides that Cohen routinely misunderstands what is political to be merely ethical, here we have some explicit affirmations by Cohen that the ethical and the political go hand in hand. Cohen had given a full account of this connection in the theory of ethics-out-of-Recht in the *Ethik*. What becomes clear in *Religion* chapter 16 is that he deems that connection to be essential for his theory of Judaism as well.

Law and the Messianic Politics of "Isolation"

In such discussions of Maimonides, as in his discussions of law in Judaism in general, Cohen must perpetually skirt the risk of making Judaism appear to be "merely" a political entity. He must avoid the appearance of making Spinoza's mistake of (as Cohen put it in his Spinoza essay) regarding all biblical laws as political laws, and disregarding their role as religious laws. This would explain why, in the midst of his discussion of Maimonides in the chapter on "Law," Cohen abruptly launches into a narration of modern Jewish political-intellectual history (RV 415ff./357ff.). In seeking to account for the purpose of law, Cohen has no prior established political history, or definition of Jewish political life, at his disposal. Insofar as he concedes, with Maimonides, that there *is* a public-political aspect to the legitimate inquiry into the reasons for the "commandments," he must also define what he means by "political" in a way that avoids the Spinozist pitfall of understanding Judaism as merely a national-political constitution. The modern Jewish history that Cohen now goes on to tell in the chapter amounts to a determination of politics in a new, messianic and universalist sense.

This history told by Cohen "begins" with "the time of the German Enlightenment." Here, as mentioned earlier, Cohen describes Mendelssohn's failing as having reduced Judaism to its law (RV 415/357).

He focuses in on a dilemma, an "apparent contradiction" between two views of Judaism:

(1) The view he attributes to Mendelssohn: that Judaism is an "*isolated*" and particularist "nation," whose "isolation" was and perhaps continues to be the necessary condition of the persistence and thriving of Judaism (or monotheism) as such. In this connection, Cohen underscores the importance of investigating the legitimacy of (law as) "isolation" – and thus also interrogating what "isolation" means – for Jewish existence. For Cohen, considering the ongoing value of isolation by means of law is one of the chief purposes of the *Religion* book as a whole:

> It belongs to the theoretical problems of this book that we do not evade the question of whether the burden of isolation is not also in the future incumbent upon the further existence and development of Jewish monotheism. (RV 418/359)

(2) The view that Judaism has a "messianic mission" that is *universalist* and oriented to humanity (RV 418/359).

From Law as "Isolation" to Jewish Nationalism

Cohen's argument across chapter 16 indeed relies heavily on a description of law in terms of "isolation" – a description that seems at first glance to belong to the register of the sociology or history of religions. According to this model, "isolation" by means of law was necessary to the establishment and survival of Jewish monotheism (RV 417–18/359). Early in the chapter, before introducing the term "isolation" that dominates in its later pages, Cohen announces that in asking about the significance of the laws (including cultic laws) in Judaism, "deep historical problems are to be considered":

> As it says in Balaam's blessing concerning Israel, "a people, living alone [*einsam*],[53] and it does not reckon itself among the nations" [Num. 23:9], so the history of Israel proceeded and so it must be conceived/grasped [*begriffen*]. Only in this way is it somewhat explainable that the nation [*Nation*] and with it the religion was able to preserve itself. If the mores of life had promoted matrimonial and economic community [i.e., with other peoples] at an earlier time, it would not be at all conceivable that this people of faith could preserve itself. This historical motif ought to be able,

53 Cohen renders לְבָדָד as "einsam," meaning "lonesome" or "solitary," as distinct from Luther's translation "abgesondert," meaning "separate" or "separated off."

> in the simplest way, to bring the great question that has continually been directed at the reasons for the commandments – a question which Maimonides so convincingly explicated – to a decisive solution. The historical instinct of the nation erected this protective wall [*Schutzmauer*] against the leveling of that which was its own [*Nivellierung des Eigenen*] and guarded it against complete destruction.... The law in its rigid strictness, as well as in its living pliancy, can be understood only in its historical significance, in which it is a model example for the problem of cultural-historical influence in general, that is, [for] whether the ideas or the mores and customs are the prevalent forces of the persistence and development of spiritual phenomena. (RV 397/341–2)

In this passage early in the "Law" chapter, it sounds as though Cohen's observation about the Jewish people's isolation is meant as a historical-sociological explanation for why the commandments emerged and persisted. But in the final pages of the chapter, it emerges that the function of this observation is of a different order. Already in his review of Lazarus, Cohen had used the image of a protective "fence" to describe the function of the law. He remarks there that religious reform, with its process of "rejection of external ritual works," by no means represented a "loosening of the fence" that would risk "making barren" the "garden" of Judaism. On the other hand, he notes that the prevalent danger of anti-Jewish "hatred" has led "in our days" to the recognition "that one might appreciate anew, and with greater insight, the protective value of the fence":

> Unfortunately it must be conceded that we had overestimated the maturity of the age. We are unfortunately not yet in the days [*Vortagen*] of the messianic age. And hence the fence must continue to be cultivated, with wise discretion. And gratitude toward the fence, which is grounded in the most profound feelings of piety, can never be extinguished among us. (PJS 26–7)

Recall that in the same review of Lazarus, Cohen had, in rejecting the idea of a particular Jewish ethics, angrily exclaimed that there has never been such a "ghetto" as a "spirit of Judaism" (PJS 8). Now, in considering the "isolating" function of Jewish law in the *Religion*, Cohen invokes the "not yet" of the messianic age in order to defer to a time in which the "fence" of the law might no longer be called for, and in order to call for a slowing of the progress of religious reform in dismantling that fence. Jewish "isolation" as a function of a Jewish-universalist messianic mission is now revived by Cohen in the political history of Judaism that he narrates, whose purpose, again, is to resolve or "sublate" (*aufheben*) the "apparent contradiction" between isolation and universalism – to show that Jewish "isolation" and Jewish messianic universalism are not at odds with each other.

The first stage in that history is represented by the so-called Reform answer to the dilemma: According to that answer, Judaism is not a nation (*Nation*) but a religion, and as a religion, it is universalist. The Reform project was to overcome Jewish isolation, the idea of Judaism as a nation, by affirming that Judaism is a religion. The agenda of reforming religious observance – that is, of relativizing law – was thus a program of overcoming Jewish "isolation" – toward the goal of ensuring full citizenship and participation in society. This was a program for a "religion" that could function as "the historical preliminary stage to the messianic future of Judaism." That is, here "religion" denotes a messianic universalism that was supposed to improve the older, seemingly damaging conception of Judaism as a nation "isolated" by virtue of a particular law (Gesetz) (RV 418/359–60).

Cohen's political history of modern Judaism next moves to analyzing what he calls a Zionist "episode," which reacted to the idea of Judaism as a religion by affirming Jewish nationhood in a new sense. Here, as Cohen describes it, the concept of "nation" became politicized, in line with the European liberal national revolutionary movements that were attempting to establish nation-states in place of old monarchies. "Nation" accordingly came to mean the same thing as state (RV 418–19/360). Part of the struggle for Emancipation had consisted in demonstrating that Jewish religion – Cohen here alludes to prayers expressing a hope for attaining Zion – did not seek a "restoration of the Jewish state" (RV 419/360). But now, the general European tendency to conflate the notions of nation and state, or nation and politics, along with increasing anti-Jewish oppression and violence, became too great for the earlier resistance to Jewish nation-statism to hold.

A New Universalist Politics of "Nationality"

In Cohen's political history of modern Judaism, then, the Zionist option favors particularism, by aspiring to a Jewish national state[54] at the expense

54 The "consequence" – that "the Jewish nation too demanded a Jewish state" – must be understood as a "paradoxical" one in view of what for Cohen is a clear disjunction between Jewish nationhood and the notion of statehood: "The two concepts [nation and state] entered into a reciprocal relationship [*Wechselwirkung*]. The nation demands the state, and the state demands the nation" (RV 419/360–1). Further on, Cohen explains what it means for "nation" and "state" to be "reciprocal concepts," *Wechselbegriffe*, which for Cohen also means concepts in correlation: "The nation is the nation of the state, and the state is the state of the nation." Each of the concepts thus constitutes the other concept's "unity" (RV 421/362).

of "religion," as messianic universalism. Cohen thus recalls and revives the opposition bequeathed to Jewish thought by the era of Emancipation and Reform – that between nation and religion – and endorses Reform's decision in favor of religion. Against the conflation of statehood and nation, Cohen asserts a new politics proper to religion: this political alternative is "messianism" as a "factor in world history" (RV 419–20/361).

Thus, where he had earlier rejected the standard politicization of the concept of Judaism in the manner of Spinoza and (he claims) Mendelssohn, Cohen now uses the term "religion" to name a world politics of a different order. As a result of this, the idea of "isolation" of the "law" takes on a new significance, in line with this differently defined politics that Cohen aligns with "religion":

> Does the concept of nation have exclusively the political meaning ...? Can the concept of the nation not have another meaning, which does justice to isolation insofar as the latter must be maintained for the sake of religion and can be maintained above all through the law? (RV 419–20/361)

Accordingly, Cohen proposes a resolution of the dilemma between national particularism and religious universalism by proposing that Jewish nationhood and isolation can be understood and maintained in a way that is not particularist, but that furthers the project of religion as messianic universalism. Universalism calls for "nationality" as distinct from "nation." In the midst of the World War, still being waged at the time he is writing, Cohen sees signs of this "other view of the meaning of the nation" – its meaning as a waystation toward a confederation of states, toward messianism becoming a "factor in world history" (RV 420/361). Some of the transformation, he contends, began to take place at the eve of the war, as by that time, the concept of "nation" had become denaturalized and idealized. Cohen's description of this improvement of the concept of "nation" sounds as though it could have been lifted from his own conception of the ethico-politics of Allheit, developed in his *Ethik*:

> Originally, the nation was thought as the natural givenness of a tribe [*Volksstamm*]. Politics taught and compelled the abandoning of this meaning of the word and the acceptance of the nation as a generative and formative concept [*Erzeugungs- und Gestaltungsbegriff*] of the state. (RV 420/361)

We can recognize here the idea from the *Ethik* that ethically significant concepts, those oriented to Allheit, including that of the state, emerge and become effective by processes of conceptual *Erzeugung*, generation. "State" is the "idealization" and "purification" of the concept of "nation," which has shed its "earthy odor" (*Erdgeruch*) (RV 420/361). This also goes with Cohen's argument, in the *Ethik*, for state, as opposed to Volk and nation, as an ethically-politically constitutive concept.[55]

About these developments on the eve of the war, Cohen writes: "Hence nation and state became identical." This is a repetition of a conceptual change that, a page earlier, he had decried in the context of Jewish political life. In that context, he had cautioned that Judaism ought not to become "political" in the sense of embracing statehood and thus of remaining within particularity. In the present narrative, however, the assimilation of the concept of nation to that of the state is part of "another" trajectory of politicization, one that functions as a waystation to the messianic-political world-historical ideal of international federation.

In the intensification of antagonisms in war, Cohen sees a new chance at peace, and with it (here a "virtue is born out of necessity") the hope for an "expansion of the concept of the state," which Cohen also calls its "maturation," into the idea of a "confederation" or "league" of states (*Staatenbund*). This development, which entails the "uniting" and "inner harmonization" of peoples, would be a transcending of "isolation": "The states could not remain isolated" (RV 420/361). The anticipated overcoming of the nation-state would be the "completion" or "perfection" (*Vollendung*) of the very idea of the state – which, we recall, also represents the ethical horizon of Allheit in Cohen's *Ethik*.[56]

In "replacing" the concept of the "nation" (RV 421/362), "nationality" denotes, in the first instance, a plurality internal to the state. Here we can think of "states" that comprise many peoples or "nationalities" – the classic example of the time (which is also the one that Cohen seems to have in mind[57]) being the Austrian multinational state. Second, "nationality"

55 ErW 34, 250–3, 255. Steven Schwarzschild highlights this aspect of Cohen's ethical and political theory in "Democratic Socialism," 425, 429. Harry van der Linden comments on Cohen's "patriotism" in "Hermann Cohen's Political Philosophy and the Communitarian Critique of Liberalism," available at http://digitalcommons.butler.edu/facsch_papers/66, pp. 11–12; published in French translation in "L'École de Marbourg," ed. Fabien Capeillères and Jean Kahn, special issue, *Cahiers de philosophie politique et juridique*, no. 26 (1994).

56 In *Deutschtum und Judentum*, Cohen argues that the fact that the concept of the state points to the international-law idea of the *Staatenbund* shows – retrospectively, as it were – that the concept of the state exceeds any naturalistic definition, and is non-identical to that of the nation. JS2: 273.

57 See Cohen's citation of this example in "Religion und Zionismus" (alternate title: "Zionismus und Religion," 1916), JS2: 322. (Also in *Werke* 17. Page references to the JS edition are included in the *Werke* edition.) Hartwig Wiedebach's reservations about the relevance of the Austrian example here are based on his justified objection to projecting the widespread opposition between "cultural nation" (*Kulturnation*) and

refers outward to a plurality of nation-states that takes on the tasks of confederation and peace. These two meanings are conjoined for Cohen: In parallel to the movement toward a confederation of states or harmonization of peoples, he advocates a concurrent movement *within* the state or individual nation: an embracing of the foreign. (Thus he opposes the völkisch-organicist attitudes according to which the "foreign body" is a "cancerous defect that threatens the organism of the states" [RV 420/362].) While the state corresponds to one nation, and vice versa, a "nationality" is not identified with a "state."[58] The confederation of states "needs peoples" in the plural (RV 421/362), and the state itself "is dependent on nationalities." Judaism exists politically, according to Cohen, as Jewish nationality, which is an indispensable support of Jewish religion as a messianic-universalist project (RV 421–2/362–3). (Cohen also warns – with implicit reference to race theories prevalent at the time – that to connect the idea of nation to that of "race" poses a "danger," because of the "exclusivity" that is demanded from the state in the name of "race.")

In view of this, Judaism should be seen as a "nationality" that needs no state, that exists within individual states (RV 421/362), and that thus brings forward the universalist world-historical task.[59] This nationality is, in other words, not a goal in itself, but exists for the sake of religion in its universalist meaning.

"political nation" (*Staatsnation*) onto Cohen's term, and thus don't invalidate Cohen's use of the Austria example. Wiedebach, *Die Bedeutung der Nationalität für Hermann Cohen* (Hildesheim: Olms, 1997), 7–8; translated by William Templer as *The National Element in Hermann Cohen's Philosophy and Religion* (Leiden: Brill, 2012), 1–2. The definition of nationality as a plurality internal to the state is likely quite standard for Cohen's time. For example, the German geographer Alfred Kirchhoff, in considering the origins of the term "nationality" and weighing its utility, understands it to be a "relative concept," whereas "nation" is an "absolute" concept, such that there may be multiple nationalities within the nation-state. Kirchhoff, *Zur Verständigung über die Begriffe Nation und Nationalität* (Halle: Buchhandlung des Waisenhauses, 1905), 62. Cohen agrees with this usage, as is evident from his claim in "Religion und Zionismus" that "the state unifies not nations, but nationalities" (JS2: 322). The idea of "nationality" is associated with the risk of fragmentation within the nation-state; but it also offers a means for a group not of the dominant nation to be accorded specific self-governance rights ("autonomy"), which was also sometimes sought for the Jews as a "nationality." See Nathan Birnbaum [Mathias Acher, pseud.], "Jüdische Autonomie," *Ost und West* 6, no. 1 (January 1906): 1–6; and the translated excerpt and editor's preface in *Jews and Diaspora Nationalism. Writings on Jewish Peoplehood in Europe and the United States*, ed. Simon Rabinovitch (Waltham, MA: Brandeis University Press, 2012), 45–55.

58 RV 421/362. Cohen, "Religion und Zionismus," 322.

59 We will return in chapter 6 to Cohen's emphasis on cosmopolitanism and the embrace of the foreign in his theory of Judaism.

Cohen illustrates his understanding of Jewish nationality as a support of religion with a dictum from Saadya Gaon, "Our people is only a people through its teachings,"[60] which he elucidates as follows:

> In this necessary disposition of nationality *for* religion lies [the] idealizability [of nationality]. And [nationality's] share in ideality consists only in religion. (RV 422/363, emphasis added)

Thus, the people's existence, or "nationality," is "only" for the sake of "religion," which is a universalist project. This is a direct contestation of the premise of Zionism, which, as we saw, is understood by Cohen to have relied on a mistaken "idealization" of the nation, in the direction of particularity and nation-statehood. Nationality, in other words – and as acknowledged by "the most profound Jewish minds/intellects" – is not an end in itself (*Selbstzweck*), but is necessary "only as the indispensable means for the preservation of religion."

However, Cohen specifies that Jewish nationality or existence should remain the support of Jewish religion only on the following condition:

> There can arise ... no doubt that nationality must remain the necessary basis for the preservation of Jewish religion *as long as it* [i.e., Jewish religion] *stands in opposition/contrast to other forms of monotheism.* (RV 422/363, emphasis added)

60 In parentheses, Cohen reproduces the full formulation from Yehudah Ibn Tibbon's Hebrew translation of Saadya Gaon's *Book of Doctrines and Beliefs*: אומתנו איננה אומה כי אם בתורותיה. *Toroteha,* which Cohen translates as "its teachings" ("seine Lehren"), is usually translated as "its laws," as in Alexander Altmann's rendition: "Our people, the Children of Israel, are a people only by virtue of our laws." The line appears as part of Saadya's canonical argument for why "the laws of the Torah shall never be abrogated." Saadya Gaon, *The Book of Doctrines and Beliefs,* trans. Alexander Altmann (1946; repr., Indianapolis: Hackett, 2002), 112. Cohen refers to this argument and praises Saadya for it a few paragraphs later, when discussing the classic question of whether the law is "necessary" or "eternal" (RV 424/365). But by initially excerpting and interpreting Saadya's line in the way that he does, Cohen underscores that he wishes to re-embed the traditional Jewish-philosophical question about the eternity of law ("a prevailing problem in the Jewish Middle Ages") into his theory of Jewish modern political existence as a universalist "religion," which he has defined by way of "nationality."

In parallel passages in *Deutschtum und Judentum* (1915/1916) and in "Das Gottesreich" (1913), Cohen translates Saadya's line as "Our nation is a nation only through its teaching[s]" and similarly interprets it as reflecting universalist messianism as a "basic idea" of Judaism, in the sense that the teachings shall transcend the people and become effective universally: "The final meaning and content of our teachings is the subordination of the nation under humanity." JS2: 265, JS3: 174.

Does Cohen, then, anticipate a time in which the plurality of "religions of reason" will merge into a single, universal religion of reason? We quickly learn that this is not his view. Just as "nationality" entails plurality, and just as the state, when properly understood, "depends on nationalities," here, Cohen similarly insists on a plurality of religions of reason.

Cohen had laid the ground for this idea in the introduction to *Religion of Reason*, when he elaborated the method of drawing on the "sources of Judaism" in order to conceive of religion in its relationship to morality and reason. Those methodological reflections in the introduction go hand in hand with the programmatic statement that Judaism is not the sole, unique religion of reason (RV 39/34).[61] It would be "impermissible," he writes, to seek to "replace" Judaism with a different monotheism: Plurality and "the manifold of cultural phenomena" are to be embraced, and studied for their "share in reason." The "thought of the absolute" must be rejected. The very "idea [*Gedanke*] of wanting to replace one religion with another" is a "historical *Ungedanke*," wholly unacceptable. Instead, the "philosophy of history" – which we can here take as a temporary name for Cohen's own philosophical project developed out of historical sources in the *Religion* – "defends against the idea of absoluteness" by researching the "share of reason" in "the manifold of cultural phenomena" (RV 422–3/363–4). Accordingly, if the preservation of Judaism remains indispensable, remains "a historical necessity," this is a necessity "out of the principle of reason" (RV 423/364), that is, *insofar as Judaism is demonstrably a "religion of reason."*[62]

---

61 That statement accords with the fact that Cohen certainly wished this work to be titled "Religion of Reason" – with no definite article – despite the erroneous insertion of the definite article in the first edition (1919), so that in the first ten years after its publication (up until the second revised edition was published in 1929), the book was mistakenly referred to as *Die Religion der Vernunft* ... (*The Religion of Reason* ...). All this is explained by the editor of the revised second edition, Bruno Strauss, in his editorial postscript, RV 625/xlii–xliii. Cf. Schwarzschild, "The Title of Hermann Cohen's 'Religion of Reason,'" 7–8. Cohen does privilege the monotheistic religions, however, and also ascribes to Judaism an "originarity" (*Ursprünglichkeit*) in relation to other monotheistic religions. Cohen's use of this term, given its role in his "logic of origin" (discussed in chapter 1), underscores the methodological nature of his treatment of this question in the introduction: that is, if Jewish monotheism functions as a generative origin (*Ursprung*), this would be in line with Cohen's explication in the introduction of how a philosophical study of religion, and/or of Judaism, must approach its "sources" (RV 39/34). See the discussion in Seeskin, *Autonomy in Jewish Philosophy*, 160. For a critical assessment of Cohen's claim that Judaism is not the sole, unique religion of reason, see Robert Erlewine, *Monotheism and Tolerance: Recovering a Religion of Reason* (Bloomington: Indiana University Press, 2010), 140–2.

62 Emphasis added. "If indeed, however, out of the sources of Judaism, Judaism can be proved a religion of reason, then the continuation [*Fortbestand*] of Judaism is, conceptually, secured" (RV 422/364).

It follows that the condition we encountered above – that Jewish religion is to be preserved on the basis of Jewish nationality "as long as [Jewish religion] stands in opposition to other forms of monotheism" – does not mean that Jewish nationality is to be preserved for as long as no universal religion of reason comes to replace it. Rather, the clause expresses the very project of the book *Religion of Reason*. Explaining what he means by Judaism's "opposition to other forms of monotheism," Cohen continues:

> What is in question here is nothing other and nothing less than the particular value [*Eigenwert*] of Jewish monotheism itself,

that is, its distinctive character "in opposition to" "other forms of monotheism" (RV 422/363). To demonstrate that distinctive character and value of Jewish monotheism is the task of the *Religion*. That Judaism *is* a religion of reason is the thesis to be demonstrated by the book. At the same time, that Judaism *be* a religion of reason is the hoped-for outcome of Cohen's effort in the book, to be attained if the understanding of Judaism laid out in the book – Judaism as a messianic-universalist force in world history – is taken seriously and becomes effective in the world.

Thus, the book *Religion of Reason* is itself the messianic-universalist project that it describes throughout its pages, and here in particular, in defining and defending "isolation in the law."

Conclusion

In the "Law" chapter of the *Religion*, Cohen resolves the apparent contradiction between Jewish particularism and Jewish messianic universalism by reinterpreting and revaluing "isolation." Isolation now no longer denotes a particularism (or a "ghetto," as Cohen sometimes calls it) or a susceptibility toward nation-statism, but becomes necessary for the sake of universality.

Viewed in the terms of the original dilemma between particularism and universality, isolation had been a synonym, or a characteristic feature, of law. Now that the necessity of Jewish existence has been refounded or projected in a new sense – the sense and project of a religion of reason – what role, if any, does law have to play in that project?

Having painted a picture of Judaism as religion of reason in the horizon of universality, Cohen considers the following objection:

> Isolation in the world of culture [or simply: in the world understood in terms of "culture" or as something "cultural"; *Kulturwelt*]! Does such a demand, made from the point of view of the law, not amount to a condemnation of Judaism? (RV 425/366)

Cohen's answer consists in recasting what Jewish "isolation in the law" means. It is not to be understood as an "isolation *from the point of view of* the law." That is, it is not law that demands the isolation, because law is not necessary in itself, but is only necessary relative to what Cohen has been calling "nationality" and "religion." "Isolation," Cohen specifies, is instead "demanded" from the point of view of "pure monotheism" (RV 425/366). When monotheism is at stake, "the world," *die Kulturwelt* – the world-historical project in which the religion of reason has a share – "is itself at stake" (RV 426/366). Thus, the "isolation" demanded is demanded not for the sake of a particular people's life – not for the sake of the law itself – but for the messianic achievement of the religion of reason as a universalist project.[63]

Looking back at the path of Cohen's argument in the *Religion of Reason*, we can see that it rests on a redefinition and revaluing of the political in Jewish existence. Law (Gesetz) is understood not as the particular law of a polity or a nation(-state), but instead as serving religion, which in turn is understood as a universalist international politics. The "isolation" of Jewish law is thus an essential facet of Jewish existence in the sense that it prepares, and defers, and represents the ultimate unity of humanity. Because Jewish religion, as *a* religion of reason, is necessarily bound up with Jewish nationality, law is indeed necessary for a "political" reason, if we understand "politics" to comprise the "world politics" of nationalities and confederation among states.[64]

This messianic logic of political realization through law, furthermore, also points back to the alterity or messianicity of law that we encountered in the *Ethik*: Alongside Recht, Cohen's main term for showing how ethics relates to law, we found there that the idea of Gesetz/nomos shows up when Cohen reworks the notion of autonomy, meaning self-legislation or

63 My reading of this passage thus differs somewhat from that of George Kohler, who glosses it as follows: "It is monotheism that enables cultural interaction in the first place, therefore monotheism must be preserved at the price of the inconvenient cultural isolation of the Jews" ("Finding God's Purpose," chap. 7, 244). Cohen does not seem to be thinking of an "interaction" among cultures (although to be sure his remarks about the necessary plurality of "nationality" and the embrace of the foreign would be consistent with a call for interaction), but he regards monotheism/religion of reason to mean the same thing as sustaining and bringing forward the *Kulturwelt* as a world-historical project. There is also no indication that he views the isolation of law as an inconvenience or as a price to be paid. Indeed, Cohen denounces attempts to ask whether law poses "hindrances to the ease of cultural interchange" as a false "consideration" or concession (*Rücksicht*) that is an "opportunism and eudaemonism" (RV 426/366).

64 This point has recently been forcefully argued by Miguel Vatter – chiefly with reference to *Deutschtum und Judentum* – in "Nationality, State and Global Constitutionalism in Hermann Cohen's Wartime Writings," in *100 Years of European Philosophy Since the Great War*, ed. Rory Jeffs, Jack Reynolds, and Matthew Sharpe (New York: Springer, 2017).

giving oneself one's own law (nomos). We saw that autonomy is the self's positing of its purpose or telos, and denotes a futural task of realizing freedom, and that law/Gesetz/nomos is a kind of possibility that is generative and futural, a task that belongs to the self in guiding the self *and* is at the same time other than that self. This idea of a futural law is what enabled Cohen's analysis, in the *Ethik*, of Recht as the domain in which ethical concepts and principles are generated.[65] To that analysis of the idea of law or legality as a force toward, or from, otherness and the future in the horizon of what Cohen calls Allheit – the legal community toward which ethical action is oriented – we now are able to add the sense of "law" that emerges from the chapter of that title in *Religion of Reason*: law as the future realization of a messianic humanity, by way of Jewish "nationality."

The two senses of futurity of law – one in relation to a general theory of law (Recht), the other in relation to Jewish philosophy of religion – indicate what Cohen's philosophy offers for a Jewish political thought. A Cohenian political thought in this vein would transcend both the particularist concept of the political imputed by Cohen to Spinoza, and the idea of politics applied by Leo Strauss in his critique that Cohen reduces law (the nomos tradition) to ethics. In that sense, then, rather than ethicizing or depoliticizing law – as is sometimes claimed[66] – Cohen's account of law in Judaism proposes a Jewish existence that is in fact geared toward generating a new, universalist politics.

---

65 Although I cannot develop a full analysis of it here, Cohen's depiction, toward the end of *Religion* chapter 16, of Jewish law/Gesetz as a "lever," which not only "supports" but "generates" or "fuels" the teaching, similarly parallels the structure of ethics being generated out of law/Recht that we find in his *Ethik*. In introducing the idea of law as a generative "positive lever," Cohen says he is supplementing the notion of the protective "fence around the teaching," which we saw him discuss earlier in the chapter. Here, as well as earlier in the chapter, Cohen is also building critically on Leopold Zunz's characterization of law as a "symbol" in the latter's 1843 essay "Thefillin." A prominent intervention in the debates about religious reform, Zunz's essay argued that Jews ought not to abandon observances such as laying tefillin. RV 398–9/342–4, 429–30/369–70. Zunz, "Thefillin" (1843) in *Gesammelte Schriften*, vol. 2 (Berlin: Louis Gerschel, 1876), 172–6.

66 See, for example, the editors' prefatory note to the selections from Cohen's *Ethik* and his *Religion* included in Leora Batnitzky and Yonatan Y. Brafman, eds., *Jewish Legal Theories: Writings on State, Religion, and Morality* (Waltham, MA: Brandeis University Press, 2018), 29. While, as the editors observe, law has a different status in relation to ethics and politics in Cohen's systematic ethical philosophy than it does in his theory of Jewish religion – a difference, I have been arguing, that can be analyzed to some extent by attending to the difference between Recht and Gesetz – I have sought to show here that Cohen's theory of law in Judaism nevertheless involves a "political task." See also Leora Batnitzky, "Hans Kelsen and Hermann Cohen: From Theology to Law and Back," in *The Foundation of the Juridico-Political*, ed. Ian Bryan, Peter Langford, and John McGarry (New York: Routledge, 2016), 53.

Chapter Five

Against "Affective Expansiveness": Cohen's Critique of Stammler's Theory of "Right Law"

The previous chapter showed Cohen to be making a decisive argument, in the course of the "Law" chapter of *Religion of Reason*, for a Jewish political task, a Jewish politics that is oriented toward a messianic universal humanity. I suggested that this Jewish politics takes shape in Cohen's argumentation by way of a kind of substitution of one meaning of "law" by an entirely other meaning. In the course of the argument I traced, Cohen's vehement objections to a politicization of Judaism à la Spinoza, in which "law" applies to the Jewish nation as a particularity, for the sake of its material and temporal advantage and good fortune, is replaced by an understanding of a law of "religion," serving a universalist international politics.

A move Cohen makes in his attack on Spinoza's politicization of Judaism, in the famous polemical "Spinoza" essay of 1915, is worth a second look: At one point in the essay, Cohen criticizes Spinoza's view that the law that is given to the Jews is bound to a promise of "temporal happiness" and "prosperity" for their state, and is merely for the sake of a material, political advantage[1] by asking rhetorically: "Are the laws only *state laws*, or are they also laws of *faith/belief* [*Glaube*]?" What Cohen finds objectionable above all is that Spinoza fails to acknowledge any universalist aspect to Jewish election.[2] Thus, Cohen contends that Spinoza ignores

1 Baruch Spinoza, *Theological-Political Treatise*, 2nd ed., trans. Samuel Shirley (Indianapolis: Hackett, 2001), 38. Cf. *Spinoza's Theologico-Political Treatise*, trans. and ed. Martin D. Yaffe (Newburyport, MA: Focus Publishing, 2004), 34. Discussed by Cohen in "Spinoza über Staat und Religion, Judentum und Christentum" (1915), JS3: 328, translated by Robert S. Schine as *Spinoza on State and Religion, Judaism and Christianity* (Jerusalem: Shalem Press, 2014), which includes the JS pagination.

2 At best, Cohen finds Spinoza to be making contradictory claims on this score. See Cohen, "Spinoza," JS3: 335.

the fact that God's covenant with Abraham promises: "You shall become a blessing for all families of the earth."[3] Instead, Cohen writes, Spinoza identifies God's political covenant with the Israelites as merely an instance of "egotism," "utilitism," and "opportunism." Consistently with this, Spinoza regards all biblical laws as political, as state laws, and is not interested in whether biblical laws have any relevance for general human morality. Cohen's prime example for this is that Spinoza, as he puts it, "does not remember" (to which he adds in parentheses, "but does he really not remember?") "that the Talmud invented and erected the laws of the sons of Noah" – laws whose purpose according to Cohen was to avoid excluding the non-Jewish peoples from divine law.[4] In particular, according to Cohen, Spinoza ought to have "remembered" that the concept of the Noahide represents "a main objection to his entire theory."[5]

Postponing a more detailed discussion of the category of the Noahide, and Cohen's interest in it, to the next chapter, for now let us note that, as part of his argument against Spinoza, Cohen identifies a mistaken politicization of Jewish law with a forgetting of the non-Jew, that is, of the foreigner. We can connect this with the argument we traced in the "Law" chapter of the *Religion*: Judaism is a religion insofar as it is a "nationality" (and not, in Cohen's terminology in that chapter, a "nation"); and "nationality" entails plurality, the embrace of the "manifold of cultural phenomena" for their "share in reason" (RV 423/364). In the argument of the *Religion*, embracing this plurality is what it means for Judaism to be a messianic-universalist project.

In this chapter, we return to the argument of Cohen's *Ethik* in order to bring out the logic by which he is able to align a positive principle of law (Recht) – which is a law-as-politics – with an immediate, indispensable "remembering" of the foreigner. With this, we are continuing to address the question posed at the end of chapter 2 in view of the tacit demand for a notion of legality informed by Judaism (Gesetz) alongside the notion of Recht – the system of law or "right" that the *Ethik* is principally concerned with. We asked in chapter 2 whether a positive notion of law in Judaism might be articulated in Cohen's writings that corresponds to his criticism of a system of law/Recht that lacks the notion of "legality" – Gesetz as something futural and heteronomous. After showing, in the previous chapter, that for Cohen law/Gesetz in Judaism names

3 Gen. 12:3 (New Revised Standard Version): "I will bless those who bless you, and the one who curses you I will curse; and in you all the families of the earth shall be blessed." Cohen, "Spinoza," JS3: 328–9.

4 Cohen, "Spinoza," JS3: 330.

5 Cohen, "Spinoza," 345.

the transcending of the particular politics of the nation-state toward an inter-national messianic politics of universalism, we now return to the notion of Recht, which (as laid out in chapter 1) was the main term in Cohen's overall argument that ethics is rooted in law and generated out of law. This term, Recht, scarcely appears in the works on Judaism – as is consistent with the conventional use of the term Gesetz to talk about law, halakhah, in Judaism. Yet it would appear that if Cohen had any notion that Judaism could be a source of a law that could sustain ethics, this would need to correspond to something in Judaism that could be termed Recht – law in the sense of a juridical system, a system of public legal institutions.

In the next and final chapter of this book, I will suggest that the category of "the neighbor" and the problem of "love-of-neighbor," as these are treated both in the *Ethik* and in the Jewish writings, best represents the presence of Recht – law as a system in a horizon of *Allheit*, and generative of ethics – in Cohen's philosophy of Judaism. That is, the neighbor – which Cohen understands in conjunction with love-of-the stranger – best embodies, within the terms of Cohen's Jewish philosophy, the main argument of the *Ethik* about law in its relation to ethics. I shall argue that it is by looking at Cohen's treatments of love-of-neighbor in the Jewish writings alongside the main argument of the *Ethik* that we can fully appreciate one of the most important and distinctive aspects of the latter work: Cohen's rejection of ethical models based on what he called "affective expansion" as a key part of his argument that ethics is generated out of legal institutions. The purpose of the present chapter is to lay out Cohen's critique of those legal models, and to do so in particular by tracing in the *Ethik* his vehement critical response to the influential legal theory of Rudolf Stammler – a figure who had, at least for a time, a close association with Cohen and Natorp and the Marburg School – as well as explicating the background and significance of that critical response.

Juridico-Ethics Is Not "Expansive"

As we saw in chapter 2, a core principle for Cohen in the *Ethik* is that ethics is oriented to Allheit (his term for the kind of universality that characterizes ethical life as being in common). Ethics consists of the correlation of the human individual with Allheit. This correlation, which, we saw, is also a "generation" by way of "hypothesis," is opposed to a conception of the individual as a function of plurality. Plurality (*Mehrheit*) is a numeric concept, while Allheit refers to a "unity" (*Einheit*) that is not countable, not an individuality (*Einzelheit*) (ErW 233). Allheit is a unity that is posited of the ethical subject from the start, and not an aggregate of individual subjects. "Plurality" for Cohen refers to plural entities or "particularities" and thus aligns with particularism, which in his view can only be damaging to the ethical project (ErW 60).

The correlation of the individual with Allheit is to be thought of as a kind of infinite – or better, "non-quantifiable" – "summation" or gathering. Crucially, Cohen opposes to such a movement any tendency to argue that ethics is a function of *expanding* our point of view from ourselves to a consideration for others. Ethics is not a matter of expansion or expansiveness. Cohen explains this objectionable tendency with reference to the "prejudice" in favor of "individuality," particularly the mistaken view that only the "individual person" can be a legal subject. For Cohen, as we saw in chapter 1, this view is untenable because it entails psychologism, naturalism, and even biologism: As soon as we privilege the individual person as the ethical subject, we are compelled to speculate about that person's psyche (and, he adds – I would say, only half-jokingly – their physiology as well[6]) as a factor in ethical subjectivity; and we also open up ethical theory to controversies about the "reality of the 'I'" (ErW 235). (Here we may recall Cohen's objection to the idea that ethics is a "law in our members" [ErW 99].)

The way out of this dilemma is not to further "hypostasize" the individual "I," but to come to a more precise understanding of specifically

6 Here is Cohen's suggestion for analyzing the problem of this "prejudice" in favor of the individual person "psychologically":

> Man wird versucht, schon *psychologisch* gegen dieses Vorurteil anzugehen. Wie steht es denn mit dem Stoffwechsel dieser ehrenwerten Person? Und mit dem Wechsel normaler und gesteigerter, sowie geminderter geistiger Regsamkeit in ihr? Und mit den Stufen der Aufmerksamkeit und des vollen wachen Bewusstseins?

> It is tempting to approach this prejudice, for a start, *psychologically*. How do things stand with this esteemed person's metabolism [*Stoffwechsel*]? And with the alternation [*Wechsel*] of normal and intenstified, as well as diminished mental activity in them? And with the levels of attention and of full waking consciousness? (ErW 235)

See also the quotation reproduced below from ErW 241, in which Cohen likens the idea that we can "expand" our intensity of affect to imagining the capacity of a "large stomach" – an analogy that must be read in conjunction with Cohen's contempt for any denunciation of socialism for being merely a "question of the stomach" (*Magenfrage*), that is, a kind of eudaemonism (ErW 295). Steven Schwarzschild discusses this remark and contextualizes it in debates about socialism in "The Democratic Socialism of Hermann Cohen," *Hebrew Union College Annual* 27 (1956), 419; included in *The Tragedy of Optimism: Writings on Hermann Cohen*, ed. George Y. Kohler (Albany: State University of New York Press, 2018).

ethico-legal subjectivity (which Cohen aims to do with his reflections on the legal person, discussed in chapter 1). In particular, Cohen criticizes the psycho-physiological view that bases an account of ethics in the individual person's capacity to "expand" their perspective outward from self-centeredness and willfulness. Such expansions are said to "begin from affect and, nourished by affect, generate/produce an object that they can therefore also only give to affect, or give back to affect" (ErW 235).

Cohen takes patriotism, "the concept of fatherland," to be an example for "a means for such an expansion of the self." In that sense, "the egotism of the individual is dulled by [the concept of fatherland]; the idea of a collectivity is ignited." Although Cohen welcomes the idea of patriotism in principle,[7] he also warns of the "grave dangers" of this "salutary cultural concept." Cohen raises the question of how to negotiate the "antinomy" between patriotism or particularism – or, more precisely, the "affect" of love-of-country – and cosmopolitanism, or universalism (ErW 235–6). (Below, we will see that Cohen actually credits the biblical prophets with having raised this essential question.) In line with his rejection of Gierke's organicist theory of *Genossenschaft*,[8] here too Cohen insists that the legal person is not the result of "affective expansion." The "legal value" of the concept of the legal person lies in its having nothing to do with "devouring and absorption." That is, by adopting the legal person as the model for ethical subjectivity, Cohen is rejecting the idea that a single entity may reach for collectivity by "externalizing" itself or its own individuality (ErW 236):

> It must not be a matter of expanding the stages of affect [*Affektstufen*] such that the "I," as if it possessed a large stomach, were supposed to take up into itself ever more particularities and were supposed to expand itself in them.

7 See Michael Zank, *The Idea of Atonement in the Philosophy of Hermann Cohen* (Providence, RI: Brown Judaic Studies, 2000; repr. Brown Judaic Studies Open Humanities Book Program, 2020), 283, https://repository.library.brown.edu/studio/item/bdr:1111035; and Eggert Winter, *Ethik und Rechtswissenschaft: eine historisch-systematische Untersuchung zur Ethik-Konzeption des Marburger Neukantianismus im Werke Hermann Cohens* (Berlin: Duncker & Humblot, 1980), 339–42. For a critical discussion of nationality in Cohen's works, see Hartwig Wiedebach, *Die Bedeutung der Nationalität für Hermann Cohen* (Hildesheim: Olms, 1997), including analyses of Cohen's attitude to love-of-country in the *Ethik* and elsewhere, at 123–6; translated by William Templer as *The National Element in Hermann Cohen's Philosophy and Religion* (Leiden: Brill, 2012), 97–9.

8 See the discussion in chapter 1.

> Nicht um Verbreiterung der Affektstufen darf es sich handeln, so dass das Ich, als hätte es einen großen Magen, immer mehr Partikularitäten in sich aufzunehmen und in ihnen sich zu erweitern hätte. (ErW 241)

The collectivity resulting from such expansion would again be a plurality, and not a collectivity of Allheit. Furthermore, it would be a volatile collectivity, since what can be expanded can also be contracted to selfishness again.

By the same token, ethical subjectivity is not a function of some kind of "humble diminution" (ErW 236). Thus, legal personhood is not based on any affect,[9] but is purely an "action of the will," a "legal action." Ethical self-consciousness is the "self-consciousness of pure will," based on the "*logical* meaning of the legal person" (ErW 237), which, as we saw earlier, is the logic of hypothesis.

Cohen extends his analysis of legal personhood as generative of ethical subjectivity also to the category of the state; he views the legal person as yielding the concept of the state (ErW 256). Thus, what he demonstrates regarding the generation of will as an "ethical hypothesis" in the case of the Genossenschaft is also what is called for in the generation of the "will of the state," as an expression of Allheit (ErW 243). Cohen underscores that it is precisely insofar as ethics is oriented to Allheit and does not pursue the particularist logic of pluralities – it is, after all, state that is the ethically relevant category, and not people/Volk (ErW 257) – that "the science of law expands to become the science of the state," political science (ErW 71). The "concept of state" yielded by that of the legal person "teaches" that ethics cannot be generated on the level of natural human individualities (ErW 256).[10]

---

9 Cohen mentions "the religious affects" here, in particular "love of God" (ErW 236), a notion that receives detailed treatment in his writings on Judaism.

10 Cohen applies this understanding to his assessment of the significance of Jewish political emancipation, in his commemorative essay on the 100th anniversary of the 1812 edict giving Jews in Prussia full citizenship rights: "It is only in the unity of the state that the individual can found for itself its own most profound unity.... It is only right/law with respect to the state [*das Recht am Staate*] that generates *human right* with respect to the culture of humanity." Only thanks to the edict granting citizenship are Jews no longer only human beings (this notion being a "religious abstraction") but become "persons" in a juridical sense (*Rechtspersonen*). Cohen, "Emanzipation. Zur Hundertjahrfeier des Staatsbürgertums der preußischen Juden (11. März 1912)," JS2: 221, 222. For a critical view of this aspect of Cohen's ethical theory, see Robert Gibbs, "Jurisprudence Is the Organon of Ethics," in *Hermann Cohen's Critical Idealism*, ed. Reinier Munk (Heidelberg: Springer, 2005), 210–12.

The "Relative" Morality of "Community"

As mentioned earlier, in favoring the legal person, or the Genossenschaft/association, as the model of ethical subjectivity, Cohen was deliberately bypassing any possible appeal to the category of community or *Gemeinschaft*, which is a hallmark of an organicist social theory of the kind that he systematically avoids.[11] (Steven Schwarzschild sees Cohen's rejection of this term in light of a disagreement with Ferdinand Tönnies, who famously put forward the opposition between Gemeinschaft, an organic and authentic kind of collectivity, and *Gesellschaft* [society], an artificially instituted form of collectivity. But Tönnies commented in his review of Cohen's *Ethik* that "as far as I know, and about this I have no reason to be surprised," Cohen was clearly not familiar with this conceptual distinction.[12]) For Cohen, ethical subjectivity, as oriented toward Allheit, cannot be adequately accounted for by the term Gemeinschaft, in that the notion of "Gemeinschaft" promotes the "relative" morality of plurality.

We can best understand what is at stake in Cohen's dismissal of a "relative" morality by identifying and clarifying the view that he is opposing. As has been observed by Schwarzschild and Eggert Winter, among others, numerous remarks in the *Ethik* point to the prime target of (or the prime occasion for) this dismissal of "relative" morality. Cohen is reacting vehemently to the work of Rudolf Stammler, specifically his work of legal philosophy *Die Lehre von dem richtigen Rechte,* published two years before his own *Ethik.*[13]

---

11 See ErW 76–7, 236–41, 249–50, 484–6, 489, 573–6. I touched on this contrast between *Genossenschaft* and *Gemeinschaft* in chapter 1 above. The preference for "'Genossenschaft' to both 'Gesellschaft' and 'Gemeinschaft'" was also noted by Steven Schwarzschild, "Introduction" to Cohen's *Ethik,* in *Werke,* vol. 7 (1981), XXXI*n6; included in *The Tragedy of Optimism.* It seems, however, that Cohen does not especially object to the term *Gesellschaft* – though he does explain it in terms of *Genossenschaft* (ErW 254).

12 Schwarzschild, "Introduction" to Cohen's *Ethik,* XXXI*n6; Winter, *Ethik und Rechtswissenschaft,* 320n147, citing Ferdinand Tönnies, "Ethik und Sozialismus," *Archiv für Sozialwissenschaft und Sozialpolitik* 29 (1909): 905. Not surprisingly, Tönnies himself finds that that which Cohen wishes to call *Genossenschaft* "in my own thinking belongs instead to *Gemeinschaft*" (912).

13 Rudolf Stammler, *Die Lehre von dem richtigen Rechte* (Berlin: J. Guttentag, 1902); translated by Isaac Husik as *The Theory of Justice* (New York: MacMillan, 1925). Although Stammler published a second edition of this work in 1926, I will be referring throughout only to the 1902 edition (LrR). Translations are almost all my own, though I supply parallel page references to the English translation. In

Stammler and Cohen

Rudolf Stammler (1856–1938) was an influential jurist and legal theorist who, at least at some point during his intellectual development, had a close relationship with the Marburg School of Neo-Kantianism. (The nature of this relationship has been characterized variously. In his 1994 study of the philosophy of law of Marburg Neo-Kantianism, Claudius Müller observes that over time, scholars' initially frequent characterization of Stammler as having "emerged from" that school gave way to a more differentiated view that he "stood in some proximity" to Natorp and Cohen, but was by no means a member of the school.[14])

---

particular, I am translating Stammler's term "richtig" – applied to law (Recht) – with "right," and not, as has often been done, with "just." (Thomas Willey also adopted this practice in his discussion of Stammler in *Back to Kant: The Revival of Kantianism in German Social and Historical Thought, 1860–1914* [Detroit: Wayne State University Press, 1978], 124–30.) Thus, I refer to Stammler's theory of "right law," and not, as in the translated title of this work, to his "theory of justice." See also note 27 below.

On the general significance of Stammler for Cohen's *Ethik*, see Schwarzschild, introduction to Hermann Cohen, *Ethik des reinen Willens*, XV*–XVII*; and Winter, *Ethik und Rechtswissenschaft*, 20–4, 262, 322, and 322n159. Stammler's oeuvre is discussed, and its relationship to Marburg Neo-Kantianism (specifically Cohen and Natorp) explored, in the following works: Claudius Müller, *Die Rechtsphilosophie des Marburger Neukantianismus. Naturrecht und Rechtspositivismus in der Auseinandersetzung zweischen Hermann Cohen, Rudolf Stammler und Paul Natorp* (Tübingen: Mohr Siebeck, 1994); Matthias Wenn, *Juristische Erkenntniskritik. Zur Rechts- und Sozialphilosophie Rudolf Stammlers* (Baden-Baden: Nomos, 2003); Wolfgang Kersting, "Neukantianische Rechtsbegründung. Rechtsbegriff und richtiges Recht bei Cohen, Stammler und Kelsen," in *Neukantianismus und Rechtsphilosophie*, ed. Robert Alexy, Lukas H. Meyer, Stanley L. Paulson, and Gerhard Sprenger (Baden-Baden: Nomos, 2002). An important resource for assessing this relationship is Paul Natorp, "Recht und Sittlichkeit. Ein Beitrag zur kategorialen Begründung der praktischen Philosophie. Mit besonderem Bezug auf Hermann Cohens 'Ethik des reinen Willens' und Rudolf Stammlers 'Theorie der Rechtswissenschaft,'" *Kant Studien* 18 (1913) (an essay discussed above in chapter 1). Brief, but useful discussions of the topic may be found in Peter A. Schmid, "Das Naturrecht in der Rechtsethik Hermann Cohens," *Zeitschrift für philosophische Forschung* 47, no. 3 (1993): 410–1n15; Peter A. Schmid, *Ethik als Hermeneutik. Systematische Untersuchungen zu Hermann Cohens Rechts- und Tugendlehre* (Würzburg: Königshausen & Neumann, 1995), 55–7; and Helmut Holzhey, "Analytische Hermeneutik und reine Rechtslehre. Die Transformation neukantianischer Theoreme in die reine Rechtslehre Kelsens," in *Hermeneutik und Strukturtheorie des Rechts*, ed. Michael W. Fischer, Erhard Mock, and Hermut Schreiner (Stuttgart: Steiner, 1984), 103–6.

14 Müller, *Rechtsphilosophie des Marburger Neukantianismus*, 3.

Stammler was a professor at Marburg from 1882 to 1884, during which period he "sought out contact" with Cohen and with Natorp, who was at that time Privatdozent under Cohen and with whom Stammler had a long-standing personal friendship.[15] (Following the intellectual break between Stammler and Cohen, it was Natorp who sought to mediate between their positions, including by publishing "Recht und Sittlichtkeit" [1913], a joint review of Cohen's *Ethik* and Stammler's *Theorie der Rechtswissenschaft* [1911].)[16]

Cohen's critical idealism and his reconstruction of Kant had had a decisive influence on Stammler.[17] As has been shown by Matthias Wenn, Stammler credits Cohen with having made the essential distinction, in studying a given thought, between studying its structure and studying its genesis – that is, between systematic and genetic inquiry. Writing retrospectively about his intellectual debt to Cohen in 1923 (and thus long after the intellectual break between the two thinkers, and of course also after Cohen's death in 1918), Stammler recalls a key lesson he learned from Cohen: To ask what is "objectively contained" in a given thought or idea requires initially suspending the question of "how [that thought] may have come to be."[18] Stammler thus credits Cohen with having clearly defined the project of philosophy, as an inquiry into the conditions of possibility of experience and of knowledge, in opposition to that of psychology (an opposition familiar from our discussion of Cohen's ethico-legal philosophy in chapter 1).

For Stammler, this core principle of *Erkenntniskritik* (critique of cognition/knowledge) applies not only to the "causal sciences" such as the

15 Wenn, *Juristische Erkenntniskritik*, 22, 77. See also Helmut Holzhey, *Cohen und Natorp*, vol. 1, *Ursprung und Einheit. Die Geschichte der "Marburger Schule" als Auseinandersetzung um die Logik des Denkens* (Basel/Stuttgart: Schwabe, 1986), 26. Volume 2 of this work, subtitled *Der Marburger Neukantianismus in Quellen*, includes letters that document the conflict between Stammler and Cohen, as well as Natorp's stance; see for example, 312, 314–18, 319, 331, 360, and 363.

16 Rudolf Stammler, *Theorie der Rechtswissenschaft* (Halle: Buchhandlung des Waisenhauses, 1911). See Winter, *Ethik und Rechtswissenschaft*, 24n38; Holzhey, *Cohen und Natorp*, 1:326n35.

17 See Wenn, *Juristische Erkenntniskritik*, 54, 58–9, 76–8, for an account of Stammler's "imprecise" crediting of Cohen's book *Kants Theorie der Erfahrung* (1871), which Wenn argues is somewhat misaligned with the actual impact of Cohen's ideas on Stammler's thinking.

18 Rudolf Stammler, "Die grundsätzlichen Richtungen der neueren Jurisprudenz" (1923), in *Rechtsphilosophische Abhandlungen und Vorträge*, vol. 2 (Charlottenburg: Pan Verlag Rolf Heise, 1925), 374; translated as "Fundamental Tendencies in Modern Jurisprudence," *Michigan Law Review* 21 (1923): 864. Discussed by Wenn, *Juristische Erkenntniskritik*, 54, 58–9.

natural sciences – that is, to descriptive claims – but also to what he calls *Zweckwissenschaften*, which is typically translated as "teleological science." Teleological science makes normative claims, or claims about "finality," that is, claims about relationships between means and ends.[19] These are distinct from claims about causality, which are the purview of natural science. Understood from the point of view of *Erkenntniskritik*, the claims of teleological science are not psychological claims, or any kind of empirical claims.

Stammler uses this distinction between causality and finality to grasp the category of "willing," which he defines as the "positing of an object that is to be effected/to be put into effect," which is to say, the positing of a "purpose."[20] Stammler conceives of the conceptual pair "means [*Mittel*] and ends/purpose [*Zweck*]" as "originary (in the logical sense!) forms of thought." As originary, logical forms, or forms of thought, means and ends have an equivalent status to that of the conceptual pair "cause and effect," which Stammler understands as "order-producing ways [i.e., types] of corporeal cognition."[21] This allows Stammler, as Julius Stone puts it, to grasp "willing" as a "basic category of thinking about law and justice," that is, as a transcendental condition of thought.[22] To understand legal science as a (teleological) science is to approach it from the point of view of what is common to all sciences: that they "bring the manifold to a conceptual unity."[23] Stammler characterizes this feature in terms of a conceptual or logical "ordering": "The concept of science and that of the fundamental unified ordering of our world of ideas/thoughts [*Gedankenwelt*] is one and the same."[24] Teleological science, as a logical inquiry into "ends" or "purposes," would thus examine the "ways of thought" that are involved in "willing" and would determine the

19 See the explanation by Julius Stone, *Human Law and Human Justice* (Stanford: Stanford University Press, 1965), 170, citing Stammler, *Lehrbuch der Rechtsphilosophie*, 3rd ed. (Berlin/Leipzig: de Gruyter, 1928), 57. Claudius Müller notes that in seeking to establish a "logic of teleological science," Stammler is adapting an idea from Natorp's logic. Müller, *Rechtsphilosophie des Marburger Neukantianismus*, 145.

20 Rudolf Stammler, *Lehrbuch der Rechtsphilosophie*, 1st ed. (Berlin/Leipzig: de Gruyter, 1922), 54.

21 Stammler, *Lehrbuch der Rechtsphilosophie*, 1st ed., 54n3.

22 Stone, *Human Law*, 170. Cf. Müller, *Rechtsphilosophie des Marburger Neukantianismus*, 145–6; and Jes Bjarup, "Continental Perspectives on Natural Law Theory and Legal Positivism," in *The Blackwell Guide to the Philosophy of Law and Legal Theory*, ed. Martin P. Golding and William A. Edmundson (Malden, MA: Blackwell, 2005), 294.

23 Müller, *Rechtsphilosophie des Marburger Neukantianismus*, 145–6.

24 Stammler, *Theorie der Rechtswissenschaft*, 59, 66, as cited by Müller, *Rechtsphilosophie des Marburger Neukantianismus*, 146.

relationships among the ends to which willing is directed. Stammler understands this enterprise to be one that formally conceptualizes human striving and desire.[25]

The distinction between causal and teleological accounts of willing is thus a way of distinguishing a psychological account of a decision or an action from a logical account of the same action. For Stammler, the teleological account makes a claim about, or posits a hypothetical relationship between, a "right purpose" and a "right means." (This is distinct from a "causal" hypothetical claim about the suitability of a given means to some particular purpose.)[26]

Similarly to what we saw in Kelsen, Stammler is concerned to define law apart from any appeal to morality (LrR 52–3/40–1). The theory of law, and of "right law" (or justice[27]), is to proceed as a formal method, without reference to the material that it is applied to. Thus, it is a mistake to appeal to something other than law, such as equity (*Billigkeit*), in order to demand that a law or a judgment materially conform to it in order to meet the standard of "rightness" (LrR 49–50/37–8). At most, "law" (Recht) or "valid law" (*geltendes Recht*) on the one hand, and "equitable law" on the other can be said to be two different ways of referring to the selfsame statute: "Law" refers to the positive statutes on the books, whereas "equitable law" refers to the same statute "but in its objective justification." The process of determining such an objective justification is the method that Stammler seeks to establish: the "universally valid, formal method" of determining the "rightness of a law" (*die Richtigkeit eines Rechtes*).[28] We have no way of determining whether a given statute is "right," unless we take into account the internal structure or nature of law/statute as such: the fact that it expresses a "juristic willing" in relation to a posited end, and is thus by its very nature an "attempt to be right law."[29]

25 Müller, 146, drawing on *Theorie der Rechtswissenschaft*, 64.

26 Here I am following the explanation of Wenn, *Juristische Erkenntniskritik*, 66–7.

27 Julius Stone articulates (his "exasperation" at) the interpretative problem raised by Stammler's use of the adjective "richtig" (which I have been rendering as "right") alongside the standard German term that is generally translated as "just," "gerecht," without clarifying what difference he intends to capture with these separate terms (*Human Law*, 170–1). The possible gap between the two terms is obscured by Husik's and others' translation of Stammler's "richtig" as "just," including Husik's translation of Stammler's book *Die Lehre von dem richtigen Rechte* as *The Theory of Justice.*

28 Cf. LrR 116–17/89–90, and the discussion in Holzhey, "Analytische Hermeneutik," 105.

29 Rudolf Stammler, "Wesen des Rechtes und der Rechtswissenschaft," in *Die Kultur der Gegenwart. Ihre Entwicklung und ihre Ziele*, ed. Paul Hinneberg, Teil II, Abteilung VIII: *Systematische Rechtswissenschaft* (Berlin/Leipzig: Teubner, 1906), XLIV.

If we recall that Cohen in the *Ethik* began from a rejection of classic ways of linking law and morality, we can see a key agreement with Stammler on this score. Both thinkers reject a classic natural-law attempt to ground law in morality.[30] On the other hand, the positivism of Kelsen that we discussed briefly in chapter 1 also provides a useful point of reference for understanding Stammler's approach: Kelsen had defined a legal norm as a hypothetical relationship between two claims (e.g., a contract takes place when "a merchant writ[es] a certain letter to another merchant, who writes back in reply" [RR 17/8]). Similarly, Stammler defines a norm as a hypothetical relationship between "right purpose" and "right means," and with this definition avoids relying on the category of morality to understand the nature of law or statute. Yet, if we consider the appeal to "rightness" that is bound up with this definition, Stammler does not look much like a positivist. As Julius Stone points out, in reading Stammler, we must distinguish the characteristically Neo-Kantian interest in establishing "a priori categories of thought ... independent of experience, which make experience possible," and in Stammler's case, the "pre-experiential categories or 'pure forms' of thinking about law," from "the field of experience of positive law" itself. The categories of thought, such as the teleological character that Stammler ascribes to volition, "do not arise from" the experience of positive law or statute; rather, they are transcendental conditions of such law.[31] To ask, as Stammler's "theoretical" account of law does, how we can tell whether positive law is a "right means to right ends" is, as he himself puts it, a distinct enterprise from developing a "technical" account of the "meaning and actual content" of positive law, of statutes and legal institutions "as we find them" ("gesetztes Recht, wie es da ist").[32]

---

30 See LrR 116–17/89–90.

31 Stone, *Human Law,* 169.

32 LrR 3/3 and 34/26; cf. 278–80/212–15. Peter Schmid interprets this contrast between "theoretical" and "technical" legal science as a rejection of positivistic legal science. This element is surely present in *Die Lehre von dem richtigen Rechte.* For example, Stammler clearly sets up his proposed method, which is supposed to make it possible to determine "right"/just law, explicitly against the idea that a jurist should take posited law (whether contemporary or historic) as the baseline for such a determination (LrR 35–7/27–9). However, Schmid does not make a case for why we should take Stammler's narrowly defined "technical" legal science, to which Stammler opposes his own "theoretical" legal science, as representative of actual streams of legal positivism (*Ethik als Hermeneutik. Systematische Untersuchungen zu Hermann Cohens Rechts- und Tugendlehre* [Würzburg: Königshausen & Neumann, 1995], 55–6). We can recall that Hans Kelsen was surely not interested merely in characterizing the meaning and content of legal statutes, but in understanding what makes law law. Like Stammler, Kelsen was asking a transcendental question about the conditions of possibility of law.

Stammler between Natural Law Theory and Positivism: The "Social Ideal" and the "Particular Community" (*Sondergemeinschaft*)

Thus, we can say that Stammler, like Cohen, occupies an intermediate position between a natural law theory that would ground law in morality, and a legal positivism. Stammler's insistence that he can give an account of "right law" without reference to anything outside of law appears to be qualified by his further stipulation that examining legal norms for their "rightness" entails assessing whether such norms conform to the "social ideal," which pertains to the "community of freely willing human beings" ("Gemeinschaft frei wollender Menschen"). This community is the "final" and "sole" "expression that comprehends in unitary fashion all possible purposes of persons united under the law."[33] The universality of such common willing is predicated, first, on not having any "particular content" or reflecting any specific "concrete striving." The social ideal is not the summation of concrete volitions, but expresses the idea of the objective unity of purposes of all persons who are part of a "legal union." Likewise, this idea of common willing must not be a "merely subjective" or "arbitrary" willing. Rather, we need to imagine the volitions that constitute this legal community as being willed "as ends in themselves."[34]

Many commentators have noted that this additional stipulation of a "social ideal" as part of a definition of "right law" opens the door once again to a natural law theory, which Stammler's legal theory, in its insistence on a formalist approach, was supposed to have left behind.[35] We will see that Stammler's account of the "social ideal" and of how to "span a bridge" between that ideal and its meaning for determining and producing concrete "right law"[36] also provides the basis for Cohen's most strenuous objections to Stammler's legal theory – objections that go to the heart of Cohen's own elaboration of ethics as a matter of Allheit. Indeed, these objections to Stammler help drive Cohen's critique of "affective expansion" as a basis for ethics and law, and thus also his theory of neighbor-love.

---

33 LrR 198/153: "The *content* of a norm of conduct is *right* when, in its specific situation, it corresponds to the idea [*Gedanke*] of the social ideal." Stammler calls this claim "the formula of the community of freely willing human beings," as well as "a definition of the concept of rightness of a content of law." See the discussion in Holzhey, "Analytische Hermeneutik," 105; LrR 201/156; and Stammler, "Wesen," XLIII.

34 LrR 197/153. Cf. Stammler, "Wesen," XLVI, and the discussion in Stone, *Human Law,* 173.

35 Holzhey, "Analytische Hermeneutik," 105; Winter, *Ethik und Rechtswissenschaft,* 22–3, who gives references (in 22–3n32) to earlier commentators who made similar observations.

36 See LrR 204/158; Stone, *Human Law,* 173–4.

Before turning to Cohen's critique, let us look at how Stammler intends to "span" that "bridge" between the objective universality of the "social ideal" and the concrete task of determining "right" law. Stammler's category of the "social ideal" (the "community of freely willing human beings") is neither descriptive – it is not meant to describe an empirically existing state of affairs – nor prescriptive, in that it is not meant to supply a particular, concrete legal norm or a specific legal desideratum. Rather, with this category, Stammler seeks to lay out a "formal method," to articulate a condition of possibility for determining whether a given law is "right" or just. The "social ideal" is meant to express the "highest unity ... which is the necessary condition of any grounded/well-founded judgment about right law." With the help of the method that would thereby be generated, it ought to then be possible, claims Stammler, to examine empirical legal statutes for their "rightness" and to develop concrete legal norms and "just decisions" in cases where individual desires and demands are in conflict.[37]

Stammler attempts to "systematically present" a "methodical procedure" by which such an examination would be possible.[38] To this end, he proposes to establish (1) "a system of *principles* [*Grundsätze*]," and, from there, (2) "doctrines and instructions" that are derived from those principles (LrR 203/158). Stammler's "principles of right law," together with what he will subsequently introduce as the "model of right law," are thus the mechanisms for "spanning a bridge" between the "idea of right law" and that idea's "meaning for particular questions of law."

In reviewing the basic claims contained in this complex structure of "principles" and "model" of right law, we are venturing into that area of Stammler's theory where we will best be able see the impetus for Cohen's strenuous objections to that theory, which in their turn are important for understanding Cohen's framing of the "neighbor-love" problematic.

The "principles" are articulations of the "social ideal" (the idea of a "community of freely willing human beings") and thus of the demand that conflicts between individual desires and demands be adjusted or balanced ("ein gerechtes Abwägen," LrR 203/157). A juridical consideration, writes Stammler, can and must run in two directions: it can primarily consider the point of view of the individual member of the legal community, or it can "emphasize" the fact that the individual members "belong together" in their "common goals." In fact, a "legal union"

37 LrR 201–3/156–8. Cf. LrR 203/157: "Thus the notion of the social ideal denotes only the *unity of conditions* under which a determination in juridical matters may deserve the predicate of 'rightness.'" Cf. Stone, *Human Law,* 172–3.

38 Stammler, "Wesen," XLVIII.

(*rechtliche Verbindung*) or community always comprises both of those directions or aspects (LrR 205/159), and the very notion of the "social ideal" "points to this dual direction of thought" (LrR 206/159). With this dualism of the social ideal, Stammler envisions those who are unified in the idea of a legal community ("die rechtlich Verbundenen") – those "who in rightness [*in Richtigkeit*] pursue their individual aims" – in such a way that "each individual emerges as one who at the same time unconditionally respects the other and is likewise respected by him" (LrR 206/159).[39] This stipulation that a legal community should consist of parties who pursue their respective goals in a stance of "unconditional" mutual respect for each other – such that no one is by virtue of engagement in that community coerced into giving up his/her legitimate interests (LrR 206/159) – is translated by Stammler into four "principles of right law," presented as two *pairs* of principles, which derive from the dual demand for (I.) fundamental respect (*Achten*) and (II.) "right" participation (*Teilnehmen*) (LrR 208/161):

Stammler's "Principles of Right Law":[40]

I. "Principles of Respect" (LrR 208/161)	**II. "Principles of Participation" (LrR 211/163)**
I.1 "The content of a volition must not fall prey to the arbitrary will of another."	II.1 "Someone belonging to a legal union[41] must not arbitrarily be excluded from the community."
I.2 "Every legal demand may exist only in the sense that the one obligated by it can still be a neighbor to himself" (*sich noch der Nächste sein kann*).[42]	II.2 "Any legally conferred power of decision/disposing may only be excluding in the sense that the one who is excluded can still be a neighbor to himself."

The two pairs of principles (I.1/I.2 and II.1/II.2) are each *together* supposed to articulate the combination of (I) the idea of a community with

39 See also the parallel discussion in Stammler, "Wesen," XLVIII–L, and the explanations in Stone, *Human Law*, 173–4 (though some of Stone's translations of Stammler's German are misleading).

40 See also Stammler, "Wesen," LI–LII.

41 Stammler's formulation is "ein rechtlich Verbundener," meaning one who is unified (*verbunden*) with others in the legal community. Husik translates this as "a person under a legal obligation." LrR 211/263. Cf. Stone, *Human Law*, 174.

42 See next footnote.

a common purpose; and (II) the idea that human beings, as rational beings, are ends-in-themselves.[43] This combination is also articulated by Stammler as the juxtaposition or thinking-together of two proverbial principles: (I) "Each shall bear the other's burden," and (II) "Each shall bear his own burden" (i.e., everyone must look out for themselves).[44]

Principle I.1 and its corollary I.2 both articulate the requirement that an individual party not be required to relinquish their legitimate self-interest in favor of the "subjective purposes" of another party.[45] Note that Stammler here takes up the wording of a common German saying that is meant to convey the commonsense reality that I am always going to "put myself first:" "Jeder ist sich selbst der Nächste" – literally, each person is "neighbor"/the nearest (only) to himself.[46]

Principle II.1 and its corollary II.2 express the idea that the legal imperative due to which the members of the community came together in the first place, "for the common struggle for the sake of existence," "must not betray itself" in the following sense: Participation in the community must not mean that *all* one's activity will be coerced into being for the sake of the collective, and that there will no longer be any possibility to take action on behalf of one's own interests.[47] (The bifurcation of each of these demands – "respect" and "participation" – in turn into two "principles," is supposed to be a "methodological" one [LrR

43 Cf. Stammler, "Wesen," L. At LrR 285/218, Stammler specifies this requirement that each person "be able to remain a neighbor to himself": "in the sense of an *end-in-itself*, for the possibility of a *right willing*." Or, in Stone's paraphrase: "The person obliged must remain 'an end in himself, so as to make possible just willing'" (*Human Law*, 174). In other words, Stammler has defined "right willing" as entailing that persons obliged to a legal community exercise their will in such a way that they themselves are ends-in-themselves; this is simply what it means for them to be a community of *freely willing* persons.

Note that Stammler translates this condition of freely willing into "remaining a neighbor to oneself," and thus recasts it as a necessary limitation placed upon their obligations to the legal community. Only if each person obligated to the legal community "remains a neighbor to him- or herself" is the (formula of the) legal community an expression of "right" or just law. See the end of this chapter for my fuller reading of this phrase in view of its invocation of biblical love-of-neighbor and in light of Cohen's critical response to Stammler.

44 Stammler, "Wesen," L.

45 Stammler, LI.

46 Cf. Cohen's comment on this saying in "Der Nächste. Bibelexegese und Literaturgeschichte" (1914/1916), *Werke* 16: 70.

47 This is my reading of the following explanation: "Es [i.e., das rechtliche Gebot, welches die einzelnen zu einem gemeinsamen Kampfe um das Dasein vereinigt] würde aber in einen Widerspruch geraten, wenn es zu gleicher Zeit den Einzelnen dem sozialen Zusammenschlusse zwangsweise unterwürfe und ihn doch im besonderen Falle als einen solchen behandelte, der *ausschliesslich* rechtliche Pflichten hätte" (LrR 211).

208/161]. "Methodologically," I.1 and II.1 have in common that they describe a state of existence/affairs, and I.2 and II.2 have in common that they describe a manner of execution [LrR 211/163].)

Continuing with his task of constructing a "bridge" between the "idea of right law" and its applicability to particular issues of law, Stammler next introduces "the model of right law": The "principles" were supposed to lack any reference to "particular content" and were merely "emanations" or "derivations" of the "idea of right law," such that that idea of right law could be made productive for social-political life (LrR 276/211). Stammler repeatedly insists that, in their claim to universal validity, the "principles" are not in themselves directly applicable to concrete legal issues (e.g., LrR 276–77/211–12).

For this reason, "the model of right law" is needed as a further mediating step. This is a name for the procedure by which open questions about "right conduct" may be "subsumed under the social ideal and its principles" (LrR 277/212). The "model of right law" is further specified by Stammler as being "the idea of a *Sondergemeinschaft*," of a "particular community" (or, in Husik's translation, "special community"; LrR 281/215), a term I will explain below.

Stammler thus envisions a four-step process by which "right law" will be "determined" (*gefunden*) in particular cases (LrR 277/212):

Stammler's "Model of Right Law"

The social ideal

The principles of right law
(principles of respect;
principles of participation)

The model of right law, i.e.,
the particular community
(*Sondergemeinschaft*)

"Justified/correct [*begründet*]
judgment in particular cases"

This procedure is supposed to be distinct from what Stammler calls the "technical" procedure used according to positivist legal theory. Yet Stammler notes a "parallel" between the two (LrR 277–8/212): Stammler's "model of right law," like the "principles," is meant to be "universal." That is, although the "model" is not empirical, it is still supposed to be, or is supposed to yield the condition of possibility for making claims about particular empirical "material" (LrR 280/214). (Positive legal reasoning, by contrast, would use models to "summarize" empirical law in order to find commonalities or "unities" among them [LrR 280/214].)

The "model of right law" conceived by Stammler is thus an intermediate entity between the "principles" and "social ideal" on the one hand and the "manifold of legally ordered/organized human life" on the other. As such, it typifies that aspect of Stammler's theory that generates a lot of objections among commentators. For instance, Peter Schmid writes: "However, Stammler does not succeed in bridging the gap between formal idea of law and concrete legal norm, despite his intentions to the contrary, because the principles and models of right law, as the emanations of the formal idea of law (cf. [LrR] 213), must in the end remain abstract and general and cannot found a concrete normative order."[48]

Most notable for understanding Cohen's response to Stammler, however, is Stammler's equation of the "model of right law" with the "idea of the particular community," the *Sondergemeinschaft.* The idea here is that for "right" law or "right" decision, on the basis of the abstract, universal "principles of right law," to be recognized or undertaken at the level of the concrete "manifold of legally ordered life," the standard of "rightness" must be conceived along the lines of an operation that adjudicates a dispute between two parties: two (or more) "persons, who confront each other in divergent willing." The required mental operation would be one in which the quarreling parties are "posited" as being "in a community" in which each party asserts its wishes, which are in turn disputed by the other party. In this thought experiment, it is a matter of conceiving how this confrontation (*Auseinandersetzung*) about the disputed

48 Schmid, "Das Naturrecht," 411n25. Stone is also critical: "Stammler found corresponding difficulties in his neo-Kantian theory of justice to those which have faced Hans Kelsen in his neo-Kantian theory of the internal structure of the law, namely, difficulties of application to the existential world." "Stammler himself admitted that he had not produced a criterion of certain or easy application...." "Stammler does not satisfactorily bridge the gap between his *a priori* ['social ideal'], 'the principles [of right] law' derived therefrom, and the empirical conflict of claims to which they are supposed to offer a just solution." Stone, *Human Law,* 175, 177, 177–8. For more on the last objection, see 179–80.

matter can proceed "along objective lines."[49] In other words, having imagined the disputing parties as making up a "particular community," the task would then be to apply the "principles of right law" to the working out of the dispute (LrR 284/217). In line with Stammler's earlier stipulations about how the "model" is supposed to work, the mental working out of how a dispute is to be carried out by means of the construct "particular community" is not a positivistic procedure, but a transcendental condition of possibility for the "rightness" of law, a conceptual aid and abstract method, which is at most analogical to actual concrete legal examples or scenarios (LrR 282–4/216–17).

Cohen's Critical Response to Stammler

As two figures who occupy an intermediate position between natural law theory and legal positivism, both Stammler and Cohen were prone to being criticized for being, in fact, natural law theorists, despite their disavowals. We considered some of these criticisms of Cohen in chapter 1. In fact, Cohen himself in the *Ethik* charges Stammler with having insufficiently thought through the legacy or share of historic natural law theory in the contemporary theory of law. He contends there that Stammler's way of objecting to the idea of natural law consists at least in part in "substituting" the idea of "right law" for natural law (*Naturrecht*) (ErW 68). Stammler, according to Cohen, thus fails to appreciate that natural law of necessity always "breaks through." This is to say that for Cohen, ethics has a necessary share in law, which must be properly accounted for. Thus, while both Cohen and Stammler reject the idea that historic, unreconstructed conceptions of morality are entities that precede and somehow have priority over any legal code – such as the ancient Greek idea of "unwritten laws"[50] – for Cohen, the idea of natural law still retains an enduring "moral" and even "sacred value." Consequently, legal science must involve a systematic reflection on its own grounds, which is to say, its connection with ethics. This "ethics of law" Cohen also calls "the law of law," or "natural law" (ErW 70).[51] In Cohen's view, Stammler mistakenly denied this enduring importance of natural law, of the question

49 "Diese jetzt Streitenden und Zweifelnden hat man zunächst in *Gedanken* in eine Gemeinschaft zu setzen, in welche jeder sein umstrittenes Wollen einzubringen hat, auf daß in objektiver Richtlinie die Auseinandersetzung erfolgen könne" (LrR 281/215).

50 ErW 68, cf. ErW 263.

51 Hence, Peter Schmid at one point characterizes Cohen's project as one of "critical natural law" (*kritisches Naturrecht*); see "Das Naturrecht," 421. Winter, *Ethik und Rechtswissenschaft,* 24, gives a similar characterization.

of law's relation to ethics, by failing to see that his own notion of "right law" in fact seeks to rethink that relationship. Stammler asserts that the theory of "right law" completely leaves behind the question of the place of ethics in law; he does not frame his own project as providing a new answer to that very question. Cohen's project in the *Ethik*, by contrast, is to correctly determine the relationship of ethics to law, apart from the natural law tradition – and, indeed in such a way that "ethics must lead us not back to natural law, but to positive legal science" – in the critical-idealist sense of science that I elaborated in chapter 1.[52]

Related to his objection that Stammler's idea of "right law" mistakenly detracts from a project of exploring the proper role of morality, or the legacy of natural law, in the philosophy of law, is Cohen's argument that what Stammler calls "right law" must be grounded in ethics, and that philosophy of law must itself involve a moral philosophy, from the start and throughout (ErW 225–6):

> Ethics must accomplish/implement itself [*sich durchführen*, i.e., carry itself out – D.H.] as philosophy of law.... Legal science, including the theory of the state [*Staatslehre*, i.e., political science], requires ethics.... Legal science requires ethics for its own foundation [*zu ihrer eigenen Grundlegung*].

– declares Cohen, in contrast with what he takes to be Stammler's project of "right law": "to make law [']right['] without seeking, positing,[53] and retaining/securing [*festhalten*] the ground of rightness unambiguously in ethics" (ErW 225). That is, regardless of how Stammler's "rightness" or (to take its standard English translation) "justice" is supposed to be conceived or achieved according to his schema, for Cohen, such a notion can be coherent only if grounded in ethics or moral philosophy:

> Philosophical, systematic ethics does not come afterwards, after legal science has established itself and has made itself [']right['].[54]

52 I have benefited from Schmid's discussion of these passages in *Ethik als Hermeneutik*, 56, although my interpretation here differs from his. See also the parallel discussion in Schmid, "Das Naturrecht," 408–9, 414; and the alternative interpretation by Holzhey in "Analytische Hermeneutik," 104–5.

53 In the first edition, Cohen writes "determining" (*festsetzen*) instead of "positing" (*setzen*).

54 ErW 1st ed.: 214. In the second edition, a version of this sentence is embedded in a much longer new paragraph. As Helmut Holzhey points out in his editorial note to the *Werke* edition of ErW, with only three years between the first edition (1904) and the second (1907), Cohen made almost no substantial changes. One major exception is that he elaborated much more fully his critique of Stammler, particularly the passage I am looking at here, on pp. 225–6 in the second edition. See "Editorische Bemerkung," ErW XXXVI*.

By way of explanation, Cohen suggests that to think of ethics, or "rightness" as "coming after" or "lagging behind" legal science would be tantamount to thinking of logic as "coming after" "mathematical natural science" – a reference to the parallel structure between Cohen's casting of law as the ground or factum of ethics and natural science as the ground/factum (*Faktum der Wissenschaft*) of theoretical philosophy.

While this methodological point made by Cohen may be insufficiently coherent or convincing on its own – given especially what we found in chapter 1 to be the "methodological circularity" of Cohen's own procedure in his ethico-legal philosophy – it gains plausibility and force if we consider how Cohen goes on to substantiate it. Here is the continuation of the paragraph I quoted above, in which Cohen denounces Stammler's project of "right law" as one that seeks "to make law [']right['] without seeking, positing, and retaining/securing [*festhalten*] the ground of rightness unambiguously in ethics":

> [To do so] is to give up, to surrender ethics and philosophy. It must not be conceded that law [first[55]] self-sufficiently and completely independently goes its own way and that, whether beforehand or afterward,[56] there may come an ethics, *as the ethics of the individual and of conviction*. By means of this purported self-sufficiency of law ethics would be robbed of its most proper task. (ErW 225, emphasis added)

This is immediately followed, by way of explanation, by the declaration that was a major focal point for our discussion of autonomy, conviction, and the role of legality in chapter 2:

> For there is no conviction without action; no individual in the ethical sense without legal community [*Rechtsgemeinschaft*]. (ErW 225)

As discussed in chapter 2, the *second* sentence of this two-sentence declaration encompasses Cohen's understanding of ethics as a project that is rooted in law (Recht), in the science of law. This understanding is based on the idea that action in some sense issues from law and Allheit/universality. The *first* sentence expresses a sort of corollary to the second: If a condition of ethical action is its orientation to Allheit, then action must not be thought of as being rooted in a psyche or a conviction – as

---

55 This word appears in the first edition only.

56 In the first edition, instead of "whether beforehand or afterward," Cohen writes, "only afterward." ErW 1st ed.: 214.

if the conviction were the cause of the action, and the action merely the externalization of a conviction.

Adding on to our earlier discussion of this two-part declaration – its combination of an insight about conviction and action with an insight about the orientation of ethical action toward law and collectivity or universality – we are now in a position to understand why it is made at *this particular point* in the *Ethik*, that is, as part of the critical response to Stammler, and thus as a combined insight to which Cohen's confrontation with Stammler gives rise. Taking that confrontation into account, we can now highlight a further corollary contained in sentence 2: Ethical action or ethical will must not be thought of as individual at all, but as pertaining to a legal community from the outset. Although this point does not initially seem strictly distinct from sentence 2 ("no individual in the ethical sense without legal community"), when seen as part of Cohen's critical response to Stammler, it acquires a weight of its own. This is because Stammler's notion of a "social ideal," or "community of freely willing human beings," is based on the notion of a specifically "*social* will," in accordance with the task of determining the "rightness" of the "common ends [*Zwecke*]" of that community. This "social will," as "a communal positing of ends," is defined by Stammler as "a willing *of a particular kind*" ("ein *besonders geartetes* Wollen").[57] "Social willing" is thus distinguished from individual, private "moral willing" (*sittliches Wollen*); they are for Stammler two distinct "tasks of [']right['] willing."

Individual, moral willing is for Stammler an essentially private "wishing" that essentially does not "manifest itself externally." Whether this willing or wishing is "good or evil" depends on "purity of character, purity and truth of the innermost [sphere]." Attaining such "purity," integrity, or self-sincerity is accordingly the moral task of the individual, supported by moral teaching (*sittliche Lehre*), but pertaining to the moral subject's "inner life."[58] "Social willing" is similar to what we saw regarding the "social ideal": It denotes the "regulating order that joins/links/unites [*verbindet*] several human beings to a common pursuit of ends." It is thus "a willing *for others.*" If moral philosophy analyzes and guides the inner work of the individual moral subject toward sincerity and purity of character in the service of "good" private willing, it is the theory of "right law" that is supposed to guide the goodness of "social

57 Stammler, "Wesen," XXXIX.

58 Stammler, "Wesen," XX.

will," in particular by determining the "right manner of cooperation [*Zusammenwirken*]."[59]

The distinction between individual will and social will is thus what undergirds Stammler's understanding of how "right law" is determined, namely as a process in which particular, individual interests are "weighed against" each other "in the interest of the community" (LrR, 196–7/152), as well as Stammler's understanding of the heuristic "particular community" (Sondergemeinschaft) as the means toward determination of "right law."

It should be clear from this account what Cohen mainly would have found objectionable in Stammler's theory. Beyond his somewhat vague formulation of the main complaint that I presented above – that a philosophical ethics must not be a separate project from a philosophy of law – Cohen's declaration "there is ... no individual in the ethical sense without legal community" shows us specifically his opposition to the idea that an *individual* morality is something essentially distinct from *social* or collective action. Stammler had aligned philosophical ethics with individual morality, and legal philosophy (the theory of right law) with collective social action; such a division is incoherent and troubling for Cohen, for whom, we may recall, moral action is *as such* oriented to universality. It would thus be an incoherent idea to posit an individual, inherently and abidingly *private* will that would still be an object of ethical-philosophical questioning. From this we can now also see the reason for Cohen's linkage, in his critical response to Stammler, between the principle "there is ... no individual in the ethical sense without legal community" and the principle "there is no conviction without action" (ErW 225).[60]

---

59 Stammler, "Wesen," XX.

60 Paul Natorp makes clear the connection between the latter idea and the idea that ethics is founded in law when he points out that the free wish or desire to perform an action is central to evaluating that action – as a matter of premeditation or intention – in the realm of law as well as that of ethics. Natorp, "Recht und Sittlichkeit," 71–2. For a public objection by Stammler to Cohen's criticism on this point, see *Lehrbuch der Rechtsphilosophie*, 1st ed., §85, 183n6. Stammler notes that the idea of Recht elaborated in Cohen's *Ethik* is not a clear or coherent one. (*Lehrbuch der Rechtsphilosophie*, §29, 62n4). A private, vehement objection, in which he notes that "even the Talmud" explains idolatry by means of a notion of "evil desires residing in the human heart" can be found in his letter to Natorp dated 31 December 1907. (Here Stammler also remarks more generally that Cohen had still not – even in the *Ethik*'s second edition – figured out the relationship of ethics and law, accusing him of "hair-raising dilettantism *in iuridicis*" ("haarsträubenden Dilettantismus in iuridicis"). Holzhey, *Cohen und Natorp*, 2:363. Wenn defends Stammler on this point, in *Juristische Erkenntniskritik*, 270–1.

Some commentators have read the critiques Cohen leveled at Stammler's theory of "right" law variously as being misdirected[61] or as based on a fundamental misunderstanding of Stammler.[62] Wolfgang Kersting attributes Cohen's and Stammler's vehement objections to each other's theories to the very commonality of their projects, the common "task of Neo-Kantian philosophy of law" to seek a scientific foundation for law and legal science. ("It could scarcely have been expected to be otherwise. When 'pure ones' [*Reine*, i.e., Stammler and Cohen as Kantian devotees of "purity" – D.H.] are alone among themselves, things are going to get uncomfortable."[63]) Although Paul Natorp sought – both (by his own account) privately, but above all publicly, with his 1913 review essay "Recht und Sittlichkeit" – to mediate between Cohen's and Stammler's positions, he reports in private correspondence during the period in which Stammler's *Lehre* and the two editions of Cohen's own *Ethik* appeared that Cohen fails to understand Stammler properly, and even that he seems strangely blind to what is meritorious in Stammler's arguments. In private remarks to colleagues, Natorp suggests that the vehemence of Cohen's reaction was in large part gratuitous and unfounded, that is, that it went beyond any discernible substantive difference between Cohen's and Stammler's views on ethics and law.[64] Helmut Holzhey has vividly described the difficulties that Natorp and others had in their dealings with Cohen, in which the latter's "sensitivity" and vehement reactions to perceived attacks were major factors, as well as his often quite justified sensitivity to antisemitism as a possible factor in the academic politics of his time.[65] Indeed, there is an undertone of Jewish-Christian polemics to the confrontation between Stammler's and Cohen's accounts of ethics – to be addressed further at the end of this chapter.

"Relative Community" and Affective Expansiveness

Regardless of how one evaluates the contrast between Stammler's and Cohen's theories, what is at stake in that contrast is most evident when we consider carefully Stammler's "model" of the "particular community"

61 Holzhey, "Analytische Hermeneutik," 104.

62 Wenn, *Juristische Erkenntniskritik*, 272. Stammler's letter to Natorp dated 31 December 1907 expresses a similar criticism. Holzhey, *Cohen und Natorp* 2:365–6.

63 Kersting, "Neukantianische Rechtsbegründung," 27–8.

64 See Natorp's letters to Albert Görland dated 27 March 1903, 31 March 1903, and 11 December 1904, in Holzhey, *Cohen und Natorp*, 2:312–13, 317–18, 331–2, and his unpublished letter to Görland dated 6 March 1907, quoted in Holzhey, *Cohen und Natorp*, 1:36.

65 Holzhey, *Cohen und Natorp*, 1:36–7.

(Sondergemeinschaft). This model of ethico-legal reasoning diverges starkly from the most fundamental premises of Cohen's ethico-legal philosophy. Thus, looking at the notion of Sondergemeinschaft and its role in Stammler's theory provides a more solid basis for making plausible Cohen's critical response to Stammler's theory of "right law" than focusing on the broader methodological and philosophical considerations about the proper relationships of law and ethics/morality, and of the individual and collectivities such as the "social ideal."[66] Further, we will see that Cohen's efforts in the *Ethik* to develop clear alternatives to constructs such as the "particular community" reveal the substantive connection between the philosophical achievements of the *Ethik* and the key ethico-legal concept of Cohen's Jewish philosophy: "the neighbor."

Here, we return to Cohen's understanding of ethical subjectivity as a correlation of the human individual with Allheit, which must be thought beginning from the unity of the "legal person." My purpose in this chapter has been to show that this understanding is at the same time an argument against what he calls "affective expansiveness." This latter term describes any tendency to view ethical comportment as a function or capacity of expanding one's point of view from oneself to a consideration for others. For Cohen, this model of ethics as a function of "expansion" goes along with the presumption that ethics first of all pertains to the individual, and that the social or collective sphere is to be thought of as derivative of, or an extension of, the sphere of individual decision or action. This, again, is one of Cohen's major objections to Stammler: He thinks that Stammler proceeds from a mistaken separation of individual ethical will from a social ethical (legal, public) will. Cohen's objection to the "expansivist" ethical model is thus also an objection to the primacy of the individual, which for him entails psychologism and naturalism. To assert Allheit as the point of orientation for ethics is at the same time to reject the category of Mehrheit, plurality, as having ethical relevance. Plurality can only be a plurality or aggregate of individuals. By contrast, for Cohen it is the legal person or Genossenschaft that best embodies the unity of ethical subjectivity in that it is supposed to be a unity from the start, and not an entity based on, or made up of individuals.

In the *Ethik* (and elsewhere), Cohen uses the term "relative," and especially the idea of the "relative community" (*relative Gemeinschaft*) as a synonym for "plurality" in the sense I have described. Indeed, "community" itself denotes an "arbitrary and relative" summing up of

---

66 Among the commentators on the Stammler–Cohen relationship, Claudius Müller is one who has noted that "Sondergemeinschaft" is a key issue. Müller, *Rechtsphilosophie des Marburger Neukantianismus*, 138–9, 139n190.

subjects or actors (ErW 238). The notion of "relative community" is meant to capture the problematic of using an "expansivist" model or procedure to theorize ethico-legal subjectivity or agency. Where Cohen casts doubt on the relevance of the category of "community" in general for thinking about ethical subjectivity, he frequently does so by saying that the problem with "community," similarly to that of plurality, is that it is "relative." Hence, Cohen strongly objects to Stammler's positing of the "particular community" as the proper model for ethico-legal reasoning. It is as if the fact that Stammler adds the prefix *Sonder-*, "particular," to the term *Gemeinschaft* merely confirms what Cohen has known all along about the potential pitfalls of Gemeinschaft. In a long passage that I will quote selectively, Cohen sets up Gemeinschaft as a term against which to assert the "juridical association" – a synonym for the Genossenschaft – as a model of ethical subjectivity. The passage begins with the question that is already familiar from our discussion of legal personhood and Genossenschaft in chapter 1: "What is the unity of the subject"?

> Who is in these unions [i.e., in "associations," *Assoziationen*], which diverge into many legal meanings, ... the unity of the subject? Does it not seem here as though the unity would have to break apart, as if the I would become not only a pathological double-I but even would normally seem to be transformed into a *quota*-I? But can an aggregated "I" [*Sammel-Ich,* i.e., an entity that is a "collection" of "I"s – D.H.] do justice to, and correspond to the unity of the subject?
>
> Here emerges the decisive value that we must recognize in the conjunction of ethics with legal science. We have after all from the start been concerned to recognize the correlation of individual and *Allheit* as the actual problem of ethics. The ethical subject must thus be at the same time *Allheit* and individual....

Cohen continues his explanation of why the individual is unsuitable as a basis for thinking Allheit by showing the connection of individuality to plurality (Mehrheit), as well as to particularity (*Besonderheit*):

> It is merely an illusion that [the human being] is only an individual; if he is an individual, and insofar as he is an individual, he can be this only in and through the fact that the individual is, rather, the individuals. The individual cannot be thought apart from plurality. What is decisive, however, is that plurality [*Mehrheit*] not remain plurality – that is, particularity [*Besonderheit*] – but that it become *Allheit.* But where do we find an example for this *Allheit* in the historical human world? (ErW 75–6)

In answer to this last question, Cohen considers and then dismisses the idea of "humanity" as a candidate for Allheit. Next, he considers "community" (Gemeinschaft): From Plato to the religious congregation ("Gemeinde," a cognate of "Gemeinschaft") that was the precursor to the church, this turns out to be inadequate for thinking Allheit. Cohen expresses this inadequacy, again, as a matter of *particularity*:

> The church community has the particular alliance in its blood. [*Der kirchlichen Gemeinschaft steckt der Sonderbund im Blute.*] It is just this nasty [böse] example that ethics must stay away from. And recently a juristic book has, in a shocking way, made clear what ensues when one dissolves the community, guided by biblical quotations, into a structure of what are always only relative communities. Such relative particular-communities [*Sonder-Gemeinschaften*] are in fact nothing other than particularities [*Besonderheiten*]. They can never turn into an *Allheit.* (ErW 76–7)[67]

The "juristic book" to have enabled this shocking revelation is, of course, Stammler's *Lehre von dem richtigen Rechte.* We will return below to Cohen's specific accusation here that Stammler, in discussing the Sondergemeinschaft, allows himself to be "guided by biblical quotations."

While community always stands for particularity and "relativity," it is the juridical concept of Genossenschaft that for Cohen aims at true Allheit/universality (ErW 77, 240, 433).[68] Cohen's objection to the idea that ethical agency consists in a conciousness that "affectively expands" to consider the requirements of others – and, by the same token, to the idea that law should regulate agents' behavior so as to produce such expansiveness – makes this contrast plain:

> It is misleading to say that the individual should and can learn, by means of legal coercion, to expand its self-consciousness into consciousness of the

67 Cohen seems already in the first edition (1896) of his introduction to Lange's *History of Materialism* to have considered religion as a model of sociality that is non-ethical – because it "breeds particular communities [*Sondergemeinschaften*]." He retained this wording in the second edition (1902), but replaced it in the third edition (1914). EmkN 518/106.

68 At ErW 77 in particular, Cohen further aligns the "association" with the notions of "society" and "sociality" originating in Roman law. In modern times, "society" denotes the "revolutionary" forces that temper and "reform" the state and thereby "morally educate" the human race. Similarly at ErW 433: "We avoid the expression 'community' because it contains too much relativity; the juridical concept *Genossenschaft* is exact, and at the same time pours into the state the added social drop of *Gesellschaft.*" On Gesellschaft and Gemeinschaft, see also ErW 237–8.

> community. Self-consciousness should not be expanded to consciousness of the community. Rather, the concept of self-consciousness should be defined according to the concept of *Genossenschaft*, and in accordance with this model concept of law

– which is at the same time the "logical meaning of the legal person" (ErW 236–7).

The expansiveness to which Cohen objects is "affective," and the mistake we make in conceiving of an ethics based on such expansion of our consciousness is to think of ethical self-consciousness as having a "natural" origin and development. This goes along with the idea that "community" is an "analogue to nature," a "unity of moral forces," just as "nature" is conceived as a "unity and essence of forces and objects" (ErW 238–9). Community, as distinct from Genossenschaft, is based on affect; this gives it an "ambiguity" that limits its value for ethical and legal reasoning. This "ambiguity" spills over into certain types of legal personhood, such as "estate, tribe, church, and even the fatherland" (ErW 239). Cohen sees these entities as making up a "quasi-concentric net of relativities," whose particularism is commonly overlooked:

> The fatherland is based on the people [*Volk*]. The people on the tribe. The tribe on the family. The family on marriage.

The perceived naturalness of the concentric circles of marriage, family, and so on, lead to a belief in a

> path of *natural development* for self-consciousness to rid itself of its egotistical character by developing and educating itself, beginning from marriage, along the [trajectory of] family consciousness, consciousness of the tribe, of the people, and of the fatherland. (ErW 240)

We have already seen how Cohen's proposal of Genossenschaft (including its culmination in the state) as a model for ethical subjectivity is meant to generate a model for ethical subjectivity along the "opposite path" (ErW 240) from that of the purported "natural development" sketched above. Along such a path, the value or orientation of Allheit would inform ethical action from the start. Legal personhood in all its forms, including that of the state,

> teaches me to understand ... that I cannot produce the self-consciousness of the will in my natural individuality, nor in seeking to expand myself in love and enthusiasm to the stages of relative community. (ErW 256)

Accordingly, although it might be common to identify the notion of "state" with that of a "people," these are for Cohen strictly separate notions. The Volk is an example of "relative community," while moral-legal-political progress must be pursued in the name of the state, in recognition of the deficiencies of peoplehood (ErW 250).

Looking at Stammler's mobilization of the "particular community" in the context of his presentation of the "model of right law," it is easy to see that it has the very traits of an affective-expansivist model that Cohen is objecting to in the *Ethik*. Stammler's heuristic device or thought experiment of the "particular community" is supposed to allow us as legal reasoners to bring disputing parties or conflicting interests together in our mind in a quest to find the "right" or just decision or statute. Such a procedure must not only account for the separate interests, in order, for instance, to find some sort of balance between them. Because it is "right law" as such that is sought, "something higher, which encompasses one's own person" is a key ingredient in achieving "community" – by way of the imagined "particular community" (LrR 283–4/216–17). But it is clear that for Cohen, such a model of balancing interests, as self-interests – defined as individual interests against each other or against the interests of the social or legal community – would not look like a model of ethical or political progress at all. Beginning from the individual, and presupposing an individual interest that must subsequently be measured against the claim of the collective – let alone in view of a "higher" ideal – violates the fundamental presupposition of Cohen's theory of ethics out of law: that Allheit or universality, in the form of law (Recht), determines ethical subjectivity from the outset, and that a kind of juridical-universal horizon generates, or makes possible ethical action as such.

Conclusion and Transition: "Who Is My Neighbor?"

My project in this book is to trace Cohen's arguments for an ethics generated out of law, while exploring how those arguments take shape within and between both his Jewish philosophical writings and his systematic philosophy of ethics and law. With Cohen's critical response to Stammler, an important "seam" becomes visible between his Jewish-philosophical and ethico-philosophical agendas. In the next chapter, I will show how those combined agendas come to a kind of culmination in Cohen's writings on love-of-neighbor, which are among his "Jewish writings." I will begin that discussion by looking at an account of what this ethical precept means that Cohen introduces into the ethico-juridical argument of the *Ethik* – the only key place in which Cohen does so outside his works on Judaism.

As is so often the case for Cohen, the occasion to discuss neighbor-love in the *Ethik* is supplied by a need to expose what he sees as a gross misrepresentation of this biblical tradition on the part of a philosophical or theological opponent – a type of misrepresentation that he viewed as both dangerous and extremely widespread in contemporary society and culture, and which he connects to a prevalent Christian anti-Jewish trope: that Judaism is ethically deficient, and that the commandment(s) to "love" is/are "Christian" – in a sense to be specified further in the next chapter. In the case of Cohen's discussion of neighbor-love in the *Ethik*, the particular occasion to take up this topic becomes apparent when we consider that that discussion is combined with one of Cohen's sharpest denunciations of Stammler's reliance on the notion of the "relative community" or "particular community" (Sondergemeinschaft). As I will show in detail in the next chapter, Cohen finds in the prevalent interpretations of the commandment "love your 'neighbor' [*der Nächste*] as yourself" the same structure of "affective expansion" against which he argues throughout the *Ethik*. As we saw, this argument is key to his objections to the role of the "particular community" in Stammler's theory of ethico-juridical action. (Indeed, we will return in the next chapter to Cohen's rejection of the very term "der Nächste" as in itself already suggesting the faulty "expansivist" logic that he views as damaging to ethical theory.) In the midst of his discussion of love-of-neighbor, he writes of Stammler's book:

> With an unselfconscious literality the template [*Schablone*] of the neighbor is used there for the "fencing in" [*Einzäunung*] of *relative communities*, such that this ambiguous concept appears in its full danger. (ErW 218–19)

Though Cohen does not point to a particular offending passage, he doubtless is referring to the section of the first edition of *Die Lehre von dem richtigen Rechte* titled "Wer ist mein Nächster?" ("Who Is My Neighbor?"). Recall that in presenting the "principles of right law" – the two principles that limit the degree to which the individual member of a community, as an end-in-itself, must compromise its interests in favor of the legal community or the social ideal – Stammler had used the locution "can still be a neighbor to himself" ("daß [er] sich noch der Nächste sein kann") to capture the self-interestedness required as a counterbalance to communal demands (LrR 208/161, 211/163). This "neighbor" language seems inessential to Stammler's purposes, and he immediately drops it.[69]

69 Thus, in his lucid study of Stammler's legal philosophy, Julius Stone mistranslates and misunderstands the sentences in question (he has Stammler say that the individual must remain a neighbor to *others*, which is the very opposite of what Stammler

However, in the later section of the book titled "Who Is My Neighbor?" – a title modeled after the occurrence of this question in the parable of the Good Samaritan in the New Testament[70] – Stammler again picks up this language for understanding the "principles." There, he makes reference to Leviticus 19:18 ("love your neighbor as yourself"), "the famous formula of the Old as of the New Testament." He writes that to understand that "formula" in light of the "principles of right law" amounts to the project of "clarifying" "who in the [sphere of] social existence and action is, respectively, the neighbor [*der Nächste*]" (LrR 288/220). In order to weigh the individual's ethical position in relation to the collectivity, Stammler envisions each person as being "initially" at the "center" of "his circle." In the course of his social activities, this person is more closely connected with some people than with others, "spatially, and temporally," and according to the "kind" of activity engaged in. It is essential to take account of these differences in degree of connection, otherwise, Stammler explains, one would have to rewrite the neighbor-love formula as "Love the other *more* than yourself," or "Love the one who is *more distant* as you do the one who is *nearby*." These formulations according to Stammler would amount to the precept to "Do *less* good to the one nearby than you do to the one who is more foreign."

With these hypothetical rewritings of the love-your-neighbor commandment, Stammler seeks to show that the commandment misunderstands the fact that we distinguish between "near" and "far" in our choices of who to care for. The method of "right law" is supposed to avoid this mistake by placing subjects who have legal ties to one another "in concentric circles, for the purpose of appropriately establishing the particular communities [*Sondergemeinschaften*] that are here to be effected" (LrR 288–9/220–1, cf. 291/222–3). As I will discuss in greater detail in

actually says), but this does not encumber his understanding of the passage as a whole. Stone, *Human Law,* 174, 175.

70 For a brief review of what this New Testament story signifies from a Jewish perspective, see Amy-Jill Levine's commentary on Luke 10:25–37 in *The Jewish Annotated New Testament,* ed. Amy-Jill Levine and Marc Zvi Brettler (Oxford: Oxford University Press, 2011), 123, as well as, in the same volume, Michael Fagenblat, "The Concept of Neighbor in Jewish and Christian Ethics," 541–3.

Five years before this reaction by Cohen to Stammler's instrumentalization of the biblical notion of the "neighbor" – including Stammler's reference to the Good Samaritan parable (see LrR 286/218–19) – Cohen incorporated his own reading of this parable into his essay "Liebe und Gerechtigkeit in den Begriffen Gott und Mensch" (1900; "Love and Justice in the Concepts 'God' and 'Man'"), JS3: 61–2. In these pages, as in general, for Cohen, reading such a text always entails challenging Christian claims to have originated love-of-neighbor – a topic we will turn to in the next chapter.

the next chapter, Cohen's theory of neighbor-love, like his ethico-legal theory in general, seeks to overturn a model of subjectivity that negotiates, measures, or ranks its allegiances to the "near" and to the "far." It is thus clear why he would strenuously object to Stammler's approach to conceiving and explaining mutual social and ethical obligations, and why he would react with particular vehemence to Stammler's rejection of "love your neighbor" as a basis for understanding individual and social responsibility, based as it is on an interpretation of Leviticus 19:18 that runs counter to the one that Cohen consistently puts forward.[71]

Stammler's invocation of the neighbor-love commandment, including its function in the Good Samaritan parable (a text that has traditionally been read as presenting Christian morality as superior to Jewish morality) thus emerges as the very likely impetus for Cohen to have included a discussion of neighbor-love in the *Ethik* in the first place. In that discussion, Cohen cautions against applying an "unselfconscious literality" to biblical traditions, instead of developing complete interpretations not only of what they say, but of how they have come to function in contemporary religio-cultural politics. Exposing the interpretative habits of "unselfconscious literality" also exposes the "dangerous ambiguity" of the figure of the "neighbor," just as plainly as does Stammler's affective-expansivist model for social ethics.

In more than one respect, then, the short discussion of neighbor-love in Cohen's main systematic-philosophical work on ethics becomes readable as a crucial "seam" between his "general" and his "Jewish" philosophies. The next chapter studies this treatment of neighbor-love in the *Ethik* and moves from there to exploring the origin, historical contexts, and significance of Cohen's treatments of neighbor-love within his Jewish writings.

---

71 As Steven Schwarzschild mentions in his 1981 introduction to Cohen's *Ethik*, another contemporary of these thinkers, the non-Jewish Neo-Kantian philosopher Karl Vorländer, in his 1903 review of Stammler's book, seems to have presaged the criticism of Stammler that Cohen would shortly develop in the *Ethik*, when he "pointed out not only that Stammler's book positively crawled with Christian textual and historical references ... but also that his dichotomy of inner and outer man, moral and legal values, follows an entrenched Christian tradition." Schwarzschild, introduction to Hermann Cohen, *Ethik des reinen Willens*, XVII*, discussing Karl Vorländer, "Rudolf Stammlers Lehre vom richtigen Recht," *Kant-Studien* 8 (1903): 329–35.

Chapter Six

The "Neighbor" as an Institution of Law (*Recht*), from the *Ethik* to the Jewish Writings

Moritz Güdemann (1835–1918) was a prolific German-Jewish rabbi and scholar. He had studied alongside Hermann Cohen in one of the earliest cohorts of the Jüdisch-Theologisches Seminar in Breslau, and was from 1890 onwards the Chief Rabbi of Vienna. His works included intellectual defenses of Judaism against antisemitic accusations; these belong to the genre of Jewish "moral defense" that I will describe in the present chapter, and contain themes and arguments that often closely parallel those that Cohen develops, especially in his polemical writings on Judaism.

It is no surprise then that, like Cohen, Güdemann wrote about the meaning of "love your neighbor" in Judaism. He did so notably in an essay of that title ("Nächstenliebe") published in 1890 – two years after the 1888 affidavit by Cohen that is the focal point of this chapter. By way of introducing the issue motivating that essay, Güdemann tells a historically authentic anecdote, and then follows it up with a Jewish joke.

The anecdote, Güdemann reports, was related to him by Ignaz Kuranda. (Kuranda [1812–84] had been a prominent Austrian-Jewish publicist and politician, with deep roots in liberal activism on behalf of democratization in Germany and Austria, and also a leader in the Viennese Jewish community, who had himself once been involved in a highly publicized trial concerning anti-Jewish defamation.[1]) Güdemann

1 This was the Brunner-Kuranda trial (1860), in which Kuranda, who had exposed the anti-Judaism of Sebastian Brunner's publications, successfully defended himself against a libel suit brought by Brunner. See *Jewish Encyclopedia* (1901–6), s.v. "Brunner, Sebastian" (3:404), "Kuranda, Ignaz" (7:584–5); Wenzel August Neumann, *Pressprozeß Doktor Brunner – Ignaz Kuranda* (Vienna: Ludwig Mayer, 1860); and Georg Franz, *Liberalismus. Die deutschliberale Bewegung in der Habsburgischen Monarchie* (Munich: Callwey, 1955), 207, 418, 422, 513n3.

retells a story told to him by Kuranda about a conversation that took place "perhaps 14 years ago":

> My late friend Ignaz Kuranda once told me that on a train ride he took with the now deceased abbot Helferstorffer and the Austrian Minister of Culture of the time von ____, the conversation turned to the commandment "Love your neighbor as yourself." When Kuranda referred to this commandment as a rule of his religion, his Excellence replied: "But, dear friend, the sentence is to be found in the *New* Testament." Kuranda, smiling at the remark, politely pointed out that the sentence had indeed been included in the New Testament, but that it was originally to be found in the Old Testament, Lev. chap. 19 v. 18. About this claim, the minister shook his head somewhat incredulously, until the above-mentioned abbot spoke up and confirmed it.[2]

Placed at the opening of Güdemann's essay, whose purpose is to show that the commandment to love the neighbor is a part of Judaism, this anecdote is meant to illustrate the widespread view even among well-educated Christians at the time that this tradition was to be understood, either exclusively, or properly speaking, as a Christian one. When Christians claim that the commandment to love one's neighbor, despite all evidence about its prominence and significance in Judaism, "after all signifies, in the context of Jesus' discourses something completely different, more profound, more comprehensive than it does in the Old Testament and in Judaism in general," this, writes Güdemann, puts an end to all possible "scholarly discussion."[3]

Güdemann does seem to find a way out of this impasse, considering that this is the opening to an over-forty-pages-long essay on neighbor-love and stranger-love in Judaism, which will argue that the commandment to love the stranger should be understood as applying "as comprehensively as possible," and that Christian moral teachings coincide with those of Judaism.[4] But first he wants his reader to understand the impasse for what it is: what it means for Christians to hold that "Love your neighbor as yourself" is meant in a "more profound, more comprehensive" way in the New Testament than in Judaism. Güdemann wants to explain why, once such a claim is made, an end-point of all debate has been reached. He wants to make clear that all that the Jew confronted by such a Christian claim can do is to "shrug his shoulders," and why it would be "wisest" for

---

2 Moritz Güdemann, *Nächstenliebe: Ein Beitrag zur Erklärung des Matthäus-Evangeliums* (Vienna: R. Löwit, 1890), 3.

3 Güdemann, 4.

4 Güdemann, 5, 8.

that Jew "to shut [*zuklappen*] his Pentateuch and break off the discussion." Güdemann explicates this piece of advice by telling a Jewish joke:

> One knows the dispute of a Polish Jew with a Christian clergyman. The former declares Jesus' ascension to be a fable, whereupon the latter remarks that, after all, the Old Testament also relates an ascension, that of Elijah. This reproach leads the Jew to exclaim triumphantly: "Ah, but *our* ascension is real!"[5]

Güdemann comments:

> The roles are here reversed, and the role of the Polish Jew is played by the Christian.

(As explaining a joke is known to spoil it, readers who prefer not to have this brilliant joke about supersessionism spoiled for themselves are invited to skip ahead past the explanation to the next section.) The joke operates with a classic shift of the terms of the discussion. The first exchange sounds like it could belong to any classic anti-religious or inter-religious dispute. How is a religion classically delegitimized? By having its beliefs exposed as fables or myths. Likewise, the most traditional Jewish-Christian dispute – or any dispute between two religions or belief-systems – classically consists of challenges to the believability or truth of its tenets. In the joke, by characterizing Jesus' ascension as a "fable," the Jew sounds less like an opponent of Christianity and more like a typical skeptic about religion in general, insofar as religion is taken to rely on supernatural stories. Indeed, this is a classic Jewish joke, as its next line – the Christian's retort that, after all, the Old Testament also relates an ascension – plays on the idea that, with his pronouncement that Jesus' ascension is a fable, the Jew might have, in the manner of the *schlemiehl*, unwittingly pulled the rug of Judaism out from under himself.

But the Jew's triumphant reply shows him – and thus Güdemann in his deployment of the joke in his analogy – to be in possession of a more profound truth – a truth about what we today would call hegemony. To assert that "yes, but our ascension is real" – that Elijah's ascension is the real one, even as Jesus' ascension remains completely unbelievable – is absurd in light of the defining significance of Jesus' ascension for Christianity, and thus as an orienting topos of Western culture in general. The joke rightly presumes that the idea of Jesus' ascension is known to any culturally literate, even non-Christian, member of society; while

5 Güdemann, 4.

the ascension of Elijah is comparatively obscure, either a matter for biblical or theological experts or a Jewish story of secondary importance – and not, in other words, a defining theologoumenon of Judaism. The absurdity of the reply, "Ah, but *our* ascension is real," is thereby not a reflection of stupidity or ignorance. Rather, it exposes the very fact that the core elements of Christology are part of the shared storehouse of knowledge of the cultural world inhabited by the Polish Jew as well as by any Christian.

With his comment that "the roles are here reversed, and the role of the Polish Jew is played by the Christian," Güdemann admonishes the Christian world to acknowledge, first, that Christian love, or Christian ethics, traces its origins to Jewish theology and ethics; and, second, that any Christian claim along the lines of "But *our* neighbor-love is the real one!" (for which he gives a number of real-life examples in the pages that follow) betrays a willful ignorance about the centrality of neighbor-love to Judaism. The Polish Jew's attempt at unseating Christianity's dominance by demoting "its" ascension to being just one example of any number of other possible scriptural stories of ascension, and even deeming that particular example of an ascension to be an inauthentic one – is absurd in the Western Christian cultural framework. But this absurdity exposes a deeper truth about that situation of hegemony, a situation of cultural particularity that has become the measure of universality. The Polish Jew is ridiculous for effectively imagining Christianity as a cultural particularity, as the contingent and minor inheritor of an older "real" tradition about ascension. The joke about the Polish Jew is funny the way Jewish jokes classically are funny: because the Polish Jew is patently wrong. It is indeed the *Christian* ascension that is evidently the "real one."

The Jew in the joke plays at a denial of the obvious hegemony of Christianity by performing a reversal of the common supersessionist logic that Christianity applies to Judaism, whose truth it is supposed to have replaced. In telling the joke, Güdemann harnesses its powerful analysis of Jewish existence in a world in which Christian-hegemonic assertions about the moral delinquency of Judaism hold sway. Güdemann's strategy is to attempt to denaturalize this hierarchy by applying the joke to the alternative situation that will be the topic of his own analysis: "The roles are here reversed, and the role of the Polish Jew is played by the Christian." By putting the Polish Jew's response into the mouth of the Christian, Güdemann suggests that when Christians deny to Judaism a full-fledged morality, when they assert or imply, "Yes, but *our* love-of-neighbor is the real one," that judgment exposes itself as wilfully blind to the Jewish origins of, and share in "love-of-neighbor."

Güdemann's analysis is surely compelling. It allows us to understand the way in which universalist ethics as such is attached to Christianity, which functions as the unmarked neutral-universal norm – to the point that, in talking about the discursive conditions for Jews' interactions with Christians, it is even misleading to use the term "Christian" to apply to the ethical norms that are in question. To borrow some language from the project of studying "whiteness" as it has developed within critical race theory: "Christianness" is in these discourses and interactions the unmarked predicate or "unseen" quality, which becomes "seen" only from, or in view of, the positionality of the non-Christian in encounters such as the ones related in the two narratives presented by Güdemann.[6] In order to remind us of this, I will sometimes use the term "Christian-hegemonic" to refer to the unmarked universalism that cannot be equated with "Christian" as a particular predicate.

But while Güdemann's analysis is compelling, I am less certain whether his deployment of the joke could serve as an effective basis for rectifying the misrecognition, for establishing "love-of-neighbor" as proper or essential to Judaism. As an attempted solution to the misrecognition, the joke proposes a mere reversal of the hierarchy of "real" and "non-real" ascensions. On the terms of the joke itself, such a reversal is appropriately ridiculous. The joke presupposes that we know that it is the Christian ascension that is the "real one." Güdemann's joke – for all its effectiveness at exposing the hegemonic logic that governs the position of Judaism in general Christian culture – is no recipe for a recognition of Judaism as a religion whose morality is commensurate with that of Christian neighbor-love. By means of Güdemann's "reversed" mapping of the joke onto contemporary reality, the Christian plays at denying the Christianness of love-of-neighbor, of full-fledged, comprehensive and profound, ethical "love" of the other. But this reversal remains a joke, as it were, and we are indeed left with a sense that, in

---

6 See, for example, George Yancy, "Whiteness: 'Unseen' Things Seen," in *Black Bodies, White Gazes: The Continuing Significance of Race* (Lanham, MD: Rowman & Littlefield, 2008), chap. 2, and *Look, a White! Philosophical Essays on Whiteness* (Philadelphia: Temple University Press, 2012).

Also helpful in this connection is Amy-Jill Levine's use of the notions "Christian privilege" and the closely related "Christian fragility" – modeled on the notions of "white privilege" (Peggy McIntosh) and "white fragility" (Robin DiAngelo), respectively – in order to understand inadequate responses to anti-Judaism in the Gospel of John in the contemporary American context. Levine, "Christian Privilege, Christian Fragility, and the Gospel of John," in *The Gospel of John and Jewish-Christian Relations*, ed. Adele Reinhartz (Lanham, MD: Lexington Books/Fortress Academic, 2018), 87–110.

the Christian universal order, "*our*" (i.e., Christian) neighbor-love must remain "the real one!"

I have opened this chapter by presenting Güdemann's anecdote, joke, and lesson about the discourse surrounding neighbor-love as a way of introducing the discursive framework of Jewish-Christian relations that forms the context of the writings of Hermann Cohen, when they argue for and explicate a tradition of love-of-the-neighbor and love-of-the-stranger. I shall be arguing that the "fellowman" (*Mitmensch*) and the "neighbor" (*der Nächste*) must be understood as core concepts of Cohen's theory of ethics out of law (Recht). With this argument, then, I am continuing the project of determining how Judaism figures into Cohen's thinking about law. I will show how Cohen's objection to "affective expansiveness," explored in the previous chapter, leads him to take account of the biblical and rabbinic notions of love of "stranger" and so-called *Nächstenliebe* (love of neighbor) in both the *Ethik* and in the Jewish writings. In order to do so, I will devote considerable attention to the discursive context that, I have been arguing, is made evident in the way that Güdemann – this important contemporary of Cohen's – opened his own essay on love-of-neighbor, informed as it is by similar polemical concerns to those that, as we will see, first (and later repeatedly) moved Cohen to write about this notion in Judaism.

An initial focus of the following discussion will be on the treatment of the "fellowman" and "neighbor" in chapter 4 of the *Ethik*. But it is important to keep in mind that by the time Cohen published this book (1904; 2nd ed. 1907), "the neighbor" and love-of-neighbor were long-established among the core themes of his works on Judaism, on Jewish-Christian relations, and on religion in general. Cohen's critical engagement with the neighbor dates back to his 1888 expert witness testimony at the so-called Marburg Antisemitism Trial[7] and his affidavit for the court, which he published independently as a pamphlet titled "Die Nächstenliebe im Talmud" ("Love-of-Neighbor in the Talmud"). Neighbor-love subsequently figured as a central theme in two essays published before he wrote the *Ethik*: "Zum Prioritätsstreit über das Gebot der Nächstenliebe" (1894; "On the Priority Dispute Concerning the Commandment to Love the Neighbor"), and "Liebe und Gerechtigkeit in den Begriffen Gott und Mensch" (1900; "Love and Justice in the Concepts 'God' and 'Man'"). After publication of the *Ethik*, he devoted two further essays to this topic: "Gesinnung" (1910; "Conviction") and "Der Nächste. Bibelexegese und Literaturgeschichte" (1914/1916; "The Neighbor. Biblical Exegesis and

7 I refer to this trial by the name coined by its foremost historian, Ulrich Sieg.

Literary History").[8] The theme is also among those that receives detailed treatment as a constitutive feature of Judaism as "religion of reason" in the posthumously published book of that title.[9]

The purpose of this chapter is to showcase how this theme arises in Cohen's thinking, against the background of Jewish moral defense discourses as they make themselves heard in response to the new political antisemitism of the 1880s. Looking in detail at the 1888 affidavit, and to some extent at the subsequent essay, "On the Priority Dispute," will allow me to explicate in detail the general direction of Cohen's main arguments, which remain quite constant across the "neighbor" corpus.

Cohen's polemical purpose throughout his writings on the "neighbor" is to counter the prejudice that the notion of love-of-neighbor is originally and properly Christian, as well as to show, against Christian misreadings, that the Jewish tradition construes neighbor-love as applying primarily not to the fellow Jew but to the stranger or foreigner. Cohen in particular argues that love-of-neighbor ought to be understood as equivalent to love of the "stranger" (*ger*). Importantly from the point of view of the method of legal science (*Rechtswissenschaft*) that we traced in the *Ethik*, Cohen substantiates this finding by linking the biblical term usually translated as "neighbor," *re'a*, with two other terms, which he takes to be juridical categories:

(1) the biblical-rabbinic notion of the *ger* ("stranger," "foreigner") in the sense of *ger toshav*, "sojourner" or "resident alien"; and
(2) the rabbinic category of the Noahide, which Cohen analyzes as an "institution of state law" (*staatsrechtliche Institution*).

These arguments reveal, in other words, that "der Nächste" is for Cohen an institution of law/Recht.

Furthermore, we will see that "der Nächste" is more than simply an *example* of a legal institution that serves to illustrate ethical principles.

8 The essays are "Die Nächstenliebe im Talmud. Als ein Gutachten dem Königlichen Landgerichte zu Marburg erstattet" (1888; "Love-of-Neighbor in the Talmud. Submitted as an Affidavit to the Königliches Landgericht in Marburg"), in JS1: 145–74 (hereafter cited in text as NT); "Zum Prioritätsstreit über das Gebot der Nächstenliebe" (1894; "On the Priority Dispute Concerning the Commandment to Love the Neighbor"), in JS1: 175–81 (hereafter cited in text as Pr); "Liebe und Gerechtigkeit in den Begriffen Gott und Mensch" (1900; "Love and Justice in the Concepts 'God' and 'Man'"), in JS3: 43–97; "Gesinnung" (1910; "Conviction"), in JS1: 196–210 and *Werke* 15: 389–413; "Der Nächste. Bibelexegese und Literaturgeschichte" (1914/1916; "The Neighbor. Biblical Exegesis and Literary History"), in JS1: 182–95 and *Werke* 16: 53–75. A book consisting of my translations of these essays into English is currently in preparation.

9 See especially, "The Discovery of Man as Fellowman," RV chap. 8.

It is an entity or construct that, similarly to that of the "legal person," not only reflects but also generates ethics-out-of-law. My argument is that the "neighbor" – or the "fellow human being," as Cohen terms this figure in the *Ethik* – and "neighbor-love" represent a key substantial link between the theory of ethics-out-of-law in Cohen's philosophical system and Cohen's accounts of Judaism as a religion of reason (i.e., in the "Jewish writings"), with the result that Cohen's ethics and his philosophy of Judaism together can be seen as forming a theory of law that is both Recht, oriented to Allheit, and Gesetz, oriented to a messianic-political futural horizon.[10]

The Fellowman and the Neighbor in the *Ethik*

As noted in the previous chapter, the discussion in the *Ethik* of the role of the "fellowman" in ethical subjectivity is one of the places in which Cohen makes his forceful objection to ethico-legal theories that rely on ideas of a desirable "expansiveness" of the self. Similarly to Cohen's account of the legal person/Genossenschaft as the prime model of ethical subjectivity, against any notion of "community" or any other sort of "relative" or (quasi-)"natural" "plurality," the "neighbor," too, will emerge as a legal category that figures in his argument against "expansiveness" as a mode of ethical and political progress.

In the *Ethik*, Cohen turns to the notion of the fellow human being (*Nebenmensch*) as another way of asking (as he had regarding the legal person): What is the "unity of the subject," or the unity of (self-) consciousness, in ethics (ErW 204–5)? Recalling Fichte's theory of self-consciousness, Cohen reinterprets Fichte's counterposing of "I" and "non-I" in terms of his own conception of the "judgment of origin," such that the "I" can be understood as "originating" in the "other." This origination or generation of the "I" from the "other" functions as a kind of corollary to Cohen's view that ethics originates in law and in Allheit; it similarly relies on the rejection of individuality or plurality as a basis for ethics. Cohen accordingly reinterprets Fichte's idea of the non-I in a way that avoids a concept of the human being that would be based on

10 In a different vein, Paul E. Nahme also argues that the Noahide, in particular as developed in the 1888 affidavit, is a legal concept, to be understood in conjunction with Cohen's ethico-legal philosophy. Nahme, "God is the Reason: Hermann Cohen's Monotheism and the Liberal Theologico-Political Predicament," *Modern Theology* 33 no. 1 (January 2017): 134, 136. See also, more recently, *Hermann Cohen and the Crisis of Liberalism: The Enchantment of the Public Sphere* (Bloomington: Indiana University Press, 2019), chap. 4, 280ff., where Nahme places the concept of the Noahide at the center of his account of Cohen's theories of ethics, modern politics, and religion.

plurality (*Mehrheit*) (ErW 209). To establish a concept of humanity, or of a "unity" of human beings means instead to contemplate the origin of the fellowman (ErW 210–11).

To put this another way: Any ethics worthy of the name (a "pure ethics," in Cohen's terms) requires an a priori notion of the other person.[11] Accordingly, Cohen's question at this point of the *Ethik* is: What is the fellow human being (Mitmensch) as an a priori notion? Just as the self is not a pre-given object, here too empiricist theories, for which the fellowman would be an object of experience and which might imagine that fellowman as "one of the many fellow human beings," and thus as a function of plurality, are not the right starting point for a "pure" theory of will and of ethics. Like the legal person in our earlier discussion, the fellowman must instead be a "hypothesis" (ErW 211). For the notion of fellow human being – that is, the concept of the non-I – Cohen here proposes to substitute the "more precise concept" of "the other" or "other person" (*der Andere*). In line with the rejection of plurality as a basis for ethical collectivity, "the other" does not mean "*an* other," one among many. Rather, "the other," which Cohen also calls "the alter ego," is the "correlate" of the "I."

Cohen uses this notion of "the other" to strengthen his argument against the idea that the "I" is an object of experience: "Correlation" between "I" and other means: the "I" is conditioned by the "pure generation of the [concept of] the other." The other is consequently the "origin of the 'I'" (ErW 212). In introducing the concept of the other, Cohen thus further illuminates two ideas we encountered in our initial presentation of Cohen's theory of ethics out of law in chapter 1: first, that there is a "correlation between the individual and Allheit," and second, the account of the self as hypothesis – and thus as a "problem" for ethics, rather than a pre-given entity (ErW 212).[12]

This further development of the idea of "correlation" reminds us in particular that the correlates in any such reciprocal relationship must be

---

11 Cohen's geometrical analogy is helpful here: To seek to determine the notion of "other person" (Nebenmensch) (a notion that must be fundamentally presupposed for there to be an ethical theory) based on experience alone would be akin to seeking to define, based on experience alone, what a line is that connects two points (ErW 211).

12 Michael Zank helpfully puts this as follows: "Similar to Fichte, yet in a typical reversal, Cohen correlates I and non-I but makes the latter the condition for the former. Non-I as an infinite judgment [i.e., in the sense of hypothesis and origin – D.H.] generates the problem of the I which is to be determined further." Zank, *The Idea of Atonement in the Philosophy of Hermann Cohen* (Providence, RI: Brown Judaic Studies, 2000; repr. Brown Judaic Studies Open Humanities Book Program, 2020), 280, https://repository.library.brown.edu/studio/item/bdr:1111035.

thought of as "persisting in isolation," while at the same time "remain[ing] in reference to each other" (ErW 212–13).[13] The "correlative unification" (*Vereinigung*) that is envisioned here between "one and another" is not a merging. This is underscored by Cohen when he cautions against envisioning this correlation as motivated by affect; he expresses it instead as a function of law, in particular as a "legal transaction":

> In fact it is already evident in the *legal transaction* [*Rechtsgeschäft*] – in which after all it is a matter, for each of the contracting partners, of his advantage – that nevertheless the other too must be considered. Otherwise it would not be possible to attain the precision, clarity and security that are called for [*gefordert*] in the *legal action* [*Rechtshandlung*]. (ErW 213)

This legally based construal of the self-other correlation is "pure scientific thought" at work, in place of "mere affect" (ErW 213).

The Fellowman and the Stranger at the "Crossroads" of Religion and Ethics

Cohen has thus established that the notion of the fellowman, or of the other, is the condition of the self. The significance of this, he now announces, is that the question of the fellowman marks exactly the "crossroads" at which systematic ethics must take its leave from religion (ErW 213–14).[14] Yet we will see that as Cohen turns his attention, in this section of the *Ethik*, to the biblical tradition, the picture he paints of the relationship of religion to ethics is an ambivalent one. Biblical religion emerges in the *Ethik* both as something to be overcome by ethics and as a key resource for ethics to build on.

Cohen frames this section by recalling the common view that the virtue of religion is that it frees the individual from selfishness (ErW 214). But if this is indeed what religion does, then religion would be pursuing a goal that runs counter to the theory of ethics that Cohen is propounding: For if the aim of religion is to transcend the individual's selfishness, then religion must exemplify exactly the kind of thinking in terms of individuality, plurality, and the expandability from self to other that Cohen rejects. (This can be so even allowing, as Cohen does, that overcoming selfishness

13 See the analysis in Robert Gibbs, "Jurisprudence Is the Organon of Ethics: Kant and Cohen on Ethics, Law, and Religion," in *Hermann Cohen's Critical Idealism*, ed. Reinier Munk (Heidelberg: Springer, 2005), 207–8.

14 This argument is one that Cohen also makes in his "Jewish writings" on "the neighbor" – see below.

is indeed the worthy goal of religion, and that the religious concept of the unity of God means "from the beginning nothing other than the unity of humanity.") It is in this sense, then, that Cohen's philosophical ethics will have to be distinguished from the teachings of biblical religion.

That religion is a prime source of the "affective expansivist" tendency that Cohen's ethics seeks to overcome is due above all to the religious emphasis on the affect of "love" (ErW 216), which Cohen counters with his understanding of ethical subjectivity as a function of pure thought, pure will, and thus of law. Ethical subjectivity or self-consciousness "is not based in affect; it is called for/required [*gefordert*] by pure thought in the pure will. The other is called for by law [*Der Andere wird vom Recht gefordert*]." This is also to say that "the other is called for by the real [*real*] powers of scientific thought; he may not and he need not be consigned to affect, not even to love."[15] Thought must not concede "love" as an independent source of ethics (ErW 216–17).[16]

But Cohen also finds in biblical religion models for some of the core theses informing his theory of ethics out of law. Thus, just as philosophical ethics calls for "the other as the condition of the 'I,'"

> for the prophets, the other appeared as a *stranger*, who appeared to injure the unity that the *one* God was supposed to represent with respect to man [*am Menschen*]. (ErW 214)

This means that biblical religion confronts the same "antinomy" between particularity and universality as does philosophical ethics, and also yields a solution that is analogous to that proposed by juridico-ethical philosophy as Cohen has been developing it: When "religion" perceives "the stranger initially as being foreign as such [*als solcher Fremde*]," as being "different from one's own people and one's own faith," it is prompted to "destroy this appearance [*Schein*], this prejudice," by stipulating that "The stranger [*der Fremdling*, which translates the biblical term *ger*] shall be to you as the native-born [*der Eingeborene*, which translates *ezraḥ*]" (ErW 214) – Cohen's translation of the beginning of Leviticus 19:34. (Cohen in this explanation leaves out the continuation of the verse: "and

15 Accordingly, Cohen devotes a lot of attention to developing a differentiated account of exactly what is meant by "love" in the biblical tradition as it informs contemporary thought. See for example, "Liebe und Gerechtigkeit," esp. JS3: 48–75.

16 On Cohen's view that the affect of love ought to be de-emphasized in ethical theory, in favor of law, see my essay "Some Remarks on Love and Law in Hermann Cohen's Ethics of the Neighbor," in "The Ethics of the Neighbor," ed. D. Hollander, special issue, *Journal for Textual Reasoning* 4, no. 1 (November 2005), available at http://jtr.shanti.virginia.edu.

you shall love him [i.e., the stranger] as yourself." The focus on that phrase, which makes stranger-love appear to be a close analogue to "love your neighbor as yourself" [Lev. 19:18], is something Cohen reserves for his discussions of "love"-of-the-stranger in his polemical "Jewish writings" on "the neighbor" – which we will turn to below.)

A note on the term "stranger" or "foreigner" (*Fremdling*): David Novak has pointed out in his study *The Image of the Non-Jew in Judaism* two usages of the term *ger* in the Bible, and especially in the Pentateuch: (1) convert or proselyte, "one who has adopted and been adopted by Judaism"; and (2) "a political alien, a sojourner among the Jewish people having a set of limited rights and responsibilities." It is the latter meaning that is relevant to the biblical passages that Cohen focuses on. Novak further explains that the rabbinic tradition later endeavors to disambiguate the term *ger*, such that *ger tzedek* comes to be used for the first meaning (proselyte) and *ger toshav* comes to be used to refer to the "quasi-citizen of the Jewish polity," the "resident alien" or sojourner. As will become clearer when we turn to his treatments of neighbor-love in the Jewish writings, this rabbinic specification of *ger* as *ger toshav*, meaning sojourner (for which Cohen uses the German term *Beisaß-Fremdling*) or "resident alien," is key to Cohen's understanding of it.[17]

The biblical notion of the stranger in Cohen's understanding has a juridical (rechtlich) dimension, in that the prophets propagate and institute law (both Recht and Gesetz in this instance) as the foundation for the cultivation of morality (*Gesittung*); this is reflected in the precept "You shall have one law for the stranger and for the native-born in the land" (Lev. 24:22, quoted at ErW 214).[18] Here, then, Cohen's formula that there is "no individual in the ethical sense without legal community" (a focal point of the discussion in chapter 2) and his idea

---

17 David Novak, *The Image of the Non-Jew in Judaism: The Idea of Noahide Law*, 2nd ed., ed. Matthew Lagrone (Oxford: Littman Library of Jewish Civilization, 2011), 20–1. See also David Novak, "Gentiles in Rabbinic Thought," in *The Cambridge History of Judaism*, vol. 4, "The Late Roman-Rabbinic Period," ed. Steven T. Katz (Cambridge: Cambridge University Press, 2008), 658–9.

Ishay Rosen-Zvi offers an account of the complex relationship between these two meanings of *ger* in the Hebrew Bible and the Septuagint, and of how they were transformed by the rabbis. "In the Torah, Is the *Ger* Ever a Convert?" TheTorah.com, 5 April 2019. Cf. Ishay Rosen-Zvi and Adi Ophir, "*Goy*: Toward a Genealogy," *Dine Israel* 28 (2011), 75*–78*.

18 When he translates this first part of Leviticus 24:22 in "Liebe und Gerechtigkeit," Cohen, citing Ibn Ezra's explanation of it, parses it quite differently: (מִשְׁפַּט אֶחָד יִהְיֶה לָכֶם, כַּגֵּר כָּאֶזְרָח יִהְיֶה) "You shall have one law: as the stranger is, so shall the native be." ("Ein Recht soll euch sein: wie der Fremdling, so soll der Eingeborene sein.") "Liebe und Gerechtigkeit," JS3: 90.

that the self is generated from the other come together in his interpretation of the "stranger." The stranger-sojourner becomes a productive ethical category by way of a juridical principle. It is by virtue of this juridical dimension of the notion of "stranger" that in biblical religion "the stranger becomes the intermediary concept within the concept of the human being," which in turn becomes available for ethics (ErW 214–15).

Cohen finds a similar (and even "more precise and more gripping") "mediation" at work in the biblical prophets' "cosmopolitan" "love of humanity." Confronted with the existence of the "foreign people," and in opposition to the nationalistic tendency, prevalent in all "historical culture" and in politics, to equate cosmopolitanism with statelessness (with lack of a fatherland, *Vaterlandslosigkeit*), the prophets "believed themselves able to love their fatherland only by teaching love of humanity"; "indeed, they would rather have relinquished their fatherland than to lose one iota of the *one* humanity." If the "mediating concept" in attaining the concept of the human being is the "stranger" or "foreigner," the mediating concept for attaining the concept of humanity is that of the "foreign people" (ErW 215). Cohen generally construes peace in terms of a "messianic" future or task; accordingly, here he describes the "mediation" as also a "messianic opposition" between one's own nation and the "foreign peoples." This mediation toward "one humanity" is one that Cohen asserts in these pages despite the discouraging evidence, in the political realm, that it is far from imminent:

> Even if in private life one might already at least concede, for the sake of a meager beneficence, that self-consciousness also ought to encompass the other person [lit. "foreign person": *fremde Person*] as the neighbor [*den Nächsten*], in politics this [principle], applied to the foreign nation, is still taken to be sacrilege. (ErW 215)

The concept of "legal person" similarly allows for the "opposition between cosmopolitanism and patriotism" to be transcended (ErW 235–6). Accordingly, the state – which, we saw, is a form of Allheit and of the legal person (cf. ErW 256) – is not threatened in its unity by the stranger, but rather, like law in general, "calls for/requires the other" or foreigner (ErW 216).

What emerges from this account is an ambivalent picture in which biblical religion yields fruitful concepts for ethical progress but at the same time fails to reach the level of ethics. Cohen underscores that despite all the achievements of the prophets in the political realm and for the sake of a unified humanity, religion has "historically" been an ethico-political failure in this regard. Although these "sublime ideas" are capable of captivating us and reverberating in our hearts, they nevertheless, "in a political sense, effectively did not engender a historical actuality/reality at all" (ErW 215).[19]

It is religion's emphasis on the affect of "love" – which is the "highest expression with which [it] can operate" – that marks the limit of its relevance to ethico-legal theory. Although the intrinsically valuable category of the fellowman was a "discovery" made by religion, "love" contaminates that discovery. The same danger of mistaking "love" for a source for ethics is evident in the perennial misunderstanding of the notion of "love-of-neighbor," that is, of the commandment "love your *re'a* as yourself" (*ve-ahavta le-re'ekha kamokha*) in Leviticus 19:18. The problem Cohen identifies is that *re'a* has classically been translated as "der Nächste" – the superlative "the nearest" (ErW 217). This mistranslation is part of a long history of mistranslations and misinterpretations of *re'a,* which Cohen argues means simply "the other," even in the simple sense of "two nails that belong to each other" (ErW 218).[20] By virtue of this history of mistranslations, "the other" has been misleadingly transformed by the interpretative tradition into "der Nächste," "the neighbor." Cohen points to the Septuagint translation, *plesios,* which means neighbor (*Nachbar,* i.e., "neighbor" in its everyday meaning: a person living next to you) and carries the meaning of "nearness," and then to the Vulgate translation *amicus,* "friend," which he takes to be a superlativization of the Latin terms for "the near one(s)" or "the kinsmen," *proximus* and *propinqui.* The interpretations of Leviticus 19:18 implied by these terms have had, Cohen argues, devastating consequences for ethical-political life, such as the wars against non-Christian peoples (ErW 218). As we will see, Cohen views those misinterpretations as signals of the "corruptability" of love as an expression of affect (ErW 217).

---

19 Cohen makes a similar point in "Zum Prioritätsstreit": Religion was bound to fail to bring true neighbor-love to the world; thus, the task must be to found or account for (*begründen*) "true neighbor-love" independently of religion (Pr 175).

20 Richard Neudecker has reviewed the range of meanings of this term in the Bible and in biblical interpretation in "'And You Shall Love Your Neighbor as Yourself – I Am the Lord' (Lev 19, 18) in Jewish Interpretation," *Biblica* 73, no. 4 (1992). Richard Elliott Friedman has argued for a universalist understanding of the Levitical commandment in "Love Your Neighbor: Only Israelites or Everyone?" *Biblical Archaeology Review* 40, no. 5 (September/October 2014).

I discuss below the question of how to understand what this and other key biblical notions "mean" in the context of Cohen's thought.

The reference "two nails that belong to each other" is obscure. Kaufmann Kohler very helpfully speculates that it might be a reference to *re'ehu,* referring to "the other" "half" or "piece" of each animal cut in two by Abram in Genesis 15:10. Whether or not Cohen had this verse in mind, it certainly provides a good illustration of the usage of *re'a* that he is evoking. Kohler, "Die Nächstenliebe im Judentum. Eine historische Studie," in *Judaica: Festschrift zu Hermann Cohens siebzigstem Geburtstage,* ed. Ismar Elbogen, Benzion Kellermann, and Eugen Mittwoch (Berlin: Bruno Cassirer, 1912), 469.

Excursus: Cohen's Mode of Interpretation

Let us consider for a moment whether Cohen's claim about the meaning of the commandment to love your *re'a* – that is, that *re'a* applies to the human "other" in general, and not to the fellow Israelite – is "correct" in some standard historical-philological sense. The answer is that it appears to belong to a minority opinion in the history of Jewish interpretation, but it nevertheless can be located somewhere within the broad spectrum particularly of modern interpretations.[21]

---

21 Kenneth Reinhard points out, following Reinhard Neudecker and Ernst Simon, that we can speak of a "dominant strand" of Jewish interpretation of Leviticus 19:18 up until modernity, according to which *re'a* "refers exclusively to a fellow-Jew," and an alternative strand "dating at least from the ninth century (and probably much older)" that has "increasingly in modernity" been identified, according to which the *re'a* is part of a larger group and thereby "allowing the recovery of a universal ethics latent or even already active in rabbinic Judaism." Reinhard, "The Ethics of the Neighbor: Universalism, Particularism, Exceptionalism," in *Journal of Textual Reasoning* 4, no. 1 (November 2005), available at http://jtr.shanti.virginia.edu; Ernst Simon, "The Neighbor (*Re'a*) Whom We Shall Love," in *Modern Jewish Ethics: Theory and Practice*, ed. Marvin Fox (Columbus: Ohio State University Press, 1975); Neudecker, "'And You Shall Love Your Neighbor as Yourself.'" See also, by Kenneth Reinhard, "Messianism and the Neighbor," *Rosenzweig-Jahrbuch* 1 (2006), and "Die Politische Theologie des Nächsten und die Topologie des Eruv," in *Talmudische Tradition und moderne Rechtstheorie. Kontexte und Perspektiven einer Begegnung*, ed. Karl-Heinz Ladeur and Ino Augsberg (Tübingen: Mohr, 2013). (I am grateful to Kenneth Reinhard for sharing with me the original English version of the latter paper, "The Political Theology of the Neighbor and the Topology of the *Eruv*.") John J. Collins discerns a gradual trend over time toward universalization of the commandments to "love" – in the sense of treating justly – the *re'a* and the *ger*. "Love Your Neighbor: How It Became the Golden Rule," TheTorah.com (2020).

In contrast to those who discern a general or modern trend toward understanding the Levitical commandment in an increasingly universalist sense, David B. Ruderman, in introducing the strikingly "cosmopolitan" interpretation of Leviticus 19:18 by Pinḥas Hurwitz in his *Sefer ha-Brit* (1797/1807) – that "love your neighbor" applies to all human beings and that consequently "loving the non-Jew is the most Jewish thing one can do!" – underscores that this position is an anomaly in its time. Ruderman, "The Moral Cosmopolitanism of Pinḥas Hurwitz: Some Initial Conjectures," in *A Best-Selling Hebrew Book of the Modern Era: The Book of the Covenant of Pinḥas Hurwitz and Its Remarkable Legacy* (Seattle: University of Washington Press, 2014), chap. 5, and "The Book of Covenant: How to Become a Prophet," *Der Tagesspiegel*, 10 September 2010.

See also Michael Fagenblat, "The Concept of Neighbor in Jewish and Christian Ethics," in *The Jewish Annotated New Testament*, ed. Amy-Jill Levine and Marc Z. Brettler (Oxford: Oxford University Press, 2011), 541; Adam Zachary Newton, *The Fence and the Neighbor: Emmanuel Levinas, Yeshayahu Leibowitz, and Israel among the Nations* (Albany: State University of New York Press, 2001), 59–60; and Paul Mendes-Flohr, *Love, Accusative and Dative: Reflections on Leviticus 19:18* (Syracuse, NY: Syracuse University Press, 2007).

However, we should also consider the question: By what historical-philological measure does Cohen's interpretation of terms such as *re'a* need to be "correct" in order for his arguments about "love-of-neighbor" to hold? Not only do current and historical interpretations of the "love-your-neighbor" tradition diverge widely,[22] but there is more than one understanding of what it *means* to determine the meaning of a biblical term, notion, or tradition. Would it mean seeking to reconstruct what it meant to "the author," or to an immediate or proximate "audience," or to a normative community of interpreters, whether historic or transhistorical? To address such questions would by far exceed the task of the present book, but it is nevertheless important to consider what measure of correctness might apply to Cohen's own argument and to his mode of argumentation – which is to say, to his theory of Judaism as "religion of reason," as it developed throughout his writings up to the posthumously published *Religion of Reason.*

Here it is helpful to recap our earlier discussion, in chapter 3, of Cohen's systematic explication, in the introduction to the *Religion*, of what it means for philosophy to draw on "sources," and in particular on biblical-rabbinic material as "literary sources" that inform the project of understanding "the concept of Judaism":

> History as such is not decisive about the essence and distinctiveness of the concept, which has perhaps not yet been brought about and accomplished in the course of history thus far.

Cohen defines "source" here using the notion of the "*factum* of science" (discussed in chapter 1), the "experience" that serves as material for transcendental investigation (as the *facta* of legal science do for ethical inquiry). The concept of Judaism must be determined in relation to its "literary sources" or "literary history." But this cannot mean that those historical sources have "the value of criterion," since a criterion for a concept "can reside only in the concept [itself], as problem and method, as task and presupposition." (Literary) history thus serves as "the factor by virtue of which the factum is accomplished" (RV 4/3). To approach a source with a view to understanding its significance for a concept is necessarily to "pro-ject" (*vor-werfen*) that concept ahead. It means anticipating the concept in the sense of "foreclosing" (*vorwegnehmen*) it (RV 3/3).[23]

22 See the survey given by Neudecker, "'And You Shall Love Your Neighbor as Yourself.'"

23 "Es kann nimmermehr gelingen, aus den literarischen Quellen einen einheitlichen Begriff des Judentums zu entwickeln, wenn dieser nicht selbst ... als der ideale Vorwurf vorweggenommen wird."

This is how Cohen envisions arriving at, or generating the concept of Judaism, as "religion of reason" – along with all concepts constitutive of Judaism, among them "love-of-neighbor." It would doubtless be possible to examine whether Cohen's interpretations are correct according to some historical-philological measure to be specified, or in view of how they relate to the scholarly findings of his day, or of ours. Although in this chapter I will identify relevant historical contexts for Cohen's arguments about neighbor-love – in particular in the contemporaneous historical discourse of Jewish moral and legal defense that was so prevalent in the Wilhelmine era amidst growing political antisemitism – my principal approach in studying Cohen's arguments based on his interpretations of the "sources of Judaism" will be guided by Cohen's own stipulations for philosophical method, for how philosophy proceeds when it confronts a "source." It is essential to that method that although Cohen *describes* Jewish teachings – including by correcting misunderstandings of those teachings – his purpose in doing so is at the same time to produce an ethical theory that will help us grasp the conditions of possibility for moral goodness and a future political justice. In line with this, the task of determining the concept of the "neighbor" – and thus of interpreting correctly terms such as *re'a* in Leviticus – is for Cohen at the same time a task of interpreting "correctly" for the future; that is, in a manner that may serve to pro-ject and generate the concept of neighbor-love which could become effective in the future.

~

To return to looking at Cohen's discussion of love-of-neighbor in the *Ethik*, Cohen finds in the prevalent interpretations of the commandment "love your *re'a* as yourself" the same structure of "affective expansion," the same logic of degrees, that informs the ethico-legal thinking against which he argues throughout the *Ethik*. Behind the superlative, "nearest," as the name of the one who is to be loved absolutely and most intimately, there "lurks the comparative in the background" (ErW 217). The "love" that is supposed to be the source of ethics is thus a matter of degree, of "more or less." This observation is in line with Cohen's objection – discussed in detail in chapter 5 – to conceiving of the self as an entity that is capable of expansion toward others. Such a view would entail that the self is volatile, equally capable of contracting (again) to selfishness.

In critically evaluating the idea of neighbor-love, Cohen applies the principle that the other should be thought of as a correlate of the self, and thus that self and other are akin to "two halves of a whole." By contrast, the prevalent idea of neighbor-love as "love" of the "nearest" "harbors" a "skepticism"[24] about the reality or certainty or stability of the imagined "expansion of one's own self to empathy [*Mitgefühl*] with another self" (ErW 219).[25] It is the very word "der Nächste," in the history of its (mis-)interpretations, that marks this mistaken path toward ethics. Any hint of "degree" or quantifiability evokes physicality, sensuality, and thus the realm of sensual happiness (*der Sinne Glück*), which for Cohen, following Kant, is dissociated from the pursuit of the good. Even the positive quality of "Nähe," nearness, by itself already carries the "danger" of being an irrelevant or contaminating qualifier for determining the concept of the "self" in its meaning for ethics (ErW 217).

It is in the context of his discussion of neighbor-love that we find one of Cohen's sharpest denunciations of Rudolf Stammler's reliance on the notion of the "relative" or "particular community" (*Sondergemeinschaft*), discussed in detail in chapter 5. That notion is of a piece with the misunderstanding of "neighbor" as countryman; both notions run counter to the true meaning of the love commandment, which has "absolute validity" (ErW 218–19). Cohen goes so far as to insinuate that Stammler's misunderstanding of the "neighbor" as forming a part of a "precisely calculated and measured progressive scale/hierarchy of relativities" represents the kind of thinking that bears responsibility for ethical-political failure in contemporary culture. (In the last section of chapter 5, I showed how the treatment of neighbor-love in the *Ethik* is bound up with, and probably is even driven by, Cohen's critical response to Stammler.) Accordingly, Cohen criticizes Stammler's theory of "right law" as being a type of theory whose effect is to sow doubt in people's minds as to whether one really could actualize juridically the demands of religion in "bourgeois reality" (ErW 219).

Systematic ethics is called upon to address the question of why the religio-ethical project fails as a "question of life and a question of law" (ErW 215). Religion's mistaken emphasis on "love" means that despite the fact that it has made "objectively valuable" discoveries (such as the discovery of the stranger/fellowman/other as the "intermediary concept" in the concept of the human being; and the concomitant rooting of love-of-country in a messianic love-of-humanity), those "objective"

24 Cohen describes this skepticism harbored by neighbor-love as a "dishonest game of hide-and-seek" regarding whether one ought to take it seriously or not (ErW 219).

25 It is in this connection that Cohen also criticizes an ethics based on the idea of enemy-love, which – quite apart from the problematic notion of the "enemy" – is for him simply an intensified form of the expansion-by-degrees of the "I," which runs counter to his own attempt to "found the individual in an originary Allheit" (ErW 220).

discoveries made by religion are of limited value for ethical philosophy (ErW 216). Thus, Cohen asserts systematic ethics as a realm of knowledge that is methodologically strictly autonomous vis-à-vis the "language and expressions of religion." Cohen's later project of developing a systematic philosophy of (Jewish) religion in *Der Begriff der Religion* and *Religion of Reason* will build on this methodological distinction between ethics and religion.

Tracing the "Stranger" and the "Neighbor" from the *Ethik* to the Jewish Writings

As mentioned above, the argument in the *Ethik* about the significance of the biblical traditions of stranger-love and neighbor-love for ethico-legal philosophy presents, in abbreviated and partial form, an interpretation of those traditions that Cohen developed in greater detail in his Jewish writings, beginning with the essay he wrote as an affidavit for the 1888 Marburg Antisemitism Trial and published as "Die Nächstenliebe im Talmud" ("Love-of-Neighbor in the Talmud").[26] In other words, when he incorporated a discussion of the status of the biblical "stranger," and of the ambivalent tradition of love-of-neighbor into the *Ethik* in 1904, Cohen was taking up a major theme from his earlier works on Judaism, and was introducing theses that he had argued for – and would continue arguing for – in detail in his Jewish writings. Cohen's accounts of neighbor-love and stranger-love would come to make up an important element of the larger philosophical account of Judaism that he developed over the years, the full contours of which become identifiable above all in *Religion of Reason.* (This account of Judaism would also have become known to a more limited, but very influential Jewish audience,[27] in the lectures Cohen gave at the Lehranstalt für die Wissenschaft des Judentums from 1912 onwards.)

In turning now from *Ethik des reinen Willens* to Cohen's "Jewish writings," my purpose is to show that his treatments of stranger- and neighbor-love in his systematic work on ethics together with his works on Judaism present the "neighbor" as a legal-political category. The "neighbor," understood in conjunction with the "stranger," is a concept of Recht; as such, it exemplifies the main argument of the *Ethik*: that legal institutions and

26 See note 8 in this chapter.

27 The best-known member of this audience was Franz Rosenzweig, whose own theory of Judaism, which drew a great deal from Cohen's *jüdische Religionsphilosophie*, was to become arguably the most influential of the subsequent generation. I discuss Rosenzweig's reception of Cohen in chapter 1 of *Exemplarity and Chosenness: Rosenzweig and Derrida on the Nation of Philosophy* (Stanford: Stanford University Press, 2008).

concepts are the facta for ethics. This will become especially evident when we look at how Cohen deploys versions of the argument against "affective expansion" – which we have traced in the *Ethik* – in the interpretations he develops in his Jewish writings of the biblical and rabbinic notions of neighbor, stranger, and Noahide.

In order to bring out these aspects of Cohen's argument, it will be important to supply some historical and discursive context. Though the "neighbor" writings are articulations of a philosophical account of Judaism that Cohen develops over time and that culminates in the two late *Religion* books, they also constitute a body of writings in which he mounts a persistent defense of Judaism as a tradition in which love-of-the-neighbor signifies an embrace of the foreign in the name of universalism. In this regard they reflect (as has often been noted) important facets of the German-Jewish historical situation of his time: As of the 1880s, a new political, *völkisch* brand of antisemitism was asserting itself, and a Jewish community that had developed robust forms of political engagement and forums for public debate was responding in multiple ways, some of them creative and original, and some increasingly routinized. Such efforts included public initiatives on behalf of varied Jewish organizations, leaders, and publications to expose and disseminate detailed information about antisemitic attacks and to defend Judaism in the face of such attacks. Notably, much of this sort of defense took place in the context of judicial proceedings – a fact we shall return to when we discuss Cohen's involvement in the Marburg Antisemitism Trial.

My purpose in situating Cohen's writings in relationship to such phenomena is not especially to show that his writings were representative of certain discursive practices (though I will sometimes be considering to what extent his arguments resemble others that appear in key contemporaneous sources). Rather, against this background it will be possible to highlight those facets of Cohen's arguments about neighbor-love that have special significance for the ethico-legal philosophy of the *Ethik*, and that exemplify the ties between that philosophy and Cohen's philosophy of Judaism.

In reading the brief treatment of the fellowman/neighbor/stranger in the *Ethik* alongside the large corpus of accounts of neighbor- and stranger-love found in Cohen's writings on Judaism, I would like to avoid two possible temptations. The first would be the temptation to understand the brief exposition on this topic that we have been examining in the *Ethik* as merely a cultural-historical tangent to an otherwise straightforward, self-sufficient, abstract philosophical account of ethics. I would argue that concrete historical-political circumstances, juridical frameworks for political action, and attendant hopes for the future shared by many German Jews of the Wilhelmine period evidently factor into Cohen's thinking about ethics, law, and moral progress. To draw on our understanding of such factors enriches our understanding of his ethico-legal theory. Of course, this does not at all constrain our reception of that theory and our ability to reflect on its possible validity beyond those cultural and political circumstances. Looking at the theory in light of its meaning within the historic framework in which it was first deployed is in fact part of what allows us to demonstrate the force of what Cohen means by claims such as "ethics is generated out of law" or "there is no individual without legal community."

The second possible reading that I wish to avoid would treat the discussion of stranger- and neighbor-love in the *Ethik* – since it is the briefest of Cohen's expositions on the matter – as being of relatively minor importance in the entire corpus of Cohen's treatments of the neighbor. In fact, I would argue that the discussion in the *Ethik* is central to those treatments – perhaps their very center. As I seek to show by means of a combined reading in this chapter, the *Ethik* on the one hand – where the arguments about neighbor- and stranger-love form part of a full-scale philosophical demonstration that ethics is founded in law – complements the "neighbor" writings on the other hand, which provide the full account of why the neighbor is primarily a legal category with an ethical significance and purpose. Neighbor-/stranger-love in the "neighbor" writings is thus on the one hand a case in point for what the *Ethik* seeks to show: that legal institutions inform and generate ethical principles. Yet Cohen's treatment of stranger- and neighbor-love as part of the argument of the *Ethik* is of crucial importance, since it is only in that book that we get the full account of how and why it is that we ought to think of ethics as being generated out of legal institutions or legal reasoning. Thus, it is only by looking at the *Ethik* and the "neighbor" writings together that we can grasp what it *means* for the neighbor to be a legal category.[28]

Historical Context of Cohen's "Neighbor" Writings: Anti-Judaism, Anti-Talmudism, and Anti-Antisemitism during the 1880s

My discussion of Cohen's "neighbor" writings will especially emphasize the first of his public statements on love-of-neighbor, his testimony and published affidavit at the 1888 Marburg Antisemitism Trial. The theses advanced

28 The reading I am proposing here can be seen as nuancing and resolving the tension I identified between Cohen's interpretations of neighbor-love in the 1888 affidavit and in the pages on the fellowman and neighbor in the *Ethik* in "Ethical-Political Universality Out of the Sources of Judaism: Reading Hermann Cohen's 1888 Affidavit In and Out of Context," in *New Directions in Jewish Philosophy*, ed. Aaron W. Hughes and Elliot R. Wolfson (Bloomington: Indiana University Press, 2009), 237.

in that text set the stage for, and remained central to Cohen's understanding of the notion of neighbor-stranger-love and its significance. However, this trial should be understood to be more than a mere occasion at which Cohen began to engage with this notion, an occasion that by definition would remain extrinsic to the substance of that engagement. Rather, I shall show that the circumstances and discursive framing of the trial are crucial to understanding Cohen's argumentation, in that they allow us to see it as a strategic response in relation to what I will sometimes call, in a Foucauldian vein, the "dispositive" of the trial. The notion of the "dispositive" is useful, among other reasons, because it allows us to see a phenomenon such as the Marburg Antisemitism Trial, and Cohen's location in relation to the trial, as signifying an ongoing power constellation, symptomatic of Jewish-Christian relations and its politics, and not simply as an event with a beginning and an end. The antisemitism trial (which I will further explicate in view of the legal framing that made trials of this kind possible) may be seen, therefore, as conditioning Cohen's writings on "the neighbor," in a way that typifies his writings on Judaism in the horizon of Jewish-Christian difference and its politics. Cohen's responses at the trial become legible as an attempt to unsettle the prevailing conceptions of Jewish-Christian difference that governed the trial and the role that Cohen was called upon to play.

The reading I wish to develop requires some attention, then, to the conditions under which the Marburg trial took place, and to the larger phenomena of which it was a part. A full characterization of the situation of Jews in the German-speaking world in the last decades of the nineteenth century naturally would exceed the scope of the present study, and there is a wealth of scholarship on German-Jewish history of this period, including excellent introductions for non-specialists.[29] Among the larger cultural-political phenomena or developments that were important for acculturated Jews and Jewish intellectual circles, I will point to four that are most relevant to situating and interpreting Cohen's writings and other public engagements on Jewish matters:

(1) The large and diverse world of Jewish periodicals and publishing.
(2) The diversity of Jewish congregations and organizations that resulted from the rise of religious reform movements and corresponding "orthodox" counter-movements, as well as non-religious

29 See, for example Steven M. Lowenstein et al., *Integration in Dispute 1871–1918*, vol. 3 of *German-Jewish History in Modern Times*, edited by Michael A. Meyer with Michael Brenner (New York: Columbia University Press, 1996); also published as *Deutsch-jüdische Geschichte in der Neuzeit*, vol. 3, *Umstrittene Integration, 1871–1918* (Munich: C.H. Beck, 1997).

organizations formed in order to assert and defend Jewish civil and political rights.

(3) The growing number of Jewish legal defense activities in response to antisemitism. These included initiatives undertaken against denunciations of Jewish law as represented by “the Talmud” or other legal codes such as the Shulkhan Arukh under statutes prohibiting insult of religions, incitement to class warfare, and other offenses, as well as defenses mounted in the context of the reemergence of “ritual murder” accusations. (Both the attacks on “Talmud” and the “ritual murder” cases were revivals of types of anti-Jewish agitation that were thought to be long obsolete.)[30]

30 On Jewish legal defense in general, see the representative range of scholarship cited by Christoph Jahr in “Ahlwardt on Trial: Reactions to the Antisemitic Agitation of the 1890s in Germany,” trans. Deborah Cohen, *Leo Baeck Institute Year Book* 48 (2003), 68–9nn4–9. Jahr notes that “while the connection between the antisemitic movement and the Conservatives is well established, there has as yet been no systematic analysis of the effects of state and, above all, judicial action against antisemitism”; he adds that this is particularly so for the Wilhelmine period (as opposed to the Weimar Republic, for which “the state of research ... is better”) (68, 68n4). This situation is now somewhat improved, notably with Jahr’s own book *Antisemitismus vor Gericht. Debatten über die juristische Ahndung judenfeindlicher Agitation in Deutschland (1879–1960)* (Frankfurt am Main: Campus, 2011), as well as with Inbal Steinitz, *Der Kampf jüdischer Anwälte gegen den Antisemitismus. Die strafrechtliche Rechtsschutzarbeit des Centralvereins deutscher Staatsbürger jüdischen Glaubens 1893–1933* (Berlin: Metropol, 2008), and Barnet P. Hartston, *Sensationalizing the Jewish Question: Anti-Semitic Trials and the Press in the Early German Empire* (Leiden: Brill, 2005). To Jahr’s observation I would add that while many of the studies of Jewish legal defense have been oriented toward answering the question of “what worked” to combat antisemitism, or whether legal defense turned out to have been a viable method to combat antisemitism, some of the more recent studies allow us to see those phenomena in the context of legal history and legal institutions of the time, as well as of larger issues concerning the interactions between law and politics. However, I believe there is still room for more work in this direction.

Note that some of the moral and legal defense action undertaken against attacks on Judaism came from Christian anti-antisemitic activists. Christian Wiese offers a highly nuanced and detailed look at the role of the Orientalist and Protestant theologian Hermann Leberecht Strack and other theologian-scholars (especially Franz Delitzsch and Gustaf Dalman), who, while they drew on their specialized knowledge of Jewish religious sources in order to debunk anti-Jewish and anti-Talmudic accusations, were at the same time involved in missionizing to Jews, or also at the same time declared Christianity to be the superior religion to Judaism. Wiese, *Wissenschaft des Judentums und protestantische Theologie im wilhelminischen Deutschland: ein Schrei ins Leere?* (Tübingen: Mohr Siebeck, 1999); translated by B. Harshav and C. Wiese as *Challenging Colonial Discourse: Jewish Studies and Protestant Theology in Wilhelmine Germany* (Leiden: Brill, 2005), chap. 3, esp. 88–9/109–10, 112–13/136–7, 116/141.

On ritual murder accusations and trials, see Hermann L. Strack, “Blood Accusation,” in *Jewish Encyclopedia*, vol. 3 (New York: Funk and Wagnalls, 1902);

(4) The broad spectrum of Jewish scholarly and intellectual activities known as "Wissenschaft des Judentums." These activities were mounted by Jews beginning in the early nineteenth century as, on the one hand, a non-traditional mode of Jewish learning that took its lead from the principles of modern Western scholarship, and, on the other hand, an alternative or supplement to the lack of academic study of Judaism in the universities.

Across and within these four broad developments – which have been well-documented and explained in the historical scholarship – we can discern, beginning in the late 1870s and extending to the turn of the century, an intellectual and political discourse that I propose to call "Jewish moral defense." With this heading, I am referring to the varied spectrum of public initiatives – in journalistic reportage and commentary, in scholarly and popular publications on Judaism, in legal actions, in political activity, and in the work of Jewish religious groupings and coalitions – that aimed to assert, clarify, or defend the moral stature of Judaism.

Cohen's writings on the "neighbor" belong to this discourse of "Jewish moral defense" – of *Abwehr*, to use the German term of the time. In particular, in his affidavit for the 1888 Marburg Antisemitism Trial, he argued for

---

Wiese, *Wissenschaft des Judentums*, 90–1/ *Challenging Colonial Discourse*, 111–12; Johannes T. Groß, *Ritualmordbeschuldigungen gegen Juden im Deutschen Kaiserreich 1871–1914* (Berlin: Metropol, 2002); Hillel J. Kieval, "Neighbors, Strangers, Readers: The Village and the City in Jewish-Gentile Conflict at the Turn of the Nineteenth Century," *Jewish Studies Quarterly*, 12 (2005); Helmut Walser Smith, *The Butcher's Tale: Murder and Anti-Semitism in a German Town* (New York: Norton, 2002); Olaf Blaschke, *Katholizismus und Antisemitismus im Deutschen Kaiserreich*, 2nd rev. ed. (Göttingen: Vandenhoeck & Ruprecht, 1999), 90; Christina von Braun, "Und der Feind ist Fleisch geworden. Der rassistische Antisemitismus," in *Der ewige Judenhass. Christlicher Antijudaismus, Deutschnationale Judenfeindlichkeit, Rassistischer Antisemitismus*, ed. Christina von Braun and Ludger Heid, 2nd rev. ed. (Berlin: Philo, 2000), 169–71; Scott Spector, "Blood Lies: The Truth about Modern Ritual Murder Accusations and Defenses," chap. 5 in *Violent Sensations: Sex, Crime and Utopia in Vienna and Berlin, 1860–1914* (Chicago: University of Chicago Press, 2016).

On the rise of antisemitism and the responses to antisemitism in general, see Peter Pulzer, "The Return of Old Hatreds" and "The Response to Antisemitism," in Steven M. Lowenstein et al., *Integration in Dispute 1871–1918*, chaps. 7 and 8, respectively; Peter Pulzer, *The Rise of Political Anti-Semitism in Germany and Austria*, rev. ed. (Cambridge, MA: Harvard University Press, 1988); Uriel Tal, *Christians and Jews in Germany: Religion, Politics, and Ideology in the Second Reich, 1870–1914*, trans. Noah Jonathan Jacobs (Ithaca, NY: Cornell University Press, 1975); and Ismar Schorsch, *Jewish Reactions to German Anti-Semitism, 1870–1914* (New York: Columbia University Press, 1972).

the first time that Judaism has a tradition of "neighbor-love" that comprises a code of ethical conduct toward the non-Jew. The trial, along with Cohen's role in it as expert witness, was publicized and reported in detail in the Jewish (as well as general) press, and his engagement typified the role that intellectuals often assumed in the face of attacks on Judaism and Jews.

As already mentioned, the attacks in question often contained, or essentially consisted of, denunciations of Talmudic or other rabbinic literature. Their highly routinized lines of argumentation often contended that Jewish law mandated discrimination and wrongdoing against non-Jews, and in particular against Christians. In fact, the popular anti-Talmudic tracts of the 1870s revived much older (medieval and early modern) Talmud denunciations whose purpose was to portray Jews as evildoers.[31] An older, established form of anti-Jewish disputation was being reactivated and embedded into a modern-day form of political agitation, whose purpose was to disqualify Jewish participation in the German polity, that is, to undo the gains of Jewish emancipation.

Two of the most important instances were the writings of the Catholic theologians Konrad Martin and Sebastian Brunner – their *Blicke in's talmudische Judenthum* dated back to 1848, but was republished in 1876 by Joseph Rebbert[32] – and the famous tract of the Catholic theologian August Rohling, *Der Talmudjude*, which was first published in 1871 and was reprinted many times.[33] Another important instance came the following decade: a book entitled *Judenspiegel* published by a friend of Rohling, Aron Briman, a converted Jew, under the pseudonym "Dr. Justus" in 1883.[34]

---

31 See Hermann Greive, "Der Talmud, Zielscheibe und Ausgangspunkt antisemitischer Polemik," in *Antisemitismus. Erscheinungsformen der Judenfeindschaft gestern und heute*, ed. Günther B. Ginzel (Bielefeld: Wissenschaft und Politik, 1991), 306; and Wiese, *Wissenschaft des Judentums*, 89/*Challenging Colonial Discourse*, 110.

32 Joseph Rebbert, *Blicke in's talmudische Judenthum, nach den Forschungen von Dr. Konrad Martin* (Paderborn: Bonifacius, 1876). The publisher of this volume, as well as of Aron Briman's *Judenspiegel* (see note 34), the Bonifacius-Druckerei in Paderborn (where Konrad Martin had been a bishop), was according to Hermann Greive one of the most important publishers of antisemitic literature, particularly antisemitic literature with an "anti-Talmudic orientation." See Greive, "Der Talmud," 306.

33 August Rohling, *Der Talmudjude* (Münster: Russell, 1871). On Rohling's biography and anti-Jewish activities, see Isak A. Hellwing, *Der konfessionelle Antisemitismus im 19. Jahrhundert in Österreich* (Vienna: Herder, 1972), 71–183; and Hartston, *Sensationalizing the Jewish Question*, 190ff.

34 Aron Briman [Dr. Justus, pseud.], *Judenspiegel* (Paderborn: Bonifacius, 1883). According to the subtitle, this book promises to expose "100 newly discovered laws of the Jews still in effect today, concerning the dealings of Jews with Christians." For a discussion of the impact of Rohling and Briman, see Stefan Lehr, *Antisemitismus – religiöse Motive im sozialen Vorurteil* (Munich: Kaiser, 1974), 32ff.

This book was an attack on the *Shulkhan Arukh*, and was also reprinted many times.[35] These publications inspired, either directly or indirectly (i.e., because their claims were cited or reproduced by others), much in the way of Jewish moral defense activity, and occasioned a number of trials, including the Marburg trial in which Cohen took part. They had in common a focus on what sort of conduct toward non-Jews was prescribed in the Talmud or Shulkhan Arukh. The guiding interpretative principle was to present precepts in those texts that referred to, or were thought to refer to, Gentiles as dictating Jewish attitudes and actions toward Christians in contemporary times, and thus to paint a picture of what the Brunner/Martin book termed "Talmudic anti-Christianity."[36] To quote

---

35 George Y. Kohler, "Manuel Joel in Defense of the Talmud. Liberal Responses to Religious Antisemitism in Nineteenth-Century Germany," *Hebrew Union College Annual* 79 (2008, published 2010): 142.

36 As cited in Tal, *Christians and Jews in Germany*, 89. Tal (90ff.) explains that the anti-Jewish agitation on the part of Catholic theologians was also a function of the conflicts of the time between the Wilhelmine state and Catholic interests, the so-called *Kulturkampf*, and was in particular an instrument of "ultramontane" Catholicism. See also the discussion in Hermann Greive, *Geschichte des modernen Antisemitismus in Deutschland* (Darmstadt: Wissenschaftliche Buchgesellschaft, 1983), 50–72.

Olaf Blaschke similarly explains Catholic antisemitism in the Wilhelmine political context, including the function of anti-Talmudism and of Rohling's writings in particular, as simultaneously an attack on Bismarck's *Kulturkampf* and on political liberalism (and even to some extent an attack on inner-Catholic opposition to Papal infallibility, represented by the Old Catholics in the wake of the First Vatican Council). Blaschke, *Katholizismus und Antisemitismus*, 59ff. Blaschke cites in particular a Catholic anti-Talmud pamphlet dating from 1876 (largely a reproduction of Rohling's theses), which illustrates to what extent "Talmud," and in particular its "morality," came to stand in for all that threatened the lives of Christians. Blaschke paraphrases and quotes as follows:

> Possessions [*Hab und Gut*], honor, and family of the Christian are given over to the "Talmud Jew." But he will not be satisfied with this, for "the murder of Christians is openly preached in the Talmud." Now, in the *Kulturkampf*, it must be lamented that "the morality of the Talmud is flourishing especially, ..." "Hence the Christian press cannot work enough on the enlighenment of Christians about the Talmud and Talmudic Judaism. When the Christian peoples' eyes are opened to this, opened completely, then a good step toward improvement ... will have been made.... (*Was lehrt der Talmud?* [Münster, 1876], 14–15, 21, 23–4, paraphrased and quoted in Blaschke, 60)

Similarly, Blaschke carefully traces the increasing acceptance and use of the term "antisemitism" among Catholics who took antisemitic positions in the 1880s and 1890s. The adoption of the term "antisemitism" to describe one's own anti-Jewish rhetoric seems to have been made possible thanks to its subordination to or explanation by way of *Christenschutz*, "the protection of Christians" (113–17).

For a discussion of parallel phenomena in Austria, see Kurt Schubert, *Geschichte des österreichischen Judentums* (Vienna: Böhlau, 2008), chap. 6.

Joseph Rebbert's preface from his 1876 reedition of this book, which was intended to persuade politicians and voters that the civil rights that had been extended to Jews ought to be revoked, as the emancipated Jews were harmful to society:[37]

> Where above all ought the deeper reason [for this harm] to be sought? Where else but in the doctrines, in particular the moral doctrines, of the Talmud.... About this moral law [*Sittengesetz*] of the Talmud our people, and specifically our voters and representatives, *must* be clearly instructed.[38]

Of the three above-mentioned works, Rohling's *Der Talmudjude* certainly had the widest and longest-lasting impact, even though in its content it was not original, but was based on a much older work, *Entdecktes Judenthum* (1701) by Johann Andreas Eisenmenger.[39] With five editions published by 1880, and seventeen editions by 1922,[40] Rohling's book was well received by the public, including the Catholic press in Austria (Rohling was at the time a professor of Semitic Languages at Charles University, the German university in Prague), and even received some recognition as a work of scholarship.[41] In the meantime, in 1883 Rohling made an official request to testify at the infamous Tiszaeszlár blood libel trial "that the shedding of non-Jewish virgin blood is an exceedingly holy act for the Jews," which gained him further notoriety.[42]

There were numerous counterattacks, of which I will mention only two famous examples: (1) The initiatives of Franz Delitzsch, most importantly a pamphlet published in 1881 defending Judaism against

---

37 Rebbert, *Blicke*, 1–5.

38 Rebbert, *Blicke*, 4–5.

39 Pulzer, *Rise of Political Anti-Semitism*, 157, and Wiese, *Wissenschaft des Judentums*, 89n2/*Challenging Colonial Discourse*, 110n2. For a history and brief characterization of this work, see Zvi Avneri, "Eisenmenger, Johann Andreas," in *Encyclopaedia Judaica*, 2nd ed. (2007).

40 Kohler, "Manuel Joel," 142, 142n3.

41 Pulzer, *Rise of Political Anti-Semitism*, 157. Olaf Blaschke documents the reach of Rohling's anti-Talmudism and argues that it was a phenomenon that was highly representative in particular of Catholic antisemitism, in *Katholizismus und Antisemitismus*, 91ff.

42 Josef S. Bloch (ed.), *Acten und Gutachten in dem Prozesse Rohling contra Bloch*, vol. 1 (Vienna: Breitenstein, 1890), 105, cited in Hellwing, *Der konfessionelle Antisemitismus*, 107–8. Rohling was here repeating a claim from Briman's *Judenspiegel*. See Hellwing, *Der konfessionelle Antisemitismus*, 100–5, and Franz Delitzsch, *Schachmatt den Blutlügnern Rohling und Justus* (Erlangen: Andreas Deichert, 1883), 19–20, 22–34. See also *Encyclopaedia Judaica*, 2nd ed. (2007), s.v. "Rohling, August"; Kieval, "Neighbors, Strangers, Readers," 72; Joseph S. Bloch, *Erinnerungen aus meinem Leben*, vol. 1 (Vienna: R. Löwit, 1922), 81.

Rohling's depictions, which itself was published in seven editions during its first year of publication.[43] Delitzsch also issued a statement, which was published along with statements by many other Protestant theologians and text scholars, in response to the Tiszaeszlár accusations, refuting the view that the Talmud mandates ritual use of Christian blood.[44] (2) A highly publicized legal proceeding initiated in 1883 in Vienna, where Rabbi Joseph Samuel Bloch successfully provoked Rohling into bringing charges against himself for having, in newspaper articles attacking Rohling and challenging his expertise, disgraced Rohling's honor.[45] With eminent theologians indicating they would discredit Rohling, and Bloch having amassed a great amount of evidence against him, Rohling finally withdrew the charge in 1885, shortly before the trial was to begin.[46]

By 1885, then, the trial being prepared in Vienna, as well as the Tiszaeszlár trial, had yielded a large corpus of writings and much publicity around Rohling's claims, and the polemics and legal defense activities around Rohling's *Talmudjude* and Briman's *Judenspiegel* continued for years afterwards.[47]

---

43 Franz Delitzsch, *Rohling's Talmudjude beleuchtet* (Leipzig: Dörffling & Franke, 1881). Cf. Spector, "Blood Lies," 226–7.

44 See Delitzsch, "Lässt sich die Ansicht, dass die Juden Christenblut zu rituellem Zwecke verwenden, irgendwie aus dem Talmud begründen?" in *Christliche Zeugnisse gegen die Blutbeschuldigung der Juden* (Berlin: Walther & Apolant, 1882). Stefan Lehr gives an overview of Rohling's individual attacks on the Talmud, together with references to parallel defamations in other antisemitic tracts, demonstrating that one can locate in the antisemitic literature "a certain storehouse of arguments and accusations, which, in varied form or new configurations, recur in almost all works of religious-antisemitic agitation." Lehr, *Antisemitismus*, 40ff.

45 Kohler, "Manuel Joel," 143; Bloch, *Erinnerungen*, 1:84; Schubert, *Geschichte*, 84; Spector, "Blood Lies," 222–6.

46 Pulzer, *Rise of Political Anti-Semitism*, 157; "Rohling, August," in *Encyclopaedia Judaica*.

47 See, for example, Christian Wiese's discussion of a pamphlet published by Hermann Strack ten years after the Rohling affair in response to the dissemination in 1892 of a flier entitled "Talmud-Auszug (Schulchan-Aruch)" ("Talmud Extracts [Shulkhan Arukh]"). Wiese, *Wissenschaft des Judentums*, 89–90, 113/*Challenging Colonial Discourse*, 110–11, 137. Strack reports that the state prosecutor declined his request that legal action be taken against distribution of this flier containing defamatory allegations – that Judaism requires the murder of non-Jews – with the explanation that the claims attributed to the Talmud in the flyer were a matter of legitimate, and thus legally protected, scholarly debate, as evidenced by the works of Rohling, the author of the *Judenspiegel*, and others. That Rohling is supposed to have been discredited in Vienna in 1883–5 makes no difference to the court's answer to Strack, which states that no "reasonable doubts" have been raised against his scholarly opinions of what the Talmud's laws say. Strack, "Die Juden, dürfen sie 'Verbrecher von Religions wegen' genannt werden?" (Berlin: Hermann Walther, 1893), 11–12. See also the treatment in Jahr, *Antisemitismus vor Gericht*, 135–6.

Since the anti-Talmudism of Rebbert, Rohling, Briman, and others was focused on exposing Judaism as mandating immoral and criminal behavior by Jews toward non-Jews, one of the core tasks that emerged as a goal of Jewish defense initiatives was to demonstrate “Talmudic ethics.” This task was on the one hand a rhetorical, argumentative, and scholarly one: Jewish periodicals and books and pamphlets written for a wider reading public confronted the denunciations of Judaism and characterizations of Talmudic precepts at various discursive levels, from supplying general knowledge, to giving spirited moral defenses in a popular vein, to producing detailed philological-historical and theological refutations of the claims Martin, Rohling, Briman, and others were making about the Talmud – claims that presented themselves as resting on philological-historical expertise in reading the ancient and medieval texts that made up the Jewish legal tradition. Thus, Bernhard Jacobsohn, in an 1879 book recording the activities of the Deutsch-Israelitischer Gemeindebund (DIGB; the first broad-based organization representing Jews in Germany) circa 1876, writes that one decisive response planned by the organization to the Catholic anti-Jewish literature of the time, “which in the main drew on Rohling’s *Talmudjude*,” was “to explain before all the world that this work lacks any scientific/scholarly [*wissenschaftlich*] basis.” This was to occur in particular by means of a tract that would be not only a “refutation” of Rohling’s claims but “a tract of enlightenment on a large scale, that is, ... a [published] work about the ethics of the Talmud.” Jacobsohn, writing in 1879, adds that this idea “still awaits its implementation.”[48] He reports that, in general, it was the educative efforts to sway public opinion, for example, by disseminating scholarly works that refuted anti-Jewish arguments, that were the focus of the DIGB’s work (as opposed to legal defense activity).[49]

---

48 Bernhard Jacobsohn acknowledges the work *Professor Rohlings Falschmünzerei auf talmudischem Gebiet* by Philipp Bloch (Posen: Merzbach, 1876), despite its having provided a strong argument against Rohling, as having made only a small “installment payment” or “introduction” toward the promised effort, which he projects to be a much larger work. Jacobsohn, *Der Deutsch-Israelitische Gemeindebund nach Ablauf des ersten Decenniums seit seiner Begründung von 1869 bis 1879. Eine Erinnerungsschrift* (Leipzig, 1879), 30–1. On the DIGB, see Steven M. Lowenstein, “The Community,” chap. 5 in Lowenstein et al., *Integration in Dispute 1871–1918*, 138–9; Schorsch, *Jewish Reactions*, 30–6.

In fact, some of the antisemitism trials of the 1880s succeeded because the defense or the court could point to Rohling’s “scholarship” as unrefuted. See Pulzer, “The Return of Old Hatreds,” 218, regarding an 1880 case in Dresden and the case of Franz Holubek in 1882 in Vienna.

49 Jacobsohn, *Der Deutsch-Israelitische Gemeindebund*, 40.

The DIGB was generally viewed as having been a successful first instance of broad-based Jewish civic organization in the Kaiserreich, but this organization, along with the very notion of such an institution, also faced challenges, especially from Orthodox quarters.[50] Moritz Lazarus (as of 1874 a professor of philosophy at the university in Berlin) seems to have been cognizant of those structural challenges when, in seeking a means to combat antisemitism at a time when the Berlin Antisemitism Dispute, launched by Heinrich von Treitschke in late 1879, was in full swing,[51] he proposed something more modest, and more local: In December 1880, he approached 200 leading figures in the Berlin Jewish community with the idea of a coordinated response to antisemitism. In his address to this very short-lived[52] "December Committee," which he published shortly afterwards, he explains that the committee's purpose should be to have an inner-Jewish (albeit public) discussion of how to confront antisemitism, as well as, among other things, to work toward the "elevation of Judaism, presentation of its ethical standpoint before the eyes of non-Jews and Jews," that is, "that we tell [and] present to the rest of the non-Jewish world what our moral creed, our moral doctrines, consist of."[53]

It was not until 1885 that the DIGB succeeded, as part of a defense initiative in which Lazarus was again involved, in producing a public statement of Jewish moral principles.[54] (This was worked out between December 1883 and December 1885 – a period, we may recall, that saw the intensification of antisemitic attacks and anti-antisemitic defense with the Tiszaeszlár case and the subsequent Rohling proceedings in Vienna.) The statement "Fifteen Basic Principles of Jewish Moral

50 Lowenstein, "The Community," 138–9; Schorsch, *Jewish Reactions*, 30–6.

51 See Marcel Stoetzler, *The State, the Nation, and the Jews: Liberalism and the Antisemitism Dispute in Bismarck's Germany* (Lincoln: University of Nebraska Press, 2009). As I discuss in the introduction to this book, Cohen himself weighed in on this dispute, with "Ein Bekenntnis in der Judenfrage" (1880; JS2: 73–94), his first publication on a Jewish topic.

52 Pulzer, "The Return of Old Hatreds," 217–18; Schorsch, *Jewish Reactions*, 59–65; Jahr, *Antisemitismus vor Gericht*, 151–2.

53 See the text of Moritz Lazarus's two-part address on 1 and 16 December 1880, published as *Unser Standpunkt. Zwei Reden an seine Religionsgenossen* (Berlin: Stuhr, 1881), 26. Christoph Jahr has also located a police transcript of the address; see Jahr, *Antisemitismus vor Gericht*, 152n172.

54 See Schorsch, *Jewish Reactions*, 73–4; Moritz Lazarus, *Die Ethik des Judentums* (Frankfurt am Main: Kauffmann, 1898), 176–7, translated by Henrietta Szold as *The Ethics of Judaism*, part 1 (Philadelphia: Jewish Publication Society, 1900), 234; Wiese, *Wissenschaft des Judentums*, 91–2/*Challenging Colonial Discourse*, 113–14; J. Hertzberg, "Die 15 Grundsätze der jüdischen Sittenlehre. Ihre Entstehung und ihre Würdigung," in *Allgemeine Zeitung des Judentums* 83, no. 18 (2 May 1919): 182 (this source was uncovered by Wiese, 91n7).

Doctrine" ("15 Grundsätze der jüdischen Sittenlehre") was meant to publicize principles of morality contained in Judaism for the purposes of moral and legal defense against anti-Jewish agitation, as well as to serve as a statement of Jewish conviction that would raise consciousness among Jews about the Jewish sources of those moral principles. The Basic Principles were officially endorsed by many other Jewish leaders and associations across Germany and Austria.[55] They thus came to be regarded as an extremely valuable instrument of moral defense – particularly in view of the fact that they received endorsement from leaders across the spectrum of religious observance (i.e., including both Reform and Orthodox leaders), and their influence was felt for years afterwards by people who were concerned about having effective tools for combating antisemitism.[56]

"Love Your Neighbor" in Jewish Moral Defense

Given that the need for a moral defense of Judaism came about in large part due to allegations that Judaism condones crimes against non-Jews, it is not surprising that a central tenet of the Basic Principles is that Judaism requires just treatment of all, regardless of national or religious affiliation. The precept "love your neighbor as yourself" appears prominently as having this meaning, and the list of principles names specific kinds of moral comportment toward all others that neighbor-love is taken to entail.[57]

We find a parallel approach in another broad-based declaration of moral principles that was issued at around the same time as the Principles statement. The 1884 assembly of sixty-eight Liberal/Reform rabbis

55 Hertzberg details that the majority of Austrian rabbis approved the Principles, as did the chief rabbis of London and Paris. Hertzberg, "Die 15 Grundsätze," 182; cf. Schorsch, *Jewish Reactions*, 73–4.

56 As evidenced by J. Hertzberg's 1919 retrospective appreciation, "Die 15 Grundsätze." As Christian Wiese has pointed out, in 1900 Hermann Strack, as part of the essay "Sind die Juden Verbrecher von Religions wegen?" ("A Defense of Judaism in the Service of Effective Missionizing to Jews") reported on this 1883–5 initiative and reproduced the Fifteen Basic Principles in full, as well as a further rabbis' statement on Jewish morality dating from 1893, including a complete list of the signatories. Strack argued that these statements were "authoritative" moral teachings for "contemporary Judaism." Strack, *Sind die Juden Verbrecher von Religions wegen?* (Leipzig: Hinrich'sche Buchhandlung, 1900), originally published in Strack's journal, *Nathanael. Zeitschrift für die Arbeit der evangelischen Kirche an Israel* 16 (1900). Cf. Wiese, *Wissenschaft des Judentums*, 115–16/ *Challenging Colonial Discourse*, 140.

57 See the list of the Fifteen Basic Principles as reproduced in Lazarus, *Ethik des Judentums*, 409–12/*Ethics of Judaism*, part 1, 302–6, esp. Principle 2.

in Berlin ("Rabbiner-Versammlung")[58] was even more explicit than the authors of the Fifteen Basic Principles (adopted a little later, in 1885) in presenting Jewish moral principles in conjunction with an interpretation of "love your neighbor" in Leviticus. This gathering had as one of its three objectives to issue a declaration "concerning the interconfessional position of Judaism." A declaration was drafted as follows:

> In the name of and with the aid of the one and only God the assembly of German rabbis declares, with reference to the denigrations which in recent years have heaped hatred and prejudice on the moral doctrine of Judaism, the following:
>
> The commandment of *Nächstenliebe* (love-of-neighbor) which in Leviticus 19:18 is proclaimed with the words: "And you shall love the neighbor as yourself. I am the Eternal" and which is called by Hillel, the great master, the quintessence of the entire Jewish teaching,[59] refers not only to the fellow member of one's tribe or of one's faith [*Stammes- oder Glaubensgenossen*], but rather is, just as is the case for the commandment of justice proclaimed in Lev. 24:22 ("Let there be one law, let the stranger be as the native-born, for I am the Eternal, your God"[60]), to be regarded as an unrestricted statute/law [*Satzung*] that encompasses all human beings.
>
> Anyone who proclaims his humanity in doing justice, practicing love, and walking humbly with God is regarded in Judaism, even if he has been born in a different creed, as truly pious and as having a share in eternal blessedness, according to the Talmudic saying that has permeated Jewish consciousness: "The pious among the peoples also have a share in eternal blessedness."[61]

---

58 Although the 1884 Rabbiner-Versammlung was not intended to be restricted to Liberal/Reform rabbis, and was not to include discussion on any contentious matters concerning religion, according to a contemporary newspaper report, no Orthodox rabbi accepted the invitation. *Allgemeine Zeitung des Judentums* 48, no. 20 (13 May 1884): 321.

59 Referring to the famous story in Tractate Shabbat 31a of the Babylonian Talmud, in which Hillel answers the gentile who demands "that you teach me the whole Torah while I stand on one foot": "What is hateful to you, do not to your fellow; that is the whole Torah, while the rest is the commentary thereof; go and learn it" (slightly modified from the Soncino translation, ed. I. Epstein). Cf. Collins, "Love Your Neighbor: How It Became the Golden Rule."

60 My English translation here of Leviticus 24:22 follows the German phrasing used in the Declaration. A more conventional translation of the same verse, drawing on the wording of the Revised Standard Version (RSV), New Revised Standard Version (NRSV), and NJPS translations, would be: "You shall have one law [*mishpat*] for the sojourner/alien/stranger [*ger*] and for the citizen/native [*ezraḥ*], for I am the Lord your God." ("NJPS" refers to: *JPS Hebrew-English Tanakh*, 2nd ed. [Philadelphia: Jewish Publication Society, 1999].)

61 The source is Tosefta Sanhedrin 13. See *Verhandlungen und Beschlüsse* (see note 62), 89–90, and the discussion in Novak, *Image of the Non-Jew*, 147–8.

> These teachings are the fundamental determinations for the position/stance of Judaism vis-à-vis those of other faiths. If however there are to be found, here and there, in Jewish writings spanning millenia, statements that do not correspond to these fundamental principles, then they are to be regarded as the opinions of individuals, or they were occasioned by the pressure of the times, and have no binding force.[62]

An important difference among the various moral defense initiatives of this period is the degree to which it was felt to be necessary to relate the principles ascribed to Judaism to Talmudic or other authoritative texts. This difference is visible when one compares the Fifteen Basic Principles (1885), and the terms in which they were discussed and appreciated, to the declaration of the 1884 Rabbiner-Versammlung. The statement of Basic Principles cites the commandment to "love your neighbor" and includes further language evocative of Scripture, but makes no further explicit mention of any scriptural or rabbinic sources. Although after the Principles were drafted, an additional committee convened to substantiate each of the principles with biblical and Talmudic proof texts in order to publish those separately, Lazarus, who had drafted the final version, was opposed to such a strategy.[63] He viewed it as a strength of the

---

62 *Verhandlungen und Beschlüsse der Rabbiner-Versammlung zu Berlin am 4. und 5. Juni 1884* (Berlin: Walther & Apolant, 1885), 17–18.

63 The resulting publication was Samuel Kristeller, *Belegstellen zu den Grundsätzen der jüdischen Sittenlehre* (Berlin, 1891). For the background to this, see Hertzberg, "Die 15 Grundsätze," and Schorsch, *Jewish Reactions*, 73–4, 233n58. As Schorsch points out, Lazarus expressed his opposition to this project in a letter to Kristeller dated 17 April 1888. Lazarus characterizes the relationship of ethical precepts and their supposed Jewish sources in terms that illustrate well the reasons for Cohen's bitter critique of Lazarus's *Ethik des Judentums*, discussed in chapter 4 above:

> The question "Where does it say this?" not as a matter of historical scholarship, but posed in the sense that through a quotation the truth, the justification, the validity of the proposition is to be produced, is to me positively horrifying. For our moral conviction, and thus also for the conviction of those whom we wish to instruct morally, it is certainly immaterial whether its content is already "said" someplace, whether it is found 3000 or 100 years ago, or at the present hour. In truth not all that today belongs to our moral conviction is already "written" – Our *Sätze* [i.e., the Fifteen Principles – D.H.] include teachings which were not yet thought, in this sense and in this version, in bygone times and not even 100 years ago, not even by a Kant or a Mendel[s]sohn.... To the question "Where did you get this from?" there is only one veritable answer: From our own spirit, which, raised through the literature and history of our ancestors and of all other peoples, created, on the basis of this education and its sources, this moral conviction by means of its own spiritual and moral deed.

Principles that they lacked references to proof texts. Such a stance was also apparent in Lazarus's 1880 address to the "December Committee" about the urgent need for a statement of Jewish ethics. That need, he explained, is not only a defensive need, but is just as urgent for Jews themselves, who are in danger of falling prey to "ignorance about our own ethical essence." To this, however, he adds:

> As concerns the otherwise so interesting book, the Talmud, it must be known that it is not a law book for us, and never has been; for it is a collection of the most varied kind. Knowledge of its content is extremely rare among German Jews, just as the greatest part, by far, of what it states has become for us a historical note. Many statements that are found in it were often made under oppressive conditions, during cruel wars and arduous persecutions. The Talmud is not a book of religion [*Religionsbuch*], and these statements are not a law. As regards *our* doctrine of morality, we need after all only point to that which we actually teach.[64]

(Lazarus goes on to mention some standard textbooks of the time that were used for instruction about Judaism and about Jewish moral doctrine.) Lazarus here in 1880 advocates raising awareness of Jewish morality by "point[ing] to that which we actually teach," as opposed to referring to sources such as the Talmud with which most Jews are unfamiliar, and adds that he does not regard the Talmud as a binding book of law or a religious book.

By contrast, the declaration issued only four years later at the 1884 Rabbiner-Versammlung not only had as its focus the interpretation of the

---

A reason Lazarus gives for this stance is that moral teachings are always developing and improving, so that referring to "older" proof texts or commandments limits the reach and potential of contemporary morality. See Ingrid Belke, ed., *Moritz Lazarus und Heymann Steinthal. Die Begründer der Völkerpsychologie in ihren Briefen* (Tübingen: Mohr Siebeck, 1971), 175–8.

64 Lazarus, *Unser Standpunkt*, 26–7. We find similar sentiments reported in the memoirs of Josef Samuel Bloch, who had led the defense activities against Rohling. Bloch tells of a Jewish leader of the time, Josef Ritter von Wertheim, "who still dragged the intellectual legacy of the age of Enlightenment and Haskalah with him," voicing his disapproval of Bloch's stance toward antisemitism by saying, "You defend the Talmud too much; we are not familiar with it, and we don't want it anymore." Bloch, *Erinnerungen*, 1:144. As Scott Spector has pointed out, the public "Talmud Disputes" such as the Rohling affair in Vienna corresponded to a "tug-of-war" even "within individual [Jewish] consciousnesses" "between associations oriental and homely, primitive and contemporary, alien and familiar," given that acculturated Jews were likely to know "more of the Talmud from Rohling's reports," through the coverage of the dispute in the daily press, "than from any personal knowledge, and the Talmud Dispute offered them an alien and primitive image of themselves." Spector, "Blood Lies," 225.

biblical precept of neighbor-love as signifying just treatment of all humanity, but also argued that that interpretation extends into the Talmudic corpus. Perhaps the intervening years, from 1880 to 1884 (which saw the increased attention to Rohling's anti-Talmudic book in connection with the Tiszaeszlár affair and the trial preparations in Vienna) had contributed to a sense of urgency beyond the task of defending Jews and Judaism from attack. The task now extended to elaborating an understanding of the Talmud that would support that sort of defense.[65] This is illustrated by Manuel Joel, the president of the Rabbiner-Versammlung, in his opening address, where he explains the objective of the declaration (*Erklärung*[66]) and the "interconfessional position of Judaism." Commenting that much had been achieved in defending Judaism against antisemitism thanks especially to Christian scholars whose defense tracts were based on knowledge of, and reverence for the Old Testament, Joel cautions that such defenses left unaddressed those antisemitic discourses that claimed to rely on post-biblical Jewish texts. Christian responses to antisemitism often entailed a valorization of biblical and especially prophetic texts, and a concomitant willingness to discredit post-biblical Judaism – of which Talmud was taken to be an expression – as representing a decline. Joel draws consequences from this as follows:

> One is happy to attribute all kinds of things to the Talmud. Now, on the one hand we have nothing to talk about in this regard, considering the program of our assembly – I mean that aspect which is an internal matter; according to the objectives of this assembly we need not demonstrate that the Talmud maintained the Mosaic foundation in rite and ceremony. That is not relevant here. What we do need to say is that the saying "you shall love the neighbor as yourself" runs through the Talmud just as it does the scriptures of the Old Testament.... In my view, we are required to declare/explain [*erklären*] that. Are we required to declare that? ...
>
> And furthermore, in answer to the question "Should we explain/declare?" – what is ordinarily said? "To whom do you wish to explain?" After all, he who is honest knows the score regarding the principles of Judaism, ... [and] he who

65 Ismar Schorsch traces parallel efforts to combat the negative reputation of Talmudic texts and rabbinic traditions in scholarship of the 1880s on the part of both Jews and non-Jews, including by means of editions and translations. Schorsch, "Missing in Translation: The Fate of the Talmud in the Struggle for Equality and Integration in Germany," in *Wissenschaft des Judentums Beyond Tradition: Jewish Scholarship on the Sacred Texts of Judaism, Christianity, and Islam*, ed. Dorothea M. Salzer, Chanan Gafni, and Hanan Harif (Berlin: de Gruyter, 2019), 171–5

66 Note the role of the verb *erklären* – which means both "to declare" and "to explain" – in the quote below.

> is not honest does not wish to know. But, colleagues and gentlemen ..., do you not know that the majority does not belong to either group? They are honest, but do not have the capacity to tell themselves how the matter actually stands. Is there not a large number of people to whom it is constantly recited that Judaism has this or that terrible principle, has this or that ruinous teaching? And you know, too, how this is done: one takes a sentence from the massive material of Jewish writings and says: See! that is the *corpus delicti*![67]

The difference that emerges between the downplaying of Talmudic and halakhic sources in the Fifteen Basic Principles (1885) and this argument by Joel at the 1884 Rabbiner-Versammlung reflects an important dilemma faced by those engaged in defense against anti-Jewish defamation based on claims about the Talmud or other halakhic/rabbinic texts:[68] In order to defend Judaism against attack one could follow the lead of Lazarus speaking in 1880 to the December Committee, by relativizing or denying the definitive or binding character of the Talmudic corpus, or of traditional halakhic texts more broadly, for contemporary Jewish life. Even when the attack involved denunciations of "Talmud," Lazarus's suggestion could seem viable, since halakhah had waned in importance for the growing number of non-Orthodox Jews. Since discrediting antisemites generally rested in part on falsifying their claims about Judaism, one could bypass Talmudic passages that appeared to mandate discrimination or mistreatment of non-Jews as irrelevant to current Jewish practice, on the grounds that the Talmud was *in general* irrelevant to contemporary Judaism. For a court seeking to evaluate whether particular anti-Talmudic claims defamed Judaism, this could provide a convenient way to bracket the question of whether the claims about the Talmud were true.[69]

---

67 *Verhandlungen und Beschlüsse der Rabbiner-Versammlung*, 8–9.

68 This dilemma has been well identified by George Y. Kohler in a study that examines the 1888 affidavit by Cohen to which we are about to turn, along with Manuel Joel's own affidavit in an earlier "Talmud" trial in 1877 (published in *Meine in Veranlassung eines Processes abgegebenen Gutachten über den Talmud* [Breslau: Schletter'sche Buchhandlung, 1877]), and Joel's attempt to set the record straight about the Talmud's stance toward non-Jews in *Gegen Gildemeister*, published in 1884, the year of the Rabbiner-Versammlung, over which Joel also presided. Kohler points out that Joel's 1877 affidavit was submitted for the earliest court case concerning Rohling's *Talmudjude*. The case took place in Silesia, where Joel was at the time the liberal rabbi of the Breslau Jewish Community. Kohler, "Manuel Joel," 142. Thus, Joel's remarks, quoted above, in his 1884 presidential address to the Rabbiner-Versammlung certainly drew on personal experience with legal defense against anti-Talmudism.

69 This is illustrated by Kohler in his description of an 1884 court case in Bonn, concerning publication of a rhymed version of Briman's *Judenspiegel*. Kohler, "Manuel Joel," 144–5.

On the other hand, the view reflected by the 1884 Declaration, as we saw in Joel's address to the assembly, is that it was desirable to defend Judaism against defamatory claims by showing that the Talmudic tradition mandates ethical treatment of non-Jews, rather than excluding references to the Talmud, as Lazarus recommended. This other approach would thus directly confront Rohling's argument that "Talmudic law was still the binding authority for Jews and legally even took precedence over Scripture."[70] George Y. Kohler has identified an antisemitism trial that took place in Silesia in 1877, in which Manuel Joel, as an expert witness, was perceived by Orthodox critics as denying the ongoing significance of halakhah for Jewish life, as part of a strategy for confronting antisemitism. Like the Marburg Antisemitism Trial of 1888, this trial concerned anti-Talmudic allegations – quoted by the defendant directly from Rohling's *Talmudjude* – to the effect that Jews were permitted to commit crimes against non-Jews.[71] Joel's affidavit – which was requested from him as a response to an earlier affidavit that had been submitted by Rohling himself – presented the Talmud as merely the historic basis of a subsequently changeable Jewish law.[72] He was attacked in a long, three-part editorial in the leading Orthodox weekly *Der Israelit*: "How a Rabbi Defends the Talmud and Vilifies the Talmudists."[73] As Kohler points out, "the main point of contention between" Orthodoxy/traditional Judaism of the time and liberal/Reform movements "on the theological level was the Oral Law and its interpretation, that is, the Talmud." Thus, unbeknownst to the German court, the very choice of a liberal rabbi such as Joel to serve as an expert witness played into the intra-Jewish dispute about the status of halakhah and the Talmud.[74] (Kohler finds in Cohen's 1888 affidavit – to which I will turn below – a similar kind of argument, and points out that Cohen got measured approval from Orthodox circles.[75]) This dilemma between a Jewish defense strategy that affirmed the divine

70 Kohler, "Manuel Joel," 148, drawing on Rohling, *Talmudjude*, 6th ed. (Münster: Russell, 1877), 35–9.

71 Joel, *Gutachten über den Talmud*, 1. Kohler, "Manuel Joel," 148–51.

72 As Kohler points out, Joel's characterization of the Talmud as "containing the doctrines and opinions that cover a span of 1000 years, beginning with Ezra in 500 B.C.E. and including 1000 names of Sages that express their views" – that is, as a collection of "opinions and views of mere mortals" that could evolve over time into a variety of halakhic positions – went against the traditional understanding of "the Talmud as being first and foremost the word of God." Joel, *Gutachten über den Talmud*, 3; Kohler, "Manuel Joel," 149–50.

73 "Wie ein Rabbiner den Talmud vertheidigt und die Talmudisten schmäht," *Der Israelit* 43 (1877), no. 36: 867–71; no. 37: 889–91; nos. 38/39: 919–21, discussed by Kohler, "Manuel Joel," 149.

74 Kohler, "Manuel Joel," 149.

75 Kohler, "Manuel Joel," 153.

and binding nature of the Talmud and one that severed the link between Talmud and conceptions of "Jewish morality" illuminates the obstacles faced in general by those who sought to form broad-based representative Jewish organizations in the Kaiserreich, and will help us situate Cohen's first public response to anti-Talmudic antisemitism, in Marburg in 1888.

The Marburg Antisemitism Trial and the Law against "Blasphemy" (*Gotteslästerungsparagraph*)

The polemical terrain I have sketched, on which Jewish moral defense discourses developed, was a decisive context for the 1888 Marburg trial that led Cohen to publish his first essay on neighbor-love, "Die Nächstenliebe im Talmud" ("Love of Neighbor in the Talmud").[76] The trial concerned an event that took place in December 1886 – three years after Rohling's statements in response to news of the Tiszaeszlár affair had led to legal proceedings in Vienna, and one year after those proceedings had concluded. The Marburg court case was thus being built exactly during the volatile period in which the anti-Talmudism of Rohling, Briman, and others, as well as the rhetoric of those who defended against it, were very widely discussed. Thus, it is not surprising that the Marburg trial itself – which was also highly publicized – also typified, and even directly drew on the polemics surrounding Rohling and his detractors.[77] Further, Cohen's testimony at the trial incorporated a similar – and in some points identical – line of defense to those represented by the Fifteen Basic Principles and, to an even greater extent, by the "interconfessional" Declaration of the 1884 Rabbiner-Versammlung.

The Marburg Antisemitism Trial was also typical of the polemics surrounding anti-Talmudism in a further respect. Like the other court cases mentioned above, it concerned an alleged act of defamation regarding

76 In his same-day report from the trial in *Die Jüdische Presse*, Hirsch Hildesheimer indicates that the pamphlet publication (Hermann Cohen, *Die Nächstenliebe im Talmud. Ein Gutachten dem Königlichen Landgerichte zu Marburg erstattet* [Marburg: N. G. Elwert'sche Verlagsbuchhandlung, 1888]) was already in preparation at the time of the trial. Hirsch Hildesheimer [H.H.], "Eine Anklage wegen Beschimpfung der jüdischen Religion," *Die Jüdische Presse* (26 April 1888).

77 For instance, the prosecutor's speech (as recorded in Hildesheimer, "Eine Anklage") invoked the Vienna case explicitly and mentioned the "extensive book" of materials produced by Bloch's attorney, Josef Kopp, to defend Judaism against Rohling's defamations (Josef Kopp, *Zur Judenfrage nach den Akten des Prozesses Rohling-Bloch*, 3rd. ed. [Leipzig: Julius Klinkhardt, 1886]). Referring to these materials helped the prosecutor make the argument that ever since anti-Talmudic allegations had appeared as part of anti-Jewish agitation, no amount of searching had ever turned up "that passage in the Talmud according to which extortion and cheating of non-Jews is permitted."

Jewish norms of conduct toward non-Jews. The accused was a schoolteacher, Ferdinand Fenner, who was reported to have claimed publicly (specifically at an antisemitic rally) that the Talmud specified that Mosaic Law was binding only for interactions among Jews and thus condoned crimes against non-Jews.[78] A stenographer employed by the local Jewish community documented what was said at the rally, after which Leo Munk, the chief rabbi in Marburg, brought it to the attention of authorities, who subsequently initiated proceedings.[79]

This sequence of events thus followed a pattern that was already becoming standard for Jews responding to antisemitic incidents. As already mentioned, by the 1880s, Jews were regularly turning to the judiciary as a means of confronting antisemitic agitation.[80] One legal avenue

78 Details of the case are summarized in the editorial note to the posthumous edition of Cohen's "Die Nächstenliebe im Talmud," JS1: 338–9, and are laid out in detail by Ulrich Sieg in "'Der Wissenschaft und dem Leben tut dasselbe not: Ehrfurcht vor der Wahrheit.' Hermann Cohens Gutachten im Marburger Antisemitismusprozeß 1888," in *Philosophisches Denken – Politisches Wirken. Hermann-Cohen-Kolloquium Marburg 1992*, ed. Reinhard Brandt and Franz Orlik (Hildesheim: Olms, 1993). Sieg also discusses the case in *Aufstieg und Niedergang des Marburger Neukantianismus: die Geschichte einer philosophischen Schulgemeinschaft* (Würzburg: Königshausen & Neumann, 1994), 155–7, and in "Der Talmud vor Gericht. Die ideengeschichtliche Bedeutung des Marburger Antisemitismusprozesses," in *Religiöse Minderheiten. Potentiale für Konflikt und Frieden*, ed. Hans-Martin Barth and Christoph Elsas (Hamburg: EB-Verlag, 2004). Further important sources for the trial are Hildesheimer, "Eine Anklage," as well as the reports published in the *Allgemeine Zeitung des Judentums* on 3 and 10 May 1888 (both with the dateline Marburg, 25 April 1888, the date of the trial.).

For the general context of antisemitic political agitation in Marburg and the surrounding region, see Sieg, *Aufstieg und Niedergang*, 154–5, and Thomas Klein, *Der preußisch-deutsche Konservatismus und die Entstehung des politischen Antisemitismus in Hessen-Kassel (1866–1893)* (Marburg: Elwert, 1995).

79 Munk brought the matter, and the transcript of Fenner's speech, to the Marburg school authorities, together with the complaint that children in the Jewish school were being harassed by students from Fenner's school using rhetoric similar to Fenner's, while a Jewish community leader brought it to the attention of the public prosecutor (Staatsanwalt), who initiated proceedings. Sieg, "Die Wissenschaft," 229–30; and *Der Prozeß Fenner nach den Akten dargestellt und beleuchtet* (Marburg: Verlag des "Reichs-Herold," 1888), 17–18, which contains the text of Munk's complaint to the school authorities. (Sieg has verified that despite the fact that *Prozeß Fenner* is itself an antisemitic tract produced in the wake of the trial and that it editorializes throughout, the wording of Munk's complaint is reproduced accurately.)

80 The procedure would become even more routinized in the following years, and especially after 1893, the year that the Centralverein deutscher Staatsbürger jüdischen Glaubens (CV) was founded as a Jewish organization one of whose central tasks was anti-defamation. The CV established a legal defense department whose job was to solicit and receive reports about antisemitic incidents in order to examine them for the purpose of seeking legal remedies where appropriate. See Schorsch, *Jewish Reactions*, 123ff.

was prosecution under Section 166 of the Criminal Code, the law known as the *Gotteslästerungsparagraph* (Law Against Blasphemy), or alternatively as the law against "insults of a religion" (against *Religionsbeschimpfungen*), which was the crime for which Fenner was tried at Marburg.

My interest here is to understand the trial as a prime site in which Cohen developed his analyses of love-of-neighbor in Judaism, and in how Cohen's expert witness testimony functioned discursively at the trial. In seeking to understand the trial and Cohen's precise position by virtue of being called as an expert witness at this trial, I will find it helpful to use the idea of a "dispositive" – in the Foucauldian sense of the term *dispositif*, in alternation with such formulations as "discursive framework."[81] To think of the framework of the trial – including the power relations that produce and are produced by such a trial – as well as the range of possible meanings of this trial as a result of one or more "dispositives" allows for a consideration of the possible scope Cohen had in responding and acting at the trial, and to read his response in view of his function at the trial, as a strategic response within a specifically constituted discursive space. To that end, let us briefly consider the nature and background of

81 I deliberately avoid the English term "apparatus," which has often been misleadingly used to translate Foucault's notion of *dispositif*. The latter notion draws on the ordinary meaning of the French word, which refers to the manner in which the parts of an apparatus or mechanism are arranged or ordered. This idea may be applied to socio-political-cultural or media phenomena or constellations so as to interpret them as a function of a plan or a strategy or a purpose according to which the elements are "disposed" (i.e., arranged, ordered). However, unlike our ordinary use of such terms as "plan" or "strategy," the notion of *dispositif* does not rely on the idea that states of affairs can be traced to particular intentions of individual or collective subjects, nor on causal or teleological accounts of states of affairs or developments that might have led to them. Rather, the *dispositif* allows for an analysis of the "interplay" of power relations and processes as in a kind of network, as well as of the "effects," "intentional and unintentional," that are thereby "produced" and can be "re-utilised" in their turn. See the classic text in which Foucault elaborates the meaning of *dispositif*: the July 1977 interview published that same year under the title "Le jeu de Michel Foucault," reprinted in *Dits et écrits*, vol. 3: *1976–1979*, ed. D. Defert and F. Ewald (Paris: Gallimard, 1994); translated by Colin Gordon as "The Confession of the Flesh," in *Power/Knowledge: Selected Interviews and Other Writings, 1972–1977*, ed. Colin Gordon (New York: Pantheon, 1980), 195–6. Foucault uses the notion extensively in *La Volonté de savoir* (Paris: Gallimard, 1976), translated by Robert Hurley as *The History of Sexuality Volume I: An Introduction* (New York: Pantheon, 1978). See the explanation given by Joannah Caborn in "On the Methodology of Dispositive Analysis," *Critical Approaches to Discourse Analysis Across Disciplines* 1 (2007): 112–23. I have also been helped in my understanding of this notion by consulting Franziska Koch, *Die "chinesische Avantgarde" und das Dispositiv der Ausstellung: Konstruktionen chinesischer Gegenwartskunst im Spannungsfeld der Globalisierung* (Bielefeld: Transcript, 2016), chap. 1.

Section 166, the statute that spells out the offense of which Fenner was accused, which read as follows:

> Whoever publicly, by insulting expressions, blasphemes God, causes scandal [*Ärgernis*], or whoever publicly insults one of the Christian churches or another existing religious association enjoying incorporation rights within the territory of the Reich, or its institutions and customs, and likewise, whoever, in a church or in another place designated for religious gatherings acts in a profane manner, shall be punished by imprisonment not to exceed three years.[82]

Criminal laws against blasphemy were of course historically widespread in European legal codes. (Some remain in place in some form to this day.) But the way they became "modernized" or secularized varied. As I have discussed in greater detail elsewhere,[83] the 1871 version of Section 166 (which was modeled on a similar law in the 1851 Prussian Criminal Code[84]) is an early case of a blasphemy law that was "pluralized" so as to include, in addition to any Christian church, "any other religious association enjoying incorporation rights." The German case thus stands in contrast to legal systems in which the offense was abolished or became obsolete, or in which it remained restricted to the one state religion (as was the case all the way to 2008 in the United Kingdom, for the Church of England[85]). Whereas historically, the crime of blasphemy presupposes a single divine authority, and a worldly authority as its extension, Section 166 specifies that it is not only "the Christian churches" but

---

82 Section 166 of the German Criminal Code of 1871, cited according to *Strafgesetzbuch mit 777 Nebengesetzen* (Munich: Biederstein, 1949), 51. My English translation partly follows the one given in *The Statutary Criminal Law of Germany: A Translation of the German Criminal Code of 1871 with Amendments* (Washington, DC: War Department, 1946), 109–10. The wording of this statute was kept in the Criminal Code of the Federal Republic, and was unaltered up until 1969.

83 In Hollander, "Ethical-Political Universality"; and two unpublished papers: "Debating the Criminalization of Blasphemy and the 'Protection' of Minority Religions: Section 166 of the German Criminal Code" (presented at the American Academy of Religion, Montreal, November 2009), and "Neighbor-Love as an Object of Protection? Hermann Cohen and Secularized Blasphemy Law" (presented at the Ludwig-Maximilians-University of Munich in May 2017).

84 See Martin J. Worms, *Die Bekenntnisbeschimpfung im Sinne des §166 Abs. 1 StGB und die Lehre vom Rechtsgut* (Frankfurt am Main: Peter Lang, 1984), 93.

85 Regarding the repeal of the blasphemy law in the U.K., and its effective replacement by a law against incitement of religious hatred, see Jeremy Patrick, *The Curious Persistence of Blasphemy: Canada and Beyond* (PhD diss., Osgoode Hall Law School, 2013), 42–4; and Yvonne Sherwood, *Biblical Blaspheming: Trials of the Sacred for a Secular Age* (Cambridge: Cambridge University Press, 2012), 43–9.

also "other religious associations" that merit protection against certain kinds of attack or profanation. That is, a law whose original purpose was to help secure allegiance to a single authority, to the one God, and, by extension, to the state church, became employable as an instrument in the service of religious pluralism, the protection of multiple religious entities – at least insofar as such entities had otherwise already been granted institutional recognition ("incorporation rights") by the state. Furthermore, Section 166 was, practically from its inception, understood and employed as a means for protecting the "feelings" of religious groups and for promoting inter-religious harmony.[86] This understanding doubtless came about principally because of the need to ease tensions between Protestants and Catholics in what was effectively a bi-confessional state.

At least as of 1882, Section 166 was also understood to apply to Judaism as a recognized religion. It thus became available as a tool for protecting Judaism from "insult"/"offense."[87] However, based on the wording in the opening to Manuel Joel's affidavit for the above-mentioned antisemitism trial, it is evident that Section 166 was being applied to Judaism, at least on that one occasion, as early as 1877.[88]

Recalling the strategic choice described above, as to whether a defense against anti-Talmudic allegations ought to explicitly confront the content

86 For example, the published "motives" for Section 166 state that "any act of blasphemy comprises an injury of the religious feeling of others" and that this feeling has a rightful claim to legal protection in order to preclude "the opinion ... that the state has no concern for the preservation of this religious feeling among the people," and that the state must not be perceived as regarding such feeling with "indifference." *Motive zu dem Entwurfe eines Strafgesetzbuches für den Norddeutschen Bund* (Berlin: Verlag der Königlichen Geheimen Ober-Hofbuchdruckerei, 1869), 96, which is also cited in the 1882 Reichsgericht decision referenced in *Entscheidungen,* 79 (see note 87 following).

87 Ismar Schorsch notes that "as early as 1882 the Imperial Court [Reichsgericht] had recognized Judaism in Prussia as an incorporated religious community and therefore protected by Section 166." Schorsch, *Jewish Reactions,* 129. For the decision in question, see *Entscheidungen des Reichsgerichts in Strafsachen* 6 (Berlin: de Gruyter, 1882), 77–81, esp. 81. In justifying its decision, the court relied on principles articulated in the Prussian Criminal Code of 1851 and in the Prussian "Allgemeines Landrecht," as well as on the 23 July 1847 Prussian law regulating the status of the Jews ("Gesetz über die Verhältnisse der Juden").

88 In introducing the published version of the affidavit, Joel describes the case in the terms of the crime defined by Section 166: "Ein Redacteur ... war angeklagt worden, in einem Artikel *die Juden in ihrer Eigenschaft einer mit Corporationsrechten innerhalb des Bundesgebiets bestehenden Religionsgemeinschaft beschimpft zu haben*" (Joel, *Gutachten über den Talmud,* 1, emphasis added). In other words, the charges brought before the court are, stated exactly in the language of Section 166, the "insult" of Judaism considered as a "religious association with incorporation rights."

of anti-Talmudic claims, the framework of a Section 166 prosecution would have certainly favored doing so. According to Section 166, in order for an "insult/defamation of a religion" to have taken place, it had to be shown that the object of the attack was an essential component of that religion. Thus, the only possible strategy for using the statute to prosecute someone who had denounced the Talmud would have been to portray the Talmud as an essential part of Judaism, and in particular as essential to Jewish law.[89]

The incriminating statement by Ferdinand Fenner was typical of antisemitic claims of the time to the effect that Jewish law condones crimes against non-Jews. The decisive passage was the following:

> Most of you acknowledge that the Jews hold the Talmud to be their law[90] and that it says in the Talmud: "the law of Moses is valid only from one Jew to another; for [treatment of] the *Goyim* it is not applicable! Him [sic] they may rob, cheat, etc. ... A good Jew does what the Talmud tells him; in that case he is in our eyes a scoundrel. If he does not do so then he is in the eyes of the Jews a scoundrel. Either way, he is a scoundrel.[91]

Again, typically for antisemitism trials of the period, the court appointed expert witnesses, whose scholarly knowledge about Judaism and Talmud presumably qualified them to advise the court as to (1) whether an attack on the Talmud amounted to an attack on Judaism, and (2) whether the defendant's claims about Talmud were true – the two criteria that had to be met for the incident to be a Section 166 offense. In the court's wording, the expert witnesses were asked to testify:

> 1) Whether the prescriptions contained in the Talmud, pertaining to religion/faith [*Glaube*] and to morals, are to be regarded as binding

89 Hirsch Hildesheimer in his report on the Marburg Antisemitism Trial ("Eine Anklage") accorded great significance to this trial based on the fact that, because this prosecution concerned insulting attacks against the Talmud, a German court was for the first time considering and deciding whether an insult of the Talmud was (punishable as) an insult of the Jewish religion. However, presumably the 1877 trial discussed above, for which Joel wrote his *Gutachten*, was an earlier such occasion. Whether there were other earlier cases is not possible to determine with certainty.

90 Or: "that the Talmud is the book of laws [*Gesetzbuch*] of the Jews," according to the version recorded in Hildesheimer, "Eine Anklage."

91 From an archival document that, according to Sieg, is likely the transcript of Fenner's speech. Sieg, "Die Wissenschaft," 247n90, 249. (There is no closing quotation mark in this transcript.) The same passage appears in Hildesheimer, "Eine Anklage," as the basis for bringing Section 166 charges, as well as in the report from the trial in *Allgemeine Zeitung des Judentums*.

> commandments for believing/practicing [*gläubige*] Jews and whether an insult of the Talmud is to be regarded as an insult of the Jewish religious community [*Religionsgemeinschaft*], or of an institution of the same.
>
> 2) Whether the Talmud states: "Mosaic law is valid only between one Jew and another; it does not apply to *Goyims* [sic], who Jews may steal from and cheat." (NT 145)

The prosecution's nomination of Hermann Cohen was accepted, as was the defense's nomination of the antisemitic professor of oriental languages from Göttingen, Paul de Lagarde.[92]

A Turning of the Tables: Jewish Exclusivism on Trial

Considering that the "pluralization" of the original offense of blasphemy or "insult of a religion" in Section 166 had as its purpose to protect Judaism from attack and thus to promote the peaceable life of Jews among Christians, it is striking that in 1888 a Section 166 trial created a situation in which Cohen, as the expert witness who was supposed to testify in support of the "Jewish" side that an offense against Judaism had indeed taken place, was called to account for whether Judaism, and in particular Jewish law, was in its turn sufficiently hospitable to the non-Jew. Thus, as I have argued elsewhere, the trial was the site of a turning of the tables.[93] While its formal legal purpose was to protect Judaism from attack, its effect was to put Judaism on trial, as it were, for its purported hostility to Christians.[94]

In order to grasp the force of Cohen's specific response to this situation, it is helpful to see this situation as an instance of what the political theorist Wendy Brown has pinpointed as the paradigm of tolerance discourse. Building on the observation that tolerance as a public or political discourse always marks its object as "deviant, marginal, or undesirable by virtue of being tolerated," Brown argues that tolerance discourse should be seen "as a strand of depoliticization in liberal democracies." One of

92 For a brief introduction, see Pulzer, *Rise of Political Anti-Semitism*, 78–9. For a full biography, see Ulrich Sieg, *Deutschlands Prophet. Paul de Lagarde und die Ursprünge des modernen Antisemitismus* (Munich: Hanser, 2007); translated by Ann Marianiello as *Germany's Prophet: Paul de Lagarde and the Origins of Modern Antisemitism* (Waltham, MA: Brandeis University Press, 2013). Lagarde's involvement in the 1888 Marburg trial and its aftermath is treated at 256–72/202–14.

93 I first developed elements of this reading in "Ethical-Political Universality," 234ff.

94 A similar point is made by Gesine Palmer in "Judaism as a 'Method' with Hermann Cohen and Franz Rosenzweig," in "Hermann Cohen's Ethics," ed. Robert Gibbs, special issue, *Journal of Jewish Thought and Philosophy* 13, nos. 1–3 (2004): 51.

the mechanisms of tolerance discourse that Brown identifies is its tendency to "naturalize or culturalize" the sources of group conflict. Thus, essentialized group identities are envisioned as being, by virtue of essential differences from each other, inherently in conflict. Such conflicts are then what call for the practice of tolerance in order to harmonize over the differences.[95] Thus, the notion of tolerance is predicated upon, and must in that sense presuppose and produce as naturally preexisting, the conflicts that it is supposedly designed to address – above all that between cultural particularity and universality. In other words, the notion of tolerance posits a universality with respect to which the object of tolerance functions as a particular. To "tolerate" the particular thus amounts to a claim about the extent to which that particular conforms to the universal. Drawing on Brown's understanding of the mechanisms of tolerance discourse allows us to see that when the Marburg court called for a statement as to whether the defendant's recorded claim – that the Talmud sanctions wrongdoing toward non-Jews – was true, a juridical-discursive framework was produced in which, depending on the answer to that question, the particular ethical code could either be reconciled with, that is, "tolerated" by the universal order, or be found lacking.

If the task that was thus effectively assigned to Cohen in the Marburg courtroom was to demonstrate that the "particular" Jewish ethical code measured up to the standard of "universality," the most straightforward means of achieving that objective would have been to do as texts such as the "interconfessional" Declaration and the Fifteen Principles had done: to show that the Talmud and Judaism mandate ethical treatment of non-Jews. There are indeed parallels between Cohen's testimony and those earlier statements, in that he argues that Judaism is universalist in its very essence and in its definitive expressions – that is, that "love your neighbor" is a precept that applies not only to members of one's own "tribe or faith" (*Stammes- oder Glaubensgenossen*) but to all human beings.[96] Responding to the massive corpus of anti-Jewish commonplaces, drawn

95 Wendy Brown, *Regulating Aversion: Tolerance in the Age of Identity and Empire* (Princeton: Princeton University Press, 2006), 14–15.

96 For the "interconfessional" Declaration, see pp. 220–1 above, as well as the "rationale" (*Begründung*) at *Verhandlungen und Beschlüsse*, 86–92. A slightly different draft version of the Declaration, with a draft rationale, had been widely circulated in advance of the assembly; it was published in the newspaper *Allgemeine Zeitung des Judentums* 48 no. 20 (13 May 1884): 321–2.

The second of the Fifteen Basic Principles (see note 57) is: "Judaism commands: 'Love your neighbor as yourself' and declares this commandment of love encompassing all human beings to be the main principle of the Jewish religion."

from the popular antisemitic and anti-Talmudic literature, that was mobilized at the trial (especially by way of Lagarde's affidavit[97]), Cohen's testimony and affidavit contains many detailed defenses of what traditional texts say about treatment of non-Jews, including point-by-point refutations of Lagarde's affidavit.

But if we look at the precise structure and argumentation of Cohen's affidavit, we can see him also destabilizing the framework that has been set up for him in this implicit trial of Judaism's code of conduct toward non-Jews. This is evident above all in the substantial introduction that precedes his direct answers to the court's questions, where we find him making two arguments in combination with each other: one about the method of philosophy, and another against Christian-supersessionist ideas about morality. Here is a key passage from that introduction:

> The hierarchy of religions is ... supposed to correspond to their position in relation to the moral ideas – not to the foundation [*Begründung*] of those moral ideas but to their plain content. This is how it came to pass that universal human morality was denied not only to the Talmud – which was known to interpret in painstaking detail every tittle of the Holy Scripture[98] – but also to its very source, the ancient covenant, the basic form of monotheistic morality: *love-of-neighbor.* (NT 148)

Cohen here effectively reads the courtroom situation as one in which he is being called upon to certify the established "hierarchy of religions," which is commonly held to "correspond to" their relative moral value – meaning, in the context of the trial, the relative moral value of Judaism

97 Lagarde's affidavit (see note 102) was submitted in advance of the trial; both Cohen and Munk referred to it in composing their own statements (cf. Hildesheimer, "Eine Anklage.") Lagarde's affidavit drew heavily on statements by Rohling in *Talmudjude* as well as on their refutations by Delitzsch in *Rohling's Talmudjude beleuchtet*; thus, in engaging with it, Cohen was dealing with the standard claims of anti-Talmudic discourse of the time. We can also see Cohen's affidavit using evidence in support of his claims that had been used elsewhere in Jewish moral defense statements. For example, he incorporates a long quote from the early thirteenth-century *Sefer Ḥasidim* by Judah ben Samuel of Regensburg that had been excerpted as representative of Jewish moral teachings in an 1845 compilation by Leopold Zunz (see NT 167–8). Part of the same quote had been used in the official "rationale" (*Begründung*) for the rabbis' "interconfessional" Declaration. See *Verhandlungen und Beschlüsse der Rabbiner-Versammlung*, 88; and Leopold Zunz, *Gesammelte Schriften*, vol. 1 (Berlin: Louis Gerschel, 1875), 65–7.

98 This refers to the tradition in Tractate bMenachot 29b that "there will arise a man, at the end of many generations, Akiba b. Joseph by name, who will expound upon each tittle heaps and heaps of laws" (שעתיד לדרוש על כל קוץ וקוץ תילין תילין של הלכות).

and Christianity. Having stated from the outset that he is answering the court's questions as a philosopher,[99] Cohen here recasts the demand to pronounce upon the relative moral value of the religions in terms of the question of what *philosophy* is, in particular in its relationship to religious history and to theology (a question that is familiar to us from his discussion in the *Ethik* of the possible contribution of biblical religion to ethical philosophy).

Cohen concedes that religious ideas are at the origin of moral ideas, but argues that the philosopher's task is to give those ideas their proper *Begründung* (foundation, grounding) and "correct" them accordingly, freed from the constraints of the positive religions and theologies (NT 147–8). Thus, while philosophy is in a sense "dependent" on theology, its task is to work out an ethics that is methodologically autonomous.[100]

But philosophy's dependence on theology, from which it must free itself, also means that it inherits and risks perpetuating theological prejudices about religious-moral systems. Continuing our reading of the above-quoted passage, these include the Christian prejudice that Jewish morality cannot a priori be assumed to measure up to "universal human morality." Cohen explicitly names the historic "denial" of such universal human morality to "the Talmud" and to the Old Testament:

> that universal human morality was denied not only to the Talmud – which was known to interpret in painstaking detail every tittle of the Holy Scripture – but also to its very source, the ancient covenant, the basic form of monotheistic morality: *love-of-neighbor.*

But Cohen's observation also pertains to the very trial at which he is testifying. If Judaism is "on trial" for whether its morality is "universal" – that

99 I am thus not an expert in the sense that it would be desirable to demand, and that would be highly desirable for the sake of the breadth and certainty of pure scientific/scholarly [*wissenschaftlich*] knowledge. I read the Talmud not as a Semitic philologian and researcher of antiquity. I am also not sufficiently familiar with the religious-philosophical literature of Jewish dogmatics to be able to make judgments as a theologian....

I nevertheless believed I ought to arm myself, with careful work, toward word and oath, and I think that in doing so I am also serving my office. For to render honor to truth, especially also to do so for the historical truths in the area of the moral ideas, has at all times been the affair of philosophy. And it is philosophy that must establish criteria for the certainty of human beliefs, and to defend them against the affects of hate as of love, as a matter of reason. (NT 145–6)

100 Cohen makes a similar point in "Zum Prioritätsstreit" (Pr 175–6).

is, for whether its moral code extends to the treatment of non-Jews – the trial, Cohen is implicitly arguing, is itself a function of supersessionist prejudice. We therefore find Cohen taking this trial as an occasion to expose that prejudice.[101]

Folded into Cohen's diagnosis of this situation and exposure of the supersessionist prejudice about relative moralities is also his delineation of a strategy for overcoming it. Philosophy, in pursuing its method of Begründung – seeking foundations for, or accounting philosophically for moral ideas – can and should avoid getting stuck in the theological habit of hierarchizing systems of morality according to the "content" of what they prescribe. The pitfall Cohen has identified here is twofold:

(a) falling prey to the supersessionism of Christian theology, according to which Judaism *of necessity* will be morally deficient with respect to the dominant norms, by virtue of the "content" of its "moral ideas," so that "the hierarchy of religions" can be maintained in a "corresponding" hierarchy of how those moral ideas are classified; and
(b) a failure of philosophical method, consisting of inventorizing the "content" of "moral ideas" rather than seeking their foundations, for example, in working out principles of morality. For:

> the difference among moral systems by no means resides primarily in the content of precepts, but principally in their *foundation* [*Begründung*] and derivation from a general basic idea, the so-called moral principle.

Accordingly, moral philosophy has the "task" "everywhere to discover the governing principle – and with it to illuminate historical research" (NT 147).

As we see in the passage quoted above, Cohen situates the prevalent misunderstanding of neighbor-love in just this hegemonic Christian morality.

The "Neighbor" and the "Stranger" (Cohen contra Lagarde and Delitzsch)

Before continuing to look at how Cohen confronts the dual mistake he identifies, let us pause to ask *why* Cohen mentions "love-of-neighbor" at this

101 A reading of the 1888 affidavit that is very compatible with my own in this regard has been undertaken by Liliana Ruth Feierstein, who classes it among the foremost works of Jewish thought to tackle the question of the "other." *Von Schwelle zu Schwelle: Einblicke in den didaktisch-historischen Umgang mit dem Anderen aus der Perspektive jüdischen Denkens* (Bremen: Edition Lumière, 2010), 109–11.

early point in the affidavit. Why, indeed, does the "neighbor" turn out to be a topic or focal point in the affidavit at all, such that the title Cohen chooses for its published version becomes "Love-of-Neighbor in the Talmud"? After all, the court was requesting a learned opinion about the stance of Judaism toward *non-Jews.* We may find the beginning of an answer in the fact that in the course of the affidavit – as, indeed, in all his texts that treat neighbor-love – we learn that Cohen in fact sees the ethical value of Judaism as centering in its treatment of the "*stranger.*" The precept "Love your neighbor as yourself" is relevant to Cohen's arguments about this central teaching because of its consistency with the teachings about love-of-the-stranger. Neighbor-love is thus of secondary importance in establishing what those teachings mean: At best, as we learned from the *Ethik,* Leviticus 19:18 is a neutral formulation about how one ought to treat "all" others; at worst, the pervasive misconstrual of *re'a* as fellow Israelite or "nearest" would have to make Leviticus 19:18 a most unfortunate place to begin a disquisition on what Judaism teaches about how to treat non-Jews. In view of this, one could imagine Cohen instead structuring his entire discussion around the question of the "stranger" and associated concepts, in order to directly answer the court's second question, about what the Talmud in fact teaches about the treatment of non-Jews. Why, then, is the resulting essay not "Die Fremdenliebe im Talmud," that is, "Love-of-the-Stranger in the Talmud"?

This may be explained if we understand Cohen's affidavit, in its entirety, as a response to Lagarde. In other words, we must read the general contours of Cohen's argumentation – and not only the passages where Cohen mentions Lagarde explicitly – as motivated by the requirement to refute Lagarde and thus the widespread defamatory image of Judaism that Lagarde's testimony exemplifies. In particular, in answering the court's second question – whether the Talmud permits crimes toward non-Jews – Lagarde had quoted a claim from Rohling's *Talmudjude* in order to "corroborate" the rhetoric of the defendant:[102]

> It is permitted to an Israelite, says the Talmud, to wrong a goy, for it says: You shall not wrong your neighbor (Lev. 19:13).[103]

---

102 The Rohling-Delitzsch exchange is centrally relied upon by Lagarde: He reasons that since the accused presumably has no firsthand familiarity with the Talmud, he must have drawn his denunciation of Jews from "the current literature of antisemitism, especially the book of Professor Rohling." Lagarde therefore devotes his affidavit to passages in Rohling "which the accused can cite in his favor" and "at the same time take[s] account of what [Delitzsch] presented in his opposing treatise *Rohlings Talmudjude.*" Paul de Lagarde, "Ein Gutachten," in *Mittheilungen,* vol. 3 (Göttingen: Dieterichsche Universitätsbuchhandlung, 1889), 11.

103 Lagarde, "Ein Gutachten," 12. Cf. Rohling, *Talmudjude* (1st ed., 1871), 24.

Giving the appearance of "balance" to his answer, Lagarde then turns to what was probably the most prominent defense of Judaism against Rohling's attacks, that published by Franz Delitzsch, a theologian whose scholarly refutations of anti-Talmudism were highly respected among Jews.[104] Yet in his refutation of the claim by Rohling – quoted by Lagarde – Delitzsch nevertheless interprets the love commandment in Leviticus 19:18 to apply to the fellow Israelite, the *Volksgenosse.* According to Delitzsch, "it is only Christianity that has taught that the human being as such is the 'neighbor' of the human being, without regard to peoplehood [*Volkstum*]," such that

> Old Testament morality is not yet Christian morality.... The legal doctrine of the Talmud is based on the distinction between Israel and the peoples, and measures the comportment of the Israelite toward the member of his own people [*Volksgenosse*] and his comportment toward the stranger/foreigner on a different scale.[105]

This classic supersessionist claim by Delitzsch about the origin of love-of-the-neighbor in the deficient "Old Testament morality," along with the fact (though it is not mentioned explicitly by Cohen) that Lagarde uses it in his affidavit explains why Cohen chooses love of the neighbor as the topic of his own affidavit. It also provides the occasion for the passages we have already looked at in which Cohen debunks Christian supersessionism regarding morality.

Like the Fifteen Principles and the Rabbis' Declaration, then, Cohen's affidavit seeks not only to refute specific defamatory claims about Jewish teachings concerning the treatment of non-Jews, but is geared toward combating the widespread perception that Christianity originated the universalist ethical standard of love-of-humanity, the idea of *Nächstenliebe.* (Here, we may recall Güdemann's amusing opening to his own essay on this topic, discussed at the beginning of this chapter, to the effect that even educated Christians could be found to hold the view that "love your neighbor" originally appears in the New Testament.) In the discursive formations or rules that govern the Marburg trial, Cohen identifies the hegemonic Christian presumption of a "hierarchy" of moral ideas, in accordance with the established "hierarchy of religions": Love of

104 On the mixed record of Delitzsch's activities and attitudes toward Judaism, see Wiese, *Wissenschaft des Judentums*, 99–111, 123–30/*Challenging Colonial Discourse*, 122–36, 150–8.

105 Delitzsch, quoted by Lagarde, "Ein Gutachten," 13. Cf. Delitzsch, *Rohling's Talmudjude beleuchtet*, 17.

humanity is regarded as an achievement of Christianity, and is therefore taken to be not yet realized in "love your neighbor" in Leviticus:

> The hierarchy of religions is accordingly supposed to correspond to their position in relation to the moral ideas.... This is how it came to pass that universal human morality was denied not only to the Talmud ..., but also to its very source, the ancient covenant, the basic form of monotheistic morality: *love-of-neighbor.*
>
> This error is one that I must, with honest regret, attribute even to the honorable Delitzsch, who deserves gratitude to a further extent than appears currently to be recognized: because he regards it as an obligation of German theology to defend a religious document with which the Christian world is undeniably connected, against slander

– in other words, Cohen begins by acknowledging the contribution of Delitzsch's above-mentioned defense of the Talmud and of Judaism against Rohling's attacks. Then he adds:

> But for Delitzsch too the *neighbor*, as he claims Leviticus 19:18 shows, "is equivalent to the countryman [*Volksgenosse*]. (NT 148)[106]

As we saw, for Cohen, philosophy, which provides "objective elucidation/explication" of questions concerning morality, is the antidote to the "prejudice that moral systems, whether philosophical or religious, differ principally in regard to the *content* of their moral precepts" (NT 146). The proper philosophical starting point for arriving at a "judgment" about what moral precepts (*Vorschriften*) the Talmud "contains" – what it teaches about morality – is to look at how those precepts are grounded, their foundation (Begründung) or underlying moral principles. Philosophy thereby works by virtue of its *method* against the tendency of Christian thought to "hierarchize" the religions according to the "plain content" of "the moral ideas." Cohen's stipulated philosophical method allows him to step outside the superessionist framework that calls for a comparison of this type. Again, we can draw on Brown's analysis of tolerance to observe that in his very insistence on philosophical method, and in explaining what he means by philosophical method, Cohen is here breaking with the tolerance paradigm or dispositive that goes with his discursive position at the trial, a position that requires that he defend the universality of Judaism in relation to "universal" Christian norms.

---

106 Cohen is quoting Delitzsch, *Rohling's Talmudjude beleuchtet*, 17.

In other words, for Cohen, if neighbor-love has any significance for ethics, it would have to be not as one teaching among others that happens to be, historically or philologically, present in the literary corpus that serves as a source for thought. It is necessary instead to break with the discursive rules calling for an empirical finding as to whether neighbor-love is or is not present in the Jewish corpus or ethical storehouse. Philosophically speaking, neighbor-love can *only* have significance insofar as it is constitutive of ethics as such, if it is the "fundamental form of monotheistic morality" (NT 148). This is what Cohen's affidavit sets out to show, by presenting the moral principles that he views as undergirding Judaism.

As we will see, the result is a view of Judaism not as a particularity that makes a bid for tolerance within the Christian order but as a moral system that is constitutive of ethical universality as such – and that thus disrupts the order of dependence between universality and particularity established within the tolerance paradigm, which is at the same time a theological-supersessionist paradigm.[107]

In objecting to Delitzsch's misinterpretation of Leviticus 19:18 as applying only to the fellow Israelite, Cohen refers, as he does in all his writings on the "neighbor," to the Levitical prescription of "love" for the "stranger" (19:33). We can see an early version of Cohen's later argument against "affective expansion" (discussed in chapter 5) taking shape here: Cohen cautions against regarding stranger-love in v. 33 as a "correction" or a balancing-out of the "love" of the fellow Israelite that one might (mis) take to be the prescription of v. 18. It is not as though v. 18 prescribes an

107 A similar point is made by Kenneth Reinhard in his argument for drawing from Leviticus 19:18 a universalism that goes beyond canceling out, in an "early Christian" mode, "Jewish particularism in the name of a supposedly neutral conception of [humankind]." This more originary universalism would call into question the opposition between universalism and particularism as it is conventionally understood and would thereby be "the condition and horizon of the ethical." It would take the closeness of the "neighbor" in v. 18 and the "stranger" in v. 34 not as a ground for "construct[ing] a category of universality" that would neutralize exclusivism or particularism – Cohen might have called such a procedure one of "expansion" into ever more "relative communities" – but, Reinhard writes, as "bring[ing] out a certain strangeness" in the figure of the neighbor. It is this sort of strangeness, I would add – a strangeness of "the stranger" that is to be "loved" – that would be the source of the disruption of the order of dependence between universalism and particularism. Although Reinhard himself does not connect his vision for the "ethical radicalism" of "love-your-neighbor" to Cohen's texts, I see Cohen's conceptualization of the ethico-legal meaning of the biblical "neighbor" and "stranger," and his understanding of ethics-out-of-law oriented to Allheit, as being in line with the potential identified by Reinhard. Reinhard, "The Ethics of the Neighbor."

exclusivist neighbor-love, which is subsequently neutralized, as it were, or is rendered unobjectionable because "love" of humanity is prescribed by v. 33. Such a reading would follow the model of "affective expansion" that Cohen will go on to reject in the *Ethik*, which would erect an ethical theory on the idea that the "self" should "expand" to encompass concern for the other, or should compensate, as it were, for its self-love with care for the other. Instead, Cohen insists (for reasons I already discussed) that *re'a* in v. 18 already by itself refers to all "others" (NT 148–9).[108]

As he does later in the *Ethik* and in his other essays on the "neighbor," Cohen thus points to the prophets' transcendence of the national frame to embrace the foreign peoples as a parallel to his conception of the "stranger" or the "other" as a point of origin for, or as generating ethical thinking. The prophetic teachings about the messianic unity of humanity – and their understanding of the election of Israel as ultimately signifying that unity – are evidence for the centrality of the "stranger" as a reference point of Jewish monotheism. Again, this view is a function of Cohen's understanding of how "sources" function for Jewish philosophy: The prophets must be read together with the Pentateuch to yield an understanding of Judaism. His challenge to the historian or philologist (such as Delitzsch) is: If you insist that the *re'a* is only the countryman, you also relativize the universalist messages elsewhere in Scripture, for example, in a verse such as "My house shall be called a house of prayer for all peoples" (Isa. 56:7) – a verse which for Cohen represents the prophets' opposition to the exclusivist national frame.

Generation of the Neighbor-Stranger Out of Law: The Noahide as an Institution of *Recht*

Philosophical method, as proposed by Cohen, looks at moral systems in view of their foundations and derivations from their principles. Accordingly, in the affidavit Cohen now shifts to looking at Jewish teachings for the arguments that supply the "foundational" account he seeks of core moral concepts, and thus of a new meaning of universalism, the prophetic-messianic universality of "all peoples" and "humanity." This is in contrast to the 1884 Rabbis' Declaration, which had listed the proclamation of "justice for the stranger" (in Lev. 24:22) alongside love-of-neighbor as a way of demonstrating Judaism's universalism encompassing all. That Declaration could be read as offering a kind of inventory of the "content"

108 In his essay on Maimonides, Cohen writes: "*Re'a* is the other; he is like You; *he is the You of the I*. The self is the result of the eternal relationship between I and You; the infinite ideal of this eternal relationship" (CEM 275/152).

of Jewish teachings, along with a scheme according to which Jewish morality teaches us to "expand" our sphere of care to justice for all. By contrast, Cohen begins from the concept of stranger-love, which is not just one precept among many in a catalogue of teachings that may be found "in" Judaism, but which philosophically *generates* what in the opening pages of the affidavit he terms "the moral principle":

> Love of the stranger is thus a creative moment in the emergence of the concept of the human being as the neighbor. And I must note for the history of moral ideas the following fact: that neighbor-love, or more precisely the love of one with a foreign *nationality or faith,* is a commandment of Judaism. (NT 150)

In other words, that stranger-love is a "*creative* moment in the *emergence*" of the human being as the neighbor, and thus of the moral principle of neighbor-love, is an instance of generation, *Erzeugung,* which, as Cohen will later develop in the legal philosophy of the *Ethik,* is what characterizes the emergence of ethical concepts or principles from legal concepts or institutions. The philosophical attainment of the concept of the human being in the "neighbor" by means of the concept of the "stranger" is – again prefiguring the core argument of the *Ethik* – a function of the "stranger"'s being a category of *law* (Recht). Reworked into the rabbinic concept of the "son of Noah" or "Noahide," the biblical concept of the "stranger" (*ger*) – which Cohen sees as the source and meaning of the *re'a* who is to be "loved" – becomes an "institution of state law" (*staatsrechtliche Institution*) (NT 158).

With this term, "Noahide," Cohen introduces into the discussion a rabbinic designation for a non-Jew whose status is equivalent to that of a Jew, subject to his abiding by seven laws that are regarded as binding on all humankind.[109] (In conjunction with highlighting that the Noahide is

---

109 The term "Noahide" or "son of Noah" derives from the tradition that these laws are binding on all human beings, who are all party to the covenant with Noah mentioned in Genesis 9. See Steven S. Schwarzschild, Saul Berman, and Menachem Elon, "Noachide Laws" (1972/2007), *Encyclopaedia Judaica,* 2nd ed.; Novak, *Image of the Non-Jew*; and Klaus Müller, *Tora für die Völker. Die noachidischen Gebote und Ansätze zu ihrer Rezeption im Christentum* (Berlin: Institut Kirche und Judentum, 1994).

In the enumeration given by Cohen, the seven laws consist of six prohibitions – blasphemy, idolatry, incest (other standard enumerations give a more general prohibtion, e.g., "sexual immorality"), murder, robbery, and eating a limb from a living animal – and one commandment: the establishment of courts of law (NT 158). Of course, the *empirical* standard of inclusivity represented by the rabbinic

a legal category, Cohen also frequently points out that the first Noahide commandment is "the requirement of courts of law" [NT 158–9], the requirement of *dinim* that we touched on in chapter 4.[110])

But just as he earlier argued that the universalism evidenced in the prophetic books must inform the interpretation of the Levitical commandments to "love" the *re'a* and the *ger*, Cohen's point here is not that a biblical teaching about the stranger *later developed* into a rabbinic juridical concept – that of the Noahide as the bearer of citizenship rights. Cohen interprets biblical and rabbinic texts as a continuous corpus that yields the facta for philosophy – in the way that the realm of law (Recht) yields the facta for ethics. Accordingly, he analyzes the relationship of the biblical term *ger* – of the "sojourning stranger" or "resident alien" (*Beisaß-Fremdling*) – and the Mishnaic term Noahide as one of specification, *Präzisierung*:

> The concept of the "sojourner" [*Beisaß-Fremdling*, i.e., resident alien] is made more precise [*präzisiert*] by that of the Noahide in the sense that the latter presupposes the assumption of seven obligations – six prohibitions and one commandment.

and of "correction":

> A *corrective* [*Korrektiv*] was given within the canon itself;[111] and historical conditions were able to direct and press forward to its consequent

---

concept of the Noahide (or of other concepts associated with it) falls far short of any standard we would defend today, and the utility of Cohen's theorizing of true universality in Judaism would be limited if we had to take it solely as an embracing of those empirical standards. My interest here is not in the documented traditions of the Noahide, or of the biblical regulations pertaining to the *ger* or to the *re'a*, but in working out Cohen's mode of argumentation for a notion of universalism – a mode of argumentation that I trace across the "neighbor" writings and the ethico-legal theory of the *Ethik*.

110 Klaus Müller explains that the Noahide obligation that is termed in the rabbinic sources *dinim* is the obligation to set up a system of law. Müller, *Tora für die Völker*, 87. See also Cohen, "Spinoza über Staat und Religion, Judentum und Christentum" (1915), JS3: 346; and "Liebe und Gerechtigkeit," JS3: 86.

111 Emphasis added. Here Cohen adds a parenthetical note directing the reader to pp. 7 and 8 of the pamphlet edition, and thus to his argument in the introductory part of the affidavit (which I discuss above, and which can be found at NT 148–50) that reads Leviticus 19:18 (love the *re'a*) and Leviticus 19:33 (love the *ger*) in conjunction with the prophets' statements on foreign peoples and the messianic unity of humankind, such that stranger-love is the decisive "creative moment in the emergence of the concept of the human being as the neighbor" (NT 150).

> implementation: This moment is the formation that the biblical concept of the "stranger" (*ger*) has found in the Talmudic concept of the "*son of Noah.*" The institution of state law, the *Noahide*, belongs to the oldest accounts of the Mishnah. (NT 158)

The juridical concept "Noahide" makes "more precise" the meaning that is *already* contained in the notion *ger* (in the sense of *ger toshav*) – by virtue of the obligations that are placed upon (or recognized as being observed by) the Noahide and that thus define his citizenship status – known as "Noahide Laws": "The conditions thus pertain to state law [*Die Bedingungen sind sonach staatsrechtlicher Art*]...." (NT 158). Cohen particularly underscores that faith in – that is, allegiance to – the Jewish God is not among the obligations: "The Noahide is thus not a believer [*Gläubiger*], but nevertheless a citizen of the state [*Staatsbürger*]" (NT 159; cf. RV 142–3/123).

Thus, the designation "institution of state law" pertains not only to the Mishnaic term Noahide but also to the biblical notions of stranger/*ger* and "neighbor," when understood in their full significance. As a juridical notion, the neighbor-stranger-Noahide represents the "singular *factum* in the history of religious politics" – a factum that issues from the "fundamental monotheistic idea": Cohen conveys this idea by quoting the words of the eighteenth-century Christian Bible scholar Johann David Michaelis:

> Moses commands, as far as is possible for a legislator, that strangers are to be loved, and includes/conceives [*begreift* – as in *Begriff*, concept – D.H.] them quite explicitly under the name of the neighbor, who is to be loved as oneself.[112]

The "neighbor" (a term I will use from now on as a shorthand for this factum of neighbor-stranger-Noahide) as a *juridical* notion is in evidence in the Levitical commandments about the neighbor and the stranger, alluded to by Michaelis; in other biblical verses (Cohen cites several others here to illustrate various rights accorded to "strangers"); and in the Noahide laws (NT 159). With this evidence, followed up by several other examples of provisions and concepts from both biblical and rabbinic sources

112 Johann David Michaelis, *Mosaisches Recht*, 3rd ed. (Frankfurt/Main: J.G. Garbe, 1793), Teil 2, 445; translated by Alexander Smith as *Commentaries on the Laws of Moses*, vol. 12 (London: Rivington, 1814), 232. Quoted in NT 159. The passage is also quoted by Cohen in "Der Nächste" (1914/1916), JS1: 190/*Werke* 16:66.

that Cohen cites as attesting the same phenomenon (NT 159–61),[113] he is able to conclude,

> The question of the Königliches Landgericht [i.e., the court's second question, as to whether the Talmud permits crimes against non-Jews – D.H.] thus appears answered. (NT 161–2)[114]

The Universalism of Law beyond Tolerance

Both the concept of the Noahide and its "religious" counterpart, "pious of the peoples of the world," as institutions of state law, confer a status on the non-Jew that is "morally equal" to that of the Jew. For Cohen, the significance of this legal institution lies in its going beyond the demand for "tolerance." He writes:

> Thus the Noahide does not enjoy *tolerance,* neither on the part of the state nor on the part of the religion, but is, as a moral person [*sittliche Person*] equal to the Jew. (NT 160)

---

113 These include notably another Talmudic concept, *ḥasidei umot ha-olam,* "the pious of the nations of the world," which was key to Maimonides's codification of Noahide law, and which Cohen regards as a further equivalent of the Noahide (NT 160, cf. RV 383/329). (See, however, RV 141–2/122–3, which complicates this equivalence somewhat.) See also Cohen's discussion of Maimonides's understanding of this notion – in which Cohen again insists on its meaning as a concept of state law – in "Spinoza," JS3: 347–51.

In citing Maimonides's key pronouncement (from *Mishneh Torah: Hilkhot Melakhim* 8:11) that anyone who accepts the Noahide commandments is among "the pious of the nations of the world" and "has a portion in the world-to-come," Cohen names another in the list of privileged sources cited in the 1884 Rabbis' Declaration – which incorporates the Talmudic statement that Maimonides's statement about the Noahide is based on. Cf. Daniel Krochmalnik, "Der Streit um das jüdische Naturrecht. Maimonides, Spinoza, Mendelssohn und Cohen" (2000), in *Interesse am Judentum. Die Franz-Delitzsch-Vorlesungen, 1989–2008,* ed. de Vos and Siegert (Berlin: Lit Verlag, 2008), 248–9.

I am leaving aside the well-known interpretative issues surrounding the continuation of Maimonides's pronouncement, discussed for instance in Novak, *Image of the Non-Jew,* 163–4; and in Schwarzschild, "Do Noachites Have to Believe in Revelation? (A Passage in Dispute between Maimonides, Spinoza, Mendelssohn, and Hermann Cohen). A Contribution to a Jewish View of Natural Law" (1962), in *The Pursuit of the Ideal: Jewish Writings of Steven Schwarzschild,* ed. Menachem Kellner (Albany: State University of New York Press, 1990), 32–3.

114 In a separate step (which goes beyond my topic here), Cohen explains that Christians were included in the historic provisions such as extending citizenship rights to the *ger* or Noahide – that is, that the rabbinic tradition does not regard Christianity as idolatry (NT 162–5).

The apparent, manifest purpose of this argument is to explain to the court the Jewish provisions for just treatment of non-Jews. But within the argumentation of Cohen's affidavit as a whole, it serves another purpose. The claim that the Noahide's status is "equal to the Jew," rather than "enjoying tolerance" within the Jewish political order must be read together with Cohen's earlier point about the "hierarchy of religions," his questioning of a hegemonic universalism that calls on the particular community or law (Gesetz) (Judaism, "Mosaic law") to demonstrate that it measures up to the "universal" norm implicit in Christian-hegemonic theology. In view of that earlier observation, which I have argued indicates that Judaism is itself "on trial" in this proceeding, Cohen's implicit public message regarding the status of Jews in Germany is clear: A true guarantee of full citizenship status regardless of ethno-religious adherence requires going beyond "tolerance" of the Jew.[115]

But Cohen's affidavit functions as a critique of the discourse of tolerance not only in relation to the trial, or as a commentary on the Jewish citizen's interactions with state institutions. I would argue that the affidavit also marks a conscious break with the predominant lines of argument pursued by the Jewish moral defense initiatives that had been undertaken by others. After declaring that the second question of the court (whether the Talmud permits crimes against non-Jews) "appears answered," Cohen adds the following comment:

> And edifying observations and excerpts from such compilations of Talmudic ethical sayings as have been produced by experts since the time of Moses Mendelssohn, if they were appropriate here, may be deemed superfluous now that the state-law category of the Noahide has been established. (NT 162)

In view of the context and structure of Cohen's argument that I have highlighted in the affidavit, this somewhat obscure statement now becomes

115 This is confirmed by Cohen years later, in an essay commenting on the final official exoneration of Alfred Dreyfus by the French Court of Appeal in July 1906, which stood in contrast to the earlier decision of the government to pardon him. Cohen comments on the fundamental "distinction between mercy and law [*Recht*]," law founded in justice. The court decision represented the culmination of a process away from a logic whereby Christians bestowed "mercy" (which is "a partly theological, partly juridical concept") on the Jewish people, by way of the Enlightenment era's stance of "toleration" toward the Jews, and ending up at full mutual recognition and political equality among peoples. About toleration Cohen here comments that it is "an instrument of peace that is not to be denigrated, but there is nevertheless attached to it the indeterminacy of moderation and condescension." "Der geschichtliche Sinn des Abschlusses der Dreyfus-Affäre," JS2: 354–5.

readable: The "edifying observations and excerpts" can be taken to refer to statements such as the Fifteen Basic Principles and the "interconfessional" Declaration of the Rabbiner-Versammlung. In accordance with Cohen's statement about philosophical method at the outset of his text, this statement gestures toward the argument of the affidavit as one that does not principally proceed by amassing or "compiling" evidence pertaining to the *content* of scripture and rabbinic "sayings."[116] The typical purpose of such a quantitative "compilation" or accumulation would be to outweigh the charges against Jewish moral deficiency, to make up Judaism's alleged shortfall in relation to the norms of "universalism." By contrast, Cohen's retrieval of the "state-law category of the Noahide" makes such compilation "superfluous" because that category, retrieved philosophically, is the kind of "principle of morality" that founds or grounds the moral system not "of" Judaism, but of ethics as such. Ethics here is generated out of what one can call, in the terminology of the *Ethik*, a factum of law, the "state law institution" of the Noahide and its cognates, the *ger toshav* and the neighbor-stranger. That what is generated in the juridical factum is an ethics as such and not a particular morality of a people, is underscored by Cohen, for example, whenever he notes that Christian jurists such as John Selden or Hugo Grotius likewise took the Noahide laws as a resource for a theory of natural law, and that the notion of the Noahide thereby figures into the formation of the general Western legal tradition.[117]

Debate on the "Priority" of Neighbor-Love (1894)

We have seen that in his affidavit, Cohen subverts the tolerance paradigm at work in state interactions with Jewish citizens such as the antisemitism trial. We also saw that his argument for a universalism that exceeds or precedes tolerance is at the same time a challenge to prevalent Jewish moral defense strategies and deliberations. This becomes even more explicit in the essay on the topic of "love-of-neighbor" that Cohen wrote after the Marburg trial, "Zum Prioritätsstreit über das Gebot

116 The third section of the affidavit is a kind of separate addendum in which Cohen confronts specific claims in Lagarde's affidavit; however, that material does not figure into his main answers to the court's questions (NT 165–73).

117 See NT 160; "Liebe und Gerechtigkeit," JS3:59, 60; RV 143/123–4; and "Spinoza," JS3: 346. Eric Nelson discusses Grotius's and Selden's use of the Noahide laws in "Hebrew Theocracy and the Rise of Toleration," in *The Hebrew Republic: Jewish Sources and the Transformation of European Political Thought* (Cambridge, MA: Harvard University Press, 2010), chap. 3. On Selden and on Grotius as an influence on Selden in this regard, see Jason P. Rosenblatt, *Renaissance England's Chief Rabbi: John Selden* (Oxford: Oxford University Press, 2006), chaps. 6 and 7.

der Nächstenliebe" (1894; "On the Priority Dispute Concerning the Commandment to Love the Neighbor"). Polemics about anti-Judaism and anti-Talmudism continued unabated in the years between the Marburg trial and the publication of this second essay. Cohen published it in the Jewish weekly newspaper *Allgemeine Zeitung des Judentums* as a polemical response to an editorial that its editor, Gustav Karpeles, had published a few weeks earlier.[118] Karpeles was reacting to an expression of anti-Jewish prejudice in a work by the Old Testament scholar Bernhard Stade,[119] and in that context cited Cohen's 1888 affidavit as exemplifying an insufficient, unsuccessful strategy of defense against ("scholarly" or "scientific") antisemitism ("wissenschaftlicher Antisemitismus").

The "priority dispute" concerning neighbor-love referenced in the title of Cohen's essay already announces that the occasion for the essay is once again a Christian-supersessionist claim about neighbor-love: the claim that the principle of universalism originates in Christian teachings, which is an assertion of Christian "priority" regarding universalism. Jewish moral defense discourses – Cohen's, as well as Karpeles's – routinely "dispute" or debate such assertions of "priority."

In this inner-Jewish dispute, the parties agree that the assertion of Christian "priority" regarding universalism is baseless and must be challenged; where Cohen disagrees with Karpeles is about the kind of counter-argument to be made. In his *Geschichte des Volkes Israel* (1887; *History of the People of Israel*), Stade had discussed the mores (*Sitten*) of the Israelites, a people dwelling in the territory of its national God Jahwe and entrusting to this God its physical well-being, but one that is not yet in a unique sort of covenant with God. This is thus a people whose moral action can be explained as obedience to its particular God, and thus as having no aspiration to general validity. The Israelites' own view of what morality (*Sittlichkeit*) is is thus strictly relative.[120] Stade's history thus typifies Protestant-theologizing approaches of his time, according to which the text of the Bible was to be read "as a development from the particular to the universal and from the external to the internal," such that "the prophets represent a higher and more inward form of religion"

118 Gustav Karpeles, "Der wissenschaftliche Antisemitismus," *Allgemeine Zeitung des Judentums* 58, no. 20 (18 May 1894), 229–30. Cohen's response "Zum Prioritätsstreit ..." was published in *Allgemeine Zeitung des Judentums* (8 June 1894), 368–70.

119 Bernhard Stade, *Geschichte des Volkes Israel*, vol. 1, *Geschichte Israels unter der Königsherrschaft* (Berlin: Grote'sche Verlagsbuchhandlung, 1887).

120 Stade, *Geschichte des Volkes Israel* 1: 507–10. On morality, Stade writes that for the Israelites, "everything that is *Sitte* [custom, habit] is as such moral [*sittlich*] and good" and then adds in a footnote: "This is a general human conclusion – as is shown by our word *sittlich* – and a valid one" (509, 509n1).

and a normative "ethical monotheism" – with Christianity forming its authentic continuation.[121]

Stade here takes the opportunity, in a long footnote, to berate Jewish defense initiatives by "assembled rabbis" (*versammelte Rabbiner* – the reference is evidently to the 1884 Rabbiner-Versammlung and its "interconfessional declaration") for "insolently" trying to convince "the Christian public" that "commandments such as Lev. 19:18 [and] 24:22" "obligate" Jews to act morally "toward all human beings" and to assert that Judaism is therefore a religion of "love of human beings" (*Menschenliebe*). All these assertions are for Stade based on "false translations" of *re'a* and *ger*.[122] Stade concedes that those rabbis may well themselves preach universalist moral principles and act on them, "but in that case they act under the influence of Christian ethics and against the ethics of Talmudic Judaism."

The Christian Bible scholar thus poses a challenge regarding the development of Judaism toward universalism – saying, in effect, that Judaism surely did not embrace love of humanity as "early" as is claimed by contemporary Jews. But Karpeles's response likewise stays within the mode of determining developmental chronologies. Though Karpeles concurs with refutations of the Christian-favored interpretation that *re'a* means "countryman" (for which he cites Cohen's 1888 affidavit along with Güdemann's *Nächstenliebe* [1890]), he observes that they are not accepted by the other side. Therefore, he finds that to argue for Jewish universalism on such

121 I am drawing here on characterizations of Protestant biblical criticism in Daniel Weidner, "The Political Theology of Ethical Monotheism," in *Judaism, Liberalism, and Political Theology*, ed. Randi Rashkover and Martin Kavka (Bloomington: Indiana University Press, 2014) (quotations are from p. 184); Wiese, *Wissenschaft des Judentums*, 200/ *Challenging Colonial Discourse*, 241; Ran HaCohen, "'Gehörst du zu uns oder zu unsern Feinden?' (Josua 5,13). Die jüdische Auseinandersetzung mit der 'Höheren Bibelkritik,'" trans. Görge K. Hasselhoff, in *Die Entdeckung des Christentums in der Wissenschaft des Judentums*, ed. Görge K. Hasselhoff (Berlin: de Gruyter, 2010), 74–5. See also Tal, *Christians and Jews in Germany*, 191–2, and Christian Wiese, "'The Best Antidote to Anti-Semitism'? *Wissenschaft des Judentums*, Protestant Biblical Scholarship, and Anti-Semitism in Germany Before 1933," in *Modern Judaism and Historical Consciousness: Identities, Encounters, Perspectives*, ed. Andreas Gotzmann and Christian Wiese (Leiden: Brill, 2007), 148–9, 151.

122 The Rabbiner-Versammlung in its "interconfessional" Declaration indeed refers to exactly the verses in Leviticus that Stade cites. Stade, *Geschichte des Volkes Israel*, 510n3. (See also Wiese's mention of this exchange between Stade and Karpeles, *Wissenschaft des Judentums*, 116n89/ *Challenging Colonial Discourse*, 141n90.) Stade's scolding of the assembled rabbis is answered by Kaufmann Kohler in his entry on "Brotherly Love" in the *Jewish Encyclopedia*, vol. 2 (New York: Funk and Wagnalls, 1902), and it also serves as a prime occasion for Moritz Güdemann's essay on love-of-neighbor, discussed briefly at the opening of this chapter. Güdemann, *Nächstenliebe*, 4–5n1. See also A. Löwenthal, "Nächstenliebe," *Die Jüdische Presse* (30 October 1890), 1–2.

grounds is ineffective. Instead, Karpeles wants to argue that even if Stade's point were conceded – that is, even if the verses in Leviticus were not understood to be an origin of contemporary Jewish morality – Judaism would still obviously have to be seen as having "developed" "naturally" in the direction of overcoming its exclusivist morality. Indeed, he argues, recognizing that Judaism has developed in such a direction ought to give one all the more reason to embrace the notion of Judaism as morally universalist.[123]

This argument is unacceptable to Cohen. What he reacts to in Karpeles's piece is not the direct attack on himself – Karpeles's contention that Cohen's (and Güdemann's) interpretation of the biblical term *re'a* and *ger* will not make for an effective grounds on which to argue the Jewish case for universalism. Instead, what Cohen objects to is the argument from "development" that is shared by both Stade (representing the dominant historical biblical criticism of the time) and Karpeles – though Cohen does not mention either of their names in his essay. (Karpeles's stance here thus resembles that of Moritz Lazarus, whom Cohen went on to challenge in 1899 for advancing an "ethics of Judaism" without regard for Jewish textual sources or Jewish philosophy – as we also saw in Lazarus's objection to making explicit that the Fifteen Basic Principles were rooted in traditional Jewish texts.[124]) The main problem is not that Karpeles is willing to concede that universalism might not have shown up as "early" in Judaism as other Jewish defenders contend (though, to be sure, Cohen does spend part of his essay taking his reader step-by-step through a reading of Leviticus 19 in order to support his interpretation of *re'a,* as well as of key verses in Leviticus about treatment of the *ger* [Pr 178–9]). The desire to search for "early" indications of a principle of love-of-neighbor in "so-called Mosaic teaching," as well as for how that notion would have been "prepared" is an understandable one, writes Cohen – since historical research is not going to be satisfied with the image of such an idea "emerging in full panoply from the head of Jehova." But, he suggests, when "historical criticism" projects stages of development onto the sources, this is an essentially theologizing move:

> The prejudice that a document is a preparatory stage [*Vorstufe*] may suit a theological conception of a divine educational plan; in a historical investigation it is deleterious [*vom Übel*]. (Pr 176)

To seek to account for the emergence of (to use the terms of Cohen's 1888 affidavit) the fundamental principle of morality by means of a

123 Karpeles, "Der wissenschaftliche Antisemitismus," 229–30.
124 See the discussions earlier in this chapter, and in chapter 4.

causal or developmental explanation is, in effect, to impose a schema of something like "affective expansion." The theologizing version of such a schema imagines a "God" whose purview or reach expands in line with his "educational plan" – just as for historical biblical criticism, as also expressed in Stade's footnote, the Israelite religion expands from particularism to ethical universalism. For Cohen, monotheism indeed entails the value of universalism.[125] But this universalism lies in the idea that the concept of the unity of God has as its "internal necessary consequence" the idea of the unity of humankind. It was through that idea that Judaism "removed" the apparent "contradiction" between the idea of neighbor-love – that we have obligations to the human other – and that of faithfulness to God (Pr 176). "It is only out of the concept of the unity of God that neighbor-love can be grasped" (Pr 180).

As he did in his 1888 account of the "neighbor"-Noahide as a legal institution (to which he also refers his reader in "Priority Dispute"), Cohen here explicates the concept of neighbor-love as something that *could not* have arisen "by means of a political tolerance" (Pr 177). That is to say, this concept must not be thought of as arising empirically from some sufficient accumulation of experience, such as "personal contacts with other tribes and with those of different faiths," which Cohen calls "the path of political tolerance." Cohen instead frames such encounters using the methodological terminology of critical idealism, when he writes that they can at most have been the occasion for the emergence of the conceptual "*problem* of neighbor-love" (Pr 177, emphasis added). That "problem" names a philosophical task, one that can be addressed by generating ethico-legal concepts such as that of the "neighbor-stranger," perhaps one akin to the scenario that, as Cohen will write in the *Ethik*, was faced by the prophets who asserted universal love of humanity upon the nation's confrontation with the existence of foreign peoples.

We see a continuation here of Cohen's challenge to the Christian-hegemonic dispositive in which ethics as such is equated with Christianity. He builds on the argument in the 1888 affidavit that the ethical-philosophical significance of the Jewish tradition of neighbor-love cannot emerge from a *comparison* of some "content" of ethics in Judaism with Christian-"universal" ethical, but rather must be realized by means of philosophical conceptualization, as accomplished by the legal category

125 It would be possible to trace in detail Cohen's hesitation about theses concerning the "development" of Israelite religion through his many writings dealing with historical biblical criticism. For a discussion of Cohen's ambivalent relationship to the Protestant Bible scholarship of his day, see for example, Wiese, "'The Best Antidote.'"

of the neighbor/stranger/Noahide, which, as we saw, is at the origin of the ethical self. In rejecting the tolerance paradigm, Cohen is in "Zum Prioritätsstreit" rejecting – as he will later in the *Ethik* – a thinking of degrees of otherness, of degrees of my capacity to extend myself to that which is different from myself:

> But it was not by way of pedantic haggling as to how much difference [*Verschiedenheit*] one could at best *tolerate* [dulden] and, on the other hand, what minimal degree of unity one ought simply to demand – not, in other words, in so external a mechanics – that such an idea, which more than any other ideas of the human spirit has the imprint of a unified idea [i.e., that of neighbor-love – D.H.], could have come about. (Pr 177, emphasis added)

Cohen links this idea of a unity of humankind to an interpretation of Leviticus 19:18 that was proposed by Naftali Herz Wessely, the noted Haskalah author who also contributed to Moses Mendelssohn's Bible translation and commentary (known as the *Biur*). In his commentary to this verse in Leviticus, Wessely concluded that instead of the customary translation of this verse as "Love your neighbor *as yourself*," it ought to be re-translated as "Love your neighbor, *he is like you* [er ist wie du]."[126] Although Cohen remarks that he does not necessarily endorse this translation as a matter of linguistic accuracy, he embraces the idea it represents. Wessely's interpretation precludes misunderstanding the "as yourself" (*kamokha*) to mean that "love-your-neighbor" should be modeled on "giving aid to oneself" (*Selbsthilfe*), on self-love. It precludes applying a logic of "affective expansion" to the commandment to love the neighbor: "It is not a given degree of love that is commanded" in that verse, writes Cohen. Rather, Wessely's suggested

126 This is actually Cohen's particular rendering of Wessely's suggested retranslation, which in the original reads: "Liebe deinen Nächsten, der dir gleich ist" (meaning: "who is like you" or "who is equal to you"). Mendelssohn's own translation had been: "Liebe deinen Nächsten so, wie du dich selbst liebst" – "Love your neighbor as you love yourself," a formulation that accentuates the interpretative problem that much of the commentary on this verse has grappled with and that Cohen also is reacting to: Should comportment toward the "neighbor" be conceived analogously to my "love" of myself? See Moses Mendelssohn, *Sefer Netivot Ha-Shalom: Vayikra* in *Gesammelte Schriften. Jubiläumsausgabe*, vol. 17, *Hebräische Schriften II,4,* ed. Werner Weinberg (Stuttgart-Bad Cannstatt: Frommann Holzboog, 1990), 237. Cf. Wolfgang Reinbold, "Die Nächstenliebe (Lev 19,18)," in *Die Verheißung des Neuen Bundes: Wie alttestamentliche Texte im Neuen Testament fortwirken,* ed. Bernd Kollmann (Göttingen: Vandenhoeck & Ruprecht, 2010), 18; and Mendes-Flohr, "Love, Accusative and Dative," 9–10. As Adam Zachary Newton helpfully glosses Wessely's commentary in the *Biur,* Wessely's retranslation takes the function of *kamokha* (here and in other instances) to be adjectival, and not adverbial. Newton, *The Fence and the Neighbor,* 60.

translation – which actually reads "Love your neighbor, who is like you [der dir *gleich* ist, i.e., equal to you]" – illuminates the idea that in this commandment, "the equality of human beings is taught, and love derived from it" (Pr 181). The teaching of the unity of humanity is the primary teaching. Its universalist meaning is fundamental and indivisible, and thus of a different order than the logic of tolerance, which recommends or calculates an approach to the other in terms of "degrees" of otherness or foreignness.

When we read these passages together with the fuller account of the *Ethik*, we can see Cohen arguing that only if we understand the "neighbor" who is to be "loved" properly as a legal institution, as the bearer of rights regardless of their nation or faith, can the notion of "neighbor-love" be truly universal. The universality of "neighbor-love" does not lie simply in the inclusion of a sufficient number of appropriate provisions in Jewish law (or in "Talmud") so as to measure up to the "neighbor-love" of Christian normativity or universality. The anti-supersessionist argument of Cohen's affidavit breaks through the logic of tolerance that is both imposed by the dispositive of the Marburg trial and maintained by Jewish moral defense statements such as the Rabbis' Declaration.

Cohen's argument, beginning in the 1888 affidavit, for a proper philosophical refoundation of "love"-of-neighbor in a juridical principle of equal citizenship presages the *Ethik* in which, many years later, he offers a systematic account of how such a legal category functions in the discovery and promotion of ethical truths. If the argument of the *Ethik* was that ethics must be oriented toward Allheit, then the messianic universalism that is, according to Cohen, the principle of prophetic monotheism is a universalism of a different order than the hegemonic universalism that produces the "turning of the tables," and thus the demand for Jewish moral defense, at the 1888 trial.

Cohen's 1888 argument to the court that the "stranger" in Judaism is a legal category, an institution of Jewish law, is an advance, key instance of the systematic account he offers years later in his philosophical ethics and philosophy of law. This is the sense in which, I am arguing in this book, the "neighbor" essays[127] need to be read together with the *Ethik*. The presentation, as early as this 1888 affidavit, of the *ger*/Noahide

127 In order to be able to focus my demonstration, I have had to limit the present discussion to only the two earliest of these essays (with occasional cross-references to the others, which I listed in note 8 above). With requisite attention to their respective contexts and argumentative aims, I believe similar demonstrations could be made for the other texts. Such an analysis would continue to look at how the philosophico-theologico-ethical debates about the neighbor are shaped by the dispositives of supersessionist Christian-hegemonic logics and of antisemitism and anti-Talmud trials under Section 166 as a regulatory mechanism of Jewish-Christian relations, including

as a category of Recht exemplifies Cohen's objection in the *Ethik* to an ethics based on "affective expansion." This is to say that the neighbor-stranger-Noahide is more than just an example of an ethical concept generated out of law. In the sense that Cohen's ethical theory in general is aimed at showing that the orientation to Allheit essentially consists of overcoming the model of affective expansion from self to other, the neighbor-stranger-Noahide both represents and effects the generation of ethics out of law, and toward the ideal of Allheit. As has been noted before, the fact that this generation should be envisioned from the start as a function of the "resident alien" or *ger toshav* is part of what makes Cohen's ethical-political thought as timely as ever in this age in which the very notions of migration and residence demand to be thought anew.[128]

When we look at the break with "tolerance" that is articulated in the Jewish writings in continuity with the ethico-legal theory of the *Ethik* – in Cohen's theory that ethics is generated in law, in Recht – we can see that for Cohen, understanding or recasting the "neighbor" as a category of law is the only warrant for moral progress in the sphere of political conceptualization and experience. Recalling Wendy Brown's analysis of the logic of tolerance as having a depoliticizing effect, we may say that Cohen's analysis of neighbor-love retrieves the notion of law in its political meaning, for the sake of justice.

We may project this outcome back onto our study of the "Law" chapter in *Religion of Reason* (in chapter 4), which showed that for Cohen "law" (Gesetz) in Judaism must ideally be revalued and transformed into messianic politics. Continuing this trajectory – a trajectory that Cohen doesn't explicitly complete – would point toward a Recht, a system of law, that would at the same time be a futural pro-ject of Gesetz. Cohen's systematic ethico-legal philosophy was oriented to Allheit. *In combination with* his Jewish philosophy, his conception of ethics out of law is shown to be oriented, further, to a counter-hegemonic universal horizon of justice that gives the futurity and otherness of Gesetz – both internal and external to Recht – its full meaning.

---

of Jewish defense discourses. Of special interest here is the essay "The Neighbor" (1914/1916), which indirectly involves another "legal defense" trial – again one that is both a Section 166 trial and a "Talmud" trial – that of Theodor Fritsch in 1912/1913 (see Wiese, *Wissenschaft des Judentums*, 206–31/*Challenging Colonial Discourse*, 258–78).

128 See Andrea Poma, "Similarity and Diversity of the Other: The Foreigner. Topical Motives in Hermann Cohen's Ethical Idealism" (1994), in *Yearning for Form and Other Essays on Hermann Cohen's Thought*, trans. John Denton (Dordrecht: Springer, 2006), 133. For examples of important contemporary new efforts in this regard, see Andreas Cassee, *Globale Bewegungsfreiheit: Ein philosophisches Plädoyer für offene Grenzen* (Berlin: Suhrkamp, 2016), and Thomas Nail, *The Figure of the Migrant* (Stanford: Stanford University Press, 2015).

Conclusion

That ethics is founded in law is a powerful idea that at first appears counterintuitive. We seek for our legal institutions to measure up to morality – which raises the question: What is the source of morality? Hermann Cohen's theory of ethics out of law begins from the deep suspicion he teaches us to cultivate toward an ethics that seeks to ground itself in transcendent concepts or rational ideals, or in sentiments such as empathy. Such sentiments are for Cohen akin to physiological symptoms over which we have no control, at best, and which, at worst, can revert into simple egotism. Instead, Cohen proposes inquiry into juridical concepts, or facta, such as the cooperative (*Genossenschaft*), as a method of generating ethics. This is a radical challenge to the dualism of ethics and law that governs much of our thinking, according to which ethical normativity is founded on rational insight or inner conviction or external principles, while laws are the mere application of such norms to actual lives, enforced by state power but with no intrinsic connection to morality.

To reconstruct Cohen's theories and to retrieve the force and potential of his challenge to practical philosophy is, as I have shown, a complex undertaking, for it requires an exploration of what connects and what disjoins the two main corpuses of his work: his systematic philosophical writings and his "Jewish writings," culminating in the *jüdische Religionsphilosophie* formulated in the *Religion of Reason.*

On one level, Cohen charts a path for the retrieval of key terms from out of "Jewish sources," as resources for thinking universal justice. His procedure is to identify and explicate biblical and rabbinic traditions that have bequeathed to Western thought a task of negotiating ethical-political dilemmas – sometimes by way of correcting dominant Christian-informed misinterpretations of them. The point of orientation for this book has been the cluster, chain, or spectrum of notions that Cohen continually turns to in order to confront and dismantle the "dangerous ambiguity" of "the neighbor"/*der Nächste*: *re'a* – stranger – *ger toshav*/sojourner/resident alien – Noahide (*ben Noaḥ*) – citizen – notions that I have refered to in abbreviated form as the "neighbor-stranger." As discussed in the final chapter of this book, Cohen's repeated treatments of the uses and abuses of the notion of "love-of-neighbor" at the turn of the twentieth century showcased it as a powerful emblem of (Christian) hegemony. For Cohen, invocations, discussions, and sometimes even casual mentions of the "neighbor" in public discourse and biblical scholarship called for persistent analyses that looked past espousals of an ethos of toleration and religious charitability, in order to "decolonize" (to use a term from our own era) the implicit view of the (Jewish) "other" constructed by them. Cohen's analyses exposed a pervasive political logic that was predicated on anti-Judaism. Yet, as I have sought to argue in the course of this book, his analyses are not merely, or primarily, attempts at restitution or at rectifying an injustice committed toward Judaism or the Jews. Rather, they show that in eclipsing Judaism or the (Jewish) "other," (Christian-)hegemonic[1] discourse effectively obscures or blocks an essential path toward conceiving of political community as such – and thus the chances of achieving a future universal justice.

But while Cohen's reliance on such "Jewish sources" is of course essential to his writings on Jewish religion and in Jewish venues, it shows up very sporadically in his systematic philosophy. For example (as discussed in chapter 6 above), Cohen's reflection on the neighbor-stranger and his critical examination of the commandment to "love" the neighbor or the stranger have an important role in his main work on ethics and philosophy of law, *Ethik des reinen Willens* (*Ethics of Pure Will*). I have argued that the neighbor-stranger is a kind of hinge or passageway allowing us to read his ethico-legal theory together with his philosophy of Judaism. I have suggested, further, that the way in which an argument may often be found to serve as a passage or a hinge joining a "Jewish" and a "general" text could be paradigmatic for modern Jewish thought. This is a matrix for reading modern Jewish authors that both takes seriously their contributions to general philosophical (or political or cultural) discourse and takes the measure of their explorations of Judaism and Jewish existence – all without reducing or projecting one set of questions and concerns onto the other, and without seeking to harmonize possible tensions or contradictions between claims made in each realm or mode.

1 As explained in chapter 6, "Christian" here is used in a sense that is not equivalent to its standard meaning as a particular predicate.

Accordingly, my intention has been to read Cohen's ethico-legal theory as developed in the *Ethik* not as a projection of insights gained from Jewish sources, nor to present Cohen's writings on love-of-neighbor (or on other Jewish themes) as an application of his ethical theory. Instead, this book argues that to take the full measure of Cohen's theory of ethics out of law entails understanding the attempts folded into it of exposing and dismantling structures of (Christian) hegemony – an aspect that only becomes legible if we read *across* the two corpuses: the philosophical and the Jewish writings. Reading across the two corpuses in this way also allows us to understand the wealth of "occasional" pieces by Cohen – interventions in particular contemporary controversies or dilemmas concerning Jewish existence in the modern German polity – as more than just instances of advocacy for a particular community in the state. To take an example that is not directly related to the material discussed in this book (mentioned only briefly in chapter 6 above): Among Cohen's occasional writings on matters affecting Jewish civil rights is his essay in a Jewish weekly commenting on the final official exoneration of Alfred Dreyfus by the French Court of Appeal in July 1906, "Der geschichtliche Sinn des Abschlusses der Dreyfus-Affäre" ("The Historical Significance of the Conclusion of the Dreyfus Affair"). This exoneration of Dreyfus stood in contrast to the earlier decision of the government to pardon him, a pardon that according to Cohen did nothing but "contradict" the charge of treason, which thereby remained in force. On its own, Cohen's reflection on the "historical significance" of this event could be understood as a simple welcome of a turning of the political tides: the overcoming of antisemitic policy and sentiment – that is, of a policy and sentiment targeting a minority community. But when we read his lines, instead, in light of the theory of ethics out of law developed in the *Ethik*, we can discern in them this theory in action, as Cohen presents this court decision as an event in the history of justice (*Gerechtigkeit*) in general. The "contradiction" or "difference" between mercy and law (Recht), he writes, has here been sublated (*aufgehoben*). From the minority-Jewish position – following the narrow logic of "Jewish moral defense" I outlined in chapter 6 – the court decision would represent the ultimate break with a logic whereby Christians bestowed "mercy" (which is "a partly theological, partly juridical concept") on the Jewish people, by way of the Enlightenment era's stance of "toleration" toward the Jews. Instead, the larger objective of Cohen's theory of ethics guides his thinking here as well. He underscores that state power as such has been refounded on its true foundation, that of justice. When such a contradiction has been resolved, it is the French people as such whose "juridical sense" (or "sense of justice," *Rechtsgefühl*) has been set aright, as right itself – and law itself – has been found and (re-)generated. The true point of orientation of this event in juridical history is – to use a term from the *Ethik* – that of Allheit, which corresponds to full mutual recognition and political equality among peoples. After all, Cohen argues, tolerance is a one-way street, a stance exercised by the powerful on the powerless (and he finds that this tolerance is endemic among "Christian peoples" as guiding the sentiment with which they regard Judaism). One who is said to be "tolerated" is never figured in such a way that we who tolerate are at the same time also seeking tolerance from them.[2] This was the root of Cohen's critique of Rudolf Stammler's "relative communities" (discussed in chapter 5), which were to be built on nothing more than empathy. The "relative community" was thus a model of "neighboring" hinging on a persistent reference to the self, emanating outward in circles of affective expansion to encompass others. In the *Ethik* and the "neighbor" writings, Cohen shows that such a model is damaging for a proper retrieval of the "neighbor-stranger" as a juridical concept from Jewish sources. "Love" in "love-of-neighbor" must be reframed as a matter of right and justice.

When Cohen finds it important to state, in regard to Dreyfus's exoneration, that the French people's *Rechtsgefühl* has been restored, this is in line with the transcendental analysis of ethics out of law he developed in the *Ethik*: This "feeling" for Recht is not an empirical psychological datum. Rather, Cohen is here asserting a legal factum, a juridical signpost or accomplishment pointing the way toward a greater justice: in this case, the recognition of a universal citizenship that obviates any need for toleration or mercy. As Cohen puts this point some years later in another contribution to a Jewish newspaper, commemorating the 100th anniversary of the 1812 Prussian edict that gave Jews full citizenship status: "Our religion thereby ceased being a protected religion [*Schutzreligion*, akin to *Schutzjude*, the status of "protected Jew" that was sometimes granted to Jews in German lands in the centuries leading up to emancipation – D.H.] and became a *Rechtsreligion* in the state." Cohen's coinage *Rechtsreligion* for the new status of Judaism in the state corresponds to no established juridical notion. If we take *Rechtsreligion* to mean "religion by law," it would denote simply a "legalized" or "recognized" religion and thus the "great principle," as Cohen puts it, represented by the fact that the law of the state (*Staatsrecht*) has recognized "our religion." But since, as Cohen also points out, the Jewish religion could be freely practiced already prior

2 "Der geschichtliche Sinn des Abschlusses der Dreyfus-Affäre" (1906), JS2: 352–9, 354–5.

to 1812, the meaning of *Rechtsreligion* must reach beyond that of legally recognized religion. *Rechtsreligion* is here constitutive of Recht – law and state – as such.[3] What is significant about according Judaism this status is that doing so makes Recht into what it is, and what it must be. Contrary to an abstract universalism that would conceive of the granting of citizenship rights to Jews as a recognition of their universal humanity, Cohen writes that the meaning of the emancipation of the Jews is that they are emancipated "not as human beings as such" – a notion that Cohen here classifies as a mere "religious abstraction" – but "as Jews in the Prussian state."[4] This means not that a particular minority has been upgraded to full-citizen status or has had its "humanity" acknowledged. Such acknowledgments, as we also experience them today in Western political figurations of racialized and minoritized others, are volatile, unreliable, and politically empty. At best they amount to recommendations to the majority that it might wish to weigh whether its own sentiments lean toward "acknowledgment" of the other (or, as Stammler put it in the work that provoked Cohen's ire: "Who is my neighbor?") in order to be able to determine, subsequently, whether such an ideal of inclusion really can or ought to be realized juridically. For Cohen, the meaning of emancipation is that citizenship as such has been elevated and made complete when Jewish religion comes to be understood as a *Rechtsreligion*, as a ratification and a program of law/Recht as such. (In a more ceremonial declaration published on the same anniversary, Cohen can be seen to extend this point: not only was the program of law and justice [Recht, Gerechtigkeit] ratified by this edict, the edict is an inaugural step onto the great path of Recht [*Rechtsweg*], a step that "is for us a guarantee that justice cannot cease to be developed as the foundation of the Reich."[5]) This insight in the essay commemorating the 1812 edict – and thus dating from 1912, the year in which Cohen began a process of consolidating his analyses of Jewish religion, which would culminate in the book *Religion of Reason* – thus already announces a "religion of reason" that is at the same time Judaism and a horizon of (future) "religion," peace, and justice as such, associated with a plurality of religions of reason (as I have discussed in chapter 4 regarding the argument of the "Law" chapter of the *Religion*).

3 "Emanzipation. Zur Hundertjahrfeier des Staatsbürgertums der preußischen Juden (11. März 1912)" JS2: 220–33, 221–2.

4 "Emanzipation," JS2: 221.

5 Cohen contributed this statement to a collection of such statements by public figures published in "Gedenknummer zur Jahrhundertfeier der Judenemanzipation in Preußen," special issue, *Mitteilungen des Verbandes der jüdischen Jugendvereine Deutschlands* 2, no. 4 (1 April 2011), 11; *Werke* 15: 559–63.

Cohen's ethico-legal theory imagines political life as oriented to a realm of legality that generates, by virtue of the transcendental inquiry into juridical phenomena or concepts (legal science, Rechtswissenschaft), a possible ethics of universal justice. Recalling the productive circularity between law and ethics outlined in the *Ethik* (discussed in chapter 1 of this book), in which juridical experience generates the facta to be examined by legal science in pursuit of justice, I have argued that the figure of the neighbor-stranger functions in an exemplary way. Indeed, Cohen's examinations of love-of-neighbor allow us to discern lessons for a contemporary politics of hospitality. To think hospitality with Cohen is to reject any according or apportioning of rights, recognition, or sympathy to those who are figured from the outset as outsiders. Law is itself (as discussed in chapter 2 in relation to the term *Gesetz*) a generative realm of the other and of the future that constitutes the self, not as individual, but as oriented to an ethical-political universality (Allheit).

Philosophical initiatives of our own time have begun to frame the stranger and the migrant not as outsiders and exceptions; they have begun to re-conceive the space of political-juridical life as one of movement, and political life as constituted by figures that are reminiscent of the "neighbor-stranger" that animated much of Cohen's thinking about ethics, justice and politics.[6] The "stranger" is no exception for Cohen, no interruption of the native-born, territorial order; rather, it bespeaks the possibility of political and ethical action as such. Categories such as "resident alien" and "citizen" generate the key questions we need to confront today about the meaning of migration and movement in conceiving of justice. While Cohen himself did not contemplate a radical openness or calling into question of national territorial borders, his writings centered on the neighbor-stranger, founded in his theory of ethics out of law, open onto latter-day initiatives to theorize a radical hospitality in accordance with the desperate demands of our times to specify and realize the principle articulated by Immanuel Kant, and repeated by Cohen when he urged Germany to keep its eastern borders open to Jewish refugees during World War I: that "by virtue of the right to communal possession of the earth's surface on which, since it is a sphere, they cannot disperse infinitely," "no one originally has any greater right than anyone else to be in a [given] place on the earth."[7] While Kant's articulation of

6 See, for example, the "kinopolitical" project of Thomas Nail in *The Figure of the Migrant* (Stanford: Stanford University Press, 2015), also described by Nail in "Figures of the Migrant: Structure and Resistance," *Cultural Dynamics* 30, no. 3 (August 2018).

7 Immanuel Kant, "Zum ewigen Frieden. Ein philosophischer Entwurf," AA8: 358. Translation adapted from those of Mary J. Gregor, "Toward Perpetual Peace," in

the human right to infinite dispersal on the earth's surface has itself often been problematized as too limited (for Kant it amounts to a right to temporarily visit a place, and not to reside or to make a home there), the challenge it represents, endorsed by Cohen, is in our time being taken up in theories of radical hospitality and arguments for "global freedom of movement."[8] Cohen's concrete demand in 1916 – made amidst lively debate among German Jews about policies toward the Jewish population of eastern territories under German military occupation, including about whether migration into the Reich ought to be permitted to continue[9] – was a limited one, directed at offering refuge specifically to Jews from the east. Furthermore, it is made in one of his troubling wartime

---

Practical Philosophy (Cambridge: Cambridge University Press, 1996), and H. B. Nisbet, "Perpetual Peace: A Philosophical Sketch," in *Kant's Political Writings*, ed. Hans Reiss (Cambridge: Cambridge University Press, 1970), 106. Hermann Cohen, "Grenzsperre" (1916) in JS2: 378–80, 378. My assessment of Cohen here accords with that of Harry van der Linden, "Hermann Cohen's Political Philosophy and the Communitarian Critique of Liberalism," available at http://digitalcommons.butler.edu/facsch_papers/66), 6. Published in French translation in "L'École de Marbourg," ed. Fabien Capeillères and Jean Kahn, special issue, *Cahiers de philosophie politique et juridique*, no. 26 (1994).

8 Kant, "Zum ewigen Frieden" AA8: 357–8. See Andreas Cassee, "Das Recht auf globale Bewegungsfreiheit. Eine Verteidigung," in *Soziale Gerechtigkeit heute. Proceedings of Kongress der Schweizerischen Vereinigung für Rechts- und Sozialphilosophie 2013* (Stuttgart: Steiner, 2015), and *Globale Bewegungsfreiheit: Ein philosophisches Plädoyer für offene Grenzen* (Berlin: Suhrkamp, 2016). Cassee discusses this famous principle of Kant, and notes that while Kant himself seems to think that it is compatible with some sort of limitation on freedom of movement across state boundaries, he makes no clear argument for this view (*Globale Bewegungsfreiheit*, 30). One of the points of departure of Cassee's project is to ask: From Kant's premise, is there in fact a valid argument to be made for restricting freedom of movement across state boundaries?

Jacques Derrida's writings on hospitality have been central to more radical interrogations of this notion. See *Adieu à Emmanuel Levinas* (Paris: Galilée, 1997); translated by Pascale-Anne Brault and Michael Naas as *Adieu to Emmanuel Levinas* (Stanford: Stanford University Press, 1999), and *De l'hospitalité. Anne Dufourmantelle invite Jacques Derrida à répondre* (Paris: Calmann-Lévy, 1997); translated by Rachel Bowlby as *Of Hospitality: Anne Dufourmantelle Invites Jacques Derrida to Respond* (Stanford: Stanford University Press, 2000); and Judith Still, *Derrida and Hospitality: Theory and Practice* (Edinburgh: Edinburgh University Press, 2010).

9 This historical context is described in Trude Maurer, "Medizinalpolizei und Antisemitismus. Die deutsche Politik der Grenzsperre gegen Ostjuden im Ersten Weltkrieg," *Jahrbücher für Geschichte Osteuropas*, Neue Folge, 33, no. 2 (1985); Sarah Panter, *Jüdische Erfahrungen und Loyalitätskonflikte im Ersten Weltkrieg* (Göttingen: Vandenhoeck & Ruprecht, 2014), 280–8; Egmont Zechlin, *Die deutsche Politik und die Juden im Ersten Weltkrieg* (Göttingen: Vandenhoeck & Ruprecht, 1969), 260–78; Tracey Hayes Norrell, *For the Honor of Our Fatherland: German Jews on the Eastern Front During the Great War* (Lanham, MD: Lexington Books, 2017); and Steven E. Aschheim,

essays, which are always suffused with a patriotic embrace of Germany's aims in this war, an embrace that is part and parcel of Cohen's approving citation of Kant's affirmation of the human right to infinite dispersal on the earth's surface. Just as he had in his Dreyfus essay, Cohen frames his plea against closing the borders with a formulation reflecting a core principle of his ethico-legal theory: A significance of the war, he writes, is that it allows Germany to have "a share in the task of international law [*völkerrechtliche Aufgabe*]," a cosmopolitical task. "Task" for Cohen always comprises a task of generative inquiry.[10] The law here is not encountered as a preexisting, ready-to-hand instrument to be wielded; rather, Cohen, in his ethical and political and "Jewish" writings, presents legal facta as a starting point for interrogating the legal order for the purpose of achieving a greater universal justice. Thus, the ethical "ideal" of a universal "humanity" – according to which, for example, each person has no greater right to be in a place than any other – must be pursued and elaborated juridically and politically. Commenting on Kant's application of the idea of a cosmopolitan "constitution" to the right to hospitality, Cohen writes: "The positive state must be guided by the ideal image of the universal state," even when it is constrained by "political conditions."[11] The figure of the neighbor-stranger brought to the fore by Cohen's philosophy of ethics out of law likewise calls "positive" polities to account, such that they, and we, may have a share in realizing the task of universal justice.

"Strange Encounter. Germany, World War I and the Ostjuden," chap. 7 in *Brothers and Strangers: The East European Jew in German and German Jewish Consciousness, 1800–1923* (Madison: University of Wisconsin Press, 1983), esp. 173–8.

The essay "Grenzsperre" is discussed by Hartwig Wiedebach in "Das Problem eines einheitlichen Kulturbewußtseins. Zur Person des jüdisch-deutschen Philosophen Hermann Cohen," in *Aschkenas. Zeitschrift für Geschichte und Kultur der Juden* 10, no. 2 (2000): 424–6, and in *Die Bedeutung der Nationalität für Hermann Cohen* (Hildesheim: Olms, 1997), 25–6; translated by William Templer as *The National Element in Hermann Cohen's Philosophy and Religion* (Leiden: Brill, 2012), 17–18.

10 On the infinite, cosmopolitical task, including its relation to prophetic messianism, see ErW 405–11, and the discussion in Pierfrancesco Fiorato, "Notes on Future and History in Hermann Cohen's Anti-Eschatological Messianism," in *Hermann Cohen's Critical Idealism*, ed. Reinier Munk (Heidelberg: Springer, 2005). Cohen's notion of "infinite task" is itself indebted to Kant's understanding of practical philosophy as entailing an infinite progress toward fulfillment of the moral law. Cf. Kenneth Seeskin, "Jewish Neo-Kantianism: Hermann Cohen," in *History of Jewish Philosophy*, ed. Daniel H. Frank and Oliver Leaman (London: Routledge, 1997), 700.

11 "Grenzsperre," JS2: 378; Kant, "Zum ewigen Frieden," AA8: 358.

Bibliography

Adelmann, Dieter. *Einheit des Bewusstseins als Grundproblem der Philosophie Hermann Cohens* (1968). 2nd rev. ed. Edited by Görge K. Hasselhoff and Beate Ulrike La Sala. Potsdam: Universitätsverlag Potsdam, 2012.

– "H. Steinthal und Hermann Cohen." In Mosès and Wiedebach, *Hermann Cohen's Philosophy of Religion*, 1–33.

– *"Reinige dein Denken." Über den jüdischen Hintergrund der Philosophie von Hermann Cohen.* Edited by Görge K. Hasselhoff. Würzburg: Königshausen & Neumann, 2010.

– "Ursprüngliche Differenz. Zwischen Einzigkeit und Einheit im Denken von Hermann Cohen." *Archivio di Filosofia* 21 (2003): 19–40.

Adorisio, Chiara. "Philosophy of Religion or Political Philosophy? The Debate between Leo Strauss and Julius Guttmann." *European Journal of Jewish Studies* 1 (2007): 135–55.

– "Politische Philosophie als *Philosophia Prima.* Leo Strauss' Transformation von Hermann Cohens philosophischem Projekt." *Links. Rivista di letteratura e cultura tedesca* 7 (2007): 97–104.

Ahrberg, Edda, Alexander Fuhrmann, and Jutta Preiß. *Das Zuchthaus Coswig (Anhalt).* Magdeburg: Landesbeauftragter für die Unterlagen des Staatssicherheitsdienstes der ehemaligen Deutschen Demokratischen Republik in Sachsen-Anhalt, 2007.

Albertini, Francesca Yardenit. *Die Konzeption des Messias bei Maimonides und die frühmittelalterliche islamische Philosophie.* Berlin: de Gruyter, 2009.

– *Das Verständnis des Seins bei Hermann Cohen: Vom Neukantianismus zu einer jüdischen Religionsphilosophie.* Würzburg: Königshausen & Neumann, 2003.

Alexy, Robert, Lukas H. Meyer, Stanley L. Paulson, and Gerhard Sprenger, eds. *Neukantianismus und Rechtsphilosophie.* Baden-Baden: Nomos, 2002.

Altmann, Alexander. "Commandments, Reasons For." In *Encyclopaedia Judaica*, 2nd ed. (2007).

– "Commentary." In Moses Mendelssohn, *Jerusalem, Or on Religious Power and Judaism*. Translated by Allan Arkush, 143–240. Waltham, MA: Brandeis University Press, 1983.

– "Hermann Cohens Begriff der Korrelation." In *In Zwei Welten. Siegfried Moses zum fünfundziebzigsten Geburtstag*. Edited by Hans Tramer. Tel Aviv: Bitaon, 1962. Also included in Holzhey, ed., *Hermann Cohen*.

Aschheim, Steven E. "Strange Encounter. Germany, World War I and the Ostjuden." Chap. 7 in *Brothers and Strangers: The East European Jew in German and German Jewish Consciousness, 1800–1923*. Madison: University of Wisconsin Press, 1983.

Avneri, Zvi. "Eisenmenger, Johann Andreas." In *Encyclopaedia Judaica*, 2nd ed. (2007).

Barash, Jeffrey Andrew. "Politics and Theology: The Debate on Zionism between Hermann Cohen and Martin Buber." In *Dialogue as a Trans-disciplinary Concept: Martin Buber's Philosophy of Dialogue and its Contemporary Reception*, edited by Paul Mendes-Flohr, 49–59. Berlin: de Gruyter, 2015.

Bartuschat, W. "Gesetz, moralisches." In *Historisches Wörterbuch der Philosophie*. Vol. 3. Edited by Joachim Ritter, Karlfried Gründer, and Gottfried Gabriel, cols. 516–19. Basel: Schwabe, 1974.

Batnitzky, Leora. "Hans Kelsen and Hermann Cohen: From Theology to Law and Back." In *The Foundation of the Juridico-Political: Concept Formation in Kelsen and Weber*, edited by Ian Bryan, Peter Langford, and John McGarry, 40–60. New York: Routledge, 2016.

– "Hermann Cohen and Leo Strauss." In Gibbs, ed., "Hermann Cohen's Ethics." Special issue, *Journal of Jewish Thought and Philosophy* 13 (2004), nos. 1–3: 187–212.

– "The Possibility of Premodern Rationalism: Strauss's Transformation of Hermann Cohen." Chap. 5 in *Leo Strauss and Emmanuel Levinas: Philosophy and the Politics of Revelation*. Cambridge: Cambridge University Press, 2006.

Batnitzky, Leora, and Yonatan Y. Brafman. *Jewish Legal Theories: Writings on State, Religion, and Morality*. Waltham, MA: Brandeis University Press, 2018.

Baumgardt, David. "The Ethics of Lazarus and Steinthal." *Leo Baeck Institute Year Book* 2 (1957): 205–17.

Beer, Udo. *Die Juden, das Recht und die Republik. Verbandswesen und Rechtsschutz, 1919–1933*. Frankfurt am Main: Peter Lang, 1986.

– "The Protection of Jewish Civil Rights in the Weimar Republic. Jewish Self-Defence Through Legal Action." *Leo Baeck Institute Year Book* 33 (1988): 149–76.

Beiser, Frederick C. *Hermann Cohen: An Intellectual Biography*. Oxford: Oxford University Press, 2018.

– "Weimar Philosophy and the Fate of Neo-Kantianism." In *Weimar Thought: A Contested Legacy*, edited by Peter E. Gordon and John P. McCormick, 115–32. Princeton: Princeton University Press, 2013.

– "The Young Hermann Cohen." Chap. 12 in *The Genesis of Neo-Kantianism, 1796–1880.* Oxford: Oxford University Press, 2014.

Belke, Ingrid, ed. *Moritz Lazarus und Heymann Steinthal. Die Begründer der Völkerpsychologie in ihren Briefen.* Tübingen: Mohr Siebeck, 1971.

Bergmann, Samuel Hugo. *Faith and Reason: An Introduction to Modern Jewish Thought* (1961). Translated and edited by Alfred Jospe. New York: Schocken, 1963.

Berlin, Adele, ed. *The Oxford Dictionary of the Jewish Religion*, 2nd ed. New York: Oxford University Press, 2011.

Bienenstock, Myriam. *Cohen face à Rosenzweig. Débat sur la pensée allemande.* Paris: Vrin, 2009.

– "Hermann Cohen über Freiheit und Selbstbestimmung." In *Religious Apologetics – Philosophical Argumentation*, edited by Yossef Schwartz and Volkhard Krech, 503–30. Tübingen: Mohr Siebeck, 2004.

– ed. *Hermann Cohen. Le concept de philosophie.* Paris: Cerf, 2014.

– ed. "Néokantisme et sciences morales." Special Issue, *Revue Germanique Internationale* 6 (2007).

Birnbaum, Nathan [Mathias Acher, pseud.]. "Jüdische Autonomie." *Ost und West* 6, no. 1 (January 1906): 1–6.

Bjarup, Jes. "Continental Perspectives on Natural Law Theory and Legal Positivism." In *The Blackwell Guide to the Philosophy of Law and Legal Theory*, edited by Martin P. Golding and William A. Edmundson, 287–99. Malden, MA: Blackwell, 2005.

Black, Antony. "Editor's Introduction" to Otto von Gierke, *Community in Historical Perspective: A Translation of Selections from* Das deutsche Genossenschaftsrecht, xiv–xxx. Cambridge: Cambridge University Press, 1990.

Blackman, Philip, ed. *Mishnayoth*, 2nd rev. ed. Vol. 4: *Order Nezikin.* New York: Judaica Press, 1963.

Blaschke, Olaf. *Katholizismus und Antisemitismus im Deutschen Kaiserreich.* 2nd rev. ed. Göttingen: Vandenhoeck & Ruprecht, 1999.

Bloch, Joseph S. *Erinnerungen aus meinem Leben.* Vol. 1. Vienna: R. Löwit, 1922.

Bluhm, Harald. *Die Ordnung der Ordnung. Das politische Philosophieren von Leo Strauss.* Berlin: Akademie Verlag, 2002.

Boehlich, Walter, ed. *Der Berliner Antisemitismusstreit.* Frankfurt am Main: Insel, 1965.

Bouretz, Pierre. "Autour du concept de Noachide: religion et altérité selon H. Cohen." In "Religion et éthique dans la pensée de Hermann Cohen." Special issue, *Revue de l'histoire des religions* 221, no. 4 (October–December 2004): 391–420.

– *Témoins du futur: philosophie et messianisme.* Paris: Gallimard, 2003.

Brämer, Andreas. "Introduction: The Jewish-Theological Seminary of Breslau, the 'Science of Judaism' and the Development of a Middle-of-the-Road Current in Religious Judaism." *transversal* 14, no. 1 (2016): 23–5.

– "Jüdische 'Glaubenswissenschaft'. Zacharias Frankels rechtshistorische Forschungen als Herausforderung der Orthodoxie." In *Die "Wissenschaft des Judentums": eine Bestandsaufnahme*, edited by Thomas Meyer and Andreas Kilcher, 79–94. Paderborn: Wilhelm Fink, 2015.

Brafman, Yonatan Y. "New Developments in Modern Jewish Thought: From Theology to Law and Back Again." In *The Cambridge Companion to Judaism and Law*, edited by Christine Hayes, 287–314. New York: Cambridge University Press, 2017.

Brandt, Reinhard, and Franz Orlik, eds. *Philosophisches Denken – politisches Wirken. Hermann-Cohen-Kolloquium Marburg 1992.* Hildesheim: Olms, 1993.

von Braun, Christina. "Und der Feind ist Fleisch geworden. Der rassistische Antisemitismus." In *Der ewige Judenhass. Christlicher Antijudaismus, Deutschnationale Judenfeindlichkeit, Rassistischer Antisemitismus*, edited by Christina von Braun and Ludger Heid, 149–213. 2nd rev. ed. Berlin: Philo, 2000.

Brenner, Michael. "Between Hermann Cohen and Karl Marx: The Jewish Dimension of Kurt Eisner's Revolution in Bavaria, 1918–19." *Modern Judaism* 40, no. 1 (February 2020): 17–36.

Breslauer, Bernhard. *Die Zurücksetzung der Juden an den Universitäten Deutschlands.* Berlin: Levy, 1911.

Briman, Aron [Dr. Justus, pseud.]. *Judenspiegel.* Paderborn: Bonifacius, 1883.

Brocke, Michael. "Hermann Cohen gedenkt seines Vaters." *Kalonymos. Beiträge zur deutsch-jüdischen Geschichte aus dem Salomon Ludwig Steinheim-Institut an der Universität Duisburg-Essen* 21, no. 1 (2018): 10–12.

Brown, Wendy. *Regulating Aversion: Tolerance in the Age of Identity and Empire.* Princeton: Princeton University Press, 2006.

Brumlik, Micha. *"... ein Funke des römischen Gedankens ..." Leo Strauss' Kritik an Hermann Cohen.* Heidelberg: Universitätsverlag, 2008.

– "Patriotismus und ethischer Unsterblichkeitsglaube: Hermann Cohen." In *Vom Jenseits: jüdisches Denken in der europäischen Geistesgeschichte*, edited by Eveline Goodman-Thau, 129–42. Berlin: Akademie Verlag, 1997.

– "1915. In *Deutschtum und Judentum* Hermann Cohen applies neo-Kantian philosophy to the German Jewish Question." In *Yale Companion to Jewish Writing and Thought in German Culture 1096–1996*, edited by Sander L. Gilman and Jack Zipes, 336–42. New Haven: Yale University Press, 1997.

Caborn, Joannah. "On the Methodology of Dispositive Analysis." *Critical Approaches to Discourse Analysis Across Disciplines* 1 (2007): 112–23.

Carrino, Agostino. *Das Recht zwischen Reinheit und Realität. Hermann Cohen und die philosophischen Grundlagen der Rechtslehre Kelsens.* Baden-Baden: Nomos, 2011.

Cassee, Andreas. *Globale Bewegungsfreiheit: Ein philosophisches Plädoyer für offene Grenzen.* Berlin: Suhrkamp, 2016.

– "Das Recht auf globale Bewegungsfreiheit. Eine Verteidigung." In *Soziale Gerechtigkeit heute. Proceedings of Kongress der Schweizerischen Vereinigung für Rechts- und Sozialphilosophie 2013*, 55–77. Stuttgart: Steiner, 2015.

Chacón, Rodrigo. "Reading Strauss from the Start: On the Heideggerian Origins of 'Political Philosophy.'" *European Journal of Political Theory* 9, no. 3 (July 2010): 287–307.

Chignell, Andrew. "Introduction: On Going Back to Kant." *Philosophical Forum* 39, no. 2 (Summer 2008): 109–24.

Cohen, Hermann. [See also "Abbreviations" in this volume.]

– "Biographisches Vorwort des Herausgebers" (1882). In Lange, *Geschichte des Materialismus*. 7th ed. Leipzig: Baedeker, 1902.

– *Briefe an August Stadler*, edited by Hartwig Wiedebach. Basel: Schwabe, 2015.

– "Immanuel Kant. Zu seinem hundertjährigen Todestage (12. Februar 1904)." *Allgemeine Zeitung des Judentums* (12 February 1904), 76–7.

– *Der Nächste. Vier Abhandlungen über das Verhalten von Mensch zu Mensch nach der Lehre des Judentums.* Berlin: Schocken, 1935.

– *Die Nächstenliebe im Talmud. Ein Gutachten dem Königlichen Landgerichte zu Marburg erstattet.* Marburg: Elwert, 1888. Also in JS1.

– *Das Prinzip der Infinitesimal-Methode und seine Geschichte. Ein Kapitel zur Grundlegung der Erkenntniskritik.* 1st ed. 1883. 2nd ed. in SPZ 2: 1–169. 3rd ed., edited by Werner Flach, Frankfurt: Suhrkamp, 1968. 4th ed., *Werke* 5/I (1984), edited by Peter Schulthess. 5th ed., edited by Johannes Kleinbeck, Vienna: Turia & Kant, 2013.

– *Reflexionen und Notizen*, edited by Hartwig Wiedebach. In *Werke, Supplementa* vol. 1. Hildesheim: Olms, 2003.

– *Spinoza on State and Religion, Judaism and Christianity.* Translated by Robert S. Schine. Jerusalem: Shalem Press, 2014.

Collins, John J. "Love Your Neighbor: How It Became the Golden Rule." TheTorah.com. 2020.

Cooper, Julie E. "The Turn to Tradition in the Study of Jewish Politics." *Annual Review of Political Science* 19 (2016): 67–87.

Dahm, Volker. *Das jüdische Buch im Dritten Reich.* 2nd rev. ed. Munich: C.H. Beck, 1993.

von Daniels, Justus. *Religiöses Recht als Referenz. Jüdisches Recht im rechtswissenschaftlichen Vergleich.* Tübingen: Mohr Siebeck, 2009.

Delitzsch, Franz. "Lässt sich die Ansicht, dass die Juden Christenblut zu rituellem Zwecke verwenden, irgendwie aus dem Talmud begründen?" In *Christliche Zeugnisse gegen die Blutbeschuldigung der Juden*, edited by Leopold Lipschitz, 12–18. Berlin: Walther & Apolant, 1882.

– *Rohling's Talmudjude beleuchtet.* Leipzig: Dörffling & Franke, 1881.

– *Schachmatt den Blutlügnern Rohling und Justus.* Erlangen: Andreas Deicher, 1883.

Derrida, Jacques. *Adieu à Emmanuel Levinas.* Paris: Galilée, 1997. Translated by Pascale-Anne Brault and Michael Naas as *Adieu to Emmanuel Levinas.* Stanford: Stanford University Press, 1999.

– *De l'hospitalité. Anne Dufourmantelle invite Jacques Derrida à répondre.* Paris: Calmann-Lévy, 1997. Translated by Rachel Bowlby as *Of Hospitality: Anne Dufourmantelle invites Jacques Derrida to Respond.* Stanford: Stanford University Press, 2000.
– "Interpretations at war. Kant, le Juif, l'Allemand" (1989). In *Psyché: Inventions de l'autre II,* rev. ed. Paris: Galileé, 1987–2003. Translated by Moshe Ron and Dana Hollander as "Interpretations at War: Kant, the Jew, the German." In *Psyche: Inventions of the Other.* Vol. 2, edited by Peggy Kamuf and Elizabeth Rottenberg. Stanford: Stanford University Press, 2007.
Deuber-Mankowsky, Astrid. "Einleitung." Hermann Cohen, *Das Prinzip der Infinitesimal-Methode und seine Geschichte. Ein Kapitel zur Grundlegung der Erkenntniskritik,* 5th ed., edited by Johannes Kleinbeck. Vienna: Turia & Kant, 2013.
– *Der frühe Walter Benjamin und Hermann Cohen. Jüdische Werte. Kritische Philosophie. Vergängliche Erfahrung.* Berlin: Vorwerk 8, 2000.
– "Kommentar zu Hermann Cohen." In *Theorien über Judenhass – eine Denkgeschichte: Kommentierte Quellenedition (1781–1931),* edited by Birgit Erdle and Werner Konitzer, 215–27. Frankfurt am Main: Campus Verlag, 2015.
Diamond, James A. "Exegetical Idealization: Hermann Cohen's Religion of Reason Out of the Sources of Maimonides." In Hughes, "Ancients and Moderns in Jewish Philosophy: The Case of Hermann Cohen." Special issue, *Journal of Jewish Thought and Philosophy* 18, no. 1 (January 2010): 49–73.
Diner, Dan, and Michael Stolleis, eds. *Hans Kelsen and Carl Schmitt: A Juxtaposition.* Gerlingen: Bleicher, 1999.
Don, Arie. "The Role of the Jewish Law in Moses Mendelssohn's and Hermann Cohen's Philosophies of Judaism." Ph.D. diss., Concordia University, 1984.
Dufour, Eric. "Introduction: L'interprétation cohénienne de la 'Critique de la raison pure.'" In Hermann Cohen, *Commentaire de la 'Critique de la raison pure' de Kant.* Translated and edited by Eric Dufour, 1–36. Paris: Cerf, 2000.
Dyzenhaus, David. *Legality and Legitimacy: Carl Schmitt, Hans Kelsen and Hermann Heller in Weimar.* Oxford: Clarendon Press, 1997.
Edel, Geert. "The Hypothesis of the Basic Norm: Hans Kelsen and Hermann Cohen." In *Normativity and Norms: Critical Perspectives on Kelsenian Themes,* edited by Stanley L. Paulson and Bonnie Litschewski Paulson, 195–219. Oxford: Clarendon, 1998.
– "Kantianismus oder Platonismus? Hypothesis als Grundbegriff der Philosophie Cohens." *Il cannocchiale. Rivista di studi filosofici* no. 1–2 (1991): 59–87.
– *Von der Vernunftkritik zur Erkenntnislogik. Die Entwicklung der theoretischen Philosophie Hermann Cohens.* Freiburg/Munich: Alber, 1988.
Edgar, Scott. "Hermann Cohen" (2010/2015). *Stanford Encyclopedia of Philosophy.* Fall 2015 Edition. https://plato.stanford.edu/archives/fall2015/entries/cohen/

Eisner, Kurt. "Hermann Cohen" (1912). *Die halbe Macht den Räten. Ausgewählte Aufsätze und Reden*, edited by Renate and Gerhard Schmolze. Cologne: Jakob Hegner, 1969.

Elbogen, Ismar, Benzion Kellermann, and Eugen Mittwoch, eds. *Judaica: Festschrift zu Hermann Cohens siebzigstem Geburtstage.* Berlin: Bruno Cassirer, 1912.

Encyclopaedia Judaica. 2nd ed. Edited by Michael Berenbaum and Fred Skolnik. Detroit: Macmillan Reference USA, 2007.

Entscheidungen des Reichsgerichts in Strafsachen 6. Berlin: de Gruyter, 1882.

Epstein, Isidore, ed. *The Babylonian Talmud.* 18 vols. London: Soncino Press, 1961.

Erlewine, Robert. *Monotheism and Tolerance: Recovering a Religion of Reason.* Bloomington: Indiana University Press, 2010.

Fackenheim, Emil. *Hermann Cohen – After Fifty Years.* Leo Baeck Memorial Lecture 12. New York: Leo Baeck Institute, 1969.

Fagenblat, Michael. "The Concept of Neighbor in Jewish and Christian Ethics." In *The Jewish Annotated New Testament*, edited by Amy-Jill Levine and Marc Zvi Brettler, 541–3. Oxford: Oxford University Press, 2011.

"Die Familie Steinthal vom Jahre 1720 bis 1935" (family tree). 1935–1961. AR 1393 VI/4. Leo Baeck Institute Archives.

Feierstein, Liliana Ruth. *Von Schwelle zu Schwelle: Einblicke in den didaktisch-historischen Umgang mit dem Anderen aus der Perspektive jüdischen Denkens.* Bremen: Edition Lumière, 2010.

Fiorato, Pierfrancesco. *Geschichtliche Ewigkeit: Ursprung und Zeitlichkeit in der Philosophie Hermann Cohens.* Würzburg: Königshausen & Neumann, 1993.

– "Notes on Future and History in Hermann Cohen's Anti-Eschatological Messianism." In Munk, *Hermann Cohen's Critical Idealism*, 133–60.

– "Ungeschriebenes Gesetz und schriftliche Lehre. Hermann Cohen über den Palimpsest der Vernunft." *Deutsche Zeitschrift für Philosophie* 59, no. 2 (April 2011): 283–93.

Fiorato, Pierfrancesco and Peter A. Schmid, eds. *"Ich bestreite den Hass im Menschenherzen." Überlegungen zu Hermann Cohens Begriff des grundlosen Hasses.* Basel: Schwabe, 2015.

Foucault, Michel. "Le jeu de Michel Foucault" (1977). In *Dits et écrits*, vol 3: *1976–1979*, edited by D. Defert and F. Ewald. Paris: Gallimard, 1994. Translated by Colin Gordon as "The Confession of the Flesh." In *Power/Knowledge: Selected Interviews and Other Writings, 1972–1977*, edited by Colin Gordon, 194–228. New York: Pantheon, 1980.

– *La Volonté de savoir.* Paris: Gallimard, 1976. Translated by Robert Hurley as *The History of Sexuality Volume I: An Introduction.* New York: Pantheon, 1978.

Frank, Daniel H., ed. *Autonomy and Judaism. The Individual and the Community in Jewish Philosophical Thought.* Albany: State University of New York Press, 1992.

– ed. *A People Apart: Chosenness and Ritual in Jewish Philosophical Thought.* Albany: State University of New York Press, 1993.

Fraenkel, Abraham Adolf. *Lebenskreise. Aus den Erinnerungen eines jüdischen Mathematikers.* Stuttgart: Deutsche Verlags-Anstalt, 1967.

Franks, Paul. "Rabbinic Idealism and Kabbalistic Realism: Jewish Dimensions of Idealism and Idealist Dimensions of Judaism." In *The Impact of Idealism: The Legacy of Post-Kantian German Thought.* Vol. 4: *Religion,* edited by Nicholas Adams, 219–45. Cambridge: Cambridge University Press, 2013.

– "Sinai since Spinoza: Reflections on Revelation in Modern Jewish Thought." In *The Significance of Sinai: Traditions About Sinai and Divine Revelation in Judaism and Christianity,* edited by George J. Brooke, Hindy Najman, and Loren T. Stuckenbruck, 333–54. Leiden: Brill, 2008.

Franz, Georg. *Liberalismus. Die deutschliberale Bewegung in der Habsburgischen Monarchie.* Munich: Callwey, 1955.

Friedman, Richard Elliott. "Love Your Neighbor: Only Israelites or Everyone?" *Biblical Archaeology Review* 40, no. 5 (September/October 2014): 24–36.

Fuchs, Eugen. *Um Deutschtum und Judentum. Gesammelte Reden und Aufsätze (1894–1919).* Frankfurt am Main: J. Kauffmann, 1919.

Gadamer, Hans-Georg. "Hermeneutik und Historismus" (1965). In *Gesammelte Werke.* Vol. 2. 2nd ed. Tübingen: Mohr, 1993. Translated by Joel Weinsheimer and Donald G. Marshall as "Hermeneutics and Historicism." In *Truth and Method,* 2nd rev. ed., 505–41. New York: Crossroad, 1989.

– *Wahrheit und Methode* (1960), 6th ed. In *Gesammelte Werke.* Vol. 1. Tübingen: Mohr, 1989. Translated by Joel Weinsheimer and Donald G. Marshall as *Truth and Method,* 2nd rev. ed. New York: Crossroad, 1989.

Gibbs, Robert. *Correlations in Rosenzweig and Levinas.* Princeton: Princeton University Press, 1992.

– ed. "Hermann Cohen's Ethics." Special issue, *Journal of Jewish Thought and Philosophy* 13, nos. 1–2 (2004).

– "Hermann Cohen's Messianism: The History of the Future." In Holzhey et al., *"Religion der Vernunft aus den Quellen des Judentums,"* 331–49.

– "Jurisprudence Is the Organon of Ethics: Kant and Cohen on Ethics, Law, and Religion." In Munk, *Hermann Cohen's Critical Idealism,* 193–230.

– "Philosophy and Law: Questioning Justice." In *The Ethical,* edited by Edith Wyschogrod and Gerald P. McKenny, 101–16. Malden, MA: Blackwell, 2003.

Gierke, Otto von. *Das deutsche Genossenschaftsrecht.* Vol. 1. Berlin: Weidmann, 1868. Translated by Mary Fischer as *Community in Historical Perspective.* Cambridge: Cambridge University Press, 1990.

– *Deutsches Privatrecht.* Vol. 1. Leipzig: Duncker & Humblot, 1895.

– *Die Genossenschaftstheorie und die deutsche Rechtsprechung.* Berlin: Weidmann, 1887.

– *Das Wesen der menschlichen Verbände.* Berlin: Schade, 1902.

Gigliotti, Gianna. "Ethik und das Faktum der Rechtswissenschaft bei Hermann Cohen." In Holzhey, *Ethischer Sozialismus,* 166–84.

Giovanelli, Marco. "Hermann Cohen's *Das Princip der Infinitesimal-Methode*: The History of an Unsuccessful Book." *Studies in History and Philosophy of Science* 58 (2016): 9–23.

Goodman, Lenn E. *Love Thy Neighbor As Thyself.* Oxford: Oxford University Press, 2008.

– "Rational Law/Ritual Law." In Frank, *A People Apart,* 109–200.

Greive, Hermann. *Geschichte des modernen Antisemitismus in Deutschland.* Darmstadt: Wissenschaftliche Buchgesellschaft, 1983.

– "Der Talmud, Zielscheibe und Ausgangspunkt antisemitischer Polemik." In *Antisemitismus. Erscheinungsformen der Judenfeindschaft gestern und heute,* edited by Günther B. Ginzel, 304–10. Bielefeld: Wissenschaft und Politik, 1991.

Groß, Johannes T. *Ritualmordbeschuldigungen gegen Juden im Deutschen Kaiserreich 1871–1914.* Berlin: Metropol, 2002.

Güdemann, Moritz. *Nächstenliebe: Ein Beitrag zur Erklärung des Matthäus-Evangeliums.* Vienna: R. Löwit, 1890.

– "Neutestamentliche Studien. I. Jüdische und christliche Nächstenliebe." *Monatsschrift für Geschichte und Wissenschaft des Judentums* 37 [Neue Folge, 1. Jg.], no. 4 (1892–1893): 153–64.

Gurganus, Albert E. *Kurt Eisner: A Modern Life.* Rochester, NY: Camden House, 2018.

Gurwitsch, A[ron]. "Hermann Cohen und der jüdische Zeitgeist." *Frankfurter Israelitisches Gemeindeblatt* 8, no. 9 (May 1930): 359–61.

HaCohen, Ran. "'Gehörst du zu uns oder zu unsern Feinden?' (Josua 5,13). Die jüdische Auseinandersetzung mit der 'Höheren Bibelkritik.'" Translated by Görge K. Hasselhoff. In *Die Entdeckung des Christentums in der Wissenschaft des Judentums,* edited by Görge K. Hasselhoff, 63–100. Berlin: de Gruyter, 2010.

– *Reclaiming the Hebrew Bible: German-Jewish Reception of Biblical Criticism.* Translated by M. Engel. Berlin: de Gruyter, 2010.

Hamburger, Ernest. *Juden im öffentlichen Leben Deutschlands.* Tübingen: Mohr Siebeck, 1968.

Hartston, Barnet P. *Sensationalizing the Jewish Question: Anti-Semitic Trials and the Press in the Early German Empire.* Leiden: Brill, 2005.

Harvey, Steven. "Love." In *Contemporary Jewish Religious Thought. Original Essays on Critical Concepts, Movements, and Beliefs,* edited by Arthur A. Cohen and Paul Mendes-Flohr, 557–63. New York: Free Press, 1987.

Hasselhoff, Görge, and Knut Martin Stünkel. Introduction to Hermann Cohen, "Germanness and Judaism." In *Religious Dynamics under the Impact of Imperialism and Colonialism: A Sourcebook,* edited by Björn Bentlage et al., 486–502. Leiden: Brill, 2017.

Hecht, Cornelia. *Deutsche Juden und Antisemitismus in der Weimarer Republik.* Bonn: Dietz, 2003.

Heidegger, Martin. *Die Grundprobleme der Phänomenologie.* In *Gesamtausgabe.* Vol. 24. Frankfurt am Main: Klostermann, 1975. Translated by Albert Hofstadter as *The Basic Problems of Phenomenology*, rev. ed. Bloomington: Indiana University Press, 1988.

Heinemann, Isaac. *The Reasons for the Commandments in Jewish Thought: From the Bible to the Renaissance* (1949–56). Translated by Leonard Levin. Boston: Academic Studies Press, 2008.

Heis, Jeremy. "Neo-Kantianism." *Stanford Encyclopedia of Philosophy.* Summer 2018 Edition. https://plato.stanford.edu/archives/sum2018/entries/neo-kantianism.

Hellwing, Isak A. *Der konfessionelle Antisemitismus im 19. Jahrhundert in Österreich.* Vienna: Herder, 1972.

Herrera, Carlos-Miguel. *Le droit, le politique: autour de Max Weber, Hans Kelsen, Carl Schmitt.* Paris: L'Harmattan, 1995.

Hertzberg, J. "Die 15 Grundsätze der jüdischen Sittenlehre. Ihre Entstehung und ihre Würdigung." *Allgemeine Zeitung des Judentums* 83, no. 18 (2 May 1919), 181–3.

Heusler, Andreas. *Institutionen des deutschen Privatrechts.* Vol. 1. Leipzig: Duncker & Humblot, 1885.

Hildesheimer, Hirsch [H.H.]. "Eine Anklage wegen Beschimpfung der jüdischen Religion." *Die Jüdische Presse.* 26 April 1888.

Hirsch, Emil G. "Golden Rule, The." In *The Jewish Encyclopedia*, vol. 6 (1904).

Hirschfeld, H.S. "Pflichten und Gesetze der Noachiden. "*Jeschurun. Zeitschrift fur die Wissenschaft des Judenthums* 4 (1864): 1–19.

Hoffmann, Daniel. "Bemerkungen zum Begriff des Nächsten und des Feindes im Anschluß an Cohen und Levinas." *Zeitschrift für Theologie und Kirche* 86 no. 2 (April 1989): 236–60.

Hollander, Dana. "Beyond the Law into the Law." In *Babel. Festschrift for Werner Hamacher*, edited by Aris Fioretos and Urs Engeler, 250–7. Basel: Verlag Urs Engeler, 2008.

– "Buber, Cohen, Rosenzweig, and the Politics of Cultural Affirmation." *Jewish Studies Quarterly* 13, no. 1 (March 2006): 87–103.

– "'But Does He Really Not Remember?' Cohen's Revaluing of the Spinozan Politicization of Judaism." In *G.W.F. Hegel und Hermann Cohen. Wege zur Versöhnung. Festschrift Myriam Bienenstock*, edited by Norbert Waszek, 209–22. Freiburg: Alber, 2018.

– "Debating the Criminalization of Blasphemy and the 'Protection' of Minority Religions: Section 166 of the German Criminal Code." Paper presented at American Academy of Religion Annual Meeting. Montreal, November 2009.

– "Ethical-Political Universality Out of the Sources of Judaism: Reading Hermann Cohen's 1888 Affidavit In and Out of Context." In *New Directions in*

Jewish Philosophy, edited by Aaron W. Hughes and Elliot R. Wolfson, 229–49. Bloomington: Indiana University Press, 2009.

– ed. "The Ethics of the Neighbor." Special issue, *Journal for Textual Reasoning* 4, no. 1 (November 2005). http://jtr.shanti.virginia.edu/volume-4-number-1/

– *Exemplarity and Chosenness: Rosenzweig and Derrida on the Nation of Philosophy.* Stanford: Stanford University Press, 2008.

– "Hermann Cohen über die Paradoxie des Gesetzes, aus den Quellen des Judentums und des Antijudaismus." Translated by Gunnar Nissen and Anette Purucker. In *Politische Theologie(n) der Demokratie. Das religiöse Erbe des Säkularen,* edited by Ino Augsberg and Karl-Heinz Ladeur, 128–54. Vienna: Turia & Kant, 2018.

– "Is the Other My Neighbor? Reading Levinas Alongside Hermann Cohen." In *The Exorbitant: Emmanuel Levinas Between Jews and Christians,* edited by Kevin Hart and Michael Signer, 90–107. New York: Fordham University Press, 2009.

– "Neighbor-Love as an Object of Protection? Hermann Cohen and Secularized Blasphemy Law." Paper presented at the Ludwig-Maximilians-University of Munich, May 2017.

– "'Plato Prophesied the Revelation': The Philosophico-Political Theology of Strauss's Philosophy and Law and the Guidance of Hermann Cohen." In Rashkover and Kavka, *Judaism, Liberalism, and Political Theology,* 66–107.

– "Some Remarks on Love and Law in Hermann Cohen's Ethics of the Neighbor." In Hollander, "The Ethics of the Neighbor." Special issue, *Journal for Textual Reasoning* 4, no. 1 (November 2005).

– "Understanding Law ('Gesetz' and 'Recht') in Hermann Cohen, with Help from the Early Strauss." In "New Directions in the Thought of Leo Strauss," edited by Jeffrey Bernstein. Special issue, *Idealistic Studies* 44, no. 2/3 (Summer/Fall 2014, published June 2015): 263–79.

Holzhey, Helmut. "Analytische Hermeneutik und reine Rechtslehre. Die Transformation neukantianischer Theoreme in die reine Rechtslehre Kelsens." In *Hermeneutik und Strukturtheorie des Rechts,* edited by Michael W. Fischer, Erhard Mock, and Helmut Schreiner. *Archiv für Rechts- und Sozialphilosophie,* Beiheft n.F. no. 20 (1984): 99–110.

– *Cohen und Natorp.* Vol. 1: *Ursprung und Einheit. Die Geschichte der "Marburger Schule" als Auseinandersetzung um die Logik des Denkens.* Vol. 2: *Der Marburger Neukantianismus in Quellen. Zeugnisse kritischer Lektüre. Briefe der Marburger. Dokumente zur Philosophiepolitik der Schule.* Basel: Schwabe, 1986.

– ed. *Ethischer Sozialismus. Zur politischen Philosophie des Neukantianismus.* Frankfurt am Main: Suhrkamp, 1994.

– "Gott und Seele. Zum Verhältnis von Metaphysikkritik und Religionsphilosophie bei Hermann Cohen." In Mosès and Wiedebach, *Hermann Cohen's Philosophy of Religion,* 85–104.

– "Heidegger und Cohen. Negativität im Denken des Ursprungs." In *In Erscheinung treten. Heinrich Barths Philosophie des Ästhetischen,* edited by Günther

Hauff, Hans Rudolf Schweizer, and Armin Wildermuth, 97–114. Basel: Schwabe, 1990.
– ed. *Hermann Cohen.* Bern: Peter Lang, 1994.
– "Hermann Cohen: Der Philosoph in Auseinandersetzung mit den politischen und gesellschaftlichen Problemen seiner Zeit." In Brandt and Orlik, eds., *Philosophisches Denken – politisches Wirken,* 15–36.
– "Neo-Kantianism and Phenomenology: The Problem of Intuition." In Makkreel and Luft, *Neo-Kantianism and Contemporary Philosophy,* 25–40.
– "Neukantianismus und Sozialismus. Einleitung." In Holzhey, *Ethischer Sozialismus,* 7–38.
– "Die praktische Philosophie des Marburger Neukantianismus. Versuch einer moralischen Bilanz." In *Neukantianismus. Perspektiven und Probleme,* edited by H. Holzhey and E. W. Orth, 136–55. Würzburg: Königshausen & Neumann, 1993.
– "Die Religion im System der Philosophie Cohens." In *Hermann Cohen und die Erkenntnistheorie,* edited by Wolfgang Marx and Ernst Wolfgang Orth, 147–65. Würzburg: Königshausen & Neumann, 2001.
– "Der systematische Ort der 'Religion der Vernunft' im Gesamtwerk Hermann Cohens." In Holzhey et al., *"Religion der Vernunft aus den Quellen des Judentums,"* 37–59.
– "Zu den Sachen selbst! Über das Verhältnis von Phänomenologie und Neukantianismus." In *Sinn und Erfahrung: phänomenologische Methoden in den Humanwissenschaften,* edited by Max Herzog and Carl Friedrich Graumann, 3–21. Heidelberg: Asanger, 1991.
– "Zwei Briefe Hermann Cohens an Heinrich von Treitschke." *Bulletin des Leo Baeck Instituts* 12 (1969): 183–204.
Holzhey, Helmut, Gabriel Motzkin, and Hartwig Wiedebach, eds. *"Religion der Vernunft aus den Quellen des Judentums" – Tradition und Ursprungsdenken in Hermann Cohens Spätwerk. Internationale Konferenz in Zürich 1998. "Religion of Reason Out of the Sources of Judaism": Tradition and the Concept of Origin in Hermann Cohen's Later Work.* Hildesheim: Olms, 2000.
Holzhey, Helmut, and Vilem Mudroch. *Historical Dictionary of Kant and Kantianism.* Lanham, MD: Scarecrow Press, 2005.
Hommes, Ulrich. "Das Problem des Rechts und die Philosophie der Subjektivität." *Philosophisches Jahrbuch* 70 (1962/63): 311–43.
Horster, Detlef. *Rechtsphilosophie zur Einführung.* Hamburg: Junius, 2002.
Horwitz, Maximilian. 1918. *Ein Vierteljahrhundert im Kampf um das Recht und die Zukunft der deutschen Juden.* Berlin: Verlag des Centralvereins deutscher Staatsbürger jüdischen Glaubens.
Horwitz, Rivka. "Two Models of Atonement in Cohen's 'Religion of Reason': One According to Ezekiel, the Other 'Joyful in Sufferings' According to Job."

In Holzhey et al., eds., *"Religion der Vernunft aus den Quellen des Judentums,"* 175–90.

Hughes, Aaron W., ed. "Ancients and Moderns in Jewish Philosophy: The Case of Hermann Cohen." Special issue, *Journal of Jewish Thought and Philosophy* 18, no. 1 (January 2010).

Hussain, Nadeem J.Z., and Lydia Patton. "Friedrich Albert Lange." *Stanford Encyclopedia of Philosophy.* Winter 2016 Edition. https://plato.stanford.edu/archives/win2016/entries/friedrich-lange/

Hyman, Arthur. "Maimonidean Elements in Hermann Cohen's Philosophy of Religion." In Munk, *Hermann Cohen's Critical Idealism,* 356–70.

Jacobsohn, Bernhard. *Der Deutsch-Israelitische Gemeindebund nach Ablauf des ersten Decenniums seit seiner Begründung von 1869 bis 1879. Eine Erinnerungsschrift.* Leipzig, 1879.

Jacobson, Arthur J., and Bernhard Schlink, eds. *Weimar: A Jurisprudence of Crisis, Philosophy, Social Theory, and the Rule of Law.* Berkeley: University of California Press, 2000.

Jahr, Christoph. "Ahlwardt on Trial: Reactions to the Antisemitic Agitation of the 1890s in Germany." Translated by Deborah Cohen. *Leo Baeck Institute Year Book* 48 (2003): 67–85.

– *Antisemitismus vor Gericht. Debatten über die juristische Ahndung judenfeindlicher Agitation in Deutschland (1879–1960).* Frankfurt am Main: Campus, 2011.

Janssens, David. *Between Athens and Jerusalem. Philosophy, Prophecy, and Politics in Leo Strauss's Early Thought.* Albany: State University of New York Press, 2008.

The Jewish Encyclopedia. 12 vols. New York: Funk and Wagnalls, 1901–1906.

Joel, Manuel. *Gegen Gildemeister.* Breslau: Schottlaender, 1884.

– *Meine in Veranlassung eines Processes abgegebenen Gutachten über den Talmud.* Breslau: Schletter'sche Buchhandlung, 1877.

JPS Hebrew-English Tanakh, 2nd ed. Philadelphia: Jewish Publication Society, 1999.

Kajon, Irene. "Merits and Demerits of Protestant Biblical Science in Hermann Cohen's *Jewish Writings." Jewish Studies Quarterly* 7, no. 4 (Feb. 2001): 399–412.

Kalmar, Ivan. "The *Völkerpsychologie* of Lazarus and Steinthal and the Modern Concept of Culture." *Journal of the History of Ideas* 48, no. 4 (October–December 1987): 671–90.

Kant, Immanuel. [See also "Abbreviations" in this volume.]

– *Grundlegung zur Metaphysik der Sitten.* AA vol. 4. Edited by Jens Timmermann. Göttingen: Vandenhoeck & Ruprecht, 2004. Translated by Mary Gregor as *Groundwork of the Metaphysics of Morals.* Cambridge: Cambridge University Press, 1997.

– *Kritik der praktischen Vernunft.* In AA vol. 5. Translated by Mary J. Gregor as *Critique of Practical Reason,* in *Practical Philosophy,* 133–272.

– *Kritik der reinen Vernunft*. Edited by Raymund Schmidt. Hamburg: Meiner, 1956. Translated by Paul Guyer and Allen W. Wood as *Critique of Pure Reason*. Cambridge: Cambridge University Press, 1998. Translated by Norman Kemp Smith as *Critique of Pure Reason*, 2nd rev. ed. New York: Palgrave Macmillan, 2007.
– *Die Metaphysik der Sitten*. In AA vol. 6. Translated by Mary J. Gregor as *The Metaphysics of Morals*, edited by Lara Denis. Cambridge: Cambridge University Press, 2017.
– *Practical Philosophy*. Translated and edited by Mary J. Gregor. Cambridge: Cambridge University Press, 1996.
– "Zum ewigen Frieden. Ein philosophischer Entwurf." AA vol. 8. Translated by Mary J. Gregor as "Toward Perpetual Peace." In *Practical Philosophy*. Translated by Hans Reiss as "Perpetual Peace: A Philosophical Sketch." In *Kant's Political Writings*. Cambridge: Cambridge University Press, 1970.
Kaplan, Lawrence. "Hermann Cohen's Theory of Sacrifice in 'Religion of Reason Out of the Sources of Judaism.'" In Holzhey et al., *"Religion der Vernunft aus den Quellen des Judentums,"* 191–204.
Karpeles, Gustav. "Der wissenschaftliche Antisemitismus." *Allgemeine Zeitung des Judentums* 58, no. 20 (18 May 1894): 229–30.
Kaufmann, Ekkehard. "Körperschaft (juristische Person)." In *Handwörterbuch zur deutschen Rechtsgeschichte*, vol. 2, edited by Adalbert Erler et al., cols. 1147–55. Berlin: Erich Schmidt, 1978.
Kavka, Martin. *Jewish Messianism and the History of Philosophy*. Cambridge: Cambridge University Press, 2004.
Kellerman, Benzion. "Hermann Cohens 'Ethik des reinen Willens.'" *Allgemeine Zeitung des Judentums* (1905), printed serially in issues no. 3, 5, 7, 9, 11, 14, 17, 18, and 21.
Kellner, Menachem. "Torah and Science in Modern Jewish Thought: Steven Schwarzschild vs Yeshayahu Leibowitz." In *Torah et science: perspectives historiques et théoriques: mélanges offerts à Charles Touati*, edited by Gilbert Dahan, Gad Freudenthal, and Jean-Pierre Rothschild, 228–37. Leuven: Peeters, 2001.
Kelsen, Hans. *Hauptprobleme der Staatsrechtslehre, entwickelt aus der Lehre vom Rechtssatze*. 2nd ed. 1923. Reprint, Aalen: Scientia, 1960.
– *Reine Rechtslehre*. 1st ed. (1934). Edited by Matthias Jestaedt. Tübingen: Mohr Siebeck, 2008. Translated by Bonnie Litschewski Paulson and Stanley Paulson as *Introduction to the Problems of Legal Theory*. Oxford: Clarendon, 1992.
– *Reine Rechtslehre*. 2nd rev. ed. Vienna: Deuticke, 1960.
Kepnes, Steven. "Liturgical Selfhood. Hermann Cohen's Religion of Reason." Chap. 2 in *Jewish Liturgical Reasoning*, 45–77. Oxford: Oxford University Press, 2007.
Kersting, Wolfgang. "Neukantianische Rechtsbegründung. Rechtsbegriff und richtiges Recht bei Cohen, Stammler und Kelsen." In Alexy et al., *Neukantianismus und Rechtsphilosophie*, 23–68.

Kieval, Hillel J. "Neighbors, Strangers, Readers: The Village and the City in Jewish-Gentile Conflict at the Turn of the Nineteenth Century." *Jewish Studies Quarterly* 12, no. 1 (2005): 61–79.

Kirchhoff, Alfred. *Zur Verständigung über die Begriffe Nation und Nationalität.* Halle: Buchhandlung des Waisenhauses, 1905.

Kittel, Rudolf. *Judenfeindschaft oder Gotteslästerung? Ein gerichtliches Gutachten.* Leipzig: Otto Wigand, 1914.

Klein, Thomas. *Der preußisch-deutsche Konservatismus und die Entstehung des politischen Antisemitismus in Hessen-Kassel (1866–1893).* Marburg: Elwert, 1995.

Koch, Franziska. *Die "chinesische Avantgarde" und das Dispositiv der Ausstellung: Konstruktionen chinesischer Gegenwartskunst im Spannungsfeld der Globalisierung.* Bielefeld: Transcript, 2016.

Kohler, George Y. "Against the Heteronomy of Halakhah: Hermann Cohen's Implicit Rejection of Kant's Critique of Judaism." *Dine Israel* 32 (2018): 189*–209*.

– "Finding God's Purpose: Hermann Cohen's Use of Maimonides to Establish the Authority of Mosaic Law." In Hughes, "Ancients and Moderns in Jewish Philosophy: The Case of Hermann Cohen." Special issue, *Journal of Jewish Thought and Philosophy* 18, no. 1 (January 2010): 75–105.

– "German Spirit and Holy Ghost – Treitschke's Call for Conversion of German Jewry: The Debate Revisited." *Modern Judaism* 30, no. 2 (May 2010): 172–95.

– "'Die Idealisierung des Diesseits' – Maimonides' Einfluss auf das Konzept des Messianismus in Hermann Cohens Essay *Charakteristik der Ethik Maimunis.*" *Judaica* 3 (2011): 241–62.

– "Manuel Joel in Defense of the Talmud. Liberal Responses to Religious Antisemitism in Nineteenth-Century Germany." *Hebrew Union College Annual* 79 (2008, published 2010): 141–63.

– *Reading Maimonides' Philosophy in 19th Century Germany: The Guide to Religious Reform.* Dordrecht: Springer, 2012.

Kohler, Kaufmann. "Brotherly Love." In *The Jewish Encyclopedia*, vol. 2 (1902).

– "Ceremonies and the Ceremonial Law." In *The Jewish Encyclopedia*, vol. 3 (1902).

– "Die Nächstenliebe im Judentum. Eine historische Studie." In Elbogen et al., *Judaica: Festschrift zu Hermann Cohens siebzigstem Geburtstage*, 469–80.

Köhnke, Klaus Christian. *Entstehung und Aufstieg des Neukantianismus: die deutsche Universitätsphilosophie zwischen Idealismus und Positivismus.* Frankfurt am Main: Suhrkamp, 1986. Translated by R.J. Hollingdale as *The Rise of Neo-Kantianism: German Academic Philosophy between Idealism and Positivism.* Cambridge: Cambridge University Press, 1991.

Kopp, Josef. *Zur Judenfrage nach den Akten des Prozesses Rohling-Bloch.* 3rd ed. Leipzig: Julius Klinkhardt, 1886.

Krieger, Karsten, ed. *Der "Berliner Antisemitismusstreit" 1879–1881. Eine Kontroverse um die Zugehörigkeit der deutschen Juden zur Nation. Eine kommentierte*

Quellenedition im Auftrag des Zentrums für Antisemitismusforschung. 2 vols. Munich: K.G. Saur, 2003.

Kristeller, Samuel. *Belegstellen zu den Grundsätzen der jüdischen Sittenlehre.* Berlin, 1891.

Krochmalnik, Daniel. "Der Streit um das jüdische Naturrecht. Maimonides, Spinoza, Mendelssohn und Cohen" (2000). In *Interesse am Judentum. Die Franz-Delitzsch-Vorlesungen, 1989–2008,* 240–61, edited by Jacobus Cornelis de Vos and Folker Siegert. Berlin: Lit Verlag, 2008.

de Lagarde, Paul. "Ein Gutachten." *Mittheilungen.* Vol. 3, 3–23. Göttingen: Dieterichsche Universitätsbuchhandlung, 1889.

Lange, Friedrich Albert. *Geschichte des Materialismus und Kritik seiner Bedeutung in der Gegenwart.* 1st ed., Iserlohn: Baedeker, 1866. 2nd ed., 1873–5. 3rd ed., London: Kegan Paul, 1925. Translated by Ernest Chester Thomas as *The History of Materialism and Criticism of Its Importance.* London: Trübner, 1877.

de Launay, Marc B. "La controverse sur l'antisémitisme: Cohen-Treitschke." In "Religion et éthique dans la pensée de Hermann Cohen." Special issue, *Revue de l'histoire des religions,* 221, no. 4 (October–December 2004): 445–58.

– *Hermann Cohen. Une réconstruction rationnelle du judaïsme.* Geneva: Labor et Fides, 2002.

– Preface to his translation of Hermann Cohen, "Germanité et judéité." *Pardès,* no. 5 (1987).

– "'Professorenkriegsliteratur.'" *Revue de métaphysique et de morale,* no. 3 (2001): 365–82.

La Sala, Beate Ulrike. *Hermann Cohens Spinoza-Rezeption.* Freiburg: Alber, 2012.

Lazarus, Moritz. *Die Ethik des Judentums.* Vol. 1. Frankfurt am Main: Kauffmann, 1898. Translated by Henrietta Szold as *The Ethics of Judaism,* Part 1. Philadelphia: Jewish Publication Society, 1900.

– *Unser Standpunkt. Zwei Reden an seine Religionsgenossen.* Berlin: Stuhr, 1881.

Lehr, Stefan. *Antisemitismus – religiöse Motive im sozialen Vorurteil.* Munich: Kaiser, 1974.

Leibowitz, Yeshayahu. *Judaism, Human Values, and the Jewish State,* edited by Eliezer Goldman. Cambridge, MA: Harvard University Press, 1992.

Leutenbauer, Siegfried. *Das Delikt der Gotteslästerung in der Bayerischen Gesetzgebung.* Cologne and Vienna: Böhlau, 1984.

Levinas, Emmanuel. "La tentation de tentation." In *Quatre lectures talmudiques.* Paris: Minuit, 1968. Translated by Annette Aronowicz as "The Temptation of Temptation," in *Nine Talmudic Readings.* Bloomington: Indiana University Press, 1990.

Levine, Amy-Jill. "Christian Privilege, Christian Fragility, and the Gospel of John." In *The Gospel of John and Jewish-Christian Relations,* edited by Adele Reinhartz, 87–110. Lanham, MD: Lexington Books/Fortress Academic, 2018.

Levine, Amy-Jill, and Marc Zvi Brettler, eds. *The Jewish Annotated New Testament.* Oxford: Oxford University Press, 2011.

Levy, Leonard. *Blasphemy. Verbal Offense Against the Sacred.* Chapel Hill and London: University of North Carolina Press, 1993.

Liebeschütz, Hans. "Hermann Cohen: Seine Philosophie und die Zeitgeschichte." In *Von Georg Simmel zu Franz Rosenzweig. Studien zum Jüdischen Denken im deutschen Kulturbereich,* 7–54. Tübingen: Mohr Siebeck, 1970.

– *Das Judentum im deutschen Geschichtsbild von Hegel bis Max Weber.* Tübingen: Mohr Siebeck, 1967.

Loeffler, James. "When Hermann Cohen Cried: Zionism, Culture, Emotions." In *Zionism as a Cultural Movement,* edited by Israel Bartal and Rachel Rojansky. Leiden: Brill, forthcoming.

Loidoldt, Sophie. *Einführung in die Rechtsphänomenologie.* Tübingen: Mohr Siebeck, 2010.

Lorberbaum, Menachem. Introduction to chapter 14: "Conversion." In *The Jewish Political Tradition,* edited by Michael Walzer, Menachem Lorberbaum, and Noam J. Zohar. New Haven, CT: Yale University Press, 2003.

– "Jewish Collectivity and Gentile Otherness." Paper presented at "*The Ethics of the Neighbor,*" UCLA, May 16, 2004.

Lowenstein, Steven M. "The Community." Chap. 5 in Lowenstein et al., *Integration in Dispute 1871–1918.* Vol. 3, *German-Jewish History in Modern Times.*

Lowenstein, Steven M., Paul Mendes-Flohr, Peter Pulzer, and Monika Richarz. *Integration in Dispute 1871–1918.* Vol. 3, *German-Jewish History in Modern Times,* edited by Michael A. Meyer with Michael Brenner. New York: Columbia University Press, 1996. Published in German as *Umstrittene Integration, 1871–1918.* Vol. 3, *Deutsch-jüdische Geschichte in der Neuzeit.* Munich: C.H. Beck, 1997.

Löwenthal, A. "Nächstenliebe." *Die Jüdische Presse* (30 October 1890): 1–2.

Löwenthal, Leo. "Die jüdische Religionsphilosophie Hermann Cohens." *Frankfurter Israelitisches Gemeindeblatt* 8, no. 9 (May 1930): 357–9.

Lüddecke, Dirk. "Staatsidee und Revolution bei Hermann Cohen. Ein Kapitel der sozialistischen Kant-Rezeption um 1900." In *Kants Lehre von Staat und Frieden,* edited by Henning Ottmann, 113–33. Baden-Baden: Nomos, 2009.

Maimonides. *Ethical Writings of Maimonides.* Edited and translated by Charles E. Butterworth and Raymond L. Weiss. New York: Dover, 1983.

– *The Guide of the Perplexed.* Translated by Shlomo Pines. 2 vols. Chicago: University of Chicago Press, 1963.

Maitland, Frederick William. "Translator's Introduction" to Otto von Gierke, *Political Theories of the Middle Age,* vii–xlv. [Partial translation of *Das deutsche Genossenschaftsrecht,* vol. 3] Cambridge: Cambridge University Press, 1927.

Makkreel, Rudolf A., and Sebastian Luft, eds. *Neo-Kantianism and Contemporary Philosophy.* Bloomington: Indiana University Press, 2010.

Marx, Wolfgang. *Transzendentale Logik als Wissenschaftstheorie. Systematisch- kritische Untersuchungen zur philosophischen Grundlegungsproblematik in Cohens "Logik der reinen Erkenntnis."* Frankfurt am Main: Klostermann, 1977.

Maurer, Trude. "Medizinalpolizei und Antisemitismus. Die deutsche Politik der Grenzsperre gegen Ostjuden im Ersten Weltkrieg." *Jahrbücher für Geschichte Osteuropas,* Neue Folge, 33, no. 2 (1985): 205–30.

Mendelssohn, Moses. *Jerusalem oder über religiöse Macht und Judentum.* In *Gesammelte Schriften. Jubiläumsausgabe.* Vol. 8: *Schriften zum Judentum II,* edited by Alexander Altmann. Stuttgart-Bad Cannstatt: Frommann-Holzboog, 1983. Translated by Allan Arkush as *Jerusalem, or on Religious Power and Judaism* Waltham, MA: Brandeis University Press, 1983.

– *Sefer Netivot Ha-Shalom: Vayikra* in *Gesammelte Schriften. Jubiläumsausgabe.* Vol. 17: *Hebräische Schriften II,4,* edited by Werner Weinberg. Stuttgart-Bad Cannstatt: Frommann Holzboog, 1990.

Mendes-Flohr, Paul. *Love, Accusative and Dative: Reflections on Leviticus 19:18.* Syracuse, NY: Syracuse University Press, 2007.

Meyer, Michael A. "Great Debate on Antisemitism: Jewish Reaction to New Hostility in Germany 1879–1881." *Leo Baeck Institute Year Book* 11 (1966): 137–70.

Meyer, Thomas. *Vom Ende der Emanzipation. Jüdische Philosophie und Theologie nach 1933.* Göttingen: Vandenhoeck & Ruprecht, 2008.

Meyer, Thomas, and Michael Zank. "More Early Writings by Leo Strauss from the *Jüdische Wochenzeitung für Cassel, Hessen und Waldeck* (1925–1928)." *Interpretation* 39, no. 1 (Spring/Summer 2012): 109–37.

Michaelis, Johann David. *Mosaisches Recht,* 3rd ed. Frankfurt am Main: J.G. Garbe, 1793. Translated by Alexander Smith as *Commentaries on the Laws of Moses.* London: Rivington, 1814.

Moser, Adolf. *Religion und Strafrecht insbesondere die Gotteslästerung.* Breslau: Schletter'sche Buchhandlung, 1909.

Mosès, Stéphane, and Hartwig Wiedebach, eds. *Hermann Cohen's Philosophy of Religion: International Conference in Jerusalem.* Hildesheim: Olms, 1997.

Motive zu dem Entwurfe eines Strafgesetzbuches für den Norddeutschen Bund. Berlin: Verlag der Königlichen Geheimen Ober-Hofbuchdruckerei, 1869.

Müller, Claudius. *Die Rechtsphilosophie des Marburger Neukantianismus. Naturrecht und Rechtspositivismus in der Auseinandersetzung zweischen Hermann Cohen, Rudolf Stammler und Paul Natorp.* Tübingen: Mohr Siebeck, 1994.

Müller, Klaus. *Tora für die Völker. Die noachidischen Gebote und Ansätze zu ihrer Rezeption im Christentum.* Berlin: Institut Kirche und Judentum, 1994.

Munk, Reinier, ed. *Hermann Cohen's Critical Idealism.* Heidelberg: Springer, 2005.

– "The Self and the Other in Cohen's Ethics and Works on Religion." In Mosès and Wiedebach, *Hermann Cohen's Philosophy of Religion,* 161–81.

Myers, David N. "The Fall and Rise of Jewish Historicism: The Evolution of the Akademie für die Wissenschaft des Judentums (1919–1934)." *Hebrew Union College Annual* 63 (1992): 107–144.

– "Hermann Cohen and the Problem of History at the Fin de Siècle." In *Resisting History: Historicism and its Discontents in German-Jewish Thought.* Princeton: Princeton University Press, 2003.

Nahme, Paul E. "From Critical to Prophetic Idealism: Ethics, Law, and Religion in the Philosophy of Hermann Cohen." PhD diss., University of Toronto, 2013.

– "God Is the Reason: Hermann Cohen's Monotheism and the Liberal Theologico-Political Predicament." *Modern Theology* 33, no. 1 (January 2017): 116–39.

– *Hermann Cohen and the Crisis of Liberalism: The Enchantment of the Public Sphere.* Bloomington: Indiana University Press, 2019.

Nail, Thomas. *The Figure of the Migrant.* Stanford: Stanford University Press, 2015.

– "Figures of the Migrant: Structure and Resistance." *Cultural Dynamics* 30, no. 3 (August 2018): 225–30.

Natorp, Paul. "Recht und Sittlichkeit. Ein Beitrag zur kategorialen Begründung der "praktischen Philosophie. Mit besonderem Bezug auf Hermann Cohens 'Ethik des reinen Willens' und Rudolf Stammlers 'Theorie der Rechtswissenschaft.'" *Kant Studien* 18 (1913): 1–79.

Nelson, Eric. *The Hebrew Republic: Jewish Sources and the Transformation of European Political Thought.* Cambridge, MA: Harvard University Press, 2010.

Neudecker, Reinhard. "'And You Shall Love Your Neighbor as Yourself – I Am the Lord' (Lev 19, 18) in Jewish Interpretation." *Biblica* 73, no. 4 (1992): 496–517.

Neumann, Wenzel August. *Pressprozeß Doktor Brunner–Ignaz Kuranda.* Vienna: Ludwig Mayer, 1960.

Newton, Adam Zachary. *The Fence and the Neighbor: Emmanuel Levinas, Yeshayahu Leibowitz, and Israel among the Nations.* Albany: State University of New York Press, 2001.

Nipperdey, Thomas. *Deutsche Geschichte 1866–1918.* Vol. 1: *Arbeitswelt und Bürgergeist.* Munich: C.H. Beck, 1990–1992.

Noack, Hannelore. *Unbelehrbar? Antijüdische Agitation mit entstellten Talmudzitaten – antisemitische Aufwiegelung durch Verteufelung der Juden.* Paderborn: University Press, 2001.

Norrell, Tracey Hayes. *For the Honor of Our Fatherland: German Jews on the Eastern Front During the Great War.* Lanham, MD: Lexington Books, 2017.

Novak, David. "The Election of Israel: Outline of a Philosophical Analysis." In Frank, *A People Apart,* 11–50.

– "Gentiles in Rabbinic Thought." In *The Cambridge History of Judaism.* Vol. 4: *The Late Roman-Rabbinic Period,* edited by Steven T. Katz, 647–62. Cambridge: Cambridge University Press, 2008.

– "Hermann Cohen on State and Nation: A Contemporary Review." In Munk, *Hermann Cohen's Critical Idealism*, 259–79.

– *The Image of the Non-Jew in Judaism: The Idea of Noahide Law.* 2nd ed. Edited by Matthew Lagrone. Oxford: Littman Library of Jewish Civilization, 2011.

– "Das noachidische Naturrecht bei Hermann Cohen." In Holzhey et al., eds., *"Religion der Vernunft aus den Quellen des Judentums,"* 225–43

– "Universal Moral Law in the Theology of Hermann Cohen." *Modern Judaism* 1, no. 1 (May 1981): 101–17.

Ollig, Hans-Ludwig. "Neo-Kantianism." In *Routledge Encyclopedia of Philosophy.* London: Routledge, 1998.

O'Neill, Onora. "Self-Legislation, Autonomy and the Form of Law." In *Recht – Geschichte – Religion. Die Bedeutung Kants für die Gegenwart. Deutsche Zeitschrift für Philosophie*, Sonderband 9, edited by Herta Nagl-Docekal and Rudolf Langthaler, 13–26. Berlin: de Gruyter, 2004.

Orlik, Franz. *Hermann Cohen (1842–1918). Kantinterpret, Begründer der "Marburger Schule," Jüdischer Religionsphilosoph. Eine Ausstellung in der Universitätsbibliothek Marburg vom 1. Juli bis 14. August 1992.* Marburg: Universitätsbibliothek Marburg, 1992.

Ott, Sieghart. "Ist die Strafbarkeit der Religionsbeschimpfung mit dem Grundgesetz vereinbar?" *Neues Juristisches Wochenblatt* nos. 14/15 (1966): 639–41.

Palmer, Gesine. "'Freud vermoralisiert die Psychologie'. Eine Randnotiz von Franz Rosenzweig im Lichte der Antinomismusdiskussion von Jacob Taubes." Lecture held at a workshop on Jacob Taubes, Zentrum für Literatur- und Kulturforschung Berlin, 21 February 2011. https://gesine-palmer.de/wp-content/uploads/2017/07/taubes.vortrag2.pdf.

– "Die Hörner des Heidentums. Gesetz und Opfer bei Hermann Cohen und Sigmund Freud." In *Einbruch der Wirklichkeit*, edited by Jens Mattern. Berlin: Vorwerk 8, 2002.

– "Judaism as a 'Method' with Hermann Cohen and Franz Rosenzweig." In Gibbs, ed., "Hermann Cohen's Ethics." Special issue, *Journal of Jewish Thought and Philosophy* 13, nos. 1–2 (2004): 37–63.

– "Präskription und Deskription. Autonomie be Sigmund Freud und Hermann Cohen." In *Torah – Nomos – Ius: Abendländischer Antinomismus und der Traum vom herrschaftsfreien Raum*, edited by Renate Haffke, Christiane Nasse, Gesine Palmer, and Dorothee C. von Tippelskirch. Berlin: Vorwerk 8, 1999.

Panter, Sarah. *Jüdische Erfahrungen und Loyalitätskonflikte im Ersten Weltkrieg.* Göttingen: Vandenhoeck & Ruprecht, 2014.

Parmod, Maximilian. *Antisemitismus und Strafrechtspflege.* Berlin: Siegfried Cronbach, 1894.

Pascher, Manfred. *Einführung in den Neukantianismus. Kontext, Grundpositionen, praktische Philosophie.* Munich: Wilhelm Fink Verlag, 1997.

– *Hermann Cohens Ethik als Gegenentwurf zur Rechtsphilosophie Hegels.* Innsbruck: Verlag des Instituts für Sprachwissenschaft der Universität Innsbruck, 1992.

Patrick, Jeremy. "The Curious Persistence of Blasphemy: Canada and Beyond." PhD diss., Osgoode Hall Law School, 2013.

– "Not Dead, Just Sleeping: Canada's Prohibition on Blasphemous Libel as a Case Study in Obsolete Legislation." *University of British Columbia Law Review* 41, no. 2 (2008): 193–248.

Patton, Lydia. "The Critical Philosophy Renewed: The Bridge Between Hermann Cohen's Early Work on Kant and Later Philosophy of Science." *Angelaki* 10, no. 1 (April 2005): 109–18.

Paulson, Stanley L. "Einleitung." In Alexy et al., eds., *Neukantianismus und Rechtsphilosophie.*

Peal, David. "Jewish Responses to German Antisemitism: The Case of the Böckel Movement, 1887–1894." *Jewish Social Studies* 48, nos. 3/4 (Summer–Autumn 1986): 269–82.

Pelluchon, Corine. *Leo Strauss. Une autre raison, d'autres lumières.* Paris: Vrin, 2005.

– Preface to her translation of Leo Strauss, "Cohen et Maïmonide." *Revue de Métaphysique et de Morale* 38, no. 2 (April–June 2003): 233–75.

– "Strauss and Cohen: The Question of Enlightened Judaism." *Interpretation* 32, no. 3 (Summer 2005): 219–30.

Piccinini, Irene Abigail. "Leo Strauss and Hermann Cohen's 'Arch-Enemy': A Quasi- Cohenian Apology of Baruch Spinoza." In "Strauss and Textual Reasoning," edited by Leora Batnitzky and Michael Zank. Special issue, *Journal of Textual Reasoning* 3, no. 1 (June 2004). https://jtr.shanti.virginia.edu/volume-3-number-1/

Piché, Claude. "Heidegger and the Neo-Kantian Reading of Kant." In Rockmore, *Heidegger, German Idealism, and Neo-Kantianism,* 179–207.

Pollock, Benjamin. "'Every State Becomes a Theocracy': Hermann Cohen on the Israelites under Divine Rule." *Jewish Studies Quarterly* 25, no. 2 (2018): 181–99.

Poma, Andrea. *The Critical Philosophy of Hermann Cohen* (1988). Translated by John Denton. Albany: State University of New York Press, 1997.

– "Hermann Cohen: Judaism and Critical Idealism," trans. John Denton. In *The Cambridge Companion to Modern Jewish Philosophy,* edited by Michael L. Morgan and Peter Eli Gordon, 80–101. Cambridge: Cambridge University Press, 2007.

– *Yearning for Form and Other Essays on Hermann Cohen's Thought.* Dordrecht: Springer, 2006.

Der Prozeß Fenner nach den Akten dargestellt und beleuchtet. Marburg: Verlag des "Reichs-Herold," 1888.

Pulzer, Peter. "The Response to Antisemitism." Chap. 8 in Lowenstein et al., *Integration in Dispute 1871–1918*. Vol. 3, *German-Jewish History in Modern Times.*

– "The Return of Old Hatreds." Chap. 7 in Lowenstein et al., *Integration in Dispute 1871–1918*. Vol. 3, *German-Jewish History in Modern Times.*

– *The Rise of Political Anti-Semitism in Germany and Austria*. Rev. ed. Cambridge, MA: Harvard University Press, 1988.

Rabinovitch, Simon, ed. *Jews and Diaspora Nationalism. Writings on Jewish Peoplehood in Europe and the United States.* Waltham, MA: Brandeis University Press, 2012

Rashkover, Randi. *Revelation and Theopolitics: Barth, Rosenzweig, and the Politics of Praise.* London: T&T Clark, 2005.

Rashkover, Randi, and Martin Kavka, eds. *Judaism, Liberalism, and Political Theology*. Bloomington: Indiana University Press, 2014.

Rebbert, Joseph. *Blicke in's talmudische Judenthum, nach den Forschungen von Dr. Konrad Martin*. Paderborn: Bonifacius, 1876.

Reinbold, Wolfgang. "Die Nächstenliebe (Lev 19,18)." In *Die Verheißung des Neuen Bundes: Wie alttestamentliche Texte im Neuen Testament fortwirken*, edited by Bernd Kollmann, 115–27. Göttingen: Vandenhoeck & Ruprecht, 2010.

Reinhard, Kenneth. "The Ethics of the Neighbor: Universalism, Particularism, Exceptionalism." In Hollander, "The Ethics of the Neighbor." Special issue, *Journal of Textual Reasoning* 4, no. 1 (November 2005). http://jtr.shanti.virginia.edu/volume-4-number-1/the-ethics-of-the-neighbor-universalism-particularism-exceptionalism/

– "Messianism and the Neighbor." *Rosenzweig-Jahrbuch* 1 (2006): 114–33.

– "The Political Theology of the Neighbor and the Topology of the *Eruv*." Unpublished paper. Published in German translation as "Die Politische Theologie des Nächsten und die Topologie des Eruv." In *Talmudische Tradition und moderne Rechtstheorie. Kontexte und Perspektiven einer Begegnung*, edited by Karl-Heinz Ladeur and Ino Augsberg, 31–48. Tübingen: Mohr Siebeck, 2013.

Renz, Ursula. "Affektivität und Geschichtlichkeit: Hermann Cohens Rehabilitierung des Affekts." In *Affekte und Ethik. Spinozas Lehre im Kontext*, edited by Achim Engstler and Robert Schnepf, 297–319. Hildesheim: Olms, 2002.

Riegner, Heinrich. "Hermann Cohen – Der Mensch." *Bulletin of the Leo Baeck Institute*, no. 7 (June 1959). 113–34.

Rockmore, Tom, ed. *Heidegger, German Idealism, and Neo-Kantianism*. Amherst, NY: Humanity Books, 2000.

Rohling, August. *Der Talmudjude*. Münster: Russell, 1871. 6th ed. Münster: Russell, 1877.

Rosenblatt, Jason P. *Renaissance England's Chief Rabbi: John Selden*. Oxford: Oxford University Press, 2006.

Rosen-Zvi, Ishay. "In the Torah, Is the *Ger* Ever a Convert?" TheTorah.com. 5 April 2019.

Rosen-Zvi, Ishay, and Adi Ophir. "*Goy*: Toward a Genealogy." *Dine Israel* 28 (2011): 69–122.

Rosenzweig, Franz. "Einleitung" (introduction) to Hermann Cohen, *Jüdische Schriften*. In JS1: XIII–LXIV. 1924.

– *Der Mensch und sein Werk. Gesammelte Schriften.* Vol. III: *Zweistromland: Kleinere Schriften zu Glauben und Denken*, edited by Reinhold Mayer and Annemarie Mayer. Dordrecht: Nijhoff, 1984.

– *Philosophical and Theological Writings.* Translated and edited by Paul W. Franks and Michael L. Morgan. Indianapolis: Hackett, 2000.

Ruderman, David B. *A Best-Selling Hebrew Book of the Modern Era: The Book of the Covenant of Pinḥas Hurwitz and Its Remarkable Legacy.* Seattle: University of Washington Press, 2014.

– "The Book of Covenant: How to Become a Prophet." *Der Tagesspiegel*, 10 September 2010.

Saadya Gaon. *The Book of Doctrines and Beliefs.* Abridged translation by Alexander Altmann (1946), edited by Daniel Frank. Indianapolis: Hackett, 2002.

Sander, Fritz, and Hans Kelsen. *Die Rolle des Neukantianismus in der reinen Rechtslehre: Eine Debatte zwischen Sander und Kelsen*, edited by Stanley L. Paulson. Aalen: Scientia, 1988.

Sander, Sabine. "Messianic Universalism: The Social Ethics and Dialogue Philosophy of Hermann Cohen, Martin Buber, and Karl Löwith," translated by Sarah Swift. In *Language as Bridge and Border. Linguistic, Cultural, and Political Constellations in 18th to 20th Century German-Jewish Thought.* Berlin: Hentrich & Hentrich, 2015.

Schäfer, Frank L. *Juristische Germanistik. Eine Geschichte der Wissenschaft vom einheimischen Privatrecht.* Frankfurt am Main: Klostermann, 2008.

Schildt, Bernd. "Genossenschaft, Genossenschaftsrecht." In *Handwörterbuch zur deutschen Rechtsgeschichte*, 2nd rev. ed., edited by Albrecht Cordes et al. Vol. 2, cols. 103–10. Berlin: Erich Schmidt, 2012.

Schmid, Peter A. "Das Naturrecht in der Rechtsethik Hermann Cohens." *Zeitschrift für philosophische Forschung* 47, no. 3 (1993): 408–21.

– *Ethik als Hermeneutik. Systematische Untersuchungen zu Hermann Cohens Rechts- und Tugendlehre.* Würzburg: Königshausen & Neumann, 1995.

Schorsch, Ismar. *Jewish Reactions to German Anti-Semitism, 1870–1914.* New York: Columbia University Press, 1972.

– "Missing in Translation: The Fate of the Talmud in the Struggle for Equality and Integration in Germany." In *Wissenschaft des Judentums Beyond Tradition: Jewish Scholarship on the Sacred Texts of Judaism, Christianity, and Islam*, edited by Dorothea M. Salzer, Chanan Gafni, and Hanan Harif, 167–84. Berlin: de Gruyter, 2019.

– "Zacharias Frankel and the European Origins of Conservative Judaism." *Judaism* 30 (1981): 344–54.

Schubert, Kurt. *Geschichte des österreichischen Judentums.* Vienna: Böhlau, 2008.

Schulte, Christoph, ed. *Deutschtum und Judentum: ein Disput unter Juden aus Deutschland.* Stuttgart: Reclam, 1993.

– "Jüdische Theodizee? Überlegungen zum Theodizee-Problem bei Immanuel Kant, Hermann Cohen und Max Weber." *Zeitschrift für Religions- und Geistesgeschichte* 49, no. 2 (1997): 135–59.

– "Noachidische Gebote und Naturrecht." In Holzhey et al., *"Religion der Vernunft aus den Quellen des Judentums,"* 245–74.

Schwarzschild, Steven S. "An Agenda for Jewish Philosophy in the 1980's" (1980). In *Studies in Jewish Philosophy*, edited by Norbert Samuelson, 101–25. Lanham, MD: University Press of America, 1987.

– "The Democratic Socialism of Hermann Cohen." *Hebrew Union College Annual* 27 (1956): 417–38. Also in *The Tragedy of Optimism*, 1–21.

– "Do Noachites Have to Believe in Revelation? (A Passage in Dispute between Maimonides, Spinoza, Mendelssohn, and Hermann Cohen). A Contribution to a Jewish View of Natural Law" (1962). In *The Pursuit of the Ideal*, 29–59.

– "F. Rosenzweig's Anecdotes about H. Cohen." In *Gegenwart im Rückblick*, edited by Herbert A. Strauss and K.R. Grossman, 209–18. Heidelberg: Lothar Stiehm Verlag, 1970. Also in *The Tragedy of Optimism*, 35–42.

– "'Germanism and Judaism' – Hermann Cohen's Normative Paradigm of the German-Jewish Symbiosis." In *Jews and Germans From 1860 to 1933: The Problematic Symbiosis*, edited by David Bronsen, 129–72. Heidelberg: Carl Winter, 1979. Also in *The Tragedy of Optimism*, 93–118.

– Introduction to Hermann Cohen, *Ethik des reinen Willens.* In *Werke.* Vol. 7. Hildesheim: Olms, 1981. Also in *The Tragedy of Optimism*, 119–39.

– *The Pursuit of the Ideal: Jewish Writings of Steven Schwarzschild*, edited by Menachem Kellner. Albany: State University of New York Press, 1990.

– "The Tenability of Herman [sic] Cohen's Construction of the Self." *Journal of the History of Philosophy* 13, no. 3 (July 1975): 361–84. Also in *The Tragedy of Optimism*, 69–92.

– "The Title of Hermann Cohen's 'Religion of Reason out of the Sources of Judaism" (1986). In Hermann Cohen, *Religion of Reason Out of the Sources of Judaism.* Translated by Simon Kaplan, 2nd ed., 7–20. Atlanta: Scholars Press, 1995. Also in *The Tragedy of Optimism*, 141–9.

– *The Tragedy of Optimism: Writings on Hermann Cohen*, edited by George Y. Kohler. Albany: State University of New York Press, 2018.

Schwarzschild, Steven S., Saul Berman, and Menachem Elon. "Noachide Laws" (1972/2007). In *Encyclopaedia Judaica*, 2nd ed. (2007).

Seeskin, Kenneth. *Autonomy in Jewish Philosophy.* Cambridge: Cambridge University Press, 2001.

– "Jewish Neo-Kantianism: Hermann Cohen." In *History of Jewish Philosophy*, edited by Daniel H. Frank and Oliver Leaman, 786–98. London: Routledge, 1997.

Shear-Yashuv, Aharon. "Darstellung und kritische Würdigung von Hermann Cohens Stellung zum Zionismus." *Aschkenas. Zeitschrift für Geschichte und Kultur der Juden* 10, no. 2 (2000): 443–57.

– "Hermann Cohen über Chok und Mischpat." In Holzhey et al., *"Religion der Vernunft aus den Quellen des Judentums,"* 381–402.

Sherwood, Yvonne. *Biblical Blaspheming: Trials of the Sacred for a Secular Age.* Cambridge: Cambridge University Press, 2012.

Sieg, Ulrich. *Aufstieg und Niedergang des Marburger Neukantianismus: die Geschichte einer philosophischen Schulgemeinschaft.* Würzburg: Königshausen & Neumann, 1994.

– *Deutschlands Prophet. Paul de Lagarde und die Ursprünge des modernen Antisemitismus.* Munich: Hanser, 2007. Translated by Linda Ann Marianiello as *Germany's Prophet. Paul de Lagarde and the Origins of Modern Antisemitism.* Waltham, MA: Brandeis University Press, 2013.

– "Der frühe Hermann Cohen und die Völkerpsychologie." *Aschkenas. Zeitschrift für Geschichte und Kultur der Juden* 13, no. 2 (2003): 461–83.

– *Die Geschichte der Philosophie an der Universität Marburg von 1527 bis 1970.* Marburg: Hitzeroth, 1988.

– "Der Preis des Bildungsstrebens. Jüdische Geisteswissenschaftler im Kaiserreich." In *Juden, Bürger, Deutsche. Zur Geschichte von Vielfalt und Differenz, 1800–1933*, edited by Andreas Gotzmann, Rainer Liedtke, and Till van Rahden, 67–95. Tübingen: Mohr Siebeck, 2001.

– "Der Talmud vor Gericht. Die ideengeschichtliche Bedeutung des Marburger Antisemitismusprozesses." In *Religiöse Minderheiten. Potentiale für Konflikt und Frieden*, edited by Hans-Martin Barth and Christoph Elsas, 128–43. Hamburg: EB-Verlag, 2004.

– "Das Testament von Hermann und Martha Cohen. Stiftungen und Stipendien für jüdische Einrichtungen." *Zeitschrift für neuere Theologiegeschichte* 4 (1997): 251–64.

– "'Der Wissenschaft und dem Leben tut dasselbe not: Ehrfurcht vor der Wahrheit.' Hermann Cohens Gutachten im Marburger Antisemitismusprozeß 1888." In Brandt and Orlik, eds., *Philosophisches Denken – Politisches Wirken*, 221–49.

Simon, Ernst. "The Neighbor (*Re'a*) Whom We Shall Love." In *Modern Jewish Ethics: Theory and Practice*, edited by Marvin Fox, 29–56. Columbus: Ohio State University Press, 1975.

– "Zu Hermann Cohens Spinoza-Auffassung." *Monatsschrift für Geschichte und Wissenschaft des Judentums* 79 (1935): 181–94. Also in *Brücken. Gesammelte Aufsätze.* Heidelberg: Lambert Schneider, 1965, 205–14.

Simon, Toni. 1959. "Hermann Cohens Elternhaus." LBI Manuscript Collection (MS 1001). Leo Baeck Institute Archives.

Singer, Isidore, and Julius Greenstone. "Laws, Noachian." *The Jewish Encyclopedia*, vol. 7 (1904).

Smith, Helmut Walser. *The Butcher's Tale: Murder and Anti-Semitism in a German Town*. New York: Norton, 2002.

– *German Nationalism and Religious Conflict: Culture, Ideology, Politics, 1870–1914*. Princeton: Princeton University Press, 1995.

Solomon, Norman. "Cohen on Atonement, Purification and Repentance." In Munk, *Hermann Cohen's Critical Idealism*, 395–411.

Spector, Scott. "Blood Lies: The Truth about Modern Ritual Murder Accusations and Defenses," chap. 5 in *Violent Sensations: Sex, Crime and Utopia in Vienna and Berlin, 1860–1914*. Chicago: University of Chicago Press, 2016.

Spinoza, Baruch. [*Tractatus theologico-politicus*.] Translated by Samuel Shirley as *Theological-Political Treatise*, 2nd ed. Indianapolis: Hackett, 2001. Translated and edited by Martin D. Yaffe as *Spinoza's Theologico-Political Treatise*. Newburyport, MA: Focus Publishing, 2004.

Stade, Bernhard. *Geschichte des Volkes Israel*. Vol. 1: *Geschichte Israels unter der Königsherrschaft*. Berlin: Grote'scher Verlagsbuchhandlung, 1887.

Stammler, Rudolf. [See also "Abbreviations" in this volume.]

– "Fundamental Tendencies in Modern Jurisprudence." *Michigan Law Review* 21 (1923): 623–54, 765–85, 862–903.

– "Die grundsätzlichen Richtungen der neueren Jurisprudenz" (1923). In *Rechtsphilosophische Abhandlungen und Vorträge*, vol. 2, 333–92. Charlottenburg: Pan Verlag Rolf Heise, 1925.

– *Lehrbuch der Rechtsphilosophie*, 1st ed. Berlin/Leipzig: de Gruyter, 1922. 3rd ed. Berlin/Leipzig: de Gruyter, 1928.

– *Die Lehre von dem richtigen Rechte*. 1st ed. Berlin: J. Guttentag, 1902. Translated by Isaac Husik as *The Theory of Justice*. New York: MacMillan, 1925.

– *Theorie der Rechtswissenschaft*. Halle: Buchhandlung des Waisenhauses, 1911.

– "Wesen des Rechtes und der Rechtswissenschaft." In *Die Kultur der Gegenwart. Ihre Entwicklung und ihre Ziele*, edited by Paul Hinneberg. Teil II, Abteilung VIII: *Systematische Rechtswissenschaft*, I–LX. Berlin/Leipzig: Teubner, 1906.

The Statutary Criminal Law of Germany. A Translation of the German Criminal Code of 1871 with Amendments. Washington, DC: War Department, 1946.

Steiner, Stephan. "Die Eröffnung der symbolischen Dimension. Zum Streit um Hermann Cohens Gesetzesinterpretation." Unpublished paper.

Steinitz, Inbal. *Der Kampf jüdischer Anwälte gegen den Antisemitismus. Die strafrechtliche Rechtsschutzarbeit des Centralvereins deutscher Staatsbürger jüdischen Glaubens 1893–1933*. Berlin: Metropol, 2008.

Steinthal, Salomon. "Aus Hermann Cohens Heimat." *Allgemeine Zeitung des Judentums* 82, no. 19 (10 May 1918): 222–5. Reprinted in *Jüdisches Gemeindeblatt für Anhalt und Umgegend* 3, no. 4 (4 November 1927).

Stern, Josef. *Problems and Parables of Law: Maimonides and Nahmanides on Reasons for the Commandments (*Ta'amei Ha-Mitzvot*)*. Albany: State University of New York Press, 2012.

Still, Judith. *Derrida and Hospitality: Theory and Practice.* Edinburgh: Edinburgh University Press, 2010.

Stoetzler, Marcel. *The State, the Nation, and the Jews: Liberalism and the Antisemitism Dispute in Bismarck's Germany.* Lincoln: University of Nebraska Press, 2009.

Stolleis, Michael. *Geschichte des öffentlichen Rechts in Deutschland.* Vol. 2: *1800–1914.* Munich: C.H. Beck, 1992.

– "Sozialrecht." In *Handwörterbuch zur deutschen Rechtsgeschichte.* Vol. 4, edited by Adalbert Erler and Ekkehard Kaufmann, cols. 1730–33. Berlin: Erich Schmidt, 1990.

Stolzenberg, Jürgen. *Ursprung und System: Probleme der Begründung systematischer Philosophie im Werk Hermann Cohens, Paul Natorps und beim frühen Martin Heidegger.* Göttingen: Vandenhoeck & Ruprecht, 1995.

Stone, Julius. *Human Law and Human Justice.* Stanford: Stanford University Press, 1965.

Strack, Hermann L. "Blood Accusation." In *The Jewish Encyclopedia*, vol. 3 (1902).

– "Die Juden, dürfen sie 'Verbrecher von Religions wegen' genannt werden?" Berlin: Hermann Walther, 1893.

– *Sind die Juden Verbrecher von Religions wegen?* Leipzig: Hinrich'sche Buchhandlung, 1900. Originally published in *Nathanael. Zeitschrift für die Arbeit der evangelischen Kirche an Israel* 16 (1900): 29–38.

Strafgesetzbuch mit 777 Nebengesetzen. Munich: Biederstein, 1949.

Strauss, Leo. [See also "Abbreviations" in this volume.]

– *Gesammelte Schriften.* Vol. 2: *Philosophie und Gesetz, Frühe Schriften*, edited by Heinrich Meier. Stuttgart: Metzler, 1997.

– "How to Study Medieval Philosophy" (1944). *Interpretation: A Journal of Political Philosophy* 23, no. 3 (Spring 1996): 319–38. A version of this essay is also included in *The Rebirth of Classical Political Rationalism*, ed. Pangle.

– "Introductory Essay" (1972) to Hermann Cohen, *Religion of Reason Out of the Sources of Judaism.* Atlanta: Scholars Press, 1995.

– "Political Philosophy and History" (1949). In *What Is Political Philosophy?* 56–77. Glencoe, IL: Free Press, 1959.

– *The Rebirth of Classical Political Rationalism: An Introduction to the Thought of Leo Strauss: Essays and Lectures*, edited by Thomas L. Pangle. Chicago: University of Chicago Press, 1989.

– *Spinoza's Critique of Religion.* Translated by E.M. Sinclair. New York: Schocken. 1965.

Tal, Uriel. *Christians and Jews in Germany: Religion, Politics, and Ideology in the Second Reich, 1870–1914.* Translated by Noah Jonathan Jacobs. Ithaca, NY: Cornell University Press, 1975.

– *Religion, Politics and Ideology in the Third Reich: Selected Essays.* London/New York: Routledge, 2004.

Thiem, Annika (Yannik Thiem). "Fate, Guilt, and Messianic Interruptions: Ethics of Theological Critique in Hermann Cohen and Walter Benjamin." PhD diss., University of California, Berkeley, 2009.

Tönnies, Ferdinand. "Ethik und Sozialismus." *Archiv für Sozialwissenschaft und Sozialpolitik* 25 (1907), 573–610; 26 (1908), 56–95; and 29 (1909), 895–930.

van der Linden, Harry. "Cohen's Socialist Reconstruction of Kant's Ethics." Available at http://digitalcommons.butler.edu/facsch_papers/42. Published in German translation as "Cohens sozialistische Rekonstruktion der Ethik Kants." In Holzhey, *Ethischer Sozialismus,* 146–65.

– "Hermann Cohen's Political Philosophy and the Communitarian Critique of Liberalism." Available at http://digitalcommons.butler.edu/facsch_papers/66. Published in French translation in "L'École de Marbourg," edited by Fabien Capeillères and Jean Kahn. Special issue, *Cahiers de philosophie politique et juridique,* no. 26 (1994), 93–118.

– *Kantian Ethics and Socialism.* Indianapolis: Hackett, 1988.

Vatter, Miguel. "Nationality, State and Global Constitutionalism in Hermann Cohen's Wartime Writings." In *100 Years of European Philosophy Since the Great War,* edited by Rory Jeffs, Jack Reynolds, and Matthew Sharpe, 43–63. New York: Springer, 2017.

Verhandlungen und Beschlüsse der Rabbiner-Versammlung zu Berlin am 4. und 5. Juni 1884. Berlin: Walther & Apolant, 1885.

Vinx, Lars. *Hans Kelsen's Pure Theory of Law: Legality and Legitimacy.* Oxford: Oxford University Press, 2007.

Vormbaum, Thomas. *Einführung in die moderne Strafrechtsgeschichte.* Berlin: Springer, 2009.

Vorländer, Karl. "Rudolf Stammlers Lehre vom richtigen Recht." *Kant-Studien* 8 (1903): 329–35.

Walter, Dirk. *Antisemitische Kriminalität und Gewalt. Judenfeindschaft in der Weimarer Republik.* Bonn: Dietz, 1999.

Weidner, Daniel. "'Geschichte gegen den Strich bürsten': Julius Wellhausen und die jüdische 'Gegengeschichte.'" *Zeitschrift für Religions- und Geistesgeschichte* 54, no. 1 (2002): 34–61.

– "The Political Theology of Ethical Monotheism." In Rashkover and Kavka, *Judaism, Liberalism, and Political Theology,* 178–96.

Weinberger, Ota. *Normentheorie als Grundlage der Jurisprudenz und Ethik. Eine Auseinandersetzung mit Hans Kelsens Theorie der Normen.* Berlin: Duncker & Humblot, 1991.

Weiss, Daniel H. *Paradox and the Prophets: Hermann Cohen and the Indirect Communication of Religion.* Oxford: Oxford University Press, 2012.

Wenn, Matthias. *Juristische Erkenntniskritik. Zur Rechts- und Sozialphilosophie Rudolf Stammlers.* Baden-Baden: Nomos, 2003.

"Wie ein Rabbiner den Talmud vertheidigt und die Talmudisten schmäht." *Der Israelit* 43 (1877) no. 36: 867–71; no. 37: 889–91; no. 38/39: 919–21.

Wiedebach, Hartwig. *Die Bedeutung der Nationalität für Hermann Cohen.* Hildesheim: Olms, 1997. Translated by William Templer as *The National Element in Hermann Cohen's Philosophy and Religion.* Leiden: Brill, 2012.

– "Hermann Cohens Auseinandersetzung mit dem Zionismus." *Jewish Studies Quarterly* 6, no. 4 (January 2000): 373–88.

– "Hermann Cohens Kindheit. Aus Anlaß seines 100. Todestages am 4. April 2018." *Kalonymos. Beiträge zur deutsch-jüdischen Geschichte aus dem Salomon Ludwig Steinheim-Institut an der Universität Duisburg-Essen* 21, no. 1 (2018): 1–9.

– "Das Problem eines einheitlichen Kulturbewußtseins. Zur Person des jüdisch-deutschen Philosophen Hermann Cohen." *Aschkenas. Zeitschrift für Geschichte und Kultur der Juden* 10, no. 2 (2000): 417–41

– "Wissenschaftslogik versus Schöpfungstheorie. Die Rolle der Vernichtung in Cohens Ursprungslogik." In *Verneinung, Andersheit und Unendlichkeit im Neukantianismus,* edited by Pierfrancesco Fiorato, 47–67. Würzburg: Königshausen & Neumann, 2009.

Wiehl, Reiner. "The Multiplicity of Virtues and the Problem of Unity in Hermann Cohen's Ethics and Philosophy of Religion," translated by Michael J. Ystad. In Makkreel and Luft, *Neo-Kantianism in Contemporary Philosophy,* 272–92.

Wiese, Christian. "'The Best Antidote to Anti-Semitism'? *Wissenschaft des Judentums,* Protestant Biblical Scholarship, and Anti-Semitism in Germany Before 1933." In *Modern Judaism and Historical Consciousness: Identities, Encounters, Perspectives,* edited by Andreas Gotzmann and Christian Wiese, 145–92. Leiden: Brill, 2007.

– "Jahwe – ein Gott nur für Juden? Der Disput um das Gottesverständnis zwischen Wissenschaft des Judentums und protestantischer alttestamentlicher Wissenschaft im Kaiserreich." In *Christlicher Antijudaismus und Antisemitismus. Theologische und kirchliche Programme Deutscher Christen,* edited by L. Siegele-Wenschkewitz, 27–94. Frankfurt am Main: Haag & Herchen, 1994.

– *Wissenschaft des Judentums und protestantische Theologie im wilhelminischen Deutschland: ein Schrei ins Leere?* Tübingen: Mohr Siebeck, 1999. Translated by B. Harshav and C. Wiese as *Challenging Colonial Discourse. Jewish Studies and Protestant Theology in Wilhelmine Germany.* Leiden: Brill, 2005.

Wilke, Carsten L. "Talmudschüler, Student, Seminarist: Breslauer rabbinische Studienlaufbahnen 1835–1870." *Aschkenas. Zeitschrift für Geschichte und Kultur der Juden* 15, no. 1 (2005): 111–25.

Willey, Thomas. *Back to Kant: The Revival of Kantianism in German Social and Historical Thought, 1860–1914.* Detroit: Wayne State University Press, 1978.

Winter, Eggert. *Ethik und Rechtswissenschaft: eine historisch-systematische Untersuchung zur Ethik-Konzeption des Marburger Neukantianismus im Werke Hermann Cohens.* Berlin: Duncker & Humblot, 1980.

Worms, Martin J. *Die Bekenntnisbeschimpfung im Sinne des §166 Abs. 1 StGB und die Lehre vom Rechtsgut.* Frankfurt am Main: Peter Lang, 1984.

Yaffe, Martin. "Autonomy, Community, Authority: Hermann Cohen, Carl Schmitt, Leo Strauss." In Frank, *Autonomy and Judaism,* 143–60.

– "Liturgy and Ethics: Hermann Cohen and Franz Rosenzweig on the Day of Atonement." *Journal of Religious Ethics* 7, no. 2 (Fall 1979): 215–28.

Yancy, George. *Black Bodies, White Gazes: The Continuing Significance of Race.* Lanham, MD: Rowman & Littlefield, 2008.

– *Look, a White! Philosophical Essays on Whiteness.* Philadelphia: Temple University Press, 2012.

Zank, Michael. "Arousing Suspicion Against a Prejudice: Leo Strauss and the Study of Maimonides' *Guide of the Perplexed.*" In *Moses Maimonides (1138–1204): His Religious, Scientific, and Philosophical* Wirkungsgeschichte *in Different Cultural Contexts,* edited by Görge K. Hasselhoff and Otfried Fraisse, 557–61. Würzburg: Ergon, 2004.

– "Cohen, Hermann." In *Routledge Encyclopedia of Philosophy.* London: Routledge, 1998.

– "The Ethics in Hermann Cohen's Philosophical System." In Gibbs, "Hermann Cohen's Ethics." Special issue, *Journal of Jewish Thought and Philosophy* 13, nos. 1–2 (2004): 1–15.

– "The Ethics of Rebuke." In Hollander, "The Ethics of the Neighbor." Special issue, *Journal for Textual Reasoning,* 4, no. 1 (November 2005).

– "Hermann Cohen und die rabbinische Literatur." In Mosès and Wiedebach, *Hermann Cohen's Philosophy of Religion,* 263–91.

– *The Idea of Atonement in the Philosophy of Hermann Cohen.* Providence, RI: Brown Judaic Studies, 2000. Digital reprint with a new introduction in *Brown Judaic Studies Open Humanities Book Program* (2020). https://repository.library.brown.edu/studio/item/bdr:1111035/

– "'The Individual as I' in Hermann Cohen's Jewish Thought." *Journal of Jewish Thought and Philosophy* 5, no. 2 (1996): 281–96.

– "New Literature on Hermann Cohen." *Jewish Quarterly Review* 98, no. 4 (Fall 2008): 566–73.

Zechlin, Egmont. *Die deutsche Politik und die Juden im Ersten Weltkrieg.* Göttingen: Vandenhoeck & Ruprecht, 1969.

Zeman, Vladimir. "Hermann Cohen's Concept of the Transcendental Method." In *Transcendental Philosophy and Everyday Experience,* edited by Tom Rockmore and Vladimir Zeman, 111–24. Atlantic Highlands, NJ: Humanities Press, 1997.

Zunz, Leopold. *Gesammelte Schriften.* Vol. 1. Berlin: Louis Gerschel, 1875. Vol. 2. Berlin: Louis Gerschel, 1876.

Index